THE RURAL LIVING HANDBOOK

AN ILLUSTRATED GUIDE
TO PRACTICAL COUNTRY SKILLS
BY THE EDITORS OF  MOTHER EARTH NEWS
INTRODUCTION BY ROY UNDERHILL

FIRESIDE

A FIRESIDE BOOK
PUBLISHED BY SIMON & SCHUSTER INC.

NEW YORK   LONDON   TORONTO   SYDNEY   TOKYO

Fireside / Simon & Schuster
Simon & Schuster Building
Rockefeller Center
1230 Avenue of the Americas
New York, New York 10020

Grateful acknowledgment is made for
permissions granted on the following material: "Erecting a Pole Building," page 40;
portions adapted from *Pole Building: A Step
by Step Guide*. Copyright © 1980 by Nor-
man Ecker, Sr., and Jeffrey L. Flanders.
"Cutting Wood With a Chain Saw," page
78, from *Barnacle Parp's Chain Saw Guide*.
Copyright © 1985 by Walter Hall. "Pruning Fruit Trees," page 106, from *Pruning
Simplified* by Lewis Hall. Copyright ©
1986 by Storey Communications, Inc.
"Fresh Chicken" (text only), page 130,
from *Stillroom Cookery*. Copyright © 1977
by Grace Firth, EMP Publications, Inc.,
McLean, VA. "Herb and Spice Chart,"
page 136, adapted from *Herbs and Spices:
How to Use Them* and *Spice Compatibility
Chart* from Three Mountaineers, Inc.,
Asheville, NC. "Ice Cream," page 158,
adapted from *Old Uncle Gaylord's Ice Cream
Book*. Copyright © 1975, 1978 by Gaylord
Willis and Ted Benhari. "Soups and
Stocks," page 164; recipe for La Soupe aux
Pois Canadienne from *American Folklife
Cookbook* by Joan Nathan. Copyright ©
1984 by Joan Nathan Gerson. Recipe for A
Soop or Pottage reprinted by permission of
Russell & Volkening as agents for the au-
thors. Copyright © 1977 by John L. Hess
and Karen Hess. "Beer," page 170; recipe
for Irish-Style Stout reprinted by permis-
sion from *Brewing Quality Beers: The Home-
brewer's Essential Guidebook*. Copyright ©
1986 by Byron Burch. "Wood-Burning
Cookstove," page 182, from *The Secret of
Better Baking* by Mary D. Chambers. Copyright © 1925 by Portland Stove Foundary
Company.

Designed by John Baxter Design
Manufactured in the United States of
America

10 9 8 7 6 5 4 3 2 1
10 9 8 7 6 5 4 3 2 1 Pbk.

Library of Congress Cataloging in Publication Data

ISBN 0-671-68370-5
    0-671-65790-9 (PBK)

Acknowledgments

As the early settlers in America knew, building shelter was best undertaken as a cooperative venture. Most times, it was a social act, a small community pitching in to build a cabin or raise a barn. Putting together this book, *The Rural Living Handbook*, has also been a social act, a shared burden which many people helped shoulder. First of all, we'd like to thank: Robin Smith ("Land Buying: Do's and Don'ts"), Chris Huck ("Surveying Your Own Land"), Silas Stillwater ("A Well-Drilling Primer"), John Vivian ("Stone Walls," "Electric Fence," "Taking on Livestock,"), David Clark ("Building A Short Log Cabin"), Steve Kohler ("Maintaining Gravel Roads"), Jake Page ("Draft Horses"), John Vara ("Choosing and Using a Tractor"), Anne Westbrook Dominick ("Organ Meats"), John Herzfeld (Annie's Southern Fried Chicken recipe on page 131), Robert C. Winians ("Rabbit Fare"), Linda Martin ("Butter"), Robert T. and Ricki Carroll ("Cheese Making"), V.B. Ramig ("Yogurt"), Marjorie Watkins ("Soups and Stocks") and Alan McNeill ("Wine").

In addition, thanks must go to *Mother Earth News* editors who, over the years, have sought not only to learn and explain the skills of country living, but to do so with fortitude and charm. Herewith, then, a roll of the drums for Bruce Woods, Pat Stone, Richard Freudenberger, Terry Krautwurst, Sara Pacher, David Petersen, David Schoonmaker, Carol Taylor, Klara Blair, Julie Brown, Wilma Dingley, Joanne Dufilho, Judy Janes, Alexis Lipsitz, Christie Lyon, Betty N. Mack, Karen Murray, Ingrid Sterner, Kathleen Seabe, Linda Patterson Eger, Bill Lessner, Donald Osby, Sandra McKee, Robert Graf, Kay Holmes Stafford, Kathy Tomlin, Helen P. McAuliffe, Richard Muehleman, Laura A. Greenburg, Rita Norton, Dennis Burkholder, Frank Sides, Susan Sides, Alfred Meyer and Judy Gold.

Finally, Managing Editor Tim Watkins, Assistant Managing Editor Liz Brennan and Chief Copy Editor Lorna Loveless deserve special praise for yoking what has often seemed an unwieldy team into a smooth, hard-pulling unit. *The Editors*

Contents

Concerning Well Springs of Wisdom and Skills' Rewards

This book is about the basic business of life: buying a place, building a home and making a living from the land. It is also a useful book for all of those who can escape from the urban madness only on weekends and vacations. You would think that, like eagles and beavers, we would be born with such elemental knowledge. But even the simple life on this planet is astoundingly complex. Our work is the same as that of our prehistoric ancestors. We must learn to perform all the sacred rituals of our tribe (get titles and building permits), we must protect our hunting grounds (hire surveyors), we must honor the forces of nature (spread the fertilizer), and we must obey the ancient taboos (don't put the privy uphill from the spring).

Living honestly, responsibly and directly with the land offers great rewards as well as making tremendous demands. I can't say that you get more enjoyment from eating a chicken you've killed for yourself, but you surely appreciate it more. No other way of life calls for such a daily range of innovating, planning ahead and evaluating risks. Get greedy (cut your windbreaks to plant more land), and you can lose big. Get cocky, and you can die. You may be able to figure out how to drive a tractor within a few minutes, but you don't want to learn from experience how a tractor can flip back over on top of you. The laws of nature haven't changed; they've just been hidden under a tangle of complications.

In spite of all we learn from reading, books can't cover everything. My own life experience was profoundly shaped by a period of "homesteading" in New Mexico. I was armed with every back-to-the-land book ever written, and I studied them all. But no book can substitute for common sense.

Once, I lost a water jug down our well. I couldn't fish it out with the well bucket, and I didn't see a stick or a grappling hook, so I decided to just climb down and retrieve it. I began to descend the shaft of the concrete casing by pushing my feet against one side and sliding my back against the other. I had made it to within a few feet of the bottom when I happened to look up. The top where I had entered was now a tiny, sky blue disk framed in blackness. I tried to go back up, but my back would not slide up the wall as easily as it had slid down. I realized my predicament quickly—but almost too late.

As my tired legs held me suspended me over the depths of icy water, I knew one thing for sure. I knew that if I were to panic, I would never get out of that well alive. I wish I could say that some ingenious insight or a dramatic rescue got me out of that well. Instead, it took an eternity of inching— painfully, wormlike, agonizingly—towards the sky. I finally emerged with the worst beating my body and self-esteem had ever taken. Experience keeps a dear school, but a fool will learn in no other.

Going down the well seems mighty stupid now, but, like a big party we held by the beaver pond, it seemed like a good idea at the time. I believe it was that particularly boisterous Fourth of July party that drove the beaver family away. The beaver dams kept the water table high enough so that our well never went dry even in the driest seasons. When the beavers left, their dams were breached, the water table dropped, and our well grew rank and dry.

Because of that fateful party, we had to tap part of a thermal spring high up the canyon. Like city people, we then had to thread a half mile of black plastic piping through the humus of the dark ravines. The spring was on federal land, and an old Spanish rancher had the rights to the water for his cattle. He was our friend and did not object, but water runs mighty thick in the dry Southwest. We were never again sure of our water supply, just because we put the beer keg too close to the beaver pond.

The beavers may be gone, but the wolves are still out there; only now, most walk on two legs. Knowledge is your best defense against being robbed by others or, more likely, by your own ignorance. You need to know what you need to have. You need substantial financial resources to buy land and equipment. You need boundless energy and stamina to endure lambing season. You need an infrastructure—fences and roads. Most folks have no idea how much of country life can be tied up in fences. And just keeping the road passable can eat your years away, unless you feel that a bad road is good protection from building inspectors.

Still, you can be independent only to a point. Even the most self-reliant cuss can be ruined by the whimsies of nature. So, it's an excellent investment strategy to diversify. It may offend the lifestyle purist, but many people live two lives, with a regular job in town and their own outdoor work in the country. Some routinely go from a morning of logging with oxen to an afternoon of logging on to distant computers.

Others mix their lives more personally. One couple I know live without electricity or telephone; farming, weaving and horse-logging in the most remote part of the lower 48 states. These same folks are pioneers into the future as well. They were among the first to benefit from the medical breakthrough of in vitro fertilization. In other words, this thoroughly country couple just became the parents of a test-tube baby.

Pick and choose the parts of the kind of life you want to enjoy, but please, stay out of wells! *—Roy Underhill, Williamsburg, VA*

To Dreamers & Doers

One or two generations are all that separate most Americans from forebears who could have written a book much like this one, if they'd only had the time. Somewhere along the line, over the course of maybe half a dozen decades, we gained more time to do as we please but lost much of the practical know-how that directed our ancestors' rural lives for generations. The hands with which you're holding this volume are almost surely less calloused and work-worn than were those of your grandparents or great-grandparents. But those same hands are almost surely less practiced in performing the essential skills of living with, and on, the land.

This book can and will teach you those skills. But perhaps more important than its function as solid how-to instruction is that it is a book of *empowerment*.

There is not a skill in *The Rural Living Handbook* that, once learned, fails to give its master power: the power of independence, the power of choice, the power of competence, the power of accomplishment. This is true no matter where or how you live, country or city, simply or not-so-simply. The principle here is fundamental: The more you can do for yourself, the more control you have over your own life and surroundings.

There is no notion quite so universally appealing. While our "service economy" may have at least partially eliminated the *need* to do for ourselves—to nurture a living from the land or to build and maintain shelter or to create items of use and beauty with our own hands—most of us still feel a deep-seated urge to do so, and we gain an abiding satisfaction in the doing.

For countless thousands, the dream of self-reliance, of living The Good Life on a small, giving plot of land, provides a nourishing goal to be lived out "some day." For countless others, it has become a reality, hard won, the result of struggling with—and learning from—every conceivable practicality. From building a barn to putting in a garden. From finding enough water to finding enough money. From clearing pasture to getting out of the driveway in the muds of April.

These people are the dreamers and doers who, for some two decades now, have shared experiences and aspirations in the pages of a unique country magazine called *Mother Earth News*. Indeed, some readers think of the magazine as an ongoing national conversation, an ultimate bulletin board full of tips, advice and know-how. And just as *Mother Earth News* is a distillation of information from country skills experts—both those on staff and those from every corner of the country—so is *The Rural Living Handbook* an updated distillation of almost 20 years' worth of *Mother Earth News*.

This book is not magic, but it *is* a kind of handyman between covers who can build and repair almost anything. It is, moreover, an enabling instrument that can lead you from wherever you are to a small place in the universe that is rich with trees, walking room and earth smells. A place that, if you care enough for it, will love you back and make your summer evenings on the front porch miracles of serenity.

The first step in that journey, obviously, is preparation. Part One of *The Rural Living Handbook* begins by pointing out the most-obvious pitfalls in searching for, surveying the boundaries of, and purchasing your country home. You'll learn what to look for—and look out for—in real-estate dealings; learn how to wisely hire, and supervise, such services as well drilling and septic system installation; and even learn how to take on, yourself, such challenging and rewarding tasks as stretching a fence, building a simple barn and bringing in firewood for your winter heat and comfort.

Also essential to building The Good Life, of course, are tools and the knowledge to use them effectively. Part Two can't take the place of years of apprenticeship in your father's workshop, but it *will* enable you to shop the local hardware store without earning the kind of blank stare that has driven many a beginner to give up and hire a contractor! Part Two begins with a short course in elementary carpentry, demystifies the chain saw and tractor and goes on to list and describe the components of a well-stocked tool shed.

And, what is rural life without a garden and a few critters? Part Three clears the way for reaping the rewards of homegrown food. Whether your interests tend toward a vegetable garden, a homestead orchard or the birds of the coop and the beasts of the field, *The Rural Living Handbook* will steer you around the most common problems and will greatly increase your chances of first-time success.

Finally, when those crops are coming in strong and the broiler chickens are ready for the ax, the *Handbook* is ready, too, with a sort of handbook within itself—Part Four: "The Country Kitchen." You'll learn the skills of curing meats; the methods of canning, freezing and drying produce; the joys of baking bread and producing other aromatic goodies; and even the delicious chemistry of brewing beers, ales and wines. Then, when you settle back in front of a good wood fire, with a cheering glass in your hand and a satisfying, home-raised dinner in your belly, raise a toast to your success and to all the other dreamers and doers of the world: Here's to you, and more power to you. Here's to The Good Life.   —*The Editors*

PART ONE

Land, Shelter and Logistics

Take some acres
or a piece of one, then
add a roof and some
bare necessities.

Land Buying: Do's and Don'ts

Don't let your enthusiasm
for an apparently "ideal" piece
of property seduce you into making
a costly mistake.

Suppose, as you eagerly scan the classified real estate listings, you suddenly spot an ad that reads: "Forty acres, year-round creek, part wooded, part cleared, some marketable timber, south-facing slopes, $26,000, low down, low monthly payments." In such a case, it would be natural to assume you had found the buy of the decade.

So let us say you decide to take a look at the place profiled in that advertisement and discover it is even better than promised. Huge trees tower overhead like a great green cathedral. You follow the creek downstream to find that it opens into a gorgeous meadow. Your heart is taken, and you're already starting to plan where to put the house and barn. This is *the place*, and—better yet—the price is right!

At this point, the owner or agent—sensing your enchantment—asks for either earnest money or a down payment. By now, you *know* the property is what you want, but, typically, you also fear that someone else is sure to buy it if you don't. As a result you prepare to shell out a big portion of your savings.

But wait. Before putting up cash that may be unrecoverable later, consider the possible pitfalls of buying *any* piece of real estate, especially undeveloped land.

Do You Have Access?

It is impossible to overemphasize the importance of access rights. Make certain beyond the shadow of a doubt that *permanent*, legal, transferable access is specified in the deed. *Never* buy any piece of property without it.

Recently, a Pennsylvania couple bought a lovely piece of land and built a house on it,

acting on a neighbor's assurances that he had no objections to their using his road to get to their property. Later, though, they had a minor disagreement with that fellow, and he promptly blocked the road, denying them access to their own property. At that point, they started walking in and out across a bordering piece of government land, only to learn from the agency in charge that they had better stop, or risk being hauled into court on trespassing charges.

Feeling increasingly hemmed in, the couple tried several other routes, each of which was eventually blocked when at least one landowner objected. Because the unfortunate couple had no money left for an expensive legal battle, they were finally forced into abandoning the place, losing the cash they'd invested.

As you can see, then, it's imperative to make sure that no one can stop you from getting to your property. If it's possible to obtain access by paying for it annually, often the case with government agencies, make certain that the right of way is irrevocable and that it is transferable to your heirs or to subsequent owners should you later decide to sell. You'll also want to find out who's responsible for the road maintenance. Believe it or not, you could be both sued and fined as a result of nicks you might make with your snowplow or of ruts created by your car or truck!

Furthermore, don't assume that access will be guaranteed because a piece of property is on a county or state road. If the right wasn't granted to the previous owner—or if no driveway has been put in yet—you may have to get permission from the county or state. Such permits are *not* always automatic, and they'll generally cost some money.

Water, Sewer and Drainage

Water and soil drainage are also critical. That creek running across your dream parcel may be lovely, but take the time to discover *whether you have the right to use it*. Your water supply could, for instance, be part of a city watershed, in which case it's possible that you'd be unable to legally use a single drop of the liquid. In addition, the law could require that all your livestock be kept several hundred feet from the creek or could prevent you from legally putting in any sort of septic tank or outhouse. In short, it's best to refrain from buying on a watershed unless you have a written statement from the city specifying your rights and you're certain you can comply with the most minuscule detail in the agreement.

Be aware, too, that outhouses are illegal in some areas, and—where this is true—a homeowner must either have a septic system installed (the location for which will be legally defined by proximity to domestic water supply and drainage) or hook up to a public sewer system.

If installing a septic system is necessary, make several percolation tests before buying any piece of land, to assure yourself that drainage is adequate and away from your water supply.

How About Easements?

It is also important to research easements: the rights and privileges that persons may have on another's land. First, find out what easements are available to you over other people's property. For example, if you're not on a county road, you'll want to know whether the easements are wide enough to meet county specifications and permit public access, in case you and your neighbors later decide to have a road put in.

In addition, you may want to make certain that easements are available for power and telephone lines. Even if such utilities aren't important to you now, they might become so later. They will almost certainly matter to potential buyers, should you ever choose to sell your spread.

Naturally, you'll also want to know what easements may apply to the land you're buying. That way, you won't plant a vegetable garden in the middle of someone else's right of way.

Utility Availability

Where utilities are concerned, you should know that if you live at a considerable distance from a power line, some companies have the right to refuse to bring in electrici-

Even the most beautiful piece of land can be a poor buy if water, mineral, timber and easement rights aren't included in the price.

ty, even if you are willing to foot the bill. In such an instance, the only alternative might be to generate your own power. The point is, know about power availability *before* you buy.

What About Mineral Rights?

Many people consider mineral rights to be minor, yet examples abound of how important they can prove to a landowner who *doesn't* hold them. In a rather extreme case in West Virginia, for instance, a man bought what he thought was an ideal piece of property. He built a beautiful home and planted a hundred acres of orchards and gardens. In short, he invested a fortune in his land, in terms of both time and money. He knew he didn't own the mineral rights to the property, but the real estate agent had assured him that they weren't important.

Some 25 years later, however, after the orchards and gardens had matured to the point where they supplied his entire income, he came home one day to find his home being bulldozed and one of his orchards already gone. Coal had been found on the land, it seems, and his deed stated plainly that the only compensation due him was the cost of the materials in the house and barns. In this situation, the hapless owner had absolutely no legal recourse.

Remember that just because no minerals of value have been found on your potential property, there's no guarantee that one or more won't be discovered later or that a new

use won't be found for currently uneconomic minerals that you know are there.

Who Owns the Timber Rights?

In most cases, timber rights don't pose much of a problem. A property owner will usually receive them *conditionally*. For example, you may be granted only enough timber to provide wood for housing and fences until the land is paid for.

However, be sure to find out whether there's a timber contract that applies to the property you are interested in purchasing. If so, extreme caution is in order. You'll want to learn when the contract expires; how many board feet the logging company is allowed to take, and of what species; and how that cutting will affect the appearance of the land. Also, be sure to find out the condition in which the loggers are required to leave the property after the harvest. Take nothing for granted, and make certain the company lives up to that agreement. Otherwise, you might come home one day to a disastrous situation.

Protect Yourself

Keep in mind that—when you do put down earnest money—you are entitled to make the final purchase dependent upon written contingencies. Just what these qualifications are will be up to you, but make sure that your earnest-money agreement covers legal access, mineral rights, timber and water, and that it requires the seller to deliver to you a deed conveying good title. Also, obtain a title search (which will tell you the legal history of the property), so that you know what encumbrances—if any—are on the land and that the seller does, in fact, own the property.

Make sure, too, that any money given to the seller goes into an escrow account and will be returned if the owner can't convey good title. Don't leave this to chance, but insist on such an agreement. Furthermore, if there's an underlying contract or mortgage on the property, get a statement in writing that it's being paid off or that you're making provision to assume it. Be aware that if this isn't specified, the holder of the mortgage has prior claim.

Additionally, you should invest in title insurance, and study that policy carefully in order to understand exactly what it says. It will, for one thing, list whatever encumbrances are on the land. See to it that the transaction is recorded at the appropriate public registry. You may, after the purchase, be able to further protect yourself by filing a Declaration of Homestead.

Though they vary from one state to another, homestead statutes are similar in intent. They are designed to preserve family homes that might otherwise be taken in times of monetary misfortune or upon the death of the head of the household. In general, this protection is available only if the declaration is filed in advance of such a catastrophe. The forms are usually available at stationery stores.

It goes without saying that when buying property you will be confronted by an often bewildering array of legalese. It will be necessary, for example, to become familiar with such terms as *binders* (often called *offers to buy* or *deposit receipts*), *mortgagor, mortgagee, graduated payment mortgage, variable rate mortgage, mortgage clause, refund clause, maintenance clause, lien, settlement clause, loan origination fee, loan discount* (or *points*), *foreclosure, quitclaim* and *acceleration clause*. It can't be emphasized enough that here is an area where conscientiousness pays off, both in terms of protecting your interests and in making you a sophisticated, rather than a naive, buyer. Be sure, then, to consult a legal encyclopedia or dictionary whenever you come across a term that isn't absolutely clear to you, and to find out from a competent real estate lawyer exactly how the term is interpreted in your particular agreement.

Community Attitudes

Finally, study the area you plan to live in as thoroughly as possible. The time spent on this research can be critical to your future peace of mind. It's amazing what going a few extra miles can sometimes mean in terms of personal happiness and opportunity. Make the effort to talk to other new residents, and ask them about their experiences. Their answers will help you make the final decision— whether to purchase or not—a sound one.

Surveying Your Own Land

Finding the fine line between theirs and yours will lead to better knowledge of your property.

As any surveyor who lives in the country will tell you, people always ask about property boundaries. The questions are varied: "How much does a survey cost?" "Can I do it myself?" "What equipment do I need?" "What do my property corners look like?" "What are the laws concerning surveying and property boundaries?" "Where are my property records?" They ask these questions not from a desire to fence and post their land but because of pride of ownership, the desire for knowledge or—sometimes—to protect themselves from the potential threat of encroachment.

Take the recent case of a man in South Carolina. For years he had lived peacefully on his 20-acre farm. Then a slick developer bought the property next door, and subdivision plans began looming on his boundaries. The man ended up paying a surveyor $1,500—just to ensure that the developer's ambitions wouldn't include any of his farm.

A thin line separates the slick developers of this world from those who prefer to live and let live—a line that is, in fact, the boundary line of your property. Your right to build or farm, your right to live on land the way you see fit, even your family dog's right to roam at will all stop at that often invisible line. And it's not particularly difficult to discern, especially with a little help. If the thought of doing your own surveying scares you, don't worry. You don't have to be a genius to find your property boundaries— just a detective.

Knowing how to find your own property markers can save you time, expense and trouble. But be aware that there's a big difference between finding established lines and setting new ones or adjusting incorrect old ones. Only a licensed surveyor is legally qualified to set or move lines.

How to Read a Property Description

You've heard it said that the job isn't over till the paperwork is done? In this job, the paperwork comes first. Don't set foot outside until you have in hand every document that could help. First on the list is the portion of your property deed called the legal description: the description in words of your property lines. And before you can understand how to decode that description, you must learn which of the two common surveying methods applies to your property. One is the metes and bounds method; the other is the public land survey system.

Metes and bounds is the most common surveying method and the one used almost exclusively in the East. Metes and bounds defines property by its boundary lines, each line consisting of direction, or bearing, and distance, or length. Here is an example:

Beginning at a point 247 feet due east of Henly Fork, thence N47W, 210 feet, thence N43E, 204 feet to an Oak, thence S47E, 210 feet to a post, thence S43W, 204 feet to the point of beginning. Containing 0.98 acres, more or less.

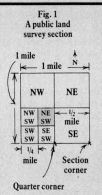

1 mile

1 mile

N

NW	NE

| NW SW | NE SW | 1/2 |
| SW SW | SE SW | mile |

SE

1/4 mile

Section corner

Quarter corner

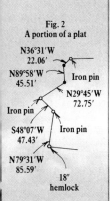

Fig. 2
A portion of a plat

N36°31'W
22.06'

N89°58'W
45.51'

Iron pin

N29°45'W
72.75'

Iron pin

S48°07'W
47.43'

Iron pin

N79°31'W
85.59'

18"
hemlock

Notice that each leg consists of both direction and distance. With a compass and a tape measure, you could walk around the perimeter.

The public land survey system evolved in response to helter-skelter settlement in Colonial times. In the 1700s, nobody knew how much land anyone owned or where it was. In northern Georgia, for instance, entrepreneurs sold over 29 million acres in a three-county area that contained only 9 million!

Thomas Jefferson solved the problem. During his presidency, the federal government sent a small army of surveyors across the Appalachians with instructions to split the frontier into squares, placing boundary markers every mile. Thus, the public land survey system consists of a checkerboard of square-mile lots, called sections. Each section contains 640 acres and a boundary marker at each corner.

To encourage people to fill up the sections, the government created homestead allotments. The basic allotment was 160 acres—a quarter section. The surveyors marked these boundaries and called them quarter-corners.

Now, all this won't help you unless you know how to read a public land description (Fig. 1). It sounds hard until you get the hang of it. Each quarter of a section bears the name of its compass location: NE, NW, SE, SW—for example, "the SW 1/4 of section 3." Want less than 160 acres? Chop the "SW 1/4" into quarters again. Each quarter-

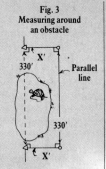

Fig. 3
Measuring around
an obstacle

X'

330'

Parallel line

330'

X'

Fig. 4
Measuring on the level

Measured distance

Level

Plumb bob

Fig. 5
Old property markers

Iron pipe

"X" etched in rock

Fig. 6
Finding a buried pin
with a compass

1/2"–1"

Buried pin

quarter is 40 acres. One of them could be named the "NE 1/4 of the SW 1/4" (shaded in Fig. 1). And so on. On occasion, adjacent quarters will be combined to yield a half: "the south 1/2 of section 27."

Thus, a public land description will not list boundary lines. Jefferson designed the system so that all boundary lines run north-south and east-west—along the quarters as well as the sections. Since section boundaries are exactly one mile long, subunit borders will be exact fractions of a mile.

Preparing for the Search

There are even better information sources than your deed. The best, though often most elusive, document you can lay your hands on is the surveyor's map, or plat (Fig. 2). The plat translates that legal confusion of numbers and terms on the deed into pictures. It may also show references to natural landmarks or give triangulation data that locate a particular point.

Plat chasing is a major pastime among surveyors. Your plat, if one exists, may accompany your deed. Or it may languish in city or county records—clerks' or surveyors' offices would be the best places to search—or reside with a previous owner. Plats of neighboring land are helpful, too. They may show the location of a common boundary.

If you live in a subdivision or built-up area, you may be wondering why your deed's legal description reads only "Lot 22, Rock

Creek Estates" or "Tract A, First Addition." But these, too, are metes and bounds surveys. The surveyors created several lots at once, so they drew one map of the whole thing. Deed descriptions merely refer to the master plat, which you will find in the public records.

You should also keep an eye peeled for early versions of your property description, surveyor's notes and descriptions of roads that border your land. Why? First, to ensure that your deed doesn't contain mistakes; second, to find out all you can about boundary markers—the key to property lines.

You are now nearly ready to step into the surveyor's shoes. First, though, you'll have to gather your equipment. You'll need a compass, long measuring tape, plumb bob, level, hatchet and some ribbon and stakes. You'll also need a willing assistant. Now check your instruments. Do they read in the same numbers as the survey? If not, you will have to translate.

Most people will have on hand the type of compass that is marked off in *azimuths*. An azimuth is a direction—from 0° to 360°—measured clockwise from due north. For example, an azimuth of 230° is roughly southwest.

Being ornery as a rule, surveyors use another system, called bearings. Bearings start with the same 360° circle but divide it into quadrants of 90° each. On either side of true north are the NE and NW quadrants. Likewise on the south: SE and SW. Every direction reads as an angle to the east or west from north or south.

Sound confusing? To get a handle on it, try translating the azimuth of 230° mentioned above. Since 180° is due south, 230° is south plus 50° beyond (to the west of). So 230° becomes "an angle from due south of 50° to the west"—or, in surveyor's shorthand, S50W. Another example: "N25E" is "an angle from due north of 25° to the east," or azimuth 25°.

On to distances. We measure lengths in feet and inches. The surveyor, however, uses either feet and tenths of a foot (be very alert for this!) or a more venerable system called chains. A chain measures 66 feet. Why 66 feet? Because it's convenient for land computations. Ten square chains equal one acre—which means to compute acreage rapidly, all you have to do is find the number of square chains, then move the decimal point once to the left. Also, one mile stretches exactly 80 chains.

A hundredth of a chain—about eight inches—is called a link. Old-timers also used a quarter-chain measure (16½ feet), calling it a rod, pole or perch.

Faced with a description written in bearings and chains when your equipment reads

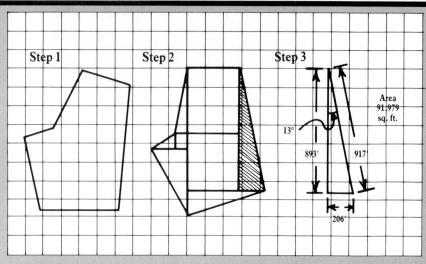

Step 1   Step 2   Step 3

Area 91,979 sq. ft.

13°

893'   917'

206'

Area Computation

If your property has a simple rectangular shape, all you need to do is a quick "length times width" calculation to find your square footage. But what about those of you with odd-shaped lots with five or 10 separate sides? Before you throw in the towel, try this method for computing your acreage.

First, make a scale drawing of your property on grid paper (Step 1). It doesn't have to be entirely accurate, but it should be large enough so you can write plenty of figures inside. Write the direction (in bearings) and distance along every boundary line.

Second, draw lines running north-south and/or east-west through every angle point. You need be concerned only with lines in the interior, and once they meet another inside line, you need draw no further.

Your polygon is now divided into rectangles and right triangles (Step 2). To figure out the area of the triangles, all you need is a math book or calculator with sine and cosine functions, the stuff of high school trigonometry. In a right triangle, the sine of

either acute angle equals the length of the side opposite divided by the length of the hypotenuse. (You'll notice that each hypotenuse happens to be a boundary line, the length of which is known.) A cosine equals the adjacent side divided by the hypotenuse.

You already know one angle of each triangle—remember, the bearing is the angle from the north-south line you drew. So if you look up the sine or cosine (whichever is appropriate) of that angle, you can use that and the length of the boundary line to solve for the remaining sides of the triangle.

For example, take the shaded triangle from Step 2; in Step 3 we find that it has a hypotenuse of 917 feet running S13E. The sine of 13° is .225. Since .225 = opposite side ÷ 917, then the opposite side = 206. Now you can use the cosine of 13°, .974, to solve for the angle's adjacent side: .974 = adjacent side ÷ 917 . . . or 893 feet. The area for a triangle is ½ base times height; in this case ½ × 206 × 893 = 91,979 square feet.

As you work, write every calculated distance on the appropriate grid line, and record the area of each subfigure inside that shape. When you add all those areas up at the end, you'll have your square footage. Divide that by 43,560, and you'll know your acreage.

---

in azimuths and feet, your brain may well reel at the prospect of translating and tramping about at the same time. It's far better to translate all the degrees and distances on paper before you set out.

Finally, the Fieldwork

Now you can begin your scavenger hunt. Step one: Always start from a known point. It must be something you can absolutely match with the written record. It may be a marker on your boundary, if someone has already positively identified it. More likely, it will be a road crossing, a section corner or

even a neighbor's marker, garnered from that plat you unearthed in the public records. Don't trust ditch lines or fence corners unless the record mentions them.

Step two: Measure off the course, direction and distance exactly as the deed says. Flag the line with your ribbons as you go. Make sure that your flags all line up straight and in the right direction. Your assistant can be a great help here. As you walk, watch out for any iron or steel objects or anything carrying electric current—they can attract the compass needle and throw your readings off. If you come to a large obstruction, you can measure a line exactly parallel to your bound-

A little care, simple equipment and a helpful partner are all you'll need to size up your land.

ary line for a short distance until you get by the obstacle (Fig. 3).

In a survey, distances are always measured on a horizontal plane, not along the ground slope. Unless you have a calculator that's well versed in trigonometry for equating slope distance to horizontal, you, too, must measure on the level. To do so whenever you're traversing hilly land, you and your assistant need to hold your tape or a measured length of string exactly level along your directional line. Use your level to determine this. Then, let the plumb bob hang vertically down from the end of the tape or string to determine where on the ground that horizontally measured distance falls (Fig. 4). Repeat as needed to accurately measure across rises and dips.

Step three: Once you've traveled the full distance in one direction, search for the boundary marker. This is always terrific fun. Will you know it when you see it? If you're lucky, your plat or deed will mention how the surveyor marked corners. If not, you're in for some Sherlock Holmes–style detective work.

You are looking for some object artificially placed in a certain spot (Fig. 5). What kind of object? If your documents omit mention of the markers, look for a date of survey, which is a clue to the type of marker used. Nowadays, surveyors use well-anchored pipes or steel rods, capped with brass, aluminum or plastic, embossed with the surveyor's registration number. But years ago they used anything handy. That included railroad spikes, wooden stakes, even broken glass, usually from a convenient whiskey bottle.

If you know you're seeking a buried pin, you can use your compass as a metal detec-

tor (Fig. 6). Stand so the compass needle is pointing due north, then turn the compass vertical so the needle points up. Keep facing north, and move the compass back and forth over the approximate pin location, holding it about a half-inch to an inch off the ground. If the needle spins downward and points to the ground—dig.

The early public land surveyors often spent months or years on the frontier and couldn't afford to carry around a load of markers. Thus the identity of their monuments varied widely. In the prairie, they filled pits with charcoal. In the mountains, where they spent most of their time hacking brush, they simply left an etched stone buried at the section corner. They would use witness trees in their notes to relocate the marker through triangulation.

In some parts of the Southwest, giant mounds of stone mark the corners. The surveyors put the soldiers who guarded them from Indians to work erecting "eternal" section corners. Often, however, Indians followed a couple of miles behind, scattering the stones as fast as the soldiers piled them.

Remember, markers don't last forever. Wooden stakes may last less than 10 years. A "10-inch pine" in ancient notes may be a 20-inch pine today—or a rotting stump.

Step four: Proceed to the next point. Don't give up if your search has so far proven fruitless. The next corner may lie in plain sight. And that's a bonus, because the more corners you find, the greater your chances of finding the remaining ones. You'll know what you're looking for and be able to zero in on it from two sides.

One possible monkey wrench that may be throwing you off: Your deed bearings may not be written in terms of magnetic north (a

compass actually points to a false North Pole). They may be written in true north (referring to the real North Pole) or even in grid north (referring to an artificial regional standard that uses parallel "north-south" lines). Then too, even magnetic north shifts some over time. So if your bearing readings seem to be causing trouble, take a compass reading between two known points of your deed or plat, and compare that to the recorded bearing. If there's a significant difference, adjust all your bearing readings as needed to compensate.

Step five: Preserve the markers you find, but DO NOT MOVE THEM. They are legal boundaries only as long as they remain where they are. You cannot move them to where you think they should be. Only a licensed surveyor can do that. The difference between you and a surveyor—besides $400 a day—is that only that person can establish property lines and testify in court as to their whereabouts. If there are serious legal problems with your boundary, you will need a surveyor.

Know Your Land

So what have you accomplished? A lot. If you found some corners, you may have staved off a boundary war with your neighbor. Show him or her what you've found, so you'll agree. Then paint a few trees nearby, or pile rocks around the spot so it doesn't go to weeds again. Don't force your grandkids to go through the same search.

Even if you didn't turn up any corners, your time hasn't been wasted. You've probably dug up some useful old records, and that's half the time and expense you'd have been paying a real surveyor for.

A Well-Drilling Primer

Most well drillers won't deliberately give you the shaft. . . .

Having a ready supply of fresh water might seem as certain as death and taxes, but any landowner who thinks that *aqua pura* automatically comes with the territory may be in for a major letdown. The truth is that most surface water is contaminated—at least to some degree—with chemicals, sewage or surface run-off.

This leaves most rural dwellers little choice but to drill a well, and even for the great majority of country folk who are traditionally independent, that option probably will involve calling in a professional driller. So if you're in the market for a well, the following information will give you some understanding of what takes place when the boring rig sets up in your front yard.

Getting Into Deep Water

The drilling of a well can be done in several different ways, although two methods—cable and rotary—probably account for nearly all the deep wells sunk today. Keeping things in perspective, however, you should know that *nondrilled* wells—which include dug, bored, jetted and driven water holes—are generally limited to 100' or so in depth, while true drilled shafts can easily penetrate several hundred feet or more.

In many areas there are three good reasons to go to the extra expense of the deeper, drilled well: First, the water is less likely to be polluted; second, such a well will probably provide a greater volume of water because of its sheer storage capacity; and finally, due to the considerable investment involved, the drillers are almost never fly-by-night contractors.

In the *cable-drilling* method, a one-ton tool bit, appropriately called a pounder, is suspended from a steel cable and dropped in 2'

strokes to shatter and crush the material beneath it, although sometimes down-the-hole air hammers are used instead. The well casing may be installed as the pounding progresses, and water is added to the hole and bailed out periodically to remove the pulverized matter that slows the bit's headway.

Rotary drilling operates on a different principle. As the name implies, a revolving drill bit—which is fastened to a series of 20' or 25' sections of heavy-walled pipe—actually cuts through the overburden. Water and compressed air are blown through the hollow drill rod as it spins, flushing a slurry of tailings out the top of the hole. In addition to turning the bit, the hydraulically powered rotary rig provides a downward force. It is also capable of hammering a casing into the newly bored hole.

In the rotary method, casing is handled somewhat differently. Instead of combining the drilling and sleeving procedures as the cable driller does, a rotary rig bores a slightly oversized shaft into which the casing is later installed. Since the walls of the hole can start to collapse before the casing can be set, the operator often must pump driller's mud (bentonite clay or a synthetic equivalent) down the shaft with the flush water to firm up the sides. Once that's completed, the tapered-tip casing can be fed into the hole and either locked into bedrock with the help of an air hammer or packed with gravel. The well is then sealed with concrete to prevent

surface water from leaking past the casing and contaminating the ground-water supply that feeds the well.

Which drilling method is better? There's no single answer to that question, but here are some facts to mull over: A rotary rig can usually punch a hole about five times faster than its cable-driven cousin. It can also go deeper with less effort and can even cut through the hardest rock with the help of carbide-tipped bits.

The cable rig, on the other hand, makes slower progress, owing to its design. It can also experience real difficulty going beyond the 150' range. The tool point is not as effective on rock, so dynamite may be needed to fracture the harder material. Finally, because it's under such stress, the casing material used with a cable drill is generally heavier, stronger and more expensive—by up to a dollar a foot—than that used in a rotary-drilled well.

In light of these facts, why would anyone want to use the cable method to drill a well? Simply because the shock of the heavy tool bit can open *fissures* in the rock, freeing up any water-bearing veins. This effectively means that a cable-drilled well may not need to be quite as deep as a rotary-bored one.

Go With the Flow

Actually, your choice of a drilling method will be dictated by which local contractor you

Pump Characteristics

Type	Total Lift (Feet)	Advantages	Disadvantages
Jet (ejector)	50–150	Simple design; easy maintenance; high capacity at low heads; compact components	Inefficient at maximum lifts; capacity reduced with increased lift; air in lines causes loss of prime; subject to freeze in extreme weather conditions
Submersible turbine	50–400	Efficient at high lifts; constant discharge; freeze protected; doesn't lose prime easily	Sensitive to abrasive matter in water; motor seals critical; subject to burnout if water level drops without warning; servicing requires removal from well
Rotary gear	50–250	Constant discharge; efficient through lift range; positive action	Sensitive to abrasive matter in water; subject to wear; low capacity
Reciprocating piston	25–600	Positive action; not overly sensitive to abrasive matter in water; high lift capability	Pulsating discharge; subject to vibration and noise; servicing requires removal from well

Hiring a well-drilling rig is an expensive proposition. Make sure you know what you need before you put money down.

tractors are often licensed by—and must answer to—the state or county government. They're bona fide business people and as such should be able to provide you with a contract that covers at least the following areas: health and environmental code compliance, liability insurance for the customer and the driller, casing specifications (including size and diameter, penetration, sand-screen protection and annular seal information), a completion date, a test-pumping report, a copy of the drilling log, itemized costs (per foot for drilling, as well as for the casing, plus any additional materials or labor charges) and a guarantee of materials and workmanship.

They Work Best Under Pressure

Unless you're one of the rare few who've been blessed with an artesian well that provides its own pressure, you're going to have to spring for a pump and pressure system to maintain a consistent delivery of water through your household plumbing network. The delivery pipe and electrical cable are standardized components and thus don't require much comment. The same holds for the pressure tank and its switch control—even though there are several different types in use.

The pump, however, might merit a bit of explanation, because the cost of operating it will be apparent long after the price of the well is forgotten. In this case, consult the adjoining table. It highlights the characteristics of the pump types you'll probably be encountering, though this listing is by no means complete.

hire. Obviously, if they all use similar equipment, your options in this area will be limited. Far more important in your quest to get the most for your investment are the price per foot, the cost and size of the casing and, ultimately, the yield of the well in gallons per minute (g.p.m.).

Unfortunately, reliable pricing information is difficult to come by, simply because the composition of the overburden varies so much from region to region. What you can anticipate with some certainty is that there'll be a minimum depth fee, usually set at 100'. Much of the expense of drilling involves the moving and setting of the rig, so even if the operator hits good water at 60', you'll probably still be charged for a 100' well.

As far as the casing goes, 5" and 6" internal diameter (i.d.) are both common sizes for a professionally drilled well, though 4" pipe isn't unheard of. Aside from cost (which might vary by a dollar a foot between sizes), the diameter of the casing is important because it's directly related to the well's storage capacity. If you think of your well as a long, thin reservoir of water, it's easy to fathom how a broader casing can store a greater volume than a narrow one. Just for reference, a 4" casing can hold about 2/3 gallon per foot; a 5-incher, just over a gallon; and a 6" one, nearly 1 1/2 gallons.

How much capacity is enough? That's tied in with the well's yield, its recovery rate and, of course, how much water your household uses. First of all, you'll need to establish your

household's minimum daily needs, which should include not only water used in bathing and drinking but that consumed by flushing toilets, washing dishes and clothes, and watering gardens, lawns, livestock or anything else outdoors—including buildings, should a fire ever occur.

Another factor, peak demand, also comes into play. It's a direct result of our tendency to use the majority of our water during specific times of the day, thus putting a huge demand on the well over a relatively short period. Rather than actually calculating this, you can simply halve what you figured your household's daily needs are and consider that estimate as your maximum hourly water requirement.

By the way, your drill-rig operator should be prepared to ensure the well's yield by making drawdown and recovery tests. This procedure of bailing or pumping the hole will tell you not only what kind of a flow you can expect from your investment but also if the delivery will be consistent.

Clearly, it's always useful to talk to neighbors who've had wells drilled on their property. Find out how deep their wells are, how much casing was used, what the cost per foot was and what kind of yield they've experienced. It would also be to your advantage to ascertain whether or not they've had any dry-spell difficulties, which would indicate that you might want to go the extra mile when you drill *your* well.

Remember, too, that professional well con-

Household Water Requirements

Use	Gallon Estimate
Full bathtub	30
Full washbasin	2
Flushed toilet	6
Average shower	25
Dishwasher	18
Clothes washer	36
Lawn watering	500
Milk cow per day	35
Horse/Beef cow per day	10
Chickens (25) per day	1.5
Sheep/Goat per day	2

Note: An alternative method of estimating indoor water use is to figure on 100 gallons per day for each person in the household.

Capping a Spring

Good water is essential to life . . . and when you live in the country, you "catch" your own.

One of the most romantic, beautiful and archetypal images of rural life is cold, fresh water bubbling up out of the ground—for drinking, watering the garden, bathing or supplying to livestock. Lucky is the country dweller who finds a vein of this "homesteader's gold" on the property, especially so if the newfound spring lies well above the house. Once capped and piped, that water will freely deliver itself to all the spigots in the home!

But discovering a usable spring on your property is only the beginning. Don't be surprised if your sense of appreciation begins to diminish when, eventually, you get around to thinking about just how to *develop* that spring. How, for instance, can you encase it to protect it from contaminants yet not simultaneously lose it by obstructing its flow? Is it high enough above your house so you won't need a pump, and strong enough so

you won't need a reservoir? Will it dry up in the summer—or freeze up in the winter? Will the health department in your area allow it to be used for drinking water?

How Good Is It?

If you've got a tiny rivulet running across your land, you've no doubt already traced it back to the spot you want—the point where the trickle first emerges from the ground. You may have a less obvious spring, though. Search your property. Is there an area particularly lush with water-loving plants—ferns, reeds or jewelweeds? Is there a "sobby spot" on your property, one of those bootsucking mudholes you normally try to avoid? Places like these may contain usable springs. There's only one way to tell: Start digging. Most times you should be able to pull rocks and move dirt until you can discover a flow-

An undeveloped spring

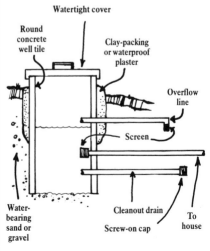

ing source for that wetness. At other times you'll very likely be forced to give up in frustration. If the land's mushy, you might want to dig a ditch running out of that soft spot to drain the area—*before* you start searching.

Once you've located your spring, the next three questions are: Is it year-round? Will it produce enough water? Is the water safe to drink?

Obviously, the only way to tell if your spring will produce water continuously is to watch it for a year—most importantly during your area's annual dry spell. All other guidelines are iffy: Has the water worn out a channel, a good flow bed, below the spring's source, or does it just look like somebody left a running garden hose on the ground for a month or two? Is the nearby plant growth distinctively lush, and can you find old roots that have grown toward the water source over an extended period of time? Are there any local residents who can vouch for that spring's reliability?

Wet-weather springs equal dry-spell frustration, so make certain you'll have year-round water before you go any further. Assuming you have a steady spring, you'll also want to know if it can provide all the water you'll need. Dam it up temporarily with a wall of mud that has a pipe section laid at the bottom, then catch the outflow from that pipe in a bucket, and time how long it takes

A porous-wall spring box

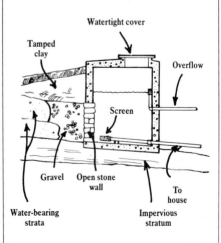

Watertight cover
Tamped clay
Overflow
Screen
Gravel
Open stone wall
Water-bearing strata
Impervious stratum
To house

A well-tile spring box

Watertight cover
Round concrete well tile
Clay-packing or waterproof plaster
Overflow line
Screen
Water-bearing sand or gravel
Cleanout drain
Screw-on cap
To house

is to make sure you're collecting only sub-surface ground water; surface water is the most likely of any to be tainted. Contact your local health department to get a water sample jar and instructions on how to use it, so you can get your water tested. The report that results will tell you if you have an excess of living pathogens in the water—things like fecal coliforms and streptococci. You may well be able to disinfect a mildly contaminated spring with an occasional bleach treatment. The health department can tell you how to do this. However, if you have reason to suspect any *chemical* contamination, you'll have to get a full water test. Has any of the land in your spring's watershed been farmed—recently or in the past? Is there an old dump above it? Either of these could mean mercury, lead, nitrate or other pollution.

Capping Time

Having located a year-round spring that passes your quantity and quality tests, it's time to cap that water source. Essentially, you want to completely encase the spring so that no surface water, small animals or debris can contaminate or clog it.

No two springs are exactly alike, but most can be classified as either a *bank spring,* one that flows out of a hillside, or a *seep spring,* one that emerges from open ground. You can encase the former by closing in the three exposed sides and adding a lid, while the latter requires a complete—four-sided and lidded—box.

Capping a bank spring requires great delicacy. You want to channel its water into a pipe as gently as you can without putting any restrictions on its flow. Otherwise it may seek another, easier, route and change course. Indeed, experienced cappers often first cap a spring temporarily, laying a length of pipe in place secured only with mud and rocks or a little concrete. Then if the water still flows a week or two later, they get on with the job.

One such experienced capper is Rick Compton, a North Carolina resident who has worked with numerous bank springs. How does Compton actually trap his springs? It varies. On one spring, he dug a horseshoe of soil out of the bank, set his water pipe down at the bottom of this shoe, built a curved rock-and-concrete wall about one and a half feet tall running back into the bank, and filled the walled-in space with rocks, leaving as many crevices and gaps between the stones as possible. He covered this stone pile with six sheets of black polyethylene and then piled dirt around and on top of that. All that is visible now at that site is a pipe coming out of the side of the hill—offering a constant

Testing the flow

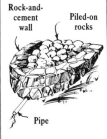

Rick Compton's "horseshoe" spring (before covering with plastic and earth)

Rock-and-cement wall   Piled-on rocks

Pipe

to draw a gallon. Since your spring may yield several times as much water in wet weather as it does in arid times, better make this measurement during a dry spell.

And exactly how much *is* enough? The household water requirements chart on page 19 notes that for indoor use you can use a ballpark estimate of 100 gallons of water per day per person in the household. Remember, though, that one of your biggest water users will be the garden or lawn: To fully water a 1,000-square-foot vegetable plot demands a whopping 600 gallons. Offhand such numbers may sound intimidating. But if that little spring dribbles out a mere gallon of water a minute, it'll give you 1,440 gallons a day!

If you want to try to increase the spring's output, the most common tactic is to keep digging back at its "spout hole" and hope you'll hit some other tappable veins. You may luck out and increase your flow—but you could also disturb the spring so much that it would change course and you'd lose it. So don't press matters. As soon as you get a water flow you can live with, quit digging.

Assuming you're pleased with your spring's output, you'll need to determine one more thing before getting to work: its *quality.* Sad to say, springwater is more likely to be contaminated than deep-well water. Indeed, the reason you want to cap a spring at the point where it emerges from the ground

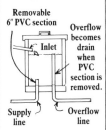

Rick's concrete tile reservoir

Removable 6″ PVC section

Inlet

Overflow becomes drain when PVC section is removed.

Supply line   Overflow line

A mechanical trencher

flow of fresh springwater, of course.

More often, Compton will dig out the spring until he hits a solid rock base, then use a cold chisel and mallet to knock a small trough in that rock to accommodate his water pipe. The conduit will be big enough—say one and one-half or two inches in diameter—to handle the spring's maximum output. He'll then build a stone-and-cement wall about a foot below the pipe's entrance end. This wall will extend back on both sides to tie into the bank and be capped with a rock or wooden lid. The wall's purpose? To enclose, but not dam, the spring. (Construction tips: While Compton is building the cement wall, he may surround the pipe with mud at

Before being capped, a spring may look like no more than a wet spot in a field.

Walling in a spring

a point above the wall, to help keep running water off the cement. To get a tight, leak-proof seal, he makes sure as he works that the rocks touch only mortar, not each other. And he uses a fairly dry, stoneless mix of three parts mortar to one part sand.)

Sometimes, of course, Compton doesn't have a solid rock base to build on. In that case, he'll again start his wall about a foot downstream of the spring—dig about a foot down at this spot and build his rock-and-cement wall up from there. He'll then lay his line in at the original water level. That way he's stopped most of the seepage that would have occurred under his wall, yet because the pool thus formed is still below the spring's

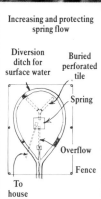

Increasing and protecting spring flow

natural water level, the piped water is still following the path of least resistance.

"All you're trying to do is to get that water to go into the pipe," Compton sums up. "As long as you don't give it any reason *not* to go into the pipe, you should be OK."

Jim Searcy is another capper, and also a North Carolinian, who says he's capped 25 to 30 springs in his time. Like Compton, Searcy says you want to do all you can to make sure "that water don't cut from you." When he's working in soft rock, he'll sometimes use the same chisel-a-trough-for-your-pipe technique Compton prefers, although Searcy is more likely to make a boxed pool at his spring sites. To do so, he'll place a big

drainpipe at the bottom of the front wall and lay up a three-sided concrete block structure, filling the blocks with cement and coating their inside surfaces with a water-sealing mixture of half mortar and half Portland cement. Then he'll lay his water line two to four inches off the bottom of his pool, perhaps build a small wooden access door in front, and lid the block structure with rocks and such to encase the pool and keep it cool. Once he's done, he'll screw a cap on the lower drainpipe (he can unscrew it anytime he wants to drain the pool for cleaning) and will put a fine screen on the inside end of the water-line pipe in the pool to keep "spring lizards and crawfish" from getting in and fouling up the lines.

Do his manmade spring pools "tempt" the water to rechannel? No, because Searcy is always careful to build his enclosures and set his water lines just far enough below the spring so that the pool never backs up to the spring itself! The box offers no resistance to the water source; it just caches a supply of the liquid right below the spring.

Searcy has also built plenty of springs at sobby spots. In those cases, he'll dig back to where the water flow is clearly visible, and around the spring he'll build a lidded, four-sided box with drain, supply line and overflow pipes.

Other Approaches (and Tips)

Both Compton and Searcy generally use a two-stage water supply approach: They encase the spring as tenderly as possible and then pipe its outflow to a separate storage reservoir. This tactic is almost always the best way to cap a low-flow spring.

Other cappers, however, cap and store their water at the same spot. This approach works best with a vigorous "boiling" spring, one with a strong flow that is not likely to reroute itself and that can keep up with peak demand, eliminating the need for a big storage reservoir. You can use such a combination spring and catchment basin with either a bank or seep spring. When capping a bank spring, you can put an inflow pipe through your uphill wall or, better yet, make the entire lower half of the basin's entrance wall porous. If you want to develop a seep spring, leave the bottom open and construct, or set in, a relatively large basin—such as a section of three-foot-diameter well tile. Either way, you'll need to lay the basin as deep as possible and use a clay or waterproof plaster packing around the ground-level sides of the basin to keep any surface water out.

It's even possible to convert an open seep into a shallow well, if you make the catchment basin large and deep enough.

Some people try to increase the flow of a

weak seep spring by burying perforated drainage tile—laid in a deep gravel bed and covered with a thick layer of impervious clay to keep rainwater out—uphill from the spring in an effort to collect and direct extra water. If you take that approach, be sure to dig a diversion ditch all the way around this tiny watershed to route surface water away from pipes.

Actually, it's a good idea to dig a diversion ditch around any spring in an open location. And if livestock or other "moving contaminants" are likely to come through this tract, construct a tight fence all the way around the spring's water-drawing area.

Here are a few *other* tips designed to help make your first spring-capping project successful:

Make sure that the overflow line is large enough to handle the spring's maximum output, that it releases water at a spot where it won't cause harmful erosion and that it is screened at its outlet to keep out small animals.

To help waterproof the insides of a reservoir or concrete catchment basin, cover its surfaces with two or three coats of one part Portland cement to three parts sand or with just a "pea soup" paste of straight (no rocks) mortar mix.

Springs can be capped with wood—our ancestors did it all the time. Use redwood or cedar, and construct the box using few or no nails. The wet lumber will swell, strengthening its seal.

You can, if desired, seal the bottom of a spring box or catchment basin by first erecting the sides and then shoveling in some well-mixed spadefuls of one part Portland cement, two or three parts sand and four parts fine gravel. The cement mix will sink to the bottom and set up.

Remember to get your water tested and, if necessary, disinfected periodically. In addition, inspect your spring often to make sure no small animals have become trapped inside.

Reservoirs

If you decide to install a reservoir, you'll want it downhill from the spring and as close to it as conveniently possible. It'll need, in descending order, inlet, overflow, supply and drainage lines. And the deeper you can sink it into the ground or the higher you can berm its sides with earth, the better—to both keep the water cool in summer and make it less likely to freeze in winter.

How *large* should a reservoir be? The rule of thumb is that it should hold at least a half-day's supply of water. You can build your own cache out of filled concrete block, or create one from any of a wide variety of materials—concrete well tiles or fiberglass storage tanks, for example.

Rick Compton often builds his own version of the well-tile reservoir—shown in an illustration. You'll notice that two of its pipes come up from below, which eliminates most cold-chiseling labor. His overflow pipe (all pipes in this design are PVC) is set into another piece right at the bottom of the reservoir; whenever he wants to drain the container for cleaning, all he has to do is pull the overflow section out. Even his supply line comes in two sections. That way, if he desperately needs a little more water during a dry spell, he can just pull out the short section of his supply line and gain access to an extra six inches of water!

Compton particularly likes using well-tile sections for reservoirs because they can be carried to those storing sites that are hard to get to by car or truck. And if the 3′ X 3′ cylinder's 150-gallon storage capacity isn't enough for a particular household, he will hook two of them up in tandem.

To Pump or Not to Pump

Assuming your reservoir or catchment basin is above your house, you'll want to determine if it's high enough to allow you to rely on gravity for your home's water pressure. That's definitely the ideal situation: You won't need to install a pump and will have neither power bills nor mechanical breakdowns to contend with.

To ascertain the height, you need a sighting level; an inexpensive one is just fine. First, measure the height of your eye from the ground. Then, starting at your house, hold the level to your eye, look in the direction of your reservoir, level the tool, and sight down it to the spot you see on the ground. Walk to that point, and sight off the level again to another ground-level spot. Repeat the procedure until you reach the reservoir, and count up the number of sightings you took. Multiply that figure by your eye height, and you'll have an approximation of the difference in altitude between your reservoir and house.

A column of water 2.3 feet high exerts one psi (pound per square inch) of pressure, so you'll need around 58 feet of altitude to get 25 psi, the minimal acceptable pressure. However, this estimate doesn't take into account friction loss, which can be influenced by both the length and the diameter of the pipe. The accompanying frictional head-loss chart can help you work in that factor. If your reservoir is below the house, or not high enough above for gravity feed, the same chart can help you size your pump.

One further note: If your pressure is more than 80 psi, you'd better decrease it, or the water force could damage your plumbing. The obvious solution would be to set the reservoir lower, nearer the house.

Problems

Perhaps the most aggravating spring-related problems occur when the temperature drops below freezing. Actually, the spring itself probably won't ever ice up, since it is bringing up moving underground water. It is the *pipes* that will freeze.

So bury all water lines good and deep, below the frost line. You can hand-dig the trench if it's a short one or if you're a glutton for hard labor. On the other hand, if the angle isn't too steep or the soil too heavily laden with rocks or tough roots, you can rent and operate a trencher—which is a sort of giant dirt-moving chain saw on wheels. Or you can just break down and pay a backhoe operator to cut the trough for you. Don't fret about spending the money: It's worth it.

Be sure, before you cover your lines, that all connections are tight. Then cover them by hand with about six inches of rockless dirt before you or a machine fills in the rest of the ditch. Otherwise, if rocks are left touching a pipe, they may eventually cut into it.

Air locks can also cause problems with a gravity feed system. If your reservoir/basin ever runs dry, you may have trouble getting water to flow down the pipe again. Of course, if you can get to sections of line easily, you can just take one apart and suck the water down. Or you can open all the house spigots and hope the in-line air will work its way out. When those tricks don't work, use a pump at either the bottom or top of the line to push or suck the air bubble from it.

The ultimate beauty of a well-capped spring is that it requires little care, yet provides a full, fresh, daily supply of the most precious and best-tasting fluid on earth.

Go With the Flow

Head Loss in PSI (and Ft.) per 100′ Sch. 40 Plastic Pipe

Flow (gallons per minute)	Pipe Diameter (In.)						
	$1/2$	$3/4$	1	$1^1/4$	$1^1/2$	2	$2^1/2$
5*	10(23)	4(9)	1(2)	0(1)	0(0)	0(0)	0(0)
10	——	11(25)	3(8)	1(3)	0(1)	0(0)	0(0)
15	——	23(53)	7(16)	2(6)	1(2)	0(1)	0(0)
20	——	——	11(26)	4(9)	2(4)	0(1)	0(0)
25**	——	——	17(39)	6(14)	3(6)	1(1)	0(0)

Note: Minimum pressure should be 25 psi. Therefore, the minimum net head (after losses are subtracted) for gravity feed is 58 feet. In pumped systems, if the pump is capable of 55 psi, the maximum tolerable pressure loss would be 30 psi.

*Weak (Better not shower and flush the john at the same time.)
**Quite strong (You can turn on everything at once!)

Example: Let's say that you have a spring 75′ above and 100′ laterally from your house, and you'd like to know what pipe to use to gravity feed. In addition, you anticipate that you might use as much as 20 gallons of water per minute (g.p.m.). To start with, $1/2″$ and $3/4″$ are out of the question . . . and if you used 1″, the net head would be 49′ (75 − 26), not enough to give sufficient pressure. A better choice is $1^1/4″$ pipe, which would give a net head of 66′ (75 − 9).

If your spring was 200′ away (while still 75′ up), $1^1/4″$ pipe would provide a marginal 57′ of head (75 − the product of 9 × 2). But $1^1/2″$ pipe would give you 67′ of head (75 − 8), which should definitely do the job.

Example: Let's say your spring lies 40′ below your house and 300′ away, so pumping is mandatory. What pipe size would you use to deliver 20 g.p.m. if your pump can push 50 psi? First of all, the 40′ climb from the spring demands 17.4 psi (40 × 0.434, the psi-per-foot value), reducing the potential output at the top to 32.6 psi. That means that the maximum pressure loss to pipe friction that you can stand (and still have 25 psi—the recommended minimum—as your final pressure) is 7.6 psi. Since you're pumping through 300′ of pipe, you can afford to lose no more than 2.5 psi (7.6 ÷ 3) per 100′ of pipe. If you wanted 20 g.p.m., you'd have to use $1^1/2″$ pipe—which has a head loss of only 2 per 100′. (You could, of course, use smaller pipe—if you want to save money and are willing to live with a lower g.p.m. rate: $1^1/4″$ pipe and 10 g.p.m., for instance.)

A well-built stone wall can serve as a monument to human cooperation.

Stone Walls

A complete guide to the construction of mortar-less stone walls

John Vivian, an author well known for his writings on many aspects of rural life, presents the following personal account.

My introduction to stonework, like beginnings in so many homesteading skills, came unexpectedly, urgently and at the wrong time. It was a rare clear morning during a rainy spring in the late '60s, and I was leaving for work from the once-derelict farm in upper Bucks County, Pennsylvania, that provided my weekend refuge from a city job.

The buildings on the place were 150-plus years old and had yard-thick stone walls. The house was stuccoed on the outside and was in fair shape, but the barn had been badly neglected. Its leaky roof rested on 10-foot-high walls that were originally constructed as a sandwich: vertical rock faces of rounded fieldstone on the outside with a mud mortar-rubble stone mix on the inside. Most of the *pointing* (mortar troweled into the cracks between rocks to retard weathering) was long gone. Winter rain and snowmelt had run in, frozen and gradually worked the mortar out, and the interior mud packing had eventually followed suit, until—in places—you could see clear through the walls. Still, the rock itself had been laid up well enough to stand through generations of rain and storm.

Till that day, that is. On walking to the car, I found that the thunderstorms that had kept me awake half the night had also washed out the southwest corner of the barn, along with half of each adjoining wall. Now the roof was kind of fluttering in the wind, ready to follow the south wall downhill.

I traded my Brooks Brothers–Florsheim city uniform for honest Sears–Endicott Johnson, hastily shored up the roof with old framing timbers and ordered up a few days of vacation from work. Then, when the yellow pages failed to produce any stonemasons at all (and the only general masonry contractor

who'd talk to me recommended that we tear the walls down and let him put up a building code–acceptable concrete-block foundation), I set about teaching myself stonemasonry the only way I could, by studying the barn foundation itself: walls that had been built shortly after the American Revolution by dirt farmers with no architecture degrees, no building codes, no engines to ease the strain—just common sense and hands-on experience, simple ramps, levers and pulleys, a team of draft animals to pull the stone boat, and strong backs unafraid of work.

My slow-learner's repair job took the better part of a week, and most sections were built and torn down and rebuilt several times before I got them *half* right. But I can honestly say that the sense of satisfaction I felt on finally completing that barn wall did more than any other single experience to move me out of the urban rat race and into a life of self-dependence on the land.

First Lessons

I'd suggest that what I did for lack of any alternative—study an existing wall and copy it—is the best way for folks to learn stone building on their own. Granted, as with most anything, a master of the trade can teach you faster (some would say *better*), and I've learned a lot from proper masons. However, stone building is a highly individual skill, so once you have the basics down, you simply have to put in time working with the stone to develop your own style.

You see, no two builders will turn the same wall out of the same pile of rock. A mortared brick wall—all plumb and square and lovely—is a work of craftsmanship, to be sure. But it's a solid chunk of ceramic assembled from identical component parts, and one of them is constructed pretty much like any other. A stone wall, on the other hand, is a combination of learned craft and an individual's intuitive response to a complex three-dimensional puzzle having an infinite number and variety of solutions. A stone wall is a work of art in the truest sense: a creation of order out of chaos, of beauty from dross—as much of an improvement on nature as may be accomplished by the hand of man.

And damn, but it is satisfying! A hard-won satisfaction, to be sure; rock weighs a lot, goes up hard and comes down harder. First of all, then, let's talk about how to keep that stone from denting you up too much as it moves in either direction.

Forewarned

Get yourself a pair of horsehide gloves, a well-fitting pair of hard-toed, high-topped boots and some stout long-legged trousers. Rock is abrasive and heavy, and building walls with it is a totally engrossing task that tempts you to forget safety. With proper outerwear you can avoid the scratches and dents—and ignore the occasional rolling stone—that could impair both your hide and your concentration. Insteps and toes are the body parts most at hazard, so proper boots are particularly important: They let you put a foot anywhere that best leverage demands without worrying about getting laid up.

Probably your most valuable piece of equipment is a healthy back. Know the old adage, Lift with your legs, not your back? Well, you can just about forget it in wall building. Instead, don't lift *any* rock at all that's bigger than you can easily heft sitting down. Roll it, slip it, slide it or flip it over end to end. Use ramps or levers or sleds. And when you must use brute force, get behind and push with your legs; bending double at the waist and heaving up on a heavy rock is an invitation to a month of forced bed rest.

Oh, yes—start off easy. Anyone in average good health can work rock. But you'll probably be employing muscles that haven't been used much before; so go slowly at first, particularly if you find, as I do, that the urge to raise stone walls comes on at the first warm spring day following a muscle-softening winter. Chances are your rock has rested where you first found it for upwards of 20,000 years minimum and is in no hurry to move. Don't rush it. The stones won't mind, and your back might.

Helpful, but not essential, are a set of rock-working tools like those shown in Fig. 1. You can find the common—and most useful—heavy mallets and brickmason's chisels at any country hardware store, or in mail-order catalogues under "Trowel Trades" or "Mason's Supplies." Locating the big pry, star drills, railroad spikes and other tools you'd need for any do-it-yourself quarrying may take a little searching. I'm told there are pointed quarrier's sledges and such niceties as wedge-and-shim splitting tools available, too, but I've never used them. If you really want to get into shaping stone, visit your local burial-monument works for advice and tool sources. And be sure to wear a long-sleeved shirt and use safety goggles during any hammer-and-chisel work. Rock chips can be sharper than a surgical scalpel, and they fly off the work at considerable speed.

Reading the Rock

Most of what I've read about stone building presumes a good supply of *table rock* (soft sedimentary rock such as shale, sandstone or perhaps a nice smooth-grained limestone that was originally laid down as sheets of alluvial silt, sand or tiny seashells at the bottom of ancient seas). Many such pieces retain their granular structure and multilayered sedimentation pattern and consequently can be easily worked into shape. (Some can be split up as even and square as a brick with little more than a hand ax!) If you are so fortunate as to have access to sedimentary stone that's good for building, God bless.

On my own Berkshire mountain plateau, there's a mix of the other two—less malleable—major rock types: igneous and metamorphic. Interspersed all too liberally through the garden loam are fieldstones, called *cobbles,* or hardheads, by local folk and *glacial erratics* by geologists. The more or less round hunks of igneous rocks were formed from minerals that melted deep in the earth's interior, cooled to become crystalline rock such as granite or feldspar and in time broke off and rolled down to us under the Pleistocene glaciers. Where bedrock pokes out of our pasture as ledge, there's a soft and greasy, easy-splitting mica schist—a metamorphic rock. Marble and slate are more familiar varieties of metamorphic stone. All are sedimentary (or other) rocks that were heated sufficiently by underground pressure to fuse, but not enough to cause a full meltdown and re-formation as igneous.

Unless you can afford to have flat rock hauled in from the nearest quarried outcropping (in which case you can doubtless afford

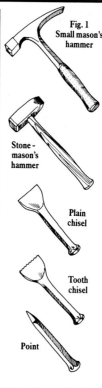

Fig. 1
Small mason's hammer

Stone-mason's hammer

Plain chisel

Tooth chisel

Point

Whether strictly utilitarian or decorative, stone endures.

your own mason to go with it), you will be building, as I did, with what you have at hand. And, unless you have a *lot* of time and patience—or a pneumatic hammer and chisel to work stones into shape—you'll probably be using your native stone pretty much as you find it.

Where's that, you ask? Unfortunately for my garden, I've never had to search out stone myself. Rocks "grow" out of our New England soil as glacial erratics are pushed skyward each year by heaving frost. If you are not so blessed, look along creeks or riverbeds, where roads cut through rolling country or wherever heavy construction is going on. Rock often crops up where someone doesn't want it and is consequently free for the taking. Even if you have to *buy* local stone, it is cheap. The loading and hauling is what'll really cost you.

Don't bother to try building a wall out of gravel or even a pile of fist-sized cobblestones. A lot of little rocks would give the wall so much travel that it would fall apart in short order. You want rocks that are a good double handful and larger—the bigger the better. To a point, that is. Some parts of the country offer great slabs of stone that need busting up, which will give you an opportunity to learn forevermore what "hard labor" really means.

To some degree, the kind and shape of

use the grandfather clause in your local zoning ordinance and building code that exempts old structures from new regs, and simply rebuild on an existing building site or foundation. I've re-piled some dandy old stone buildings into shapes and sizes that the original architect could never have imagined, and I'm now halfway through building a foundation for a satellite dish antenna (!) onto the cellar hole of an eighteenth-century root cellar on my place, no permit applied for or needed. Next, I plan to begin work on an old-style post-and-beam, mortise-and-tenon, pegged-and-slated barn on another "ancient" stone foundation—one I hadn't finished laying before the first snow fell. (Carved the date, 1787, on the cornerstone myself.)

Preparations for Building

We come at last to hands-on construction *and* to the one elemental truth of stone building. Adam Smith and Karl Marx would cringe in unison at the suggestion, but the main ingredient in a stone wall is neither the rock nor your own hard work. It's gravity. Arrange your stones in such a way that gravity keeps pulling straight down on them, and the wall will be standing long after you and I no longer can.

First, you'll need a proper foundation. The more permanent you want your wall, the more of it you must bury forever underground. The base of any wall expected to last a few hundred years must rest on bedrock if possible; otherwise on solid subsoil. So get yourself a cutting spade to slice out sod and a long-handled shovel to dig a trench.

You will find that any ground cover cuts best in early spring before its root systems grab hold; in any season, it cuts more easily when wet. Get out the sod and topsoil, and haul it to the compost pile. Then remove any loose rocks, and cut out all roots. You may want to remove nearby trees as well. If they're left standing, their roots will—in time—grow back and heave any wall made, so long as there is soil on the other side for the roots to grow into. (Roots don't much bother walls around cellar holes—there's nothing beyond to grow into.)

If you live in the Snow Belt and want the wall to be a permanent monument to the time and labor you put into it, you should dig the foundation to below the frost line. If you plan your walls as part of a building, particularly one that will house people or livestock, you absolutely *must* dig the foundation trench that deep. Simply put, winter temperatures freeze soil moisture, which expands and pushes everything above it up (such as those boulders that grow in my garden each winter). Then when soil warms in spring, the frozen water thaws and the wet

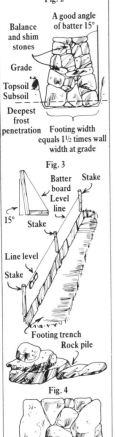

Fig. 2

A good angle of batter 15°

Balance and shim stones

Grade

Topsoil
Subsoil

Deepest frost penetration

Footing width equals 1½ times wall width at grade

Fig. 3

Batter board / Stake

Level line

15° / Stake

Line level

Stake

Footing trench
Rock pile

Fig. 4

your available rock will dictate the internal dimensions of your wall. It needn't decide *what* you build, however. There are cross-country walls in China and in Great Britain, pyramids in Mexico and in Egypt, and monuments and temples all over, each made of "dressed"—and squared and trued—stone of all varieties, laid by hand hundreds or thousands of years ago and still standing. Within an hour's drive of my own place are buildings and foundations of big stone, small stone, round stone and flat stone. I know several local fences so well made, though of potentially unstable—almost globular—field-stone, that they have lasted with no maintenance for 200 years.

The true limiting factors in wall construction are your own time and patience, your skill and confidence, the nature of the structure you are building and—one more thing—whatever the local building code has to say about all that. In some places the zoning mavens will be on you if you try to build a foot-high stone fence along your own garden path. If that happens to you, I'd suggest getting a permit to build a privacy screen; then just go ahead and do your work behind that. (Take the screen down after the next election, and no one will give a hoot.)

If there's enough rock in the neighborhood to erect a building, earlier generations will most likely have built with it. In that case,

Fig. 5

Always keep courses level.

Go up hills smoothly . . .

or in steps.

Fill dips with junk stone.

Fig. 6
OK: Stable

Thin rocks

NO: Will slide

Force

Thin rocks

Fig. 7
One over two

Two over one

Cover the joints.

Fig. 8

Avoid runs like this.

earth shrinks and sags away from solid objects. A dry stone fence—which has more flex than one secured with mortar—absorbs the up-and-down and interior motion that such alternate freezing and thawing impart each season. Even one laid without much foundation will retain its integrity for years with only an annual patrol to replace fallen top stones. On the other hand, a foundationless cemented wall will crack open the second winter. You don't want either cracks or falls with a house, barn or shed, so put *any* building on a deep foundation.

Dimensions

The more width you build into your wall per unit of height, the bigger its footprint and the more stable it will be. So dig your trench a good bit wider than the base of the wall, and make it as deep as you can manage. I plan the footing bases of my own walls to be about one and a half times their width at ground level, with a gradual upward slope, called *batter,* from base to grade (the bottom of the trench to the top). I try to build each face sloping inward at about a 15° angle from base to top (see Fig. 2).

The batter lets gravity pull the wall in on itself as well as straight down on each individual stone. No wall builder sticks to a single, strict height-to-width ratio, of course, and, often as not, the availability of rock and the use to be made of the wall will determine your dimensions. Few rocks, and the need for a high screen, make for a thin, well-thought-out wall; lots of rocks, and no need at all, produce nothing but a rock pile. Most of the massive New England stone walls that surround our place were raised mainly to provide somewhere orderly to stash an oversupply of glacial erratics—which were jutting out of the hayfield, just waiting to chip a scythe blade at mowing time—so they're good and wide. They also defined property lines. Many real estate deeds contain such language as ". . . 20$\frac{1}{3}$ chains running 67.5° along a stone wall from a large Chestnut, thence 62 feet to a blighted Elm, thence 115 yards 57.3° along a loose stone fence . . ." and so forth. Today only the stone walls remain, sad to say.

Laying Out

To lay out your wall, find a length of twine and some stakes. Be sure to line up the stakes straight, and don't skimp on them. Too few stakes and a high wind can bow out your string, and you'll end up with a curve in your wall (see Fig. 3).

If you plan a wall more than a few feet high, you may want to make genuine *batter boards,* lengths of lumber fixed to a ground-level board at the desired angle of batter. Use them repeatedly, much as a carpenter uses the square, to check the angle of what's being built. A mason's level is sometimes helpful in setting individual stones, particularly at the top course and when leveling out stone tables, benches, gates and steps.

Always keep your guide string perfectly horizontal (use a hardware store *line level*—shown in Fig. 3—for this), because you'll use it to align the layers, or *courses,* of rock in your wall, raising the line as you build. Level courses are not essential on flat ground and are hard to maintain precisely on any terrain if you're working with a lot of irregular stones. In Fig. 4, for instance, oddball, giant and partly buried boulders made flat courses almost impossible, but it's a good wall nonetheless.

Still, you want to try to keep your layers horizontal (*straight*), particularly on rolling ground, just to keep gravity pulling straight down (see Fig. 5). If you slope the courses going over a rise, in time the wall will sag downhill.

Building

With the wall laid out and the footing trench dug, the real challenge begins. Now you can start building. You will quickly agree that the more bricklike its shape, the easier a rock is to fit in. But save your heaviest thin stones to make a fine, flat top. Put your biggest and worst stones in the trench, most-irregular sides down. You may have to dig out holes at the footing bottom to accommodate the bumps ("wobbleknobs") on the real stinkers.

Try always to make the top of each course—even the underground ones—level and even, the sides parallel and square. Where you have a lot of little stuff you must use, try to alternate stacked thin rocks with thick single ones in a course, putting layers of thin rocks on each side of a single thick one, and avoiding backing multiple thins against each other where possible (see Fig. 6). Stacked thins will slide over one another, permitting the whole wall to slip off itself, much as a deck of cards will spread when pushed with the palm of your hand.

Here your affinity for the craft and your own style will begin to develop. You may find it more satisfying to lay the entire bottom course first, or you may want to lay multiple courses, always keeping the lower courses out ahead of the upper by a few stones. Some folks find in their character a persuasive need to leave a minimum of open space, so they work for hours to create as closed and bricklike a wall as they can; others can tolerate a lot of gaps; still others like gaps but will want to fill them with rubble and shims. The wall won't care which way you choose, provided the bigger rocks are laid properly.

Do it however your sense of order dictates; the wall will stand for a century or two (so long as you truly enjoy one another's company). But—fair warning—you may find, once you've tried it, that you just don't like wall building. It is hard, often sweaty labor that can leave you sore, bleeding and grubby. Rock is a coarse artistic medium, demanding little fine motor control and permitting few precise embellishments. If you don't like it, if you find that you don't get real intellectual gratification from turning a rock pile into the beginnings of a proper wall, don't force yourself to continue. Fill your trench with compost, and plant asparagus—which will provide satisfactions of a different sort.

The Following Courses

Once the base course is laid, the fun begins of making a wall grow before your eyes. And we come to a few more basic rules of wall building. For one, you don't set or lay stones; you *drop* them (from a small height). Try to lay them gently atop one another and you'll soon crush a finger in the middle. So drop the rock, and move your hands out from under—*fast.*

Always lay stones as flat as possible and ac-

Fig. 9

Tie stones (shaded) add lateral stability.

Fig. 10
Good end

Tie stones are shaded.

Fig. 11
Good corner

Early stone walls resulted when clearing fields of loose rock provided free raw materials.

cording to the old-time formula: one over two, two over one (see Fig. 7). Put another way, always cover an up-facing joint between two rocks with the solid undersurface of another. This rule applies in the vertical dimension as well: Put one beside two beside one, and so on.

Finally, no proper wall builder ever hefts a rock more than once. All the selecting and adjusting is done mentally beforehand. I am told that there are some wags who maintain that we stoneworkers just never own up to lifting a rock more than once, but they're most likely folks who've watched from a distance and have never hoisted a stone themselves. And anyone who can watch a mason at work and resist the urge to pitch in for a while—at least long enough to learn the facts—is not to be believed in any event.

Avoiding Runs, and Tying

If you fail to cover too many joints, you'll create a vertical *run,* and the wall will fold at the crease (see Fig. 8). Properly lapped, the rocks in a dry wall will shift with the seasons but will not fall out.

From time to time, and as the rock permits, *tie* the faces of your wall. That is, lay a long rock crossing the width of the wall, so as to cover all the rocks in the course below, as shown in Fig. 9. This adds lateral stability.

Some builders like to pull in giant rocks

that will fill an entire section, interrupting the courses and forming a solid pier. Presumably this helps stabilize the wall by reducing lengthwise, along-wall shift. Personally, I feel that a giant in a wall invites "fallout" the same as excessive run does, but experienced masons don't always agree. (Indeed, I'd say that they tend to disagree more often than not.)

Another topic of dispute is chinking: Do you chink *in* or *out?* That is, when rock surfaces don't mate well or where there is a substantial gap in a face, do you fill these holes with shim rocks laid big end inside the wall (chinked *out*), or do you hammer in a wedge-shaped shim from the outside (chinked *in*)? I do it both ways, and so will you, I imagine.

As you build, try to imagine the effect of gravity on each rock as you place it, *setting each stone so as to best keep gravity pulling straight down on your wall.* I like to have the rocks in all the courses angling down slightly toward the center of the wall; that is, to have rocks in each face slope in and down toward the midline a bit. Not always possible, but a help in aiding the wall to hold itself together.

Ends and Corners

The sections that make your wall-building reputation are the ends, especially the ones

that butt up to public view. I've known wall builders to haul good end stones for miles to make a lasting impression on posterity. You want the ends to hold up unaided; there's no more wall beyond them to rest against. So save the biggest of the long, squared-off stones for the ends. Then tie alternating courses in opposite directions—first face to face and then back into the length of the wall (see Fig. 10). For a really permanent end, extend your footing out in a wedge in front of the wall as far as you can.

A corner is a pair of ends built together, but here you tie alternating courses into first one and then the other length of wall. Since the wear of the seasons will have the wall heaving at the corner from both lengths, it should be stronger than a simple end. So save the best tie stones for corners (see Fig. 11). Even a giant may find good use here.

And that's about it. Let's summarize: To build a good stone wall, dig as deep a footing as you can, lay the courses parallel and level, and be sure to alternate thicknesses within them. Keep to the one-over-two principle, and tie your ends and corners well. Save the heaviest and flattest rocks for the top course (and shim the top flight well if there will be people or creatures running along your wall). Do you want to build in a gate too? Then make two ends, and hang a wooden door from hinges mortared into the cracks in the rock.

Putting up a stone building is another topic altogether, if only because the building codes enter in. Still, the wall-raising principles are the same; just increase your dimensions. A cellar is nothing but a really deep footing trench, dug square and scooped out in the middle. A doorway is two ends with a heavy timber or long, squared rock for a lintel. The front of a fireplace is a low door, and a window is a half door. You frame doors and windows, set plates and fasten roofing the same as in concrete-block construction (and there are plenty of how-to books around on that).

Frankly, I don't trust my own stonemasonry enough to try a pure dry-laid or even a mud-matrix–filled stone building. For the barn I'm planning, I'll use steel reinforcing rods and a mortar-rubble matrix inside the rock walls, which is the same principle—with a few modern embellishments—used in that old Pennsylvania Dutch barn that got me into stonework in the first place. I'll be laying a parallel set of thin but solid freestanding stone walls a few feet apart, then filling in the interior as I go.

It's a good project to think about when the snow lies thick in the pasture, so at the first sign of spring I'll be ready to tackle that rock pile out back.

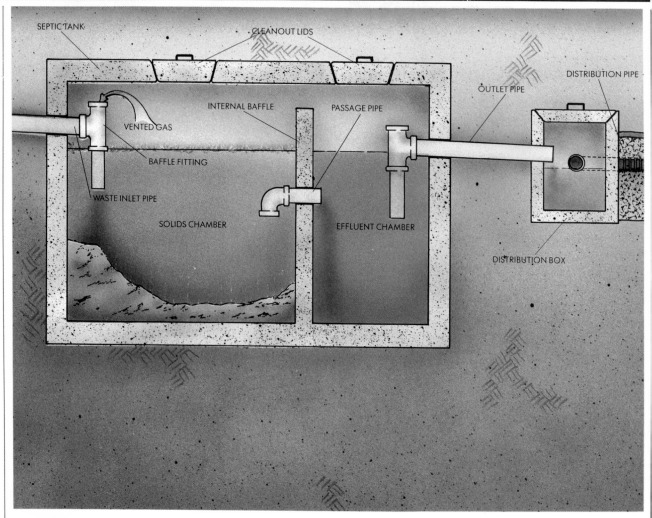

SEPTIC TANK
CLEANOUT LIDS
INTERNAL BAFFLE
PASSAGE PIPE
OUTLET PIPE
DISTRIBUTION PIPE
VENTED GAS
BAFFLE FITTING
WASTE INLET PIPE
SOLIDS CHAMBER
EFFLUENT CHAMBER
DISTRIBUTION BOX

Septic Systems

Now and again, it's best to give a little thought to a part of your water system that's usually out of sight and out of mind.

City dwellers may be able to flush and forget, but their country cousins need to know where that flushing water goes and what happens to it then. In other words, when your household waste disposal system is *literally* in your own back yard, you live with the unpleasant consequences if something goes wrong. It only makes good sense, then, to know the workings—and fixing—of that underground water workhorse, the septic system.

Almost 60 million people in America practice inexpensive and effective home-scale recycling every time they run water. Individual, on-site sewage disposal systems—"the septic" in country argot—do a commendable job of treating domestic waste through a natural biological process that eventually returns most spent water safely to its source. However, septic systems aren't perfect. Because of them, we tend to use too much water, perhaps 40% too much. Moreover, as long as the liquid is flowing in the right direction—out—we assume the plan is working, when in fact it may be broadcasting bacteria and discarded household chemicals.

The Dirty Truth

The boast of a homeowner who claims 20 years of trouble-free septic service is, sad to say, a shallow one. A properly designed septic system is *supposed* to receive occasional maintenance, usually nothing more than a cleaning every few years to remove accumulated insolubles. An untended unit can easily be overtaxed without a sign, quietly suffocating itself until it reaches a point at which it becomes less expensive to replace the system than to try to save it.

Then again, some systems are improperly designed or installed and cause their owners to face upkeep and expense beyond the norm. Frequent pumping, costly chemical treatments and mechanical handling systems shouldn't be necessary with a good installation.

Abuse of a system, however, will quickly lead to problems. No matter how conveniently paint thinners, cigarettes, hair and harsh household cleaners go down the drain, they have no place there. Foreign matter, especially nonorganic material, may never break

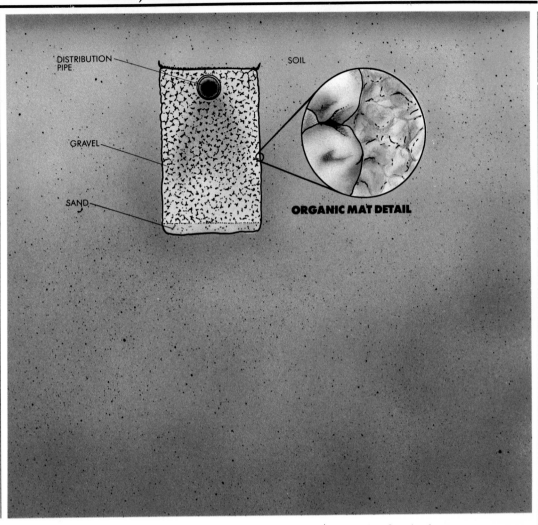

DISTRIBUTION PIPE.

SOIL

GRAVEL

SAND

ORGANIC MAT DETAIL

down and can contaminate both the system and the local water supply.

Think of the septic system as a continuation of your household drain plumbing. Every water-bearing fixture in your home is connected by drainpipe to one main line that carries the highly diluted waste material to an air- and watertight septic tank buried a foot or so beneath the soil and at least 10 feet from the house.

The tank can be constructed of precast concrete, fiberglass, steel and even stone or sealed brick. Average capacity is 750 gallons, though smaller tanks do exist. For large homes or households with more than five people or two baths, 1,000- and 1,500-gallon tanks are available.

By design, the tank has two functions. One is to serve as a settling chamber for heavy solids and as a trap for the floating grease film that rises to the liquid's surface. The other is to provide ideal conditions for the digestion and ultimate breakdown of organic waste material.

Not surprisingly, the two are dependent upon one another. In most modern tanks, internal baffles slow the flow of incoming material, allowing solids to settle. The anaerobic (meaning there's no available oxygen) environment within the chamber encourages specialized bacteria that feed on the cellulose, starches and other constituents of waste matter. These living organisms are so small that perhaps 25 million might fit in a square inch of area.

So efficient are they that within three to five days, up to 75% of a given load of solids is digested, leaving a bottom of heavy sludge and creating bubbles of methane gas which rise to the surface and further aid the decomposition of the lighter fats and greases. Excess gas is "burped" to the atmosphere through a vent in the household plumbing.

The idea is to allow relatively clear liquid, or effluent, to pass from the the tank. By far the simplest way of accomplishing this is to slow the rate of flow through it. Older tanks have a single large compartment, so management is limited. Newer designs use two chambers with a fixed passage between them. In theory, this layout traps grease and sludge in the primary chamber, keeping the secondary one clear. Three-compartment tanks with deep chambers and a reverse-flow pattern are

believed to function better yet.

Upon leaving the tank, the clarified effluent contains organic and inorganic substances, plus pathogens and bacteria that can pose a health hazard. The *absorption field,* containing a series of buried distribution pipes, disperses this liquid evenly into the earth, where it's filtered and processed by movement through the soil.

Not all that long ago, it was considered perfectly acceptable to send this waste water to a seepage pit or dry well—an unmortared brick-lined excavation, or sometimes simply a hole in the ground filled with gravel. Because such a pit allows so little control over where the effluent travels (and it may well migrate through fissures to the water table and contaminate a drinking supply), most counties now require leach fields, or beds, engineered to suit local soil conditions and terrain.

A typical network begins with a concrete *distribution box,* which allows the single pipe from the septic tank to branch equally into several capped lines, usually four-inch-diameter perforated ABS plastic or bituminous paper pipe (and sometimes vitrified clay drain tile) arranged in rows of equal length and set in a bed of gravel about two feet below the ground. Normally, several parallel trenches are dug about 10 feet apart to accept the pipe—each 24 inches wide, up to three feet deep and no more than 60 feet long.

The particular dimensions depend on the size of the septic tank, the permeability of the soil and, ultimately, the decision of the local building inspector or sanitarian. The goal is to achieve enough soil contact area to safely absorb the expected flow. That's determined, sometimes with the help of a soils engineer, by percolation tests and site analysis.

Perk tests indicate the rate, in inches per minute and under set conditions, at which the ground can absorb water. Sandy soils are particularly porous and may drain in several minutes—great for your plumbing but risky for nearby water supplies, since seeping effluent may not have time to be purified. Clay, on the other hand, may retain water for hours, inevitably causing a back-up in the system and a polluted bog on the surface.

Site or soil analyses determine seasonal water table levels, soil texture and the presence of a flood plain or layered rock—all of which affect how water will move through the earth over the course of time.

Taken together, the information can roughly establish the required absorption area, when matched to a set of standard guidelines—either the number of bedrooms, baths and garbage disposals in the house, or an estimate of average water use.

Sometimes, space limitations, grades and other physical problems may dictate a need for a modified drain-field design. Besides the standard forked pattern, a level site can be set up with a closed-loop grid or a single serpentine layout. On downslopes, equal serial distribution—in which the liquid must completely fill one lateral trench before it flows to the next—is possible with the use of drop boxes or fittings that create a "jump" between levels. Upward-sloped sites, on the other hand, can't depend on gravity to do the job; in cases like these, a pump is installed between the septic tank and the leach field, and woe to the downhill family that suffers a power outage.

Occasionally, two other features may be used to supplement a septic system. One is a dry well exclusively for gray water—the relatively clean discharge from showers, sinks and washing machines. Though there's little doubt that shunting this mildly polluted water to a separate location takes a sizable load off the septic system, local codes usually limit the use of dry wells.

A second fixture is a grease trap—a filter used between the kitchen drain and the waste line to prevent cooking fats from building up in the septic tank. Since fats and greases

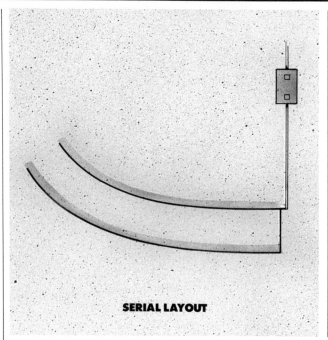

SERIAL LAYOUT

DRAIN-FIELD DESIGN
The choice of drain-field design will be dependent upon available space, terrain, soil type, household water use and the advice of the local sanitarian.

are particularly difficult for the system to digest, a trap can save a lot of grief. But so can separating the grease by hand before dishwashing.

An Ounce of Prevention

Unless you're present during the construction of your septic system, there's little you can do about its installation. But taking care of it after it's in the ground is a different story. First—even if you've never had septic problems—make it a point to find out where your septic tank and leach field are located. The tank's outline may appear as a depression in the lawn, and the field as strips of moist green. No signs? Your local health or building inspector may have a plat of your property on file. Such foresight can save you time and money when you call in the pump truck.

Second, let the absorption field do its job. Don't allow run-off from downspouts and driveways to flood the area; redirect the surface flow if you have to. Trees and deep-rooted shrubbery—along with vegetable gardens—should also be kept off the field: The roots of large growth can penetrate and clog the pipe and trenches; edible plants can absorb toxins from household chemicals. The best cover is a bed of healthy grass. Parking or driving over the space also invites trouble, since it compacts the soil and may crush a leach line.

Make a conscious effort to reduce water usage. You'll be doing your part for conservation and at the same time extending the life of your septic system. Running too much water not only floods the absorption field, but it can force grease and solids into the

lines, effectively clogging the pipes and the gravel around them. Water-saving plumbing fixtures don't cost much, and it's even less expensive to simply schedule showers, dishwashing and laundry chores over a broad period rather than bunching them up and loading the system.

Likewise, try to limit the use of your garbage disposal—or do away with it altogether. In some communities, a disposal counts as an extra bath because it requires water to operate. It also shreds food solids to a size just small enough to flow from the septic tank into the field, sometimes without being fully digested.

Probably the biggest harm to septic systems comes in the form of chemicals. Some—like petroleum distillates, pesticides and photo developers—have no business being there and should be disposed of separately. Others, such as household cleaners and bleaches, may seem harmless and probably are in small quantities. Nonetheless, bleach is a disinfectant, and many cleaners, notably bowl and tank products, contain acids and salts. Safe for plumbing? Sure. But all will kill bacteria in the septic system if used to excess.

Drain cleaners and even some products said to clean septic tanks are particularly risky if used regularly. Anything containing potassium or sodium hydroxide (lye) can affect the system's acidity/alkalinity (pH) balance and temporarily loosen and precipitate solids. The result is loss of bacteria and an accumulation of bulk at the tank inlet or in the drain field.

Brine from water softeners will alter clays in the soil, which will encourage clogging. Colored toilet paper is highly resistant to

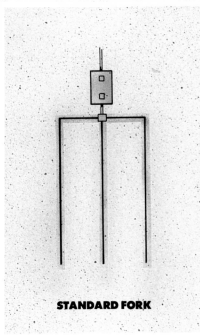

STANDARD FORK

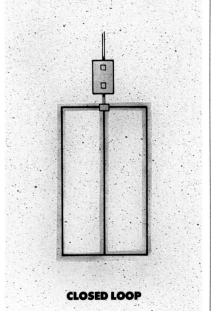

CLOSED LOOP

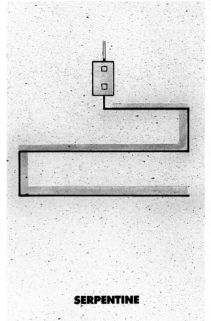

SERPENTINE

digestion (as are disposable diapers!), and coffee grounds or cat litter don't do the tank any favors either.

The question, then, seems to be what *is* good for the system? Pumping every three to five years can be considered preventive maintenance to keep the sludge level down and thwart solidification; for some households, that schedule is not frequent enough, while for others it may be overkill. The pumping contractor's on-site opinion is as

good a gauge as any, and is certainly better than waiting for the obvious signs to show up: sluggish, gurgling drains, polluted backups in ground-floor bathtubs or rank "daylighting" of effluent in the vicinity of the leach field.

Bacterial additives and liquid enzymes can do their part, but they're often misunderstood. A bacterial treatment adds millions of bacteria—to a system populated in the many billions. Enzymes, on the other hand, are

catalytic proteins produced by living bacteria; they alter the rate of digestion, not the amount that existing bacteria can consume. One additive that does neither of these things but may help the system nonetheless is plain baking soda; it tends to buffer the pH level to control short-term fluctuation.

Beyond the Obvious

Chronic problems that continue despite conservation, pumping and "first-aid" efforts can indicate several things, none very encouraging.

Faulty installation occurs more often than you might think. Out-of-plumb or reversed tanks and distribution boxes, too little (or too much) pitch in the line between the house and the tank, a line shoved against a tank baffle, or even one that enters through a right angle can affect the system's ability to accept and pass on waste water. Subsoil freezing and broken seals at the joints are also causes of in-ground difficulties.

A drain field placed in a poor location or pitched irregularly may be hindering flow. If only part of the field is receiving effluent, it's being overloaded. Ditto if the site gets inundated with subsurface run-off. Curtain drains (which divert water from a specific area) or an alternate drain field may solve the problem.

Finally, consider this: Perhaps the system was never designed for the load it's now handling. Some older houses were built with clog-prone cesspools (rather than true septic systems) and single baths. Over the years, additional bathrooms and appliances have taken their toll on what may once have been a perfectly adequate arrangement.

Soil: The Organic Treatment Plant
The biology of the system

Far from being merely a collection of minerals, healthy soil is a working community whose business it is to recycle most anything that passes by. Bacteria feed on pollutants in the waste water. Viruses, in turn, seek out bacterial hosts and live on their life fluids. Protozoa, the simplest form of animal, prey on bacteria, and nematodes—roundworms just visible to the eye—consume organic matter of any kind.

Truly, there is no better cleanser and renovator than living earth: a cleanser, because clay particles in the soil act as electrostatic filters capable of adsorbing virus pathogens before they can migrate; a renovator, because microorganisms, as they work, transform harmful microbes into carbon dioxide and soil nutrients, and also produce antibiotics.

Oxygen is critical to the absorption field and the creatures in it. Aerobic bacteria—those that thrive in a well-aerated en-

vironment—are far better suited to the chore of recycling effluent than are the anaerobic varieties. Without sufficient oxygen, aerobic bacteria and the protozoa that feed on them fall dormant or die. At this point, anaerobic bacteria, fungi and yeasts will take over.

The anaerobic organisms work more slowly and give off less heat. They also process waste material differently than the aerobic variety, creating acids and methane rather than the sugars and fixed nitrogen beneficial to the soil. Under these conditions, ferrous sulfide forms and bonds with algae and dead bacteria to make a layer of insoluble gum, called the *organic mat*, that clogs soil pores and restricts drainage. This clogging mat exists in limited measure under aerobic conditions and is important to the system as a natural filter. But when it spreads out of control in unhealthy soil, the field will ultimately fail to do its job.

Short-log construction enables a family to build a shelter without the help of heavy machinery or a large crew.

Building a Short-Log Cabin

Here's how to build a shelter with log scraps.

What would you say to a log-building technique that is so uncomplicated that British Columbia's regional recreation commission regularly employs novice builders to use it when constructing ski and camp shelters? For more than 300 years, Canadian settlers, the Hudson's Bay Company and the Royal Canadian Mounted Police have utilized it as well, proving just how adaptable and functional the method is to have survived for so long.

French-Canadians call the technique *pièce sur pièce* (piece on piece), but the term *short-log construction* is more descriptive. This method of log building doesn't require arrow-straight whole timbers 20' or 30' long, as a traditional log cabin would; instead, logs 6' and 8' in length are used to make what's essentially a post-and-beam framework that's filled in with equally short pieces laid horizontally between the posts.

For anyone, especially the would-be homebuilder with a creative bent and a tight budget, the technique has a lot going for it. For one thing, since most of the timbers are short, they can be managed by one or two people and a pickup truck; usually, only parts of the roof require logs longer than the standard vehicle bed. For another, chunks of this size can be smaller in diameter than full-length logs, making the selection process a whole lot easier. Too, trees that can't yield a sound 25' run may well provide two perfectly good 8' sections. And short logs are considerably less expensive than longer ones if you're buying felled timber—especially in areas where pulp logging is big business.

Aesthetically, the piece-on-piece method also offers a flexibility that's just not available with many other log-building techniques: Logs that are round, square or a combination of both may be used; outside corners can be dovetailed, overlapped and notched, or set into posts; the bays can be widely spaced or can be narrowed to match

Before doing any measuring or cutting, the log should be peeled and supported in a sturdy sawbuck.

SQUARE-CUTTING AN END

Cut a piece of heavy paper or builder's felt into a 18" X 72" strip. Wrap it one and a half turns around the log, match the paper's edges, and draw a line around the outer edge with indelible pencil.

Laying Out a Log

The finished cabin is snug and comfortable. Its interior sports no unnecessary decor or trim, just rustic good looks.

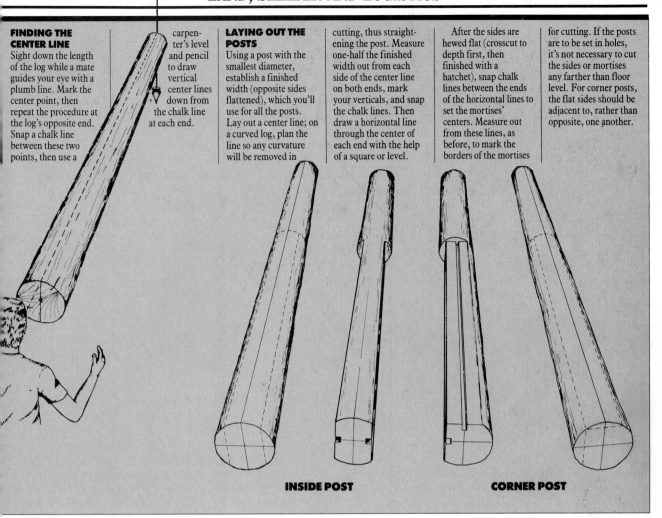

FINDING THE CENTER LINE

Sight down the length of the log while a mate guides your eye with a plumb line. Mark the center point, then repeat the procedure at the log's opposite end. Snap a chalk line between these two points, then use a carpenter's level and pencil to draw vertical center lines down from the chalk line at each end.

LAYING OUT THE POSTS

Using a post with the smallest diameter, establish a finished width (opposite sides flattened), which you'll use for all the posts. Lay out a center line; on a curved log, plan the line so any curvature will be removed in cutting, thus straightening the post. Measure one-half the finished width out from each side of the center line on both ends, mark your verticals, and snap the chalk lines. Then draw a horizontal line through the center of each end with the help of a square or level.

After the sides are hewed flat (crosscut to depth first, then finished with a hatchet), snap chalk lines between the ends of the horizontal lines to set the mortises' centers. Measure out from these lines, as before, to mark the borders of the mortises for cutting. If the posts are to be set in holes, it's not necessary to cut the sides or mortises any farther than floor level. For corner posts, the flat sides should be adjacent to, rather than opposite, one another.

INSIDE POST   **CORNER POST**

---

the width of doors and windows; and infill material between the posts needn't be strictly timber or even horizontal—rock, masonry or preinsulated panels are all acceptable—whether the structure is a cabin, barn or outbuilding.

Finally, the technique is very forgiving to the part-time builder—particularly the novice who may be juggling the demands of a paying job *and* a still-alien skill. Common sense, a good back and little else more than a chain saw, a broad hatchet, a slick and some measuring tools are collectively a fair substitute for experience. Also, short-log construction is not the kind that needs to be gone at hammer and tongs to the end; work on a wall or a section can proceed independently of efforts elsewhere. The infill logs can be precut, and in one variation the roof can be finished before the bays are even filled in.

Skin, Rack and Stack

Building a short-log cabin may not be the easiest thing anyone can do, but by tackling the job with only a couple of sharp slicks and a supply of rot-resistant red cedar, a two- or three-person crew—even one with hardly any construction experience and no knowledge of log building at all—can get off to a strong start by simply peeling the bark off those logs that are seasoned, straight and no less than 8″ in diameter.

An odd timber load will probably yield a number of solid 10″ logs about 12′ in length that can serve as anchor posts, to be sunk 3$\frac{1}{2}$′ into the earth, with 7$\frac{1}{2}$′ or more left aboveground to provide at least 6″ for top trimming.

This, of course, is just one way of anchoring the structure. Other methods, such as laying perimeter footings or using traditional stone piers, would work equally well and might even be better in some situations.

To prepare the uprights, it's easiest to use a chain saw and a hatchet to cut two flat sides; these should be the opposite faces for all posts except the corner ones, which get flattened on adjacent sides. It's important that these cuts be parallel to the center line of each log, rather than following its taper. Once that's done, a 1$\frac{1}{2}$″ X 1$\frac{1}{2}$″ channel, or mortise, is cut down the middle of each flat, using the chain saw for the rough work and

trimming up with a framing chisel.

Positioning the posts is just a matter of planning. It's necessary to line them up precisely and to diagonally brace each one temporarily. The spacing between the posts should be kept at some uniform distance—6′ or 8′—by placing boards, cut to the same length as the infill logs, between each of the uprights. String stretched between batter boards will insure that the postholes are dug accurately; by fastening the cord 1′ outside the center line of each row, it's easy to measure inward this same distance to align the marked center of each post.

After setting the posts and bracing them from outside the structure, the forms for the concrete slab can be put into place. To discourage cracking, the floor is usually divided into sections to coincide with the supports by staking treated 2 X 4s between the posts and around the perimeter. Setting two lengths of 3/8″ rebar at the edge helps hold the skirt together.

This method allows a single pour, which can be screeded along the top of the boards; they are then simply left in place. Since the floor doesn't support any real weight, the

Linking Logs

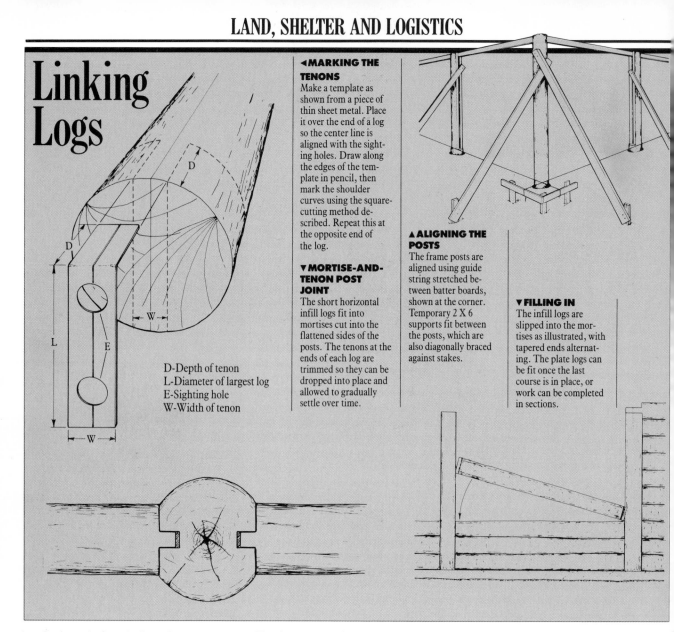

◄ MARKING THE TENONS

Make a template as shown from a piece of thin sheet metal. Place it over the end of a log so the center line is aligned with the sighting holes. Draw along the edges of the template in pencil, then mark the shoulder curves using the square-cutting method described. Repeat this at the opposite end of the log.

▼ MORTISE-AND-TENON POST JOINT

The short horizontal infill logs fit into mortises cut into the flattened sides of the posts. The tenons at the ends of each log are trimmed so they can be dropped into place and allowed to gradually settle over time.

D-Depth of tenon
L-Diameter of largest log
E-Sighting hole
W-Width of tenon

▲ ALIGNING THE POSTS

The frame posts are aligned using guide string stretched between batter boards, shown at the corner. Temporary 2 X 6 supports fit between the posts, which are also diagonally braced against stakes.

▼ FILLING IN

The infill logs are slipped into the mortises as illustrated, with tapered ends alternating. The plate logs can be fit once the last course is in place, or work can be completed in sections.

---

only threat it faces is from frost heaving, which probably won't be a problem even in extreme temperatures.

The real heart of short-log construction follows: filling in the horizontal pieces. As usual, there are a couple of ways to do this correctly. The first—cutting notches in the ends of the logs, and mortise slots in the uprights to accept 2 X 6 splines—is more of a craftsman's approach and takes patience and a good deal of practice.

The other way is far simpler and gives nearly the same results in considerably less time. It involves cutting tongues, or tenons, into the ends of the horizontal logs and merely dropping them into the waiting mortises. By trimming the logs slightly shorter than the actual distance between the grooves, one end can be started and the other raised enough to clear the top of the post. Settling should occur over time, so the logs don't have to be fastened.

The first course of logs should rest on a strip of tarpaper laid over the concrete. With other types of foundations, carefully cut sill logs would be appropriate to support a girder and floor joists, but that isn't necessary in a simple shelter. Each successive course alternates butt-to-tip with its neighbor below to minimize the natural taper of the logs.

To make trimming chores easier, it's worth the effort to choose the straight sides of any bowed log as the top and bottom; if time is short, you can merely flatten these faces rather than scribing and cutting lateral V-grooves into the bottom of each timber. Naturally, this may leave gaps of up to $^1/_2$" between the courses and may invite standing water in places. These spaces should be filled later with chink sealant—a maintenance step that's taken regularly with any log building.

Windows and doors can be either planned or treated as an afterthought. Experience shows that door frames are made most easily by placing posts on either side of the opening, one of which can be a corner or frame member. The faces needn't be mortised.

Window openings, if they're small, can be cut out from a solid wall or placed against a post. With large windows, posts should be set on either side of the casing, with a header beam or framing used above to meet the top plate log. An important step is to caulk between the casings and the logs or framework around them.

Pass the Plate

The purpose of the plate logs is to tie the tops of the posts together and provide a bearing beam for the roof rafters. In addition to the ridgepole, these might be the only long logs needed. In a pinch, short logs attached end to end by lap joints cut to rest on top of the posts will do as well as full-length

Though often the bane of the owner-builder, the inspector should find no fault with the structural aspects of this construction method.

timbers; this, in fact, is how the plate logs are joined at the corners, secured by cut lengths of $1/2''$ rebar pounded into $3/8''$ holes drilled through the joints and into the uprights below.

It takes only elementary mathematics to figure out the final post heights. Each can be trimmed $3''$ higher than the top of the uppermost horizontal course, allowing that gap to be filled by the plate logs if $3''$ flat notches are cut into their undersides. Given logs of $10''$ or more in diameter, this leaves plenty of meat for load support, even where a lap joint exists.

To evenly distribute the considerable weight of the roof over the structure (and to make it easier for a small crew to lift the longer, unwieldy rafters), a ridgepole, the familiar full-length timber supported by vertical king posts and a pair of diagonal struts, is the best choice. The temporary bracing used to hold up the kings can double as an incline when the time comes to haul the ridgepole to the top of the posts with a simple rope parbuckle. The notch and rebar method is a good way to secure the ridge to the king posts.

No special joinery is required to attach the rafters to the ridgepole or the plates. To get the upper surfaces of all the rafters to line up, just enough wood is removed from their undersides to make the tops more or less even. By temporarily spiking each set of rafter tips in place next to one another at the peak, the junctures can be cut with a chain saw to trim the ends at the proper angle. That way, it's a lot easier, after spiking the butt ends of the rafters to the plates, to line up the matching tips, drill the sockets and drive home the upper rebar spikes to finish the job.

Roofing material is a matter of choice, but for this rafter pattern, corrugated sheet roofing supported on horizontal purlin strips makes the most sense. Rough-cut 1 X 4 purlins cost less than dressed lumber and offer more strength, so that's another thing to consider when working in a rural area. Since it's unlikely that the rafters will be in a perfect plane, count on trimming down the high points and building up the low ones. The surface will probably still be somewhat wavy, but it won't show from the ground.

Though he's sometimes considered the bane of the owner-builder, the building inspector shouldn't find fault with the structural aspects of this particular construction method. An inspector who puts faith in common sense and personal experience may even prove to be a welcome source of information. In any case, learning the ins and outs of log construction using a proven method is a great way to start—especially with the experience of 300 years behind you and something to show for it when you're finished.

Erecting a Pole Building

Functional as they may be, pole buildings are also elegantly economical. When it comes to enclosing a space and protecting its contents from the elements—the definition of an outbuilding—no other construction method can do it with so few materials and so little effort. Pretty is as pretty does.

You probably won't build a house using the pole-building technique, though it does bear a resemblance to timber framing. The spindly frame doesn't lend itself to insulation, finished floors or the other amenities of buildings meant for humans. But pole building is the perfect way to put up a barn, a shed or a garage.

Along with its simplicity come other advantages: Pole building requires only basic hand tools—items a handy person is already likely to have. And there's no need to call out bulldozers, backhoes and concrete mixers. All of the construction can be done with supplies from a lumberyard and the following tools:

1. Posthole digger
2. Handsaw (good and sharp)
3. Chain saw (optional)
4. A 4' level
5. Chalk line (200')
6. Shovel
7. Large wrecking bar
8. Framing square
9. Try square

10. A good ruler
11. Tin snips
12. Two 100′ tapes
13. Hammer
14. Line level
15. Circular saw

Site Preparation

Site preparation for pole buildings is, in most cases, a fairly easy and simple process.

The site for a pole building needs to be about 5′ longer and wider than the proposed building's outside dimensions. Staking and squaring this area is done in the same manner as squaring the building's four corner posts—though the latter operation is more crucial—so area layout will give you valuable practice.

Pick an approximate place for one corner of your site, and drive a stake; this we'll refer to as stake number 1. Next, measure off the length of the area, and drive stake 2. If you wish to keep your building square to an existing landmark, such as a road, driveway or another structure, measure from the landmark to both stakes 1 and 2, making sure they are the same distance from the landmark. To locate stake 3, measure from stake 2 the appropriate distance, and attempt to form as near a right angle as you can. To complete the outline of your site, measure from stakes 1 and 3 at the same time, and at the point where the proper measurements intersect, drive stake 4.

You must now check the site for squareness, which is done by measuring the diagonals—the distances between stakes 1 and 3 and between 2 and 4 (Fig. 2). (If you don't have two tapes, or if the tapes you have won't reach between corners, a length of marked rope or unstretchable twine will do.) If the rectangle has square corners, diagonals A and B will be equal; if the diagonals aren't equal, the stakes must be adjusted so they become equal. If, for example, diagonal B is longer than diagonal A, move stakes 3 and 4 back toward stake 1, thus decreasing the length of

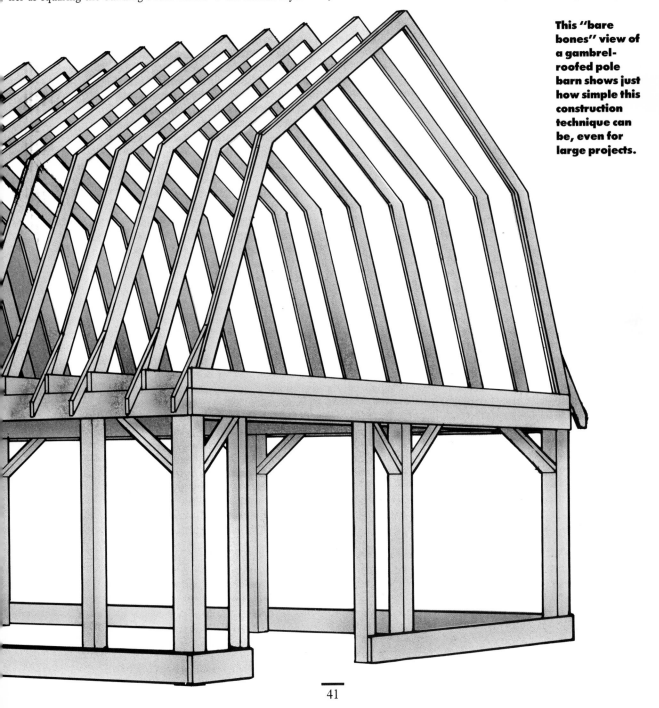

This "bare bones" view of a gambrel-roofed pole barn shows just how simple this construction technique can be, even for large projects.

consult the rafter conversion table on your framing square, which, with a given pitch, will give you the total length of the rafter. To this you need to add the length of overhang you want.

The step-off method using your framing square is the simplest way to lay out a rafter. Mark the top end first, by setting the square with 12″ on the blade and the unit of rise in the tongue both lining up on the edge of the rafter (Fig. 18). If the rafter length from the peak (on a gable) or upper overhang (on a shed) to the building line doesn't come out to an even foot measurement, measure the odd unit from the top first, and then mark down the rafter a foot at a time until you reach the building line. To mark out the notch where the rafter sits on the plate (commonly called the bird's-mouth), run your square at a right angle to the building line about a third of the way up, and mark the notch (Fig. 19). On a gable roof, you can now mark out the overhang; on a shed, continue stepping across to the lower plate, notch again, and then mark off the overhang. Cut out one rafter, and use it as a template for the others. The number needed will depend on the spacing (usually 2′ on center) and whether there will be an overhang at the ends of the shed or gable.

Shed roof rafters are simple to install, but gable rafters take a bit more effort. Start by setting up a ridgepole of appropriate length supported temporarily by 2 X 4s at the proper height (Fig. 20). Then mark the locations of the rafters along the ridgepole and the top plates. Nail rafters to the ridgepole first, then set them to the marks on the top plates, and toenail them to the plates. Wherever a rafter butts against a joist or pole, face-nail it to the wood with 16d common nails. (Steel straps add extra security in regions with high winds.) If you plan no overhangs on your gable ends, go ahead and stud in the ends at this point (Fig. 21).

The poles along the eaves will need to be trimmed to conform to the rafter slope, and since the joists will also stick out, they'll need trimming too. Roofing materials set on purlins give you a little more slack here, but the cuts still need to be pretty close.

Gambrel: Rafters for this gracefully arched roof style must be laid out, cut, joined and reinforced on site before they're lifted into place—much as trusses are set.

To lay out a gambrel rafter, place a 2 X 6 on each side of your roof deck so that the ends come out even with the edge of the joists on one end, and about 2′ to 3′ in from the edge on the other end (Fig. 22a). After measuring to see that they're identically positioned, temporarily nail them to the roof deck. Next lay out two 2 X 6s so that they run across the ends of the two you've just positioned and

so that they cross each other exactly in the middle of the deck. Mark lines through the joints at the hips and peak (Fig. 22b), and cut through the boards at the same time. The four pieces should fit tightly at the joints.

Nail pieces of 2 X 4 on both sides to form a jig for assembling the rest of the rafters. Then pull the 2 X 6s up, and use them as templates. Mark out one rafter at a time, lay the pieces in the jig, and nail them at the joints. For added strength, make plywood gussets 1′ wide and 4′ long out of ½″ plywood. Lay them at the joints, and cut them to match the angles (Fig. 22c). Glue them to the rafters, and nail them with 6d coated box nails. Do this on both sides of each rafter—except for the two end rafters, which should be gusseted only on the inside.

Set your end rafter, bracing it well and making sure it's plumb. Then set the remaining rafters, securing each one as described in the section on truss setting. Again, the poles will have to be trimmed to conform to the roof line. Then stud in the open ends under the roof. If you want them, apply tails to your gambrel roof rafters. A few styles are shown in Fig. 23.

Overhangs

To have the roof overhang the ends of the building perpendicular to the rafters, you must build *ladders*. These are boxed sections built of the same material as the rafters (Fig. 24). They rest on a framed-in end that is even with the underside of the rafters, and they're face-nailed to the end rafter so they cantilever out to form the overhang. The overhang should be about equal to the rafter spacing, and it should have spacers every 16″. Though you could run siding up between the spacers to the underside of the decking, it's simpler to close the overhang with plywood on the underside.

Roofing

There are three basic choices of material for pole-building roofs—steel, aluminum and asphalt (shingles or roll roofing). Each has advantages and disadvantages. Steel and aluminum are strong, easy to apply, relatively maintenance-free and less costly than asphalt and plywood sheathing. On the other hand, when they're used in heated buildings without good ventilation, condensation may form and the metal will sweat. Plywood and asphalt provide a tighter roof that holds heat better than metal.

All metal roofs are applied on top of purlins—2 X 4s lying broad-face down on 24″ centers perpendicular to the rafters (Fig. 25). Steel usually comes 32″ wide (which covers 30″) and up to 18′ long. Aluminum

is available in 36″ and 38″ widths and can be special ordered up to 28′ long. Steel and aluminum go on in just about the same way, so the following instructions apply to both.

The most important part of putting on a metal roof is starting the first piece square to the eaves. Allow a 1″ overhang at the eaves, making sure the measurement is equal on both sides of the piece. Fasten steel with galvanized nails (either "lead heads" or nails with neoprene washers). Aluminum goes on with aluminum nails with neoprene washers. Nail through the peaks of the ridges, drawing the nail tight enough to put pressure on the metal without flattening it (Fig. 26). Each successive piece overlaps the preceding one; nail through both.

Check as you apply each piece to see that the overhang is running the same. If the pieces begin to run unevenly, you'll have to pull them back into place. Let's say that a piece has an overhang of 1″ on one side and ½″ on the other. To even this out, use a hammer to pull the metal straight. If you wish to take the metal back toward the eaves, push the metal at the top—causing a slight bump—and nail. Then, on the bottom, stick the claw of your hammer in the rib and pull the metal toward you. If you are short on the far edge and need to bring the metal out from the eaves, reverse the procedure (Fig. 27).

When cutting steel, get a good metal blade for your circular saw, or turn an old plywood blade backward and use that. Protective goggles and earplugs are a must. Aluminum can be cut with a pair of tin snips.

If two lengths of metal are needed to reach the peak, be sure to put the top piece on last and overlap the bottom by 4″ to 5″.

At the top, the roof's two sides won't join together tightly, so a manufactured ridge cap is necessary. The cap is specially designed to fit the metal you are using and will be either a one- or two-piece cap (Fig. 28). With the cap on, a metal roof is complete.

A plywood and asphalt roof doesn't require purlins, as plywood is nailed directly over the rafters. Measure up on both end rafters approximately 47″ and strike a chalk line; this will leave a 1″ overhang. Run the plywood on this line, centering the joints on the sheets' 4′ ends over the rafters. Nail with 6d common or box nails. When the next row of plywood is applied, stagger the joints so they don't coincide with those of the previous row.

When the plywood is on, cover it with 15-pound felt, which comes in rolls and is stapled to the roof as undercoating. Next, nail aluminum drip edge around the perimeter of the roof. If you use shingles, there are excellent instructions on the package. Roll roofing is simple to install; just overlap the sheets at least 6″. If you want further expla-

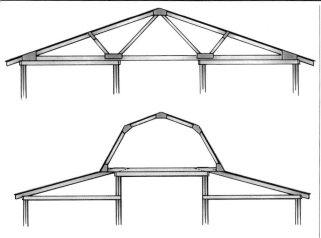

Fig. 21

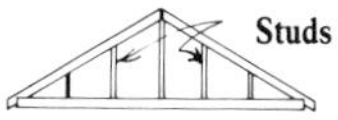

Studs

Fig. 22

3′   3′

2 X 6 s

a

Deck

Line of cuts

b

Gussets

c

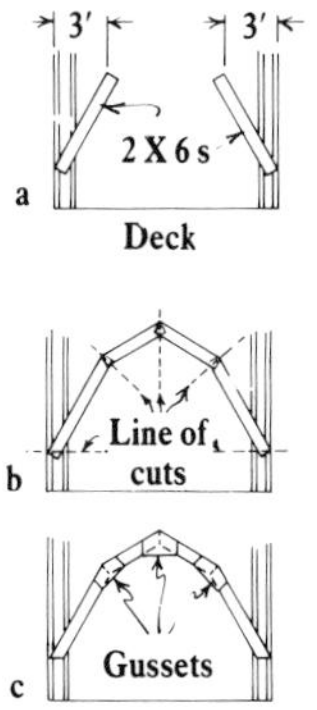

Fig. 23
Gambrel roof tails

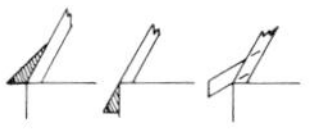

Fig. 24

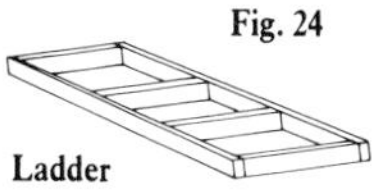

Ladder

Fig. 25

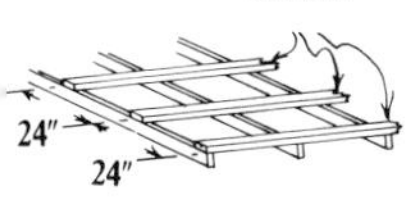

Purlins

24″

24″

Fig. 26

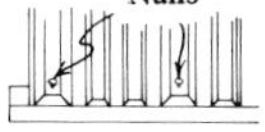

Nails

Fig. 27

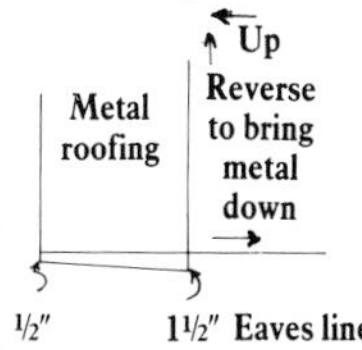

Up

Reverse to bring metal down

Metal roofing

½″   1½″ Eaves line

nation, consult your local library for a book on roofing.

Girts

Now that the roofing is on and the weather is at least partially at bay, it's time to close in the walls. Wall framing on a pole building is different from conventional construction. Instead of vertical studding, 2 X 4s—called girts—are run across the poles horizontally on the outside (Fig. 29). Girts are placed 24″ on center measuring up from the bottom plate. It's best to measure on each corner pole and strike a line to keep the girts level across the building. Where girts break, run the next one directly on top of the last, so they overlap. On the next overlap, drop back down to the previous level.

The only place studding will be necessary is in the rough openings for windows and doors. On either side of a window or doorway there must be a pole or a stud. The distance between these studs is determined by the rough opening width of the door or window. Studs are 2 X 6s placed in between the two top plates and running down onto the inside face of the bottom plate (Fig. 30). Plumb studs with the 4′ level.

To complete the framing of an opening, run pieces of 2 X 6 horizontally at the top and bottom of your opening (for a door, of course, you'll need just one piece at the top). The studding can be done before the girts are put on, with the girts sized to the opening later; or the girts can be installed first and then cut away later to reveal the opening. When the studding and girts are installed, cut blocks to run around the opening to bring the entire face of the opening flush to the girts (Fig. 31).

Siding

Of the many types of siding available, the most common on pole buildings are board-and-batten, metal, and wood sheathing.

Fig. 28
Caps

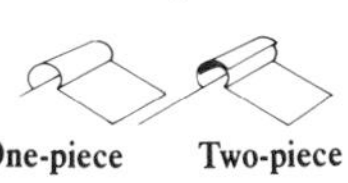

One-piece   Two-piece

Fig. 29

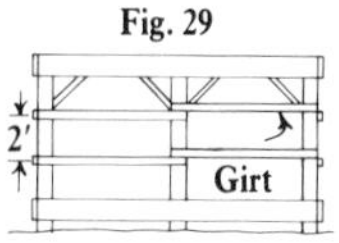

2′

Girt

Fig. 30

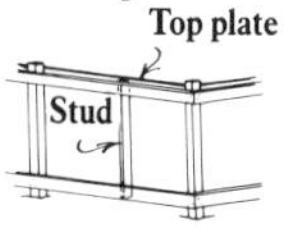

Top plate

Stud

Fig. 31

Studs

Blocks

Girt

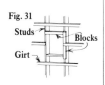

Fig. 32

Siding run

Bottom plate

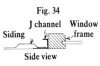

Fig. 33

Battens

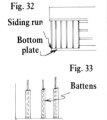

Fig. 34

J channel   Window frame

Siding

Side view

Fig. 35

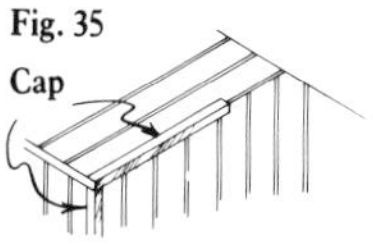

Cap

Fig. 36

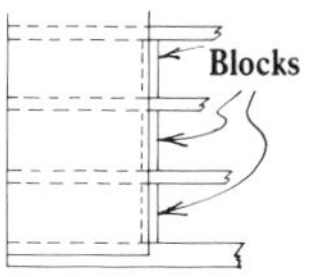

Blocks

Most rural communities have at least one small independent sawmill where you can buy rough-cut lumber suitable for board-and-batten siding at a real saving over lumberyard prices. The planks, usually 1″ thick, vary in width and are sold by the board foot (one square foot, 1″ thick). You'll also want to have a quantity of 3″ or 4″ battens cut.

Start this type of siding on a corner, plumbing the boards as you go. Fasten the planks with 8d cement-coated nails. The boards should run down onto the bottom plate without covering it completely (Fig. 32). When the planks are in place, install the windows and doors in their openings. To finish up, position battens over each siding joint. Because the rough-cut lumber will shrink when it dries, it's important to adequately cover the joints (Fig. 33).

In siding as in roofing, the metals—steel and aluminum—are applied the same way. Before you begin siding with metal, set your windows and doors. Each window and door should have a drip cap across the top and J channel down the sides and under the bottom of the window. This flashing covers the exposed edges of the siding (Fig. 34).

To install the metal, start at a corner, making sure the siding is plumb. Nail through the valleys instead of the ridges, except at joints where two pieces overlap. Use the same kind of nails recommended above for roofing metals. Always start at the bottom so any higher pieces will overlap the lower. Once the sides are on, put on the corner caps, which are 6″ X 6″ L-shaped pieces. Also, if your roof doesn't have an overhang, you'll need to run this material along the joints between the roof and siding (Fig. 35).

The last type of siding is sheathing: 4′ X 8′ sheets of plywood. The most commonly used is T-111, plywood with grooves to imitate board-and-batten siding. Again, start from the corner, and be sure to set the first piece plumb. You may want to insert backing blocks between the girts to support vertical joints between sheets. This is an optional measure but considered a good practice (Fig. 36). After the siding is on, set the windows and doors.

When cutting the angle of the roof pitch on any of these materials, use your framing square to lay out the angle. If, for instance, you have a 4:12 pitch, place the foot mark on the low corner, go up 4″ on the other angle, mark it, and draw a line from the corner through the mark.

There are any number of niceties that you can add to your pole building—from a cement floor to animal pens to a partitioned-off, weatherproofed shop. That's the beauty of a pole building. For minimal effort and expense, it encloses a space that can be adapted to myriad uses.

Electric Fence

Here's the cheapest critter-keeper of all.

Every country dweller occasionally needs to keep some creatures in and others out. But all fences are not created equal. Wooden ones demand intense labor and maintenance, the barbed-wire variety often inflicts injury on animals or installers, and welded-wire enclosures are both expensive and unwieldy. The cheapest, easiest to erect and most flexible animal containment of all replaces the pure force of a physical barrier with applied human intelligence and technology. This is none other than electric fencing.

An electric fence consists of one or more strands of bare steel wire charged to deliver a convincing (but short-lived) electric shock when touched. It can be rigged for anything from a one-strand rabbit barrier around the carrot patch to a multistrand, high-tension fence that carries enough voltage to keep a whole county of winter-hungry deer from a young fruit orchard. Moreover, there is an often overlooked advantage to electric fencing: Country people do move from time to time, and electric fence is the only form of barrier that is readily transportable.

The Fencer

The heart of an electric fence is the charger, or *fencer* (Fig. 1), which combines an electrical transformer with a timing mechanism to develop those short, sharp shocks. The current can come from a 6- or 12-volt DC battery, a small photovoltaic system or from (greatly modified) 110-volt AC household current. The most persuasive chargers are the low-impedance "Energizers" used to electrify sheep fence by the hundred-mile leg in the Australian outback. These turn 110-volt AC power into pulses of 3,000 volts at 30 amps—almost 100,000 watts of power and enough to turn a whole herd of sheep into shish kebab were each pulse not limited to a few *ten-thousandths* of a second. The typical domestic line–powered charger develops only about 4,000 volts at half an amp. This 2,000 watts is also a potentially dangerous charge, but each pulse (they come on 50

to 60 times a minute) lasts less than a thousandth of a second. Battery-powered fencers have less oomph behind them, so they release longer pulses—lasting about a half-second each—at a fraction of an AC unit's voltage.

The jolt from a typical fencer feels like being hit by a rapid-fire electric peashooter: You feel it and pull back quickly, but there is no burn or lasting pain—just a strong and unpleasant memory. And since the current pulses for only a fraction of a second, there is little danger of getting "frozen" to the wire. However, a fencer shock *can* interfere with cardiac pacemakers and such; people outfitted with them should be warned to keep their distance.

It is an absolute must to use a UL–labeled, or similarly approved, fencer to charge a fence. Such a device is effective and safe—it will blow a fuse instantly during any serious malfunction. *Don't* do as some neophyte homesteaders have done and wire an electric fence directly to a wall socket, welding transformer, model railroad speed controller or any "home-brewed" device.

How an Electric Fence Works

You'll recall from junior-high science that electricity is the flow of free electrons from

the + to the – terminal of a power source through a *conductor* such as metal (or a water-based living thing). The steel fence wire is good conducting material that's held away from other conductors such as fence posts by nonconductive ceramic or plastic *insulators*. The hot (+) post of the charger is connected to the fence. The other (–) post is wired to a stake driven into the soil. Normally, as the charger pulses with *voltage*, trying to send a charge of electrons through the wire, nothing much happens. There is no connection between the hot + post and the – return one, so there is no flow of current—no *amperage*. The circuit is *open*. Only when your curious saddle pony brushes the wire with its velvety muzzle does the circuit *close* (Fig. 2). Then a brief shot of current flows at lightning speed from the + post of the fencer to the wire, through the pony's nose, body and hooves, back through the soil and the – post of the charger. ZAP. The shock is delivered, causing the pony to pull away and reopen the circuit.

Setting Up a Garden Fence

To keep small pests out of a vegetable patch, you'll want to set up a small garden fence, the main component of which will be an economical charger. The least expensive

An electric fence is easy to put up and can be moved as needed, either to keep your livestock *in* the best pasture or *out* of the vegetable garden.

garden fencers run a low-power, *continuous* charge. These are not as powerful or as safe as those employing pulsed current, so are seldom worth buying. A typical, plug-in, pulsed charger costs more and uses an average of seven kilowatt-hours of electricity per month. Small 6-volt, battery-powered fencers cost the same as plug-in ones—if you don't count the required battery, which should last a growing season.

Buy a bag of two dozen little slotted plastic insulators, and nail them to yard-long tomato stakes. Hammer the stakes 6" deep, and string 19-gauge steel wire on the insulators and charger. This will give you a perfectly satisfactory one- to three-strand garden fence. Remember to run the wire on the outside of the posts (to keep predators from knocking the posts over). And prevent sag in the fence by guying each corner post: Attach a length of wire by its midpoint to the post top, and run it to a pair of ground stakes hammered in at a mirror image of the angle made by the fence corner (Fig. 3).

You can use more elaborate stakes, of course. Lightweight fiberglass T posts, for instance, are nonconductive—so they require no insulators—and come with clips to hold the wire (Fig. 10). They push right into the soil, pull out as easily and cost little.

Garden fencers aren't waterproof or par-

ticularly sturdy, so they must be kept under cover, preferably in a dry spot in the shed or house. You can build a weathertight box out at the garden for a battery-powered model. In any case, make sure the charger is readily visible so you can see the red blinking indicator that tells you it is operating. Most models also have a test button or a separate white blinker that indicates whether the fence circuit is open or grounded.

If your charger is a bit away from your fence, you can run a length of common insulated lamp cord between the two. Hook one of the cord's two wires up to the fence and the hot pole of the charger (turned off, of course!), and the other to the fencer's ground post and a bare metal stake. Drive this stake in as close to the fence and as deep into the ground as you can. In dry areas, that stake needs to go 8' down!

Always put a lightning arrestor between the fencer and fence—especially if the charger is inside a building (Fig. 4). It's nothing but a fuse having its own ground line that you connect to its own well-sunk steel post. (Don't just punch the little metal probe at the end of that ground line into the sod.) If the megavolts of a lightning bolt strike the fence, they'll melt the arrestor's fuse and go to ground instead of frying the fencer and possibly your house and barn too. Install a

separate lightning protector even if the fencer has a built-in one; it's easier to replace.

How many strands should you run? A single wire set about 5" above the ground should shock the muzzles, ears or underbellies of rabbits, ground hogs and raccoons. Better yet is a two-strander with the lines run 4" and 10" high. A third wire up another 6" completes a really effective back-yard garden fence. You can step over it, but most pests won't think to do so.

The three-strand garden fence will deter dogs if they're not running hard, chickens and ducks if you add wire springs or thin batten stakes every 5' or so to keep those birds from charging through, and wayward pigs and sheep (at least for a while). It won't restrain grown goats or large stock that can step right over.

The fence will require periodic maintenance. You'll have to trim grass under the wire or it will lose its zap after every heavy dew. (And once an animal has gotten through a grounded electric fence, it may ignore the shock when the juice is on.) Simply pull the stakes, move the whole fence a couple of feet to one side, mow, and then put the fence back. You'll also have to keep alert to other grounding mishaps. For instance, a branch may blow onto the wire or a wet leaf onto an insulator. If the fence light indicates a grounded condition, make a quick inspection tour or use a fence tester—a small continuity tester that lights up when the fence is delivering full power.

Planning a Pasture Fence: The Wire

A pasture fence, or one used for keeping out larger predators (such as wild dogs or deer), will need to be a good bit stouter than a simple garden fence. It should be tensioned tight enough to stay off the ground and to maintain enough resistive pressure so that an animal will take it seriously if the charger goes out for a while. You'll need strong support posts at the ends and corners, and at the tops and bottoms of any hills or culverts. That way, runs of wire can be strung tight, needing little between the main supports but battens or lightweight line posts to keep the wires separated and off the ground.

Before setting the fence, plan and clear the intended fence line so animals can see the wire and so no weed plants will short it out. If the fence crosses a well-traveled drive or private road, you can order a spring-hinged drive-through gate (Fig. 5) from a mail-order house. These dandy gadgets have charged wire dangling off horizontal members to keep any animal in check, though your vehicle can pass through at will. If you just need to drive through the gate occasionally or need a walk-through opening, you can use inexpensive spring-tensioned plastic gate handles; just cut the wire near a post and hook them on (Fig. 6). Be sure to train everyone who uses the gate to refasten the handles: If a line is left unhooked on the ground, electricity will drain out of it with each pulse.

The larger the stock, the heavier gauge of wire required; the taller the animals, the more strands; and the wilder the animals, the stronger the posts. In choosing the wire layout, put the wires where they will make best contact on the animals to be restrained. If you're running a single wire, string it at chest level so the target animal will be shocked going over or under. The top strand of a two-wire fence should hit at upper midbreast (a horse or cow's lowered nose), the other midway down to the ground, so long as the interwire space doesn't permit a careful step through. With three or more wires, run the top wire at upper mid-breast level and the others equally spaced below it.

A single or double 15- or 17-gauge wire fence should do for domesticated steers, milk cows, sheep, young goats and feeder pigs—*if* they have plenty of food, water and shade, *and* if they won't get into too much trouble if they do get out. But don't try to restrain the animals' stronger urges with such a lightweight fence. If the pasture's definitely greener next door, use at least three strands of 14-gauge wire on sturdy posts.

When building an antipredator fence, consider the invaders' habits. Deer can jump high, slink low and sneak through gaps. Still, a six-strand fence with the wires 10" apart and the bottom one no more than 8" off the ground will keep most of them out (Fig. 7). The same basic layout will repulse most coyotes, dogs or wolves. Still, some of them are great at slinking under wires, so run the bottom wire 6" off the ground. They'll even seek out dips in the ground where it's easier to squeeze under. A series of stakes hammered into a dip, strung with an extra wire, will close a big gap (Fig. 8); a loose wire dangling off a hot line will block off a small one. However, if you have serious predator problems or range stock needing strong restraints, consider high-tensile fencing.

The Posts

You can make a temporary, single-strand pasture fence with 5′ sticks sunk 18″ into the pasture soil, though you'll want to use stouter wood or steel posts for ends and corners. Using a double-headed (easily extracted) nail, hammer an insulator onto each post *before* you set it. Chip a point on one stick end with a hand ax. Then, one day when the ground is wet and easily penetrated, open holes in the soil—a 4′ pry bar works well for this—stick the posts in, and pound them down

with a sledgehammer so they will stay put.

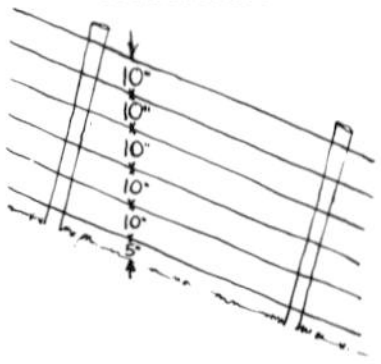

A more permanent fence with multiple wires should use stout wood or steel corner and end posts, sturdy line posts every 20′ to 50′, and battens where needed in between. Six-inch pressure-treated or creosoted wood fence posts made of cypress, red cedar, locust or other rot-resistant wood work fine. You'll need to dig their holes with a posthole digger and tamp the posts firmly in place. The corners and ends will need H or diagonal bracing (Fig. 9).

Steel and fiberglass posts (Fig. 10) are easier to set than wood ones—they just pound in. You can secure their ends and corners with diagonal braces inside or outside guy-wire rigs with tensioning sticks (Fig. 11). And there's a wide array of steel posts available. Forged U-shaped posts with holes or hooks down their length are strong and adaptable. You can install insulators on them quickly with long bolts and wing nuts. Of all the steel posts, the U type with a broadened lance foot stays put the best.

Forged T posts are about equal in cost and fence-holding strength to the U's. They use a special clip for mounting insulators, which makes for easy height adjustment. Some T posts come with spade-shaped anchor plates attached near the bottom to help secure the posts in the ground.

Self-insulating, heavy-duty fiberglass posts cost about the same as the two steel posts above, are notched so wire can be clipped right on, don't corrode, and make great line posts. They're not strong enough, though, for ends or corners.

L-shaped sheet-steel posts come next in strength and cost, followed by various types of rod-type steel posts. You can mix and match post types as your needs and pocketbook dictate.

When putting posts in, keep the line as straight as possible to make the tightening job easy. And orient posts so the insulators on a stock-containment fence point *in*, while those on a predator-control fence point *out*. You can drive steel posts in most soils with nothing but a hand sledge and a good arm, but if you have a great many to install, you may want to invest in a steel-tube, spring-loaded post driver. If you ever plan to *remove* a steel-post fence, an equally good investment is an all-purpose ratchet-type farm jack and post remover.

And Fencers

If your fence is in easy range of the house or a wired outbuilding, choose a plug-in charger. The up-front cost, energy expense and upkeep are all low. Get the most powerful fencer you can justify; it won't develop much greater deterrent, but it *will* push it out

Fig. 1
A 110-volt plug-in fencer

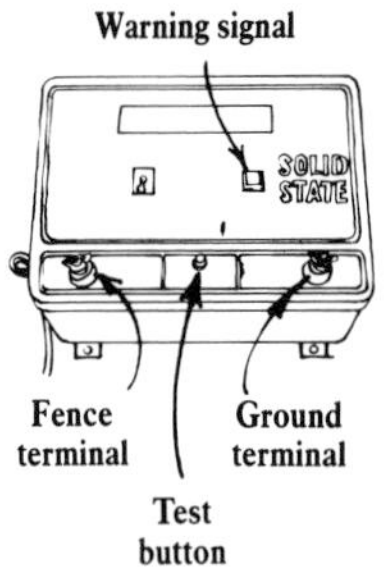

Warning signal

Fence terminal — Ground terminal

Test button

Fig. 2
Closing the circuit

Fig. 3
A garden fence

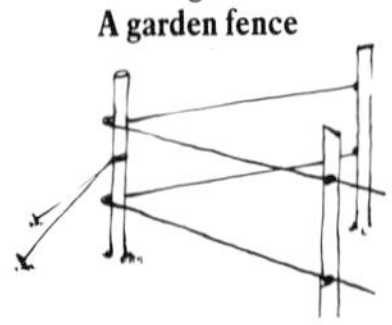

Fig. 4
Lightning arrestor

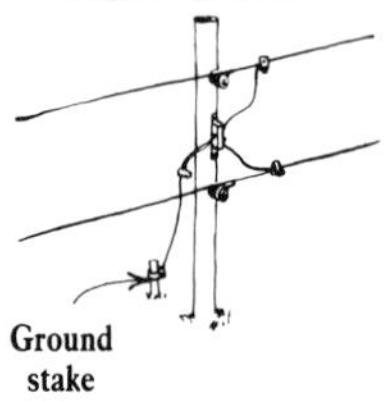

Ground stake

Fig. 5
A drive-through gate

Fig. 6
A hand gate

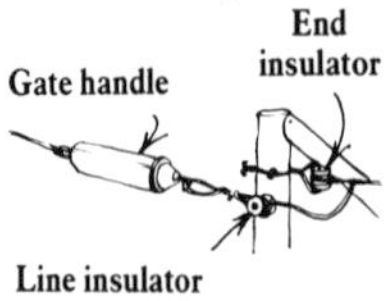

End insulator
Gate handle

Line insulator

Fig. 7
A deer fence

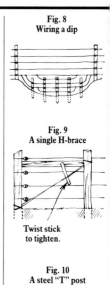

Fig. 8
Wiring a dip

Fig. 9
A single H-brace

Twist stick to tighten.

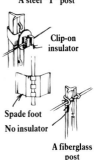

Fig. 10
A steel "T" post

Clip-on insulator

Spade foot
No insulator

A fiberglass post

Fig. 11
A guy with tensioning stick

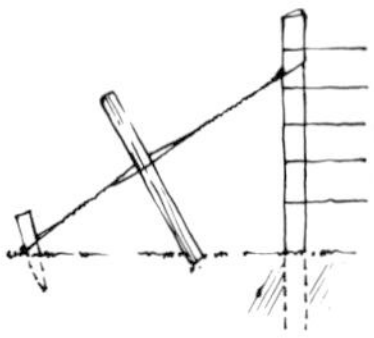

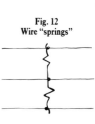

Fig. 12
Wire "springs"

Fig. 13
Fence with hot and ground wires

To fencer's hot terminal

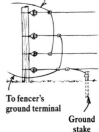

To fencer's ground terminal

Ground stake

Fig. 14
Poly wire

over greater distance and through more undergrowth. And consider getting a fencer with all solid-state circuits. It's more costly but has no parts to wear out except for the indicator lamp and the on-off switch.

For remote locations, a battery-powered fencer is best. The chargers cost about the same as equivalent line-powered models, although the expense of batteries must be considered.

The most up-to-date fencers are solar-powered and have solid-state components along with built-in gel-cell batteries that never need water. They come in 6- or 12-volt models; the 6-volt chargers have 16 PV cells, the 12-volt, 36 to 40. Starting with a fully charged battery, they should keep your fencer operating virtually forever. The battery will run down over three weeks of solid overcast weather but will perk up after only one day of full sun.

Hooking Up the Wire

Once the posts are hammered in and the fencer's ready to go, stringing the fence itself is a cinch. Attach a length of wire by a ceramic, doughnut-shaped end insulator at a braced corner or gate opening, and reel the line out, fixing it to your insulators as you

go. Don't let loops kink up in the outgoing wire, but revolve the reel as needed to keep the run smooth. And maintain just enough tension to make a taut fence. You can cut and splice wire easily whenever needed. To keep the wires separated and off the ground, set battens every 10' or 15', or put in "springs"—segments of wire crimped in a Z fashion between runs of wire (Fig. 12). If no trees or shrubs mark the course of the fence, help livestock see it by tying "flags" every few feet along the top wire. Strips of nonconductive fluorescent plastic tape work best. Tape them on or tie them tight so they don't get blown to downwind stakes.

To join fencer to fence, hook the charger's positive lead through the lightning arrestor and to the fence. Attach the negative post of the fencer and the lightning arrestor ground to a deeply buried steel ground rod as near to the fence as possible. In a multiple-wire fence, you will need to connect the fence strands together with securely wrapped wire before they go to the fencer and ground stake lines, so all wires will be uniformly charged. In very dry areas where the soil may not have enough moisture to conduct current, run alternate charged and ground wires: Hook the hot wires up to the fencer's positive lead, and the return wires up to the negative

lead (Fig. 13). Animals will get shocked when their bodies connect the two wires.

You should be sure to *train* your stock to electric fencing before you set them loose in the pasture. Scatter a little feed under and just outside a charged wire—perhaps one you've rigged up on doughnut-shaped corner insulators at the end of a pen that's large enough to allow them room to bolt when they get shocked. As they reach farther and farther for the feed, they'll get zapped on the snout. Keep that training up until the animals consistently avoid the wire. But *never* leave the training wire uncharged, or the animals will realize it can be harmless.

Poly Wire for a Fast Fence

A great new innovation is poly wire—fence line made from several strands of brightly colored plastic filament that's interwoven with thin, stainless-steel wire. It conducts superbly but is as flexible as twine. Not intended as permanent fence, it can nevertheless be strung out to make quick one-strand containments for mild-mannered stock (Fig. 14).

Another great use for poly wire is dividing your pasture into segments for controlled grazing. Such *strip grazing* has become a science in the sheep country of New Zealand and Australia. By rotating pasture segments between intensive graze and fallow time (and by eliminating shade and water so livestock have to eat grass to get fluid), farmers improve—some say *double*—pasture productivity. The grazers harvest everything edible instead of just the choicest fronds. Once the graze is down far enough to encourage new growth, but before the animals have pulled the plants out by the roots, the stock are moved to a strip of fresh browse. Long, narrow strips requiring movement of only two poly wire strands and a few battens make for the simplest strip system.

Poly wire is also the best fencing tool for breaking a wild meadow into manageable plots so you and your animals can work it into proper pasture a bit at a time. After each section has been grazed, you can go in with a scythe or lawn mower and cut down the unpalatable goldenrod, ferns and woody plants that haven't been grazed down. Then you can fertilize, lime and reseed as necessary.

Better Fencing, Electrically

The only comparative disadvantage of electric fencing is maintenance. You must service the charger as necessary, keep the fence line clean and ungrounded, and overhaul the wire and insulators from time to time. Still, building a "hot" fence is the only way to put up a heavy-duty barrier quickly and for pennies—rather than dollars—a foot.

LAND, SHELTER AND LOGISTICS

How to Build a Log Bridge

One of the most prized assets on rural property is a stream or creek, not only for irrigating crops, watering livestock and greening the landscape but for the sheer pleasure of sight and sound. Yet, to access all parts of the property, that waterway will most likely need to be crossed, perhaps even with heavy tractors or construction equipment.

The bridge described here, built of logs and flooring, is suitable for small streams and drainage ditches; there are no trusses or suspension features involved. Step-by-step instructions tell you how to build a log bridge,

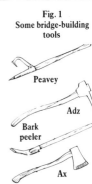

Fig. 1
Some bridge-building tools

Peavey

Adz

Bark peeler

Ax

and you'll also be able to determine just how great a load your particular span will be able to handle.

Getting Started

Throwing up an untrussed bridge is simplicity itself. Step one: Build a good base on each side of the waterway. Step two: Lay some stringer logs across the span. Step three: Add flooring. The main tools required are equally basic: a tractor or pickup truck with a chain for pulling logs, a chain saw, an ax, a bark peeler and adz, a chalk line, a shovel, a couple of peaveys and a heavy hammer. You'll also need a helper with a stout back, since bridge building is definitely a two-person job.

Of course, you'll need logs as well. The amazingly durable black locust comes highly recommended, but plenty of other woods can also do the job, assuming they've got more heartwood than sapwood. Bald cypress (old growth), Arizona cypress, catalpa, cedar, chestnut, juniper, mesquite, several of the oaks (not chestnut, Gambel, Oregon white, post or white oak), redwood, Osage orange and Pacific yew are all quite decay-resistant, especially the last two. Bald cypress (young growth), Douglas fir, honey locust, western larch, swamp chestnut oak, tamarack and eastern white, longleaf and slash pines are all moderately durable. Plan to inspect your bridge logs often if you use alder, ash, aspen, beech, birch, buckeye, butternut, cottonwood, elm, hemlock, hickory, magnolia, maple, red or black oak, sweet gum and most pines, poplars, spruces or true firs.

Cut the best and straightest logs you can

find. They should be at least a foot in diameter, not counting the bark, and have no knots in their middle halves. If you bevel the underside of each log a bit before you haul it to the bridge site, it will have less tendency to jam into the ground while being pulled.

The Base

The design of the foundation will depend on where you're building. Ideally, you'll have steep banks that rise well above the stream and that are close enough to each other to give you an acceptably short span. In such a case, dig ditches about 4′ long into both banks to receive the logs. Then lay some good-sized—say, 6″-thick—flat rocks in the troughs, and set the stringers on them (Fig. 2). Or you can pour cement for these footings instead. Try to design all this in such a way that the logs end up a little bit above ground level. That way, the approaches will slant slightly up to the bridge itself, which will help the structure shed rainwater.

If the banks taper down too gradually to the stream or if the span is slightly long, you can build out or up from the sides of the streambed using crib construction. Simply assemble a three-sided wall of logs on each creek side—with the open end stuck into the bank—as if you were making a little log cabin (Fig. 3). Be sure to notch out half the diameter of each timber where it crosses a log underneath, so the sides of the crib will fit together. You can do this roughly by eye or make accurately scribed bowl-shaped cuts. Fill in the opening behind each layer of logs with gravel and dirt as you go up. Then stack riprap—that's local quarry talk for big rocks—around the up- and downstream sides of the crib to help reduce the erosive effects of the stream.

Crib construction is also useful for raising the height of the bridge when spanning a stream that gets an unusually high run-off from heavy rains. How can you tell ahead of time if you have such a flood-prone creek? Watch the stream when it's high, talk to neighbors about how much it rises or consult your local soil conservation service. Its topographic maps will show the entire watershed and help provide an accurate estimate of peak flows.

Typical cribs are built with 90° angles, so each enclosure looks like three sides of a box. Others are built at 60° and resemble halves of hexagons. If the soil is too muddy to be contained by a wooden crib, a concrete base and reinforced block retaining wall may be called for.

The third crossing situation you're likely to encounter is over a stream with very low flow and quite shallow banks. In this case, you can't lay your stringers in ditches, since

Fig. 2
Laying the logs in the bank

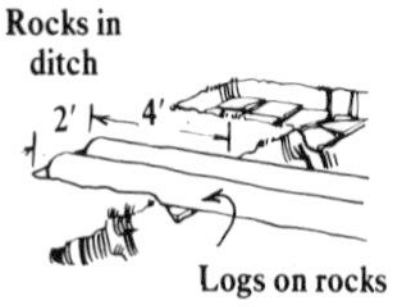

Rocks in ditch

2′ · 4′

Logs on rocks

Fig. 3
A log crib

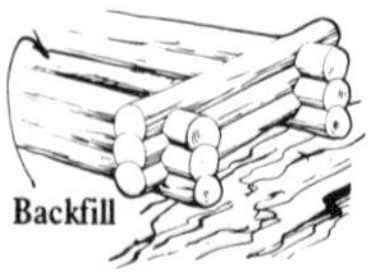

Backfill

Fig. 4
Laying bed logs

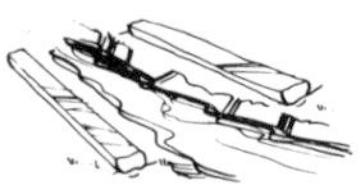

Fig. 5
Pulling a log over a creek

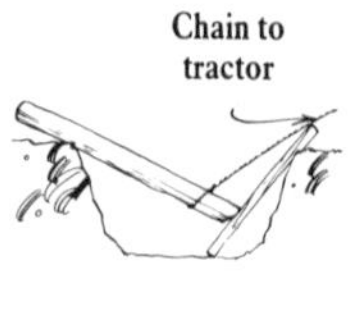

Chain to tractor

Fig. 6
Pivoting a log with peaveys

Fig. 7
Making sure the stringer tops are even

Fig. 8
Marking the logs

Fig. 9
Scoring

they'd be too low, but you don't want to build cribs either, as this would put the bridge so high you'd have to raise the road.

To handle this sort of problem, first dig out the streambed as much as possible to lower the water. Then lay bed logs (Fig. 4) *parallel* to the stream in gravel-filled dirt (for drainage). The purpose of the bed logs is to support the ends of the stringers and thus raise the bridge to a few feet above flood stage.

Level the tops of the bed logs so the stringers will also lie fairly level, both lengthwise and widthwise. Actually, it won't hurt if you have to drive a little up or down to get across your bridge. But you don't want a structure that's sloped enough to one side to cause a car to start sliding off on an icy night.

Stringers

Once the base is built, it's time to get those creek-spanning logs in place. Just how many stringers to use depends on the length of the span and the type of vehicle crossing it. For the use of cars alone, one log under each wheel track may be sufficient. For pickup trucks you might use four stringers, setting them in pairs, with the centers of the tracks 6½′ apart—the width of a truck's axle. Construction trucks may need three big timbers for each wheel path, and some builders simply use seven logs, all spaced the same distance apart. In Alaska, you can even find bridges where a whole bunch of logs are cabled together like a raft and then surfaced with small rocks. Some of those mighty structures are 80′ to 100′ long!

No matter how many logs you use, getting them across the stream probably won't be an easy task. If your banks are steep, you'll do best to get your hauling vehicle on the far side from the log. Lay a heavy plank down the slope of that side, and then pull the log until its front end falls onto the board (Fig. 5). You should be able to drag the log up that board without a lot of trouble, especially if you beveled the log's lower edge.

But if you can't get that tractor to the other side yet, run a long cable from the log to a snatch block hooked up high on the other side and back around to your pulling vehicle on the near side. Then go ahead and yank away.

In some cases the banks and water will be low enough so that the logs can be worked across with peaveys. Do this by pivoting each log: One person hooks a peavy into one end and starts it rolling, while the second person holds the other end in place with a peavy stuck into the ground (Fig. 6). You can even hook both peaveys into opposite sides of the same end of a log and drag it a short distance.

After your logs are in place, flatten the

A simple, sturdy log bridge can offer a way "to get there from here," and do so on a budget.

round tops to produce a good, level flooring surface. The first job here is getting the bark off the tops of the logs. (Some people feel you should peel all the bark off, since the logs will dry faster that way, and dry wood is stronger than green.) This job can be done with an ax, but it goes a lot faster with a bark peeler (shown in Fig. 1).

Once the stringers are skinned, focus on making sure the flattened tops are even and

level, sloping neither to the upstream nor downstream side of the bridge. To do so, first nail a spare 1 X 8 board onto the log ends at one bank. This plank should be carefully leveled and set so its top edge marks the desired trim line on the stringers (Fig. 7). Then nail another 1 X 8 on the other end, making sure that it, too, is level and is the same height above the bed log on its side as the first board is on the other side.

It will then be a simple matter to snap an accurate chalk line on both edges of each stringer by pulling the line from top to top of the 1 X 8s (Fig. 8). Do your best to draw it out *horizontally* when snapping it, or the line it marks may be off level.

With that done, use a chain saw to score each log by cutting level grooves, running from one chalk line to the other across the stringer (Fig. 9). Make those "slices" every

2" or so down the log; if you're sawing a wood that's softer than locust, you can space the cuts farther apart. Then knock out the scored sections (Fig. 10), and follow with an adz to further flatten out the log tops. An ax does work of this sort for large-scale chiseling, but the curved-blade adz is the more efficient tool.

Use a level often to make sure the timbers are reasonably flat and all cut to the same depth. When that point is reached, you can further smooth the tops with a chain saw (but don't try this unless you're adept with the tool). Lay the blade level on the wood, and let it "float" across the top by itself, putting very little downward pressure on it. Don't let it dig down in at all (Fig. 11).

Once satisfied that surfaces are smooth and level, assemble some rebar, a portable electric generator, a $1/2$" drill and a 16"-long $9/16$" bit. Use these to bore a pegging hole into each log end where it rests on the bed log. Then drive a rebar section (cut to length with a hacksaw) down in place. Such a method, while a fine way to secure your stringer logs, is dependent on the somewhat rare luxury of having electric power available at your bridge site. Just in case you don't, you can secure runners to a bed log or crib by using a brace, a bit and a lot of labor; by driving spikes into the base alongside the runners; or by notching the stringers out some on their undersides before leveling their tops.

Flooring

Once the stringers are laid, leveled and secured, you can finally start making the bridge look like one by flooring it. But before nailing planks down, check to make sure the flooring will be squared up. If you don't, by the time you reach the last board on the far side of the bridge, you may find the floor so askew that one end of the final plank fits over its stringer logs while the other end falls off.

To determine the bridge's squareness, use the 1 X 8s you nailed to the two ends of the stringers (they helped mark the leveling cuts, remember?) and two strings tacked 12' apart (or the intended width of the flooring) at the ends of those boards. Once the shape formed by those strings and 1 X 8s becomes a true rectangle, you are lined up for nailing. But how can you tell if the four sides really make a rectangle? You do it by using that piece of old carpentry lore; that is, seeing if the two diagonals across the box's inside are of equal length (Fig 12). If not, shift one or the other of those 1 X 8s slightly sideways until the diagonals do indeed match. After that, take off one string, leaving the other as a guide for placing the ends of the floorboards.

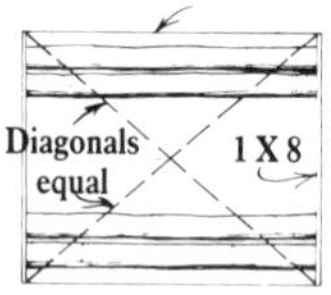

Before nailing, however, it makes great

Fig. 10
Chopping wood sections

Fig. 11
Sanding

Fig. 12
Squaring off the ends

String

Diagonals equal   1 X 8

sense to lay down a coat of roofing cement at those points where a board will lie on the stringers. That tar layer helps keep water from pooling between the wood surfaces and making the bridge rot faster. Then, stick a piece of $1/8$" Masonite on end between planks to serve as a temporary spacer (Fig. 13). The gap thus created enlarges to about $1/2$"—the desired water-shedding spacing—once green boards have dried.

Now it is time to pull out a hammer and get to nailing.

Finishing Up

When the hammering is done, trim both ends of the boards by marking cuts with the chalk line and then running down those lines with a chain saw (Fig. 14). Next, remove the 1 X 8s at the bridge's ends, trim those log ends even with the flooring, and permanently nail extra flooring boards in their stead (Fig. 15).

If for aesthetic or safety reasons you want to add handrails, you can build them easily enough out of 2 X 4s. Your railings will be

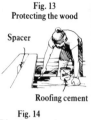

Fig. 13
Protecting the wood

Spacer

Roofing cement

Fig. 14
Trimming the ends

Fig. 15
Boarding the ends

Fig. 17
Rail braces

What Will It Hold?

This is the toughest question and the most important one: How much weight will a simple log bridge hold?

No one can answer that question for you. You are responsible for the bridge you build—after all, you're the one who's going to be crossing it. So don't complain if a loaded manure spreader falls clear through your 33' poplar span.

Still, a few standards can be offered, though in applying them you should check the data, assumptions and calculating methods for yourself.

First off, a lot will depend on the load you plan to place on the structure. What are you going to take over it? The family pickup truck? A tractor with a front-end loader? A bulldozer? A silage truck filled with 10 tons of corn? Equally obvious, you'd better be sure the bridge will be on your private property and intended solely for your personal use. If you plan to build one on a public road—no matter how far in the backwoods—you'll have to bring in a county or state road official before you can even start.

The following chart indicates the log diameter needed to hold a concrete truck loaded with 8 yards of concrete (a total weight of

around 65,000 pounds) over spans of 10' to 24'. The formulas come principally from Tedd Benson's *Building the Timber Frame House* (Charles Scribner's Sons, 1980). Since Benson's calculations were for square or rectangular green beams, an extra factor of 1.4 (the ratio of a circle's diameter to the depth of the largest square inside it) is incorporated into the calculations here to compensate for the use of round green logs. That correction factor allows you to transpose log diameter for beam depth in his equations.

There is another important assumption as well. If the structure is designed with two logs under each wheel track and the truck is centered as it goes over the bridge, each of the four logs will have to bear only one-quarter of the total load, or 16,250 pounds.

The important things to consider for calculations are the maximum imposed load a log would have to bear (call this M load) and the maximum design resistance of a log (call this M log). The equations come from Benson's formulas for a two-point load—the front and back wheels of the truck—distributed equally across a beam. Here's the result:

$$\text{M load} \leq \frac{WL}{3}$$

$$\text{M log} \geq \frac{d^3 f}{6 \times 1.4} = \frac{d^3 f}{8.4}$$

where

W = total load (16,250 pounds)

a lot sturdier, though, if you plan ahead by leaving some of the flooring boards extended at regular intervals along both sides of the bridge. That way, you can easily add outside braces for the railing (Fig. 16).

It will take four or so days' work to build this bridge, but how many years before wear and tear destroy it? There are two answers to that one. The flooring should go first. Oak boards can be expected to last from five to 10 years before they'll need to be replaced. Just remember: The more steps you take during construction to help water stay *off* the boards, the longer they'll last.

The life expectancy of the stringers will vary widely, depending on the type of wood you use. Good locust logs might last 50 years, but others could fail long before that. In other words, when the bridge starts creaking as you drive over it, when the nails come out easily or when the logs seem "punky" if you poke around underneath with a screwdriver, it's time to replace the stringers.

Whatever you do, don't take your bridge for granted until it's so far gone that somebody has an accident. Of course, if you go to all the work of cutting and hauling the logs, building up the base, laying and flattening the stringers, nailing on all the flooring and trimming up the sides and ends of your own log bridge, you'll probably never take the structure for granted. You'll more likely want to stop your car to admire it.

L = clear span (in inches)
d = diameter of log
f = maximum allowable fiber stress in bending

For the bridge to hold, the resistance must always be greater than or equal to the load (M log ≥ M load). So we can safely combine the equations to get:

$$\frac{WL}{3} = \frac{d^3 f}{8.4}$$

Rearranging this new equation to get a minimum diameter, we find that

$$d^3 = \frac{2.8WL}{f} \text{ or } d = \sqrt[3]{\frac{2.8WL}{f}}$$

The values of f for typical woods are the following:

black locust	3,600 psi
white and northern red oak	2,200 psi
Douglas fir and southern pine	2,100 psi
eastern and Sitka spruce and other pines	1,400 psi

All the f values incorporate a factor of 3.5 to allow for using green logs.

Putting these numbers together produced the accompanying chart for theoretical log diameters necessary to hold a quarter of a 65,000-pound concrete truck for 10′- to 20′-long bridges. (Note: Since the distance between the front and the first set of back wheels on most concrete trucks is 12′, a bridge under 12′ long will bear only the front or back wheels at one time, giving it about half the load calculated here.)

Supporting the Load

Theoretical length and diameter of logs to support a two-point 16,250-pound load

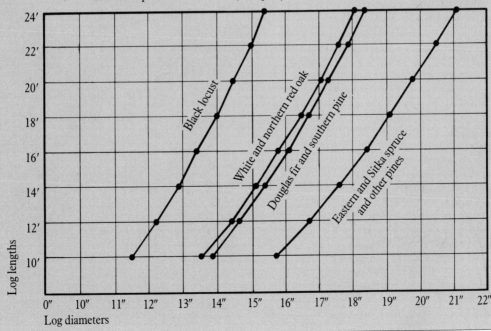

Maintain- ing Gravel Roads

Taking care of your pathway to the great big world out there

First, set the blade to cut perpendicular to your line of travel, and, working uphill, level the bumps.

Next, rotate the blade 180°, plus one adjustment stop. Draw loose material toward the center of the roadway.

Then, if too high a crown has been created, make a pass with the blade set square and horizontal.

Heavy rains, freezing and thawing and the constant wear and tear from cars and trucks all take their toll on gravel drives.

The first step toward successfully maintaining a gravel road is to realize that producing a smooth surface—the smoother, the better—is the ultimate goal. Undulations set vehicles bouncing up and down on their springs. The vertical forces generated, even though they may be too small for you to object to while riding in the vehicle, are then transferred back to the road. After enough of this bouncing activity, the road eventually worsens until it is nothing but a series of humps and gullies—the washboard effect.

The second step toward maintaining a gravel road, once you've decided to strive for a tabletop-smooth surface, is to accept the fact that you'll never be able to achieve that goal. Then make up your mind to go ahead and try anyway.

Take a look at the work site in the early morning or late afternoon, when the sun is low and the shadows are long enough to emphasize any humps in the surface. If you examine the terrain, you'll find that there is almost always a hollow just uphill from every bump. That's because, as vehicles crest the bump, their wheels become ''light'' and lose traction, causing them to spin and dig a trench on the uphill side.

One basic principle of gravel-road maintenance, therefore, is always to work toward the uphill, in order to fill in those trenches.

Maintenance Basics

If you own a tractor (almost any size other than the smallest yard and garden machine will do), the only other tool you'll need is a six-foot, rear-mounted blade that's reversible and adjustable for angle and slope. A six-footer is best because it gets about half the road's width in a single swipe and still covers the tracks of all but those of the biggest tractors. A blade much longer than six feet is hard for an inexperienced person to handle. If you don't own a tractor, try to borrow or rent one; although the principles for keeping a gravel road in good shape apply even if you're willing to do a lot of digging and raking with hand tools, a tractor makes the job infinitely easier.

Set the blade to cut, and adjust it so that it's perpendicular to the line of travel. The blade should also be sloped slightly, using the adjustment on the tractor's hitch arm, so that it cuts a little deeper at the edge of the road than it does in the middle.

Now go ahead and start grading. Tearing into that surface, when you've paid so much for gravel and waited so patiently for everything to pack down, will be scary at first; be-

If water runs under your road (through a culvert or under a bridge), keep the pathway on the downstream side of the crossing clear of debris to prevent backwash.

fore long, though, you'll wind up with a better, smoother drive.

Work each half of the road, always remembering to grade *uphill*. Then, once you've cut down all the bumps, turn the blade so that it will drag, rather than cut, and angle it to pull material into the center of the roadway. In other words, turn the blade 180° from its original position, plus one adjustment stop. And again, slope the blade slightly so that it will touch the outermost edge of the drive just before it contacts the middle.

Drag each side of the road several times, still working toward the uphill. In places where, in the previous step, you cut the top from a good-sized bump, windrows of gravel will have been left by the square-running blade; be sure to catch these piles and move them to the center. It usually takes two such passes to stir things up and get the gravel satisfactorily redistributed.

Of course, by pulling the gravel to the middle of the road with the angle and slope of the blade, you'll create a crown. There's some disagreement about the need for crown on a road, but a surface with a modest hogback sheds running water to the sides more quickly and thus reduces down-the-road erosion. Besides, the center of the drive makes a good place to store any excess gravel that you scrape up. It sure beats leaving the crushed rock to spread slowly outward into adjacent pasture, forest or lawn.

Try to leave a crown of no more than one foot, total. The best rule is this: The steeper the road, the more crown required to shed water to the sides. Drives on a flat terrain require very little crown, just enough to keep them from puddling up.

If pulling gravel to the middle has created too high a ridge or a big, loose gravel pile running down the spine of the road, a single swipe with the blade in its reversed, noncutting position should sweep the right amount of material back into the tracks where wheels will run. For this operation, set the blade perpendicular to the drive, and crank the adjuster on the hitch arm until the blade runs level.

Some Additional Tips

If the road you're determined to improve happens to be an old one—well packed or badly damaged—you may need to wire a few concrete blocks to the blade's frame to increase the tool's weight and thus its cutting and dragging power. *Never* attempt to accomplish this by having someone ride on the blade; the practice can be lethal! And if you do add weight, do so cautiously, or you may force the blade into the road's substructure. If you're moving anything as big as your fist, you're into road *building*, not maintenance.

The best time to tackle a road-blading job is shortly after an inch or so of rain has fallen. Then, the dust won't bother you, and gauging your progress will be much easier because you'll be able to see the darker, damp gravel from beneath the surface as it is scraped up. Most important, the material will quickly pack in place from the weight of traffic, rather than slither away on a lubricating film of dry dust.

If your road crosses water, a special note of caution is in order. Obviously, it's necessary to provide enough space beneath the roadway for flooding water and to keep that stream's passageway (such as a culvert pipe or the area under a bridge) cleared out. Not quite so apparent, however, is the need to keep the waterway on the *downstream* side of the crossing free of debris. Gravel, leaves and branches are likely to collect in the eddies that form below a pipe or pier. And that swirling water can do damage there in short order.

To discourage excessive wash during heavy rains, keep that crown on the road and maintain clean drainage ditches along the edges of the drive. Fill washed-out ruts by repeatedly blading gravel up to them, leaving a pile of loose material over each one. Then pack the stones into the rut, using a shovel and your own booted feet, before blading the areas smooth.

An Ounce of Prevention . . .

To keep ruts, bumps and dips from forming in your road in the first place, exercise two simple rules: 1) Drive more slowly than normal, and 2) put some weight in the rear of any pickup truck that will be using the road regularly. Speed makes vehicles bounce on their springs, which again lightens the load on the wheels on the "up" bounce, ultimately creating the dreaded washboard effect so familiar to drivers and owners of rural byways. And *any* unladen pickup truck will spin its wheels on even the slightest hill, thus digging a bone-rattling series of trenches and sending precious gravel flying every which way.

Actually, maintaining a gravel road doesn't require time so much as it does common sense and regular loving care. An average of about one hour per month will keep most drives in reasonable shape, except during an unusually wet spring or fall, when that time might double.

Certainly the effort is well worth it. By putting in just a little bit of time and work, you can enjoy your country road and avoid having to pay the local well-to-do dozer artist over and over again!

Poplar gives a bitter smoke,
Fills your eyes and makes you choke.
Apple wood will scent your room
With an incense like perfume.
Oaken logs, if dry and old,
Keep away the winter's cold.
But an ash wet or ash dry
A king shall warm his slippers by.
— Anonymous

It's a volatile question, this matter of "best" firewood, one that has kindled fiery debate among wood burners for centuries. The wood one person swears by is sure to be the wood another person swears *at*.

Truth be told, there is no clear best. Ounce for ounce and pound for pound, any given kind of firewood delivers virtually the same amount of heat as any other kind. A pound of pine, a pound of hickory, a pound of poplar, a pound of willow—each, properly seasoned, will produce about 7,000 Btu. It's *density* that makes a difference: An armload of pine weighs less than an armload of hickory, and thus yields less heat. The denser the wood, the higher the fuel value, and the higher the fuel value, the fewer trips you have to make to the woodbox to carry in an evening's warmth.

So goes conventional wood-burning lore. But Btu are only one measure of a wood's worth. Each species offers its own unique

White Birch: Fair fuel value

combination of properties: ease (or difficulty) of splitting, ash content, aroma, seasoning time, flame size, tendency to smoke or throw sparks. Black ash burns nicely, but only after a long period of seasoning. White ash needs little seasoning. Rock elm ranks high in heat value but is hard, some say impossi-

ble, to split. Aspen and balsam poplar split easily but throw off a lot of smoke.

Some woods—particularly conifers and other low-density softwoods—burn fast, releasing all their heat in a few fiery moments. Others—notably dense hardwoods such as hickory, oak and ash—burn slowly, holding their coals hot and long. Each can serve a purpose: the quick burners for kindling, for fast heat, for a batch of biscuits on a cookstove; the slow burners for a romantic flickering fireplace or for strong, steady heat in the ole box stove. Likewise, each can be managed to serve the other's function: Split hardwood extra small, and it burns hot

Maple: Fair to good fuel value

and fast. Refuel and tend your stove carefully, and low-density wood makes a perfectly acceptable heating fuel.

Probably the most important factor in choosing the "best" firewood for you is *accessibility*. Obviously, you're pretty much limited in your choice to whatever woods are available in your area. (Little wonder that fuel value charts like the one on page 60 irritate westerners, who have little access to high-ranked hardwoods and who have always heated their homes just fine, thank you, with such woods as fir, aspen and pine.) If you buy wood for heating your home, it probably pays to spend a little more to get the densest species available in your area. But if you cut and haul your own wood, the less work you can make of it the better. Is that hickory 300 yards off the road—and downhill, meaning you'd have to lug it *up*—really all that much better than the abundant yellow poplar growing (on level ground, yet) just a hoot 'n' holler from your back door? Also, consider the value of any tree—both monetary and environmental—before you cut. It's often better to thin low-grade wood from your lot for burning (or better yet, glean downed wood from construction sites and other clearing projects) than to topple healthy high-heat hardwood.

The chart can serve as a general guide to firewood based on two important considerations: relative heat value and ease of splitting. But don't forget to weigh other factors, and don't hesitate to try whatever woods—including the so-called inferior types—are

available to you. In many cases, it's not which wood you use, but how you season and burn it, that's important.

Seasoning Firewood

Freshly cut, green wood can contain anywhere from one-third to nearly two-thirds water. When wood's wet, it has to use some of its energy to boil off the moisture, leaving less energy to heat your home. Burning green wood can rob you of up to a third of your wood's potential heating value—that's millions of wasted Btu per cord.

Besides, you don't have to lug many logs around before you learn another advantage of dry wood: It's lighter—by something like half a ton or more a cord.

But contrary to long-held myth, it's *not* always necessary to let fresh wood dry a year or two to cure it properly. Time is only one factor affecting the moisture content of firewood. Different kinds of wood dry at different rates. The time of year it's cut, handling and storage methods and the climate all influence the speed and degree of drying.

Here are some tips:

Harvest firewood between late autumn and

Hickory: Good fuel value

early spring. This is the time of year when the sap in most trees is at its lowest—so there's less moisture in the wood to begin with. Also, wood dries best in breezy, low-humidity weather—a climate more typical of autumn and early spring than of summer.

Choose low-moisture and/or fast-drying wood species. Some freshly cut woods are much less "green" than others. White ash, American beech, black cherry, any of the hickories, and sugar and silver maple are low-moisture

The Art of Firewood

From forest to
fireplace: a compendium of
useful knowledge

hardwoods; Douglas fir, longleaf (Southern yellow) and red pines and Eastern spruce are low-moisture softwoods.

Also, USDA research on hardwoods shows that some species lose their moisture more quickly than others. Silver maple is the fastest drying, followed by sugar maple, ash, oak, beech, birch, cherry and hickory.

Cut your firewood to stove length, and split it. The extra work of cutting logs into short (one- to two-foot) lengths and splitting them is more than made up by their faster drying time. Studies show that split pieces dry much more rapidly than whole ones, short pieces much faster than longer ones. Also, try to keep the logs' lengths uniform; same-size wood stacks easier, looks neater and—because there are no odd-length logs sticking out of the pile to catch rainwater—stays dry better.

"Leaf-cure" summer-cut deciduous trees. You can hasten the drying of wood from trees felled during high-moisture months (May through September) by leaving the trees whole for four to 12 weeks. The foliage will draw moisture through the trunk and out the leaves (a process called transpiration). When the leaves wither and turn brown, the tree will have lost as much as half its moisture and

Douglas Fir: Fair fuel value

Beech: Good fuel value

is ready to be cut, split and stacked as usual.

Pick a dry, sunny, breezy site for stacking your wood. Choose a location away from trees, buildings or other objects that might keep the sun and wind from your woodpile, or that might drip rain onto it. If possible, position the pile perpendicular to prevailing winds.

Relative Fuel Values of Woods

Wood	Relative Fuel Value	Ease of Splitting	Wood	Relative Fuel Value	Ease of Splitting
Apple	3	▽	Box-elder	1	▽
Ash, black	2	▽	Butternut[2]	1	▽
Ash, green	2	▽	Catalpa	1	▽
Ash, white	2	▽	Cherry, black	2	▽▽
Aspen, bigtooth	1	▽	Cottonwood	1	▽▽
Aspen, quaking	1	▽	Dogwood	3	▽▽▽
Basswood	1	▽	Elm, American	2	▽▽▽▽
Beech, American	3	▽▽▽	Elm, rock	3	▽▽▽▽
Beech, blue[1]	3	▽▽▽	Fir, Douglas	2	▽
Birch, black	3	▽	Fir, balsam	1	▽
Birch, gray	2	▽	Hemlock	1	▽
Birch, white	2	▽	Hickory	3	▽▽
Birch, yellow	3	▽▽	Ironwood[3]	3	▽▽▽

Red Oak: Good fuel value

Black Walnut: Fair fuel value

Raise your woodpile several inches off the ground. To encourage air circulation and to keep fungus from attacking the wood, put your pile on an open foundation of concrete blocks, logs or shipping pallets. Also, clear any brush or tall grass from around the pile.

Stack firewood loosely in a single row. Approaches to stacking vary widely and are largely a matter of personal preference. Still, most experts say that the traditional single-row woodpile is easiest to stack and—most important—allows maximum air circulation. Lay the logs loosely, leaving plenty of air space between them. Mixing pieces of different sizes helps. To keep the stack stable, build the pile so that every log leans slightly toward the middle, allowing gravity to help keep them from rolling outward. At each end, build a "bookend" of crisscrossed logs positioned tightly together.

Cover the top—but only the top—of the pile. It's important to keep rain and snow from leaking down through the pile onto the logs and the ground beneath it. A tarp that's draped over the sides of a woodpile, however, holds moisture in and blocks airflow. Better to use a rigid cover—such as plywood, a few boards or a piece of metal roofing. It should be a bit wider than the pile itself.

Measuring Moisture Content

The moisture content of wood is expressed as a percentage ratio, comparing the weight of water in a piece of wood to the weight of that wood after all the moisture has been removed. For example, if a log weighs 15

Relative Fuel Value Key
1 = Low: 11 to 16 Million Btu per cord
2 = Medium: 17 to 20 Million Btu per cord
3 = High: 21 to 26 Million Btu per cord

Ease of Splitting Key
▽ = Piece of cake
▽▽ = Good exercise
▽▽▽ = A challenge
▽▽▽▽ = Splitting headache!

Wood	Relative Fuel Value	Ease of Splitting
Locust, black	3	▽▽▽
Locust, honey	2	▽▽
Maple, red	2	▽▽
Maple, silver	2	▽▽
Maple, sugar	3	▽▽
Oak, black	3	▽▽
Oak, red	3	▽▽
Oak, white	3	▽▽▽
Osage orange	3	▽▽
Persimmon	3	▽▽
Pine, longleaf[4]	2	▽
Pine, red[5]	2	▽
Pine, white	1	▽

Wood	Relative Fuel Value	Ease of Splitting
Poplar, balsam	1	▽
Poplar, yellow[6]	1	▽▽
Serviceberry, downy[7]	3	▽▽
Spruce, red	1	▽
Sweet gum[8]	2	▽▽▽▽
Sycamore, American	2	▽▽▽▽
Tamarack[9]	2	▽▽
Tupelo, black[10]	2	▽▽▽▽
Walnut, black	2	▽
Willow, black	1	▽▽

1. Also known as American hornbeam. 2. Also known as white walnut. 3. Also known as hardhack and hop hornbeam. 4. Also known as Southern yellow. 5. Also known as Norway pine. 6. Also known as tulip poplar. 7. Also known as shadbush. 8. Also known as red gum. 9. Also known as Eastern larch. 10. Also known as black gum.

pounds just after it's cut and 10 pounds after thorough drying, the wood's original moisture content would be calculated at 50%, like so:

$$\frac{(\text{original weight} - \text{oven-dry weight})}{(\text{oven-dry weight})}$$

$$\times 100$$

$$= \text{MOISTURE CONTENT (\%)}$$

OR

$$\frac{5}{10} \times 100 = 50\%$$

Therefore, wood that's said to have a 100% moisture content isn't all water—it's half water and half wood. A 200% moisture content means there's twice as much water as wood.

According to research, wood burns most efficiently (and cleanly) when its moisture content is between 15 and 25%.

To measure the moisture content of your firewood, cut a two- or three-inch-thick piece from the center of two or three different logs. Immediately weigh them, then put the pieces in a low (212° to 220°F) oven. Weigh them periodically until they stop losing weight. (This usually takes about a day. To avoid tying up your oven that long, you can simply put the pieces next to a wood-burning stove for a couple of days to dry them, or use a toaster oven.) Plug the recorded weights into the formula given above, and you'll be able to calculate the wood's moisture content.

You don't want to go to all that bother? Then *look* at your wood—when the ends of the pieces are cracked and checked, it's at least near dry (some types of wood check readily at the ends but take longer to dry through and through). Now pick up a couple of pieces of the same type and knock them together; in general, wet wood makes a dull *thump* (a moist bruise may be visible, too). Dry wood makes a ringing sound—music to any wood-burner's ears.

Apple: Good fuel value

Hanging a Handle
What to do when your splitting maul splits

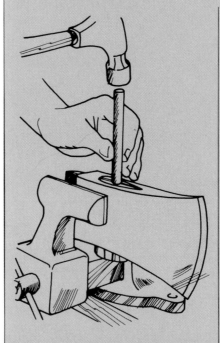

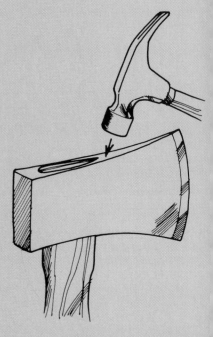

Step 1: Remove the remaining wood. Saw off the old handle as close to the head as possible. Drive out the remaining wood and the wedges with a hammer and either a steel rod, an old screwdriver or a wood chisel—or better yet, bore a few holes into the wood with an electric drill, and then punch out the remaining loosened wood. (Take care not to let the drill bit strike the metal sides or wedges.)

Step 2: Fit the new handle into the eye. With the heel of the handle on the ground, gently tap the head down onto the helve—use a block of wood and a hammer—until the head just begins to feel tight around the wood. (If the handle won't fit into the eye, carefully pare the extra wood away with a knife or rasp and try again.) Then turn the handle around, holding it just below the heel, with the head hanging free toward—but not touching—the ground. Now pound the flat end of the butt several times with a hammer. You'll feel the handle drive into the eye.

If you think splitting wood is hard work, consider the handle on your ax or maul; now *there's* a hardworking piece of equipment. But sooner or later, countless blows (both well placed and otherwise) take their toll: CRRAAAACK. Time to replace the handle.

Most hardware stores carry a good selection. Bring your ax or maul and the broken handle with you, so you can choose a replacement as near to the original as possible. Hickory is the wood of choice. Look at the butt end of the handle; the grain should run straight up and down, back to front—not diagonally or across the width. Beware painted handles that conceal the grain. Most handles come with a wooden wedge for securing the helve into the eye, but you'll also need a couple of one-half- or three-fourths-inch soft steel wedges to finish the job; buy them now if you're not sure you'll be able to use the ones in your old handle.

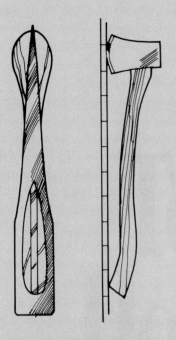 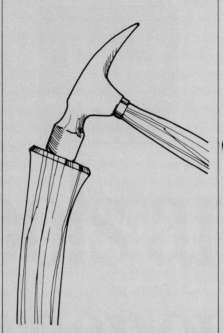 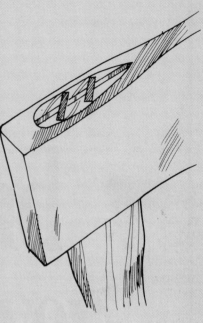

Step 3: Check the alignment.

When the handle is about a third of the way into the eye, turn the ax or maul around and, sighting from the top down, line up the tool's edge with the butt end of the handle. The edge should neatly bisect the butt end, angling neither to the right nor the left. Now lay the tool on the floor bit down; the bit should touch the floor near the *middle* of the edge. If the tool fails either test, you'll have to remove the handle and—using a spokeshave, bastard file, rasp or knife—whittle the helve until the blade lies right. Remove only a little wood at a time, though, or you'll carve away too much, making it impossible to get a tight fit.

Step 4: Drive the handle home.

When you're satisfied with the alignment, hold the tool head-downward as you did before and resume driving the handle in, striking the butt end with a hammer and checking the alignment every three or four blows. When the bit seems to be well seated on the handle's shoulder, give the butt two or three more good, hard raps. If the hammer bounces sharply off the wood and your hand holding the ax or maul smarts a bit from the shock, the head has been driven sufficiently.

Step 5: Wedge the head.

Check the blade alignment once more, and if all is OK, saw off the protruding wood about one-fourth inch above the head. Now gently tap the wooden wedge into the slot sawn into the handle's top. Even when you're careful, the wedge often splits and breaks apart; if this happens, hammer each piece in separately as best you can. When the wedge is in as far as it will go, cut or file away all surplus wood above the head. Finally, spacing them about three-fourths inch apart, drive the two steel wedges in diagonally across the wooden wedge. You now have a splitting tool straight and true, ready for hard work.

Elementary Carpentry

Building skills for the *true* beginner

A couple of summers ago, a young man in North Carolina took leave from his desk job to work with a three-man carpentry crew that was building his family's new house. He didn't know much of anything about carpentry but wanted to learn and was eager to participate.

One day during the initial framing, he sat talking with the utility company worker who was hooking up a temporary power line. "How many people you got working on your house?" he asked. "Three," the young man replied, referring to the paid crew and shyly omitting himself. "That's good," said the utility man. "Three's the perfect number. If you have any more than that, one of them's usually a lunt who does more harm than good."

What follows is intended for lunts, people who don't know a speed square from a chalk line and who might feel a bit embarrassed whenever they pick up a hammer or saw. Anybody already competent with such tools, and others, can stop reading now—you won't learn anything new. What you will find here are those basic tips that *real* carpenters don't often deign to tell beginners.

Measuring

The real secret to carpentry is to *not* misplace tools. That may sound obvious, but beginners invariably spend more time the first day hunting tools than using them. So, right off the bat, buy a tool belt.

Incidentally, a carpenter's most important tool is the ordinary *pencil*. Carpentry involves constant figuring and measuring, so if you don't have one, you won't get far.

Next in importance is the tape measure—a locking, retractable tape $3/4''$ or $1''$ wide, so it's stiff enough for long, one-person measurements, and $16'$ to $25'$ long. Notice how the metal tab on the end is slightly loose? It's not broken. Rather, that tab (Fig. 1) pushes in when you measure from the inside of a board and pulls out when you measure from the outside—so it self-corrects for its own

width. Never give that looseness another thought; just measure away. However, use the same tape for the whole job, since one tape's tab might move more than another's.

Measure twice, cut once: Even professional carpenters try to follow that axiom to avoid sawing boards the wrong length. That makes repeating a measurement before you cut mandatory for beginners. Take care to read the tape accurately, noting the right number of inches and fractions thereof. When you read a tape upside down, don't mistake $26''$ for $29''$—and don't accidentally think you're reading $7'10''$ when you're really reading $6'10''$. These are easy mistakes to make, because we normally read left to right, whereas you have to read an upside-down tape *right* to *left*.

How do you measure higher than you can reach? Let a lot of tape out so you can run it past the end point you're measuring. It'll curve back toward your hand, but as long as the tape's straight to the end point, your measurement will be straight as well (Fig. 2). Use the same tape-bending trick when you're measuring against an inside wall and can't run the measure past your end point. Or if the tape measure case is an exact width, like $2''$ or $3''$, you can just run it into the wall and add its width to the tape length you see.

Marking

Now, having measured twice, you have confirmed that you need to cut a board, say, $68^3/4''$ long. Grab that board, hook your tape over one end, run it down $68^3/4''$, and mark the cutting point with a big V whose two legs diverge from the exact point. That V, or "crow's-foot," is a more accurate way to mark an exact spot than a penciled line or dot. You might get thrown off by the width of a line or the fact that it may not be perpendicular to the board, but a V points to precisely the right spot. It also makes a big mark that is easy to see.

Next you need to mark a right angle from that crow's-foot so the whole board will be

$68^3/4''$ long. You can use a *combination square* or a big *framing square* for that, but the best tool for the job is a *speed square* (a right triangle with protruding rims on one of its sides). You can lay its rimmed side against the board, line up the right-angled side with the V mark and run the pencil down that edge for a perfectly straight, square-to-the-board line (Fig. 3).

Of course, you should first use your right-angled tool to check the end of the board that you *won't* be cutting, even though you bought your wood from the lumberyard and it's supposed to have square ends. Check it anyway—sometimes it won't. Once you've made sure that end's square (cut it square if you have to), measure those $68^3/4''$, and mark your cut.

And anytime you make a mistake and mark a line in the wrong place, be *sure* to run a squiggly pencil line all the way through the bad line when you draw the correct one. Otherwise, you'll have two lines to choose from when you cut, and—inevitably

Fig. 1
Adjustable
tape measure
tab

Fig. 2
Curving the tape

—you'll sometimes pick the wrong one.

Now suppose you're ripping (cutting with the grain instead of across it) down the length of a long board or cutting across a full-sized sheet of plywood. Sure, you can mark the V on both ends of the board, so you'll know where to start and end your cut, but your square won't reach all the way across, so how can you mark a straight cutting line between those points? The *chalk line*. This is a string that's covered with colored marking chalk. Pull the end out of its case, hook its tab over the near V on your board, run out some string (keeping it off the board), line it up on the far V, and pull it taut. Then lift the string *straight* up in the middle, keeping it taut, and let go (Fig. 4). It'll snap down against the board. Lift the string off, winding as you go, and the chalk it shed when snapped will leave a nice straight line that marks the entire length of your cut.

A few chalk-line pointers: Get a *blue* one; red chalk lines are rainproof and practically indelible. Don't use it on wet wood—damp

Fig. 3
Using a speed sqaure

Mark lines
with a V.

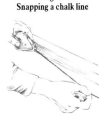
Fig. 4
Snapping a chalk line

chalk will gum up the inside of the case. If you can't hang the string's tab over a board end, drive a nail partway in at the starting point, and hook the tab over that. If you have to mark a long line, have another person snap the middle of the string while you hold the taut end. Need an *exceptionally* long mark? Have that assistant pin the string down in the middle, and then snap the line on both sides.

One more thing to consider before you cut: You'll need to support your board on sawhorses or a table. Don't brace both ends and cut in the middle; the board will sag in and trap your saw blade. Instead, support the long side of the board, as close to the cutting line as possible, then saw off the short side.

You'll have to vary that arrangement if both pieces are going to be long. Otherwise, the free-falling piece will be so heavy it'll break off before you finish cutting and leave a splintery stub. In that case, ask a friend to hold the free end. If no one's around, put a third sawhorse under the falling piece, not at its far end (remember the pinching problem) but near the middle of the falling piece, just a little toward the cut (Fig. 5).

When cutting a big piece of plywood, you can set two boards on two sawhorses, lay your plywood on top of them so the cutting line runs between the sawhorses, and then cut as little into the support boards as possible.

Cutting

Handsaw or circular saw? *Handsaws* are less popular—they're slower and more tiring to use—but they will get the job done. If you use one, concentrate on keeping it straight, and don't let its body twist sideways into the wood. Hold it at a 45° angle, start the notch with a few pulling strokes, then push and pull with an even, steady motion that lets the saw do most of the work. You can steady the board with your opposite knee and reach over to grab the waste end with your free hand right before it breaks off to keep the wood from tearing.

Getting tired? The saw may well be dull. Have it sharpened, and you'll be amazed how much stronger you suddenly become. Also, be sure you're using a *crosscut saw* (the ordinary one with lots of little teeth) for cutting across boards and a *ripsaw* (fewer and larger teeth) for cutting with the grain.

Having trouble following the line? Examine your mistake. If you're cutting a straight line but it bears left or right, the fault is yours. Practice holding the saw straight to the line while you cut. If the top of the cut is on the line but the bottom is beveled (slanted) in or out, you're not holding the saw blade vertically square to the board. Hold a square up against the blade as a guide while you cut (Fig. 6) until you develop an eye for sawing correctly. If your cuts all have curves, your saw blade is bent. Get another saw.

Circular saws (Skilsaw is a popular trade model) are definitely the most common cutting tool—but watch out, they're dangerous! *Never* let that spinning blade get near your hands, legs or any other part of your body. *Never* let it cut its own power cord. *Never* get the blade pinched in a cut—it can kick back into you. *Never* put a blade on with its teeth going the wrong way (the saw will jump out of the cut). *Don't* jam its blade guard open to "make things easier." *Always* cut with the saw on the supported side of the board, not on the one that will fall off. *Unplug* it when you want to adjust the blade or leave the worksite. In other words, treat that tool with lots of respect.

But don't be scared off: A circular saw is immensely useful. It can cut at angles. With special blades, it can saw through a variety of materials, even concrete. And it can make

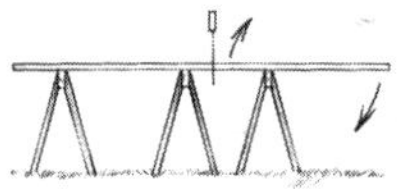

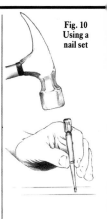

Fig. 6
Keeping a handsaw
square

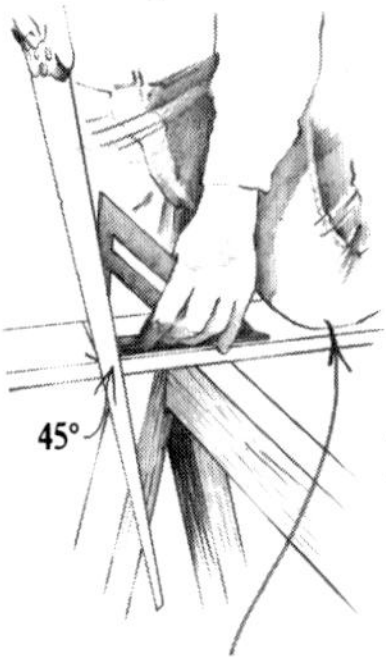

45°

Knee braces board

Fig. 7
Cutting with a circular saw

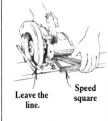

Leave the
line.

Speed
square

Fig. 8
Nails

Finishing
nail

Common
nail

Spiral nail

Fig. 9
Pulling a nail out

Block for
extra leverage

those standard straight cuts with ease.

For straight cuts, first make sure the blade is set just $1/8''$ deeper than your board. This will make the saw work more efficiently and tear the wood less. Then hold the saw so the power cord and your body are out of the way, start the motor, and let it reach full speed before the blade enters the wood. Unfortunately, the guide sights at the front of a circular saw often don't work well as guides, so you have to look around the side and watch the blade itself moving along your cutting line. That means you'll need to wear safety goggles to keep flying sawdust out of your eyes. Earplugs are good, too, for muffling the noise.

The first inch of a cut is all-important. Get it straight, and the saw will pretty much steer itself the rest of the way. If it's off your line, though, pull the saw out and start again. If necessary, hold the blade guard handle back with one hand, and push the saw evenly all the way through the wood with the other, letting it rest flush on the supported board (Fig. 7). Don't push it too hard—forcing the tool increases the risk of accident and can damage the motor. Don't try to back a circular saw out of a cut while it's running—it may kick back instead. Turn the motor off as soon as the cut is finished, but don't put the saw down until the safety guard has snapped back into place and completely covered the blade.

Leave the line. This carpenter's axiom means you want to cut just along the waste side of your penciled line, so you can still see the line on the wood piece you use. Why? Because the width of a saw cut (the kerf) can be substantial ($1/8''$ or more), so if you cut *on* the line, you'll remove wood from your measured side as well. For the same reason, don't mark a series of cuts all at once on a board: The kerf waste will throw them off. Mark one, cut one. Then mark the next, cut the next. So don't forget: Cut so the line stays on the piece you want, *not* on the waste piece.

Are you having trouble making the saw run straight across the cut? Then once you've got it lined up to start your cut, set a speed (or other) square flush against the saw's other side, and hold it there while you cut. That'll help keep your saw on course and give you a beautiful finished cut. A speed square's 45°-angled side makes an especially useful guide when you need to make 45° cuts.

Nailing

Finally, the soul (and sometimes the frustration) of carpentry: driving nails. Real carpenters can wham a nail home in two or three hits, but that skill comes with practice, *lots* of practice.

First, pick a hammer that feels comfort-

Fig. 10
Using a
nail set

Fig. 11
Toenailing

Start off
the line.

Fig. 12
Tying a taut string

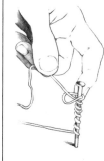

Fig. 13
Spirit level
and plumb bob

Fig. 14
Sliding T-bevel

"Level twice, build once." Constant checking—and rechecking—measurements is the key to good construction.

really tiny nail or you're in an awkward position, you might use needle-nose pliers, cardboard, putty or chewing gum to hold the nail in place.

Tap the nail to secure it, remove your hand, hit it a bit harder once or twice (not full force, or you may send it zinging off into space), and then pound it in. At first, you may tend to use your wrist too much when driving nails because that gives you finer control, fewer misses. Try instead to get your entire arm into the act with a loose, swinging motion. You'll hit with more power and tire less quickly. Also, resist choking up on the hammer to increase accuracy. Make yourself learn from the beginning how to do it right.

Is the nail going in crooked? If it's a third or more in, it's too late to reorient. Pull it out and try again. Happen again? You may be trying to nail through a knot or curved grain. If so, you'll have to predrill your hole (drill it slightly smaller and shorter than the nail) to get *any* nail to go in straight.

Is the nail bending over? That'll happen a lot if the wood's too hard to nail easily. In that case, make sure you're not using too puny a nail for the job at hand, or try rubbing soap or wax on the nails to help them slide in. Or simply eliminate the hassle by predrilling your nail holes. Of course, the problem may be that you're hammering the nailhead at an angle instead of straight on. Only practice will solve *that* problem.

In the meantime, you may be able to tap that bent nail in by carefully banging straight on its head, or you could try to straighten it out with sideways blows. If neither trick works, you've got to pull the nail out. Grab it with the claws on the back end of the hammer, put the tool's head down on the board (you can lay a putty knife or thin wood strip under the hammerhead to keep it from marring the board), and pull. If you do put a small block of wood under your hammerhead, you'll have extra leverage and pulling power—that's a big help once the nail's partway out (Fig. 9).

The nail just won't come out? This time bend the hammer down *sideways* instead of pulling it back. This'll bring out almost any nail, but it'll be too bent to reuse.

Suppose you drove the nail in just fine, but then you realized that the boards were placed wrong, so now you need to take it out. The hammer claws won't squeeze under the nailhead, so try banging the top board from the back and then the front to see if that makes the nailhead protrude enough to grip. No luck? Use a flat-faced pry bar (a wonderful tool that's often appropriately called a wonder bar), and either wedge it under the nailhead, or use it to pry the two boards apart so you can pound the nail point.

able: properly balanced and neither too heavy to use repeatedly nor too light to have much impact (try one about 16 or 20 ounces). That'll make a big difference.

Next, get the right size of nail. The rule of thumb here is that the nail should go twice as far into the second board as it traveled through the first—i.e., its length should be three times the thickness of the first board. You'll want a *common* flatheaded nail for ordinary jobs, a *spiral* (spiral-shanked) nail for extra holding power and a *finishing* (no-headed) nail for inside jobs where you don't want the head to show (Fig. 8). If your work's going to be exposed to weather, use *galvanized* nails. They resist rust.

Hold the nail in place, either with your thumb and forefinger or—if you want to protect your fingertips—between your palm-up fingers, like a cigarette. If you're nailing a

Fig. 15
Nail board ends to backing.

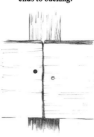

Driving a nail home in a few hits, without having to stop to straighten it, is a skill that will come with practice—lots of it.

Does the wood split when you drive a nail? If so, don't position the nails too close to the end of a board. Try to keep them at least as far away from the edge as the board is thick. Also, make sure all your nails aren't going in the same stretch of wood grain. Stagger them. Still splitting? Blunt the tip of the nail with a few hammer hits before you drive it. It'll then tear, not pry, its way through the fibers and be less likely to split the wood. *Still* splitting? It's probably time to predrill your holes again.

When you're nailing one board onto the edge or end of another (*edge* or *end nailing*), the union will be stronger if you drive your nails in at slight alternating angles rather than all straight down. The same holds true for *face nailing*, nailing two boards back to back. If the face-nailed boards are both the same thickness, you can't use the 3X rule of thumb to determine nail length. Instead, pick nails that would protrude slightly if nailed straight down, then drive them in at angles.

Actually, if appearance isn't a factor, you *can* use longer nails for face nailing and *clinch* them for a joint that just plain won't come apart. Drive the nail all the way through. Bend the nail tip over with your hammer claws. Then hammer the nail over and flat. The bent tip will stick back into the wood.

If you're doing finishing work, you don't want to have nailheads or round hammer-head marks—carpenters call them donkey tracks—in the wood, so use finishing nails with no heads. Then when the nail gets close to the wood, grab a *nail set*. It looks somewhat like an iron pencil. The "lead" fits into a dimple in the little finishing nail's top, and you hammer on the "eraser" end. Drive the nailhead a bit into the wood with the nail set (Fig. 10), and fill the resulting hole with wood putty.

Toenailing means angle nailing through one board into another. The classic toenail goes out the end of one board and into a second, right-angled one (Fig. 11). It's hard to do. You can split the board end off, drive too low or too high or push the board out of position.

To avoid these mishaps, start your nail at a spot on the board halfway up the nail's length. Drive it almost square to the wood until you get it started, then turn it to a 45° angle, and pound it on down. If the board end splits, blunt the nail tip, start higher up on the board, and/or predrill the hole. To keep your hammering from pushing the top board off-line, start that board off the line in the *other* direction to compensate ahead of time for its tendency to slide. Or start a toenail on the opposite side of the board, and alternate driving the two nails to keep the board in place. Or simply hold the board in place with your foot, a wood block or clamps.

Actually, the fact that a toenailed board tends to move comes in handy when you need to move a board over to a chalked line or nail a bowed board to a straight one. Just start a toenail in the direction you want the board to go and pound away!

One last nail tip: *Never* leave a nail in a loose piece of wood, most especially if its point is sticking out. Otherwise, sooner or later, without fail, somebody will injure either a tool or a foot on it.

Other Tools and Aids

Another surprisingly useful carpentry tool is *string*. It seems like anytime you want to establish a line to build to, you have to run out a taut length of string. Nylon is best; it's strong. To draw and tie it tight, use this trick: Drive a nail where the string needs to end, loop it around the nail eight or more times, then make another loop, draw the string through it, lay that around the nail and tighten (Fig. 12). It's remarkably easy to do and *undo* the resulting knot.

String lines often help when you want to level something—and you're leveling all the time in building. A *spirit level* and a *plumb bob* are pretty straightforward tools (Fig. 13). The former has a bubble in a vial to help you check that things are level horizontally—often simply called level—and often another vial to check that something's level vertically, or plumb. A plumb bob, a weight on a string, is good for leveling vertically or checking that one object is centered over another. Be sure to use these tools precisely. Don't let the bubble in a spirit level be just "slightly off-center." Use a level in more than one direction; for instance, make sure that post is plumb front to back as well as left to right. Make sure you're holding a level against a straight, smooth surface, a good reason to use it in more than one spot. And *recheck* something for level or plumb after you finish nailing or securing it.

Shims are little wedges of wood you use as spacers when, for one reason or another, things don't quite meet as they should. You just push the shim in the gap as far as necessary. To fill the gap completely, drive one shim in from one side and another from the other and then nail. They're the carpenter's way of cheating—and they're so useful that lumberyards call them "cedar shakes" and sell them by the bundle.

There are a few other tools that even the beginning carpenter will probably need. First is an *electric drill*. Next, *screwdrivers* come in handy all the time. You need several so you'll have the right size for the screw you're driving. Remember that if wood is quite hard, you can predrill the screw holes. Three or four *nail sets* will take care of your finish nailing needs. A *staple gun, pliers* (particularly locking pliers) and a *utility knife* (it holds razor edges for cutting) are ordinary tools with lots of uses.

A set of three or four *wood chisels* will help you in a multitude of ways. A *sliding T-bevel* (Fig. 14) is like a small square, but it has one free-moving, adjustable side. You can use it to "capture" any nonsquare angle and "transfer" it to a board you're cutting. Always double-check the transferred angle before you cut. Some kind of *plane* will help you smooth surfaces and shave off that inconvenient extra width. And *safety goggles* can save your eyes from flying chips of wood or metal. The ones with real eyeglass frames are much better than the clear, all-plastic type, which scratch and fog up easily.

Miscellaneous Tips

Always make a complete drawing of everything you plan to build. And be sure to include the thickness of the material in your calculations. If you're making a simple square box, for instance, with the two side walls inside the two end ones, those side walls will have to be cut two thicknesses shorter than the end ones to keep the box square.

Speaking of thickness, you probably already know that a 2 X 4 isn't really 2" by 4", just as a 1 X 6 isn't really 1" by 6". Boards get planed a bit from this *nominal* size in their final milling. So a 2 X 4 is actually 1¹/₂" by

Penny (d) Nail Size in Inches

Why are nails sized in "pennies"? In England, they used to be sold by the hundred. One hundred 2" nails cost six pennies, so they became known as six-penny (6d) nails!

Penny	Length	No. per Lb.
2d	1	847
4d	1½	296
6d	2	167
8d	2½	101
10d	3	66
12d	3¼	56
16d	3½	47
20d	4	30

BOX NAIL

COMMON NAIL

FINISHING NAIL

CASING NAIL

3¹/₂", and a 1 X 6 is ³/₄" by 5¹/₂".

This is why the most common 2 X 4 board, the *stud*, used to frame all those 8'-tall walls, is actually 3" shy of being 8' long. The stud in a framed wall, like the inside walls of a box, sits on a 2 X 4 and is topped by a 2 X 4. The real thickness of those two boards (1¹/₂" plus 1¹/₂") adds up to 3", so the stud has to be 3" short for a wall exactly 8' tall.

Never leave the end of a board dangling between supports in anything you build. Always nail it to something. (Add some backing, called *blocking*, if need be.) If another board's going to butt up against the first one, you'll want to cut the first board so it ends halfway across that nailing surface (Fig. 15). Then you'll have something left to nail the other board to.

Want to be sure a large corner makes a true right angle? Measure 3' out one side and 4' out the other. If the distance between those points (the hypotenuse of a right triangle) is 5', you're on the mark.

Do you want to know if any rectangular structure you've laid out—from a box to a house site—is square? Measure the diagonals. If they're equal (and, indeed, all four corners are right angles and the opposite sides are equal), you're in business.

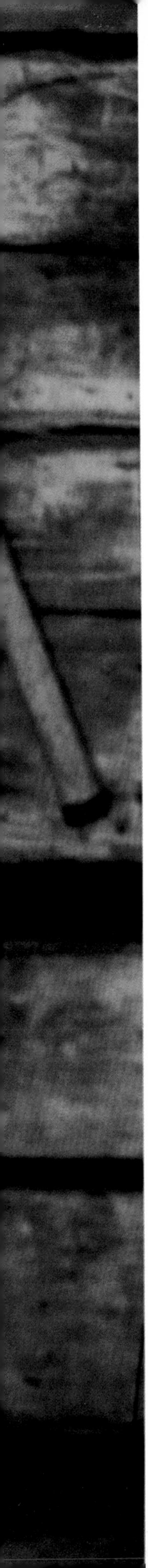

Tool Sharpening Basics

Cutting-edge advice on a vital skill

Coaxing the optimum edge from a trusted tool is a rewarding, fulfilling and strangely peaceful job.

Fig. 1
Removing nicks

Fig. 2
A single-beveled tool
Sharpen this side . . .
. . . not this one.

Fig. 3
Steeper angle = tougher edge

Lower angle = sharper edge

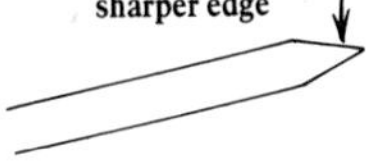

Most newcomers to the country life are intimidated by the prospect of sharpening their own tools, partly because everybody else seems to be an expert at it. Still, it is an important skill to master. You simply can't *do* many country jobs with dull tools, and you can perform any cutting task much better and more easily with a sharp one.

Tools with blades fall into two main groups—rough outdoor tools you can sharpen well enough with a file, and finer blades that need more specialized care. Filing methods will be explained first, because they take less skill, if more muscle, yet illustrate many of the principles of fine-tool sharpening. In fact, let's start by discussing tools many people have never even *thought* about sharpening—**spades** and **shovels**.

It is difficult to believe, but a sharp spade (the flat-faced digging tool) or shovel (the curve-faced one) *will* cut through dirt far more easily than a dull one. All you need is a coarse hand file. It can be either single-cut, with one set of teeth, or double-cut, with two intersecting sets of teeth. The double-cut will take more metal off with less effort; the single-cut will do a finer job.

Before you start filing, however, look at your digging tool. Is it rusted? Not good. The only thing that will ruin the edge on a tool faster than using it is *abusing* it. And nothing will pit up an edge faster than rust. So scrape off as much rust as you can with steel wool, and from now on clean off this and every tool after you use it, rubbing it lightly with oil to keep new rust from forming. This simple step will greatly extend the edges and lives of your tools.

Now for the real work. First, run your file around the top of the edge some, if need be, to smooth out any nicks you find in the blade (Fig. 1). Then consider: A shovel or spade is a single-beveled tool. It has only one sharp edge, which leads to:

Sharpening Axiom No. 1: Sharpen single-beveled tools ONLY on the beveled side (Fig. 2). You can ruin the cutting edge of the tool otherwise. In real life, you could probably rescue a rough tool like a shovel from the mistreatment of having both sides filed. But do that to your scissors or prized pruners, and they'll be headed for the junk pile.

So brace your spade or shovel well—this and almost every sharpening job will go more easily if you clamp your work with C-clamps or in a vise—and file it on the top, the beveled side. Run your file up into the blade or down the blade, whichever's easier, though try to keep your fingers out of the way. Use a file that matches the contour of the blade: a flat one for that flat-faced spade and a half-round one for the curved shovel.

What kind of angle should you sharpen at? The answer leads right to:

Sharpening Axiom No. 2: In general, sharpen the bevel at the same angle that was already there. In other words, if you can tell what angle the manufacturer or prior sharpener used, follow it. If you can't tell, move on to:

Sharpening Axiom No. 3: Sharpening at a steep angle gives a more durable edge; sharpening at a low angle gives a sharper edge (Fig. 3). The thin edge produced by low-angle sharpening will be sharper than a wider edge, but it will be more brittle as well. Since you're honing a digging tool that's likely to strike roots or rocks, a tough edge is more important than a sharp one, so sharpen your spade at a fairly high angle—say, one that puts a shine back only about one-fourth inch into the blade.

Press the file hard on your forward stroke, going the full length of the sharpening tool so you won't wear the file out in one spot. Your backward stroke should be light, little more than the weight of the tool, to keep

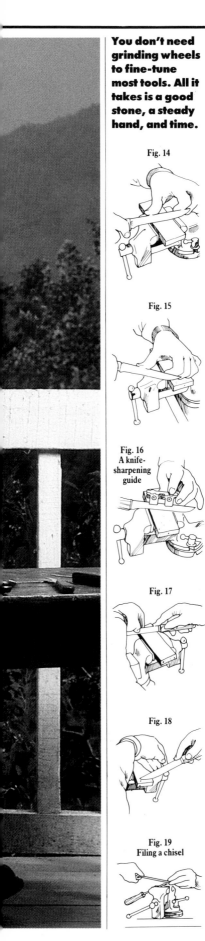

Fig. 14

Fig. 15

Fig. 16
A knife-sharpening guide

Fig. 17

Fig. 18

Fig. 19
Filing a chisel

Some other tips: Hold that thumb back-stop on the blade so the side of it touches the stone while the middle of it holds the blade at the angle you want. Sharpen by pivoting your body at the waist so you'll have your wrists and elbows locked. And you can, if you'd rather, do your rough honing by moving sections of the blade round and round in a circular motion. Underhill figures that makes it easier to keep the correct angle because you're not repeatedly lifting the blade off the stone.

If you're getting frustrated or just want to make the whole job go a lot easier, get a sharpening guide—a little blade clamp that automatically holds your knife at the right angle (Fig. 16). Buck Knives makes one, called the Honemaster, and Juranitch offers the Razor Edge Knife Sharpening Guide. Unlike many sharpening gimmicks, these two doodads work. You may just want to use them as training wheels, but beard-axer Juranitch claims no expert can sharpen a knife edge freehand as well as an amateur with a guide can. He's even proved it by having pairs of novices—his daughters, Boy Scouts, professional outdoors writers—use his guide to sharpen pocketknives and then by shaving his own face with those blades.

OK, guided or not, work that one side of the blade until you can raise a burr along the whole edge. Keep working until you get that burr—let it be your teacher.

Once you've got a full-length burr, turn the knife over and sharpen the other side by pulling the blade toward you. Your blade-hand position will have to change here. This time put your fingers behind the blade, and let your thumb press down on the side (Fig. 17). Everything else is the same. Keep a constant blade angle (the same one you had on the other side), stroke the whole blade on the stone, and lift the handle some as you get to the tip so it will get sharpened too (Fig. 18). Work that side until you raise a full burr going the other way.

Now switch to your fine stone for the finish work. Stroke once away from you (as you did at first) and once toward you. Alternate about a dozen strokes, forward and backward, on the stone. Don't press as hard on these strokes as you did on the rough-side ones. And you can keep lightening up so your last few strokes carry just the weight of the knife.

You're done—or are you? How can you tell if your knife is sharp? Well, you can run your thumb over (not down—ow!) the edge and feel if it tends to catch in your thumbprint grooves. You can hold a piece of paper by the corner and see if your knife will cut (not tear) into it. And you can try to shave hair off the back of your arm with it.

If it does all that, congratulations! You've done well. If not, repeat your steps on the fine stone. That'll probably do the trick. If it doesn't, you're most likely not holding the knife at a constant sharpening angle. Keep practicing—or get a sharpening guide.

Once you've got a fine edge, you might want to put an extra finishing touch on it by stroking it down a steel or a pair of ceramic sticks. Most of these are set at an angle. All you have to do is hold your blade vertical and run it straight down the stick, drawing the full blade against it as you do. Regular use of these last aids will help keep a good edge on a blade, but they will not fix a dull one. Put that kind back on the stone.

Now you can sharpen all the knives in your home. Most of them will take that same slight angle you put on your first blade. If you're honing a butchering knife that's going to be going through bone, put a steep angle on it so the edge won't be likely to break. If you're keening a delicate-work fillet knife, give it a very slim taper.

Let's move on and sharpen a wood **chisel** or a **plane**. Another two-stage job, rough then fine. You can do the rough work with a coarse stone, a file or a grinding wheel (if you're real careful). Remember, the most important thing: This is a single-beveled blade, so sharpen it only on the angled side or all is lost. Follow the original bevel unless you're going to be cutting into very hard wood—in which case, you'd want a steeper (tougher) angle.

Some experts recommend clamping your chisel in a vise so that the edge is horizontal, then running your file down the face of it until you raise a burr (Fig. 19). Note: Use a fine file for this operation, following the rule that the harder the object, the finer the file. (A fine file's tiny teeth can better reach into the fine pores of a hard object.) Smooth the burr off by rubbing the back side with a fine stone set flat (not at an angle), then touch up the cutting side a bit with the fine stone. If you're not too confident about your own freehand sharpening, you could use Juranitch's knife sharpening guide (but not the Honemaster) on it and be sure you'll maintain a set angle.

Enjoying the Grind

In short, simply combine the techniques given here with some serious dedication to practice. Soon you'll be able to sharpen plenty of the tools around your place.

And you'll probably do so more often than you'd think, because it gets to be an enjoyable task. There's a curious sense of peacefulness from putting an edge on a favorite blade or tool. The slow rhythm of metal stroking on stone is a calming sound, a serviceable sort of music our forefathers knew well.

Cutting Wood With a Chain Saw

How to use this rural workhorse . . . with care

Proper safety gear may seem to be hot and restrictive on some days, but it must be worn every time you start your saw.

Rural author Noel Perrin once said, "If I were to move to an old-fashioned farm, everything quaint and handmade like a scene from Old Sturbridge Village, and could bring just one piece of modern machinery with me, I wouldn't hesitate a second. I'd bring my chain saw."

Perrin was right—a chain saw is *that* important to country living.

Hazards

Many aspects of chain saw work present potential threats to your health and safety. First is the obvious danger of the cutting attachment itself. It is meant to cut wood. It will also cut flesh. When you operate a chain saw, you must constantly be alert and take whatever precautions you can. A lot of things can go wrong.

Kickback is the most common cause of wounds. It causes 30% of all chain saw injuries. Kickback occurs when the chain, as it speeds around the upper part of the nose of the bar, comes into contact with something solid (Fig. 1). When the chain is at the upper third of the nose, it can't cut efficiently, and its movement forces the bar back and up, in the direction of the operator. If for any reason you have to cut with the nose of the bar, be sure to start the cut with the lower part of the nose, and be sure the saw is running at high speed as the chain touches the work. You should definitely avoid boring or using the nose of the bar until you are familiar with operating chain saws.

When you operate your chain saw, be alert for kickback at all times. Always cut with your left elbow locked or with your arm as straight as possible. Cut only one log at a time. Take every precaution to be sure that the nose of the bar does not touch anything. Always cut as close to the engine end of the bar as possible. Use the saw's bumper spikes to grip the wood and to provide pivot and balance for the saw.

Another problem caused by the chain is the pull or push that occurs when the chain catches in the work at the middle of the bar (Fig. 2). Push occurs when the top of the bar hits the log; the chain catches in the wood, and the saw is forced violently back toward the operator. Similarly, pull occurs when the work is forward of the bumper spike; the chain catches and violently pulls the saw forward until the spike hits the wood. These two hazards are most likely to occur if the saw is not running at full speed as the chain hits the work or if the operator isn't holding the saw firmly.

Certain safety precautions can help prevent chain-caused injuries. Competence and alertness are the operator's best protection. Next is proper clothing. For most of us, ordinary snug work clothes are best. You should certainly avoid wearing bulky or loose coats, sweaters or gloves when you're working with a chain saw. Trousers should be snug and cuffless, like ordinary jeans.

The cutting chain can also cause injuries when it breaks. A chain-catching pin built into the saw can protect the operator by stopping the chain before it flies into the body. Hand guards for the front and rear handles also help. Even when a chain catcher stops the broken chain, the end can still reach the operator's right hand. Many recent chain saw designs incorporate a large guard to protect the right hand. Snug leather gloves can also help. Either goggles or a face mask and a hard hat protect the operator's eyes, face and head from flying chain.

In addition to the cutting attachment, other aspects of the chain saw present hazards to the safety and health of the operator. Any prolonged session of chain saw work in-

avoid limbs that snap back and logs that roll? What follows is a look at various woodcutting situations.

Plastic or homemade wooden wedges will be useful tools. In many cases, simply using a wedge will save a guide bar from being pinched in a cut. A pinched bar is often bent so badly that it makes continued cutting difficult or dangerous, so it is definitely to be avoided. If you're going to buck a log that's lying fairly flat on the ground so that its weight is supported by the ground for its entire length, use a wedge to keep the kerf open enough to avoid pinching the bar (Fig. 4). Or make a series of overbucks, then roll the log over, and finish from the other side. Remember to work on the uphill side and avoid cutting into the dirt.

The first thing to consider in any more complicated woodcutting problem is the stress factor. By analyzing stress conditions before cutting, many problems will be avoided.

The general rule is first to cut the side of the log where the wood is *compressed* by the stress, then cut the side on which the wood is *under tension* created by the same stress. For example, when a log is supported on only one end, the *compression* of the wood occurs on the underside of the log, while the wood in the upper portion of the log is *under tension*. On the other hand, if a log is supported at *both* ends, the compression occurs on the top side, while the tension occurs on the underside. Always stop to analyze the stress before cutting (be especially careful of tree limbs bent against the ground), and always cut the compression side first and then the tension side.

With a huge log supported on one end only, the amount of stress must be minimized the moment the cut becomes complete. A wedge won't help in this situation because it would increase the stress, rather than decrease it.

So start the cut from the underside of the log by cutting upward with the top side of the guide bar (called *pulling chain*) until you've cut about a third of the way through. Then you can finish the cut from the top of the log, and the stress at the moment the cut is complete will be considerably lessened. The log will be unlikely to split, and the cut end will simply fall free as soon as the top cut meets the bottom cut (Fig. 5). Note that this procedure is made much more difficult, even impossible, if the saw won't cut straight because of a bent bar, an improperly sharpened chain or unevenly filed bar rails.

Now suppose your large log is supported on *both* ends. The top side is the compression side, and the bottom is under tension. To avoid splintered wood and a pinched bar in this situation, begin this cut with a one-third overbuck. Then finish the cut from underneath with an underbuck (Fig. 6). Make both cuts at a slight angle so the bar isn't pinched in the kerf when the log settles. The top of the cut should angle slightly toward the end of the log that's being cut—that is, the short end. Another trick to avoid pinching the bar is to make the two cuts so they aren't directly opposite each other but are still close enough for the log to come apart when the cut is complete.

Now let's say you have two logs that are both larger in diameter than the length of the guide bar. One log is supported on both ends, the other on only one end. In both cases, you'll have to make a number of cuts in sequence. The idea in sequence bucking of thick logs is to leave a break-off hinge of uncut wood in whichever third of the log is affected by compression.

The first log is supported on both ends. Since the stress causes the compression to occur in the upper third of the log, that's where you'll want to leave the hinge. To buck this log (Fig. 7), first make a one-third cut on the far side. Then overbuck to leave a thin hinge in the upper third of the log. The third cut, on the close side of the log, brings the saw into position for the fourth cut, an underbuck. Finish with a fifth cut from underneath to take out the hinge. The log will then fall; watch your feet.

The second log is supported on one end only, so you'll want to leave the hinge in the compressed lower third of the log to prevent splitting (Fig. 8). Again, make your first cut on the far side of the log. Make the second cut an underbuck to create the hinge. The third cut is on the close side, the fourth is an overbuck, and the fifth takes out the hinge from above.

Felling a Small Tree

Practice cutting down a small tree. Pick one that's fairly straight, so you can control the direction of its fall. (It's very difficult to fell even a small tree against the direction of its lean.) Also, you want a tree that you're sure will fall in a safe direction, away from power lines, buildings, cars and such.

Next, study the tree as you're walking toward it. Try to estimate its center of gravity, its direction of lean and which side is most heavily weighted with branches. Now make sure that no one will come within the radius of the tree in any direction. Then clear a large area all around the tree. Clear away any brush or debris that could catch fire, trip you or cause kickback. Clear an escape route away from the planned direction of fall and at a 45° angle to it (Fig. 9). Don't plan on running directly opposite to the direction of fall, since the tree may well fall exactly opposite to the way you planned.

The *notch* determines and controls the direction of the tree's fall. The *felling cut* removes most of the wood still holding the tree and causes it to break and topple. The notch and the backcut must always be made so as to form a hinge of uncut wood (Fig. 10). As the tree falls, it pivots on this hinge, breaking it. *Never* cut all the way through any standing tree with a single cut, no matter what the tree's size.

Move to one side of the tree, facing the planned direction of the fall. Aim across the top of your saw, along your front handle or across the falling sights (usually cast ribs in the saw's main housing), at exactly the place where you want the tree to fall. This will correctly line up your guide bar with the trunk.

Now make the upper cut of the notch, sawing down at an angle so that the cut, when completed, will go about one-third of the way into the trunk. *Never* cut as far as halfway into a tree with any cut in the notching procedure. Doing so will make the fall uncontrollable. Next, make the lower cut to complete the notch and remove the wedge of wood. With a straight tree on level ground, make this second cut straight in to meet the first. The hinge of uncut wood will be created when you make your felling cut.

Go behind the tree to make your felling cut. This is another horizontal cut, *at least one inch* (more, for large trees) above the horizontal notch cut. It is extremely important not to make the felling cut meet the horizontal notch cut. It must be at least an inch or two higher.

When your felling cut is partway complete, insert a plastic or wooden wedge into the cut, behind your bar but not touching it, to prevent the tree from settling back onto your bar and to help control the direction of the fall. Then keep an eye on the top of the tree, and continue cutting until the tree begins to fall. Don't cut all the way through to your notch. As the tree starts to move, leave your saw on the ground and retreat quickly along your planned escape route—while glancing back over your shoulder to be sure the tree doesn't turn around and come in your direction. Remember that the butt end of the tree may kick backwards and that unseen dead branches may fall straight down or fly in any direction. Take no chances. Retreat quickly and without hesitation.

Felling Large Trees

To cut a tree with a diameter larger than, but not twice as large as, the length of your saw's guide bar, use the following method. Exercise great caution, because the technique involves making a *plunge cut* that greatly increases the r of severe kickback. This

Fig. 12
Felling a larger tree

Direction of fall
Plunge cut
Notch cut
Hinge

Pivot saw around back

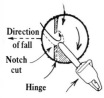

Fig. 13
Felling a big tree
Notch plunge cut: Use caution!

Direction of fall
Notch cut
Hinge

Pivot saw around back

procedure is definitely not for the novice cutter.

Make a notch, as before, though it may require four cuts to complete. You should make one-half of the upper notch cut on one side, and then move to the other side of the tree to complete it. Do the same with the horizontal cut.

After the notch is formed, make a plunge cut to one side of your planned felling cut. Start this cut about an inch or two above the base of the notch, keeping your bar horizontal. To minimize the danger of kickback, start the plunge cut with the underside of the tip of your bar, and slowly cut inward (Fig. 11). When the bar has cut a few inches into the tree, cautiously straighten the saw to begin boring straight inward with the tip of the bar, being careful to leave adequate wood for the hinge. (Your bar should bore into the tree more or less parallel with the back of your notch, not toward it.)

When your plunge cut is about halfway into the tree, proceed to complete the felling cut by sawing around the tree toward your planned escape route. In other words, make a pivot with the tip of the bar up against the hinge (Fig. 12). Insert a plastic or wooden

Always be aware of any obstacles around your feet or in the path of the saw's bar. Safe chain saw use involves avoiding any excitement.

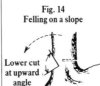

Fig. 14
Felling on a slope

Lower cut at upward angle

wedge behind your bar as soon as you pass the halfway point—but not before, as that would tend to spin the tree away from your desired angle of fall.

To fell a tree having a diameter more than twice as great as the length of your guide bar, only one additional cut is necessary. This time, the extra cut is in the notching operation and, in effect, cuts the hinge in half. Make a notch, as before. Then make a plunge cut in the back center of the notch, right in the center of the tree (Fig. 13). The plunge cut should be approximately twice the width of your guide bar.

From the felling side of the tree, make another plunge cut that meets the first, then pivot around the tree to make the felling cut. Place your wedge as early as possible, and be careful not to cut through the hinge.

Note that if you fell a large tree on a slope, you should make the bottom notch cut at an upward angle to provide more control during a long fall (Fig. 14).

And, through all your woodcutting, remember to take it easy. Take frequent breaks to keep both you and your saw sharp. That way you won't have to learn how to split wood with one hand in a cast.

Jason Rutledge prepares a field for planting, with a little help from a pair of Suffolk Punch geldings.

Draft Horses

This farmer feels that draft horses help him maintain an independence that would be impossible if he relied on power equipment.

"Come up, gentlemen," says Jason Rutledge. The two red horses heave forward into their collars. The field cultivator—called a rear-end wiggler—lurches into motion.

Rutledge proceeds into the cornfield, drawn unerringly down the rows by two Suffolk Punch geldings. As each tautly muscled leg moves and plants a round hoof in the soil, it presses 1,600 pounds into the ground. A prodigiously powerful step, but delicate as these things are measured.

Rutledge holds the reins firm. "You've gotta stay in touch with them all the time," he says, and they move quietly through the cornfield while Rutledge tells them how well they're doing. Three thousand feet up on Copper Hill in the mountains south of Roanoke, Virginia, where he lives with his wife, Sally, and two youngsters, Rutledge "orders up" all of his 76 acres with these chestnut horses. It is quiet on the mountain, and the team, plodding through the cornfield, evokes idyllic memories, old photographs, times gone by.

But Rutledge will have none of that.

"I don't want to give the impression that I'm a complete eccentric," he says as the horses stop for a breather. "These animals have a place on the modern farm. Look down there."

Between the rows of corn the soil is soft, loose, moist. "Practically no soil compaction," Rutledge says and, satisfied he's made a point, sets off again behind the team.

An intense, muscular man of 36, Rutledge

talks eloquently and often about the place of the draft horse on the farm today, especially the place of this particular kind of horse—the Suffolk Punch. Today he is one of the major breeders of this rarest of workhorses—there are fewer than 400 in the U.S., with another 200-odd in England. He owns more than 20, including a stallion and 12 brood mares. He points out that they're the only workhorses specifically bred for the farm. All the others derive from animals bred for military work—hauling knights in armor and, later, cannons.

Rutledge himself was in the military, the Navy, when he saw his first Suffolk. He was in England and saw a little boy leading a huge chestnut workhorse along a country road. Years later, he recalled the sight and felt driven to find out more about that powerful but docile horse.

What the sailor saw was a descendant of Crisp's horse of Ufford, a stallion foaled in 1768 and the foundation horse of the breed, making Suffolks among the oldest known breeds of heavy horses—certainly the breed with the oldest continuous studbook. They arose to fill the needs of farmers in the then remote area of England comprising Suffolk and Norfolk counties, a region bordered on three sides by the North Sea and on the fourth by a boggy region called the Fens. For many years, there were practically no sales of the horses outside the area, so the breed remained pure—and relatively unknown.

What kind of draft horse did frugal English yeomen breed to take on the rigorous task of plowing their heavy clay soil? For one thing, they look different, even to the untrained eye. They run true to color. They are all chestnut. The official association for these animals won't register one that isn't within some seven hues of chestnut, from gold to liver, or one that has any other color on it (except a small white blaze or star or a splash of white on the ankles or fetlocks). Compared to the Percherons and Clydesdales you've seen hauling beer wagons, these horses are smaller and rounder (hence the British word *punch*). In a sense, they look friendlier.

An expert notices that they seem short of back and short of leg, with especially heavily muscled forearms and thighs. The shoulders are upright—positioned for power, not speed. Also, the forearms and thighs are comparatively longer than those of other workhorses. As a result, to extend their legs forward, Suffolks need to lift them two and a half to three degrees of angle less than another horse, a modification that promotes power and movement with less action. These are horses that aren't likely to get stuck in the mud. Too, their coats are smooth down to the hooves: no long hair near the ground to collect mud and dirt. A special advantage is

that, being smaller, they eat considerably less than other breeds of heavy horses.

It was 1978 when Jason Rutledge and his wife, Sally, dreamed their "Suffolk dream" and bought a few mares from "the killer man" at the ominous place where horses stop off before becoming horsemeat. One of the mares turned out to be pregnant, and two years later Jason and Sally found an Amish man who traded them a stallion for the colt.

Rutledge was born to farms and farming—he learned land lessons from his "grampaw," known as Uncle Willie and now in his 80s. "Farming's made up the majority of my income for 15 years," Rutledge says. "Hay's one of my main crops . . . cabbage, tobacco. Got a little orchard, apples and some peaches." And, he adds, "I breed and sell Suffolks." He gets around $2,500 for what he calls an average purebred, but in truth, he says, "I'll take all the traffic will bear."

How powerful are the relatively small Suffolks? Rutledge takes some of his horses to pulling matches around Virginia and the surrounding states. Weighing in at about 1,600 pounds, they tend to be above the cut-off point (which is exactly 1,600 pounds), so they usually have to compete with the much larger heavyweights. So far, Rutledge's horses have not won in that class, but one of his teams has come in second, hauling 7,000 pounds of dead weight the required $26\frac{1}{2}$ feet in the required time, only a few hundred pounds behind the winners.

Rutledge goes to the contests to make the breed better known. Suffolks almost disappeared in the 1950s when mechanized equipment virtually wiped workhorses off the farm altogether. Also, he confesses, those contests are "my kind of hot-rodding. You get those animals pulling 7,000 pounds, screeching along the ground . . . that's a power trip."

Is it bad for the horses? "It can be, if you overdo it," says Rutledge. "Or if you don't have the right equipment." Each of his horses has its own collar, painstakingly fitted to produce the least friction on the animal's neck and shoulders—the same collar for pulling or farm work. No antiquarian, he uses specially designed nylon and leather harnesses. "Leather for where you need the harness to have a memory; nylon for give and strength." The nylon stretches, relieving the sudden shock in pulling, and it lasts longer.

Once, a woman came up to Rutledge to scold him for mistreating his horses by entering them in a pulling contest. Feisty as ever, he put his fingers in a circle on the horse's haunch. "See that?" he asked. "That's about the size of an Alpo dog food can. That's where this horse would be if he weren't out here. Do you suppose he'd rather be out here pulling and entertaining people

or in the Alpo can?" Rutledge has pulled out of contests when he thought the conditions were wrong. "I don't ever want to hurt these animals." One of his Suffolks, obtained from another breeder, has a bobbed tail, a cosmetic custom that evidently makes the horse's haunches look larger and more powerful. "That's just plain stupid cruelty," he explains in anger. "That's the end of their spinal column those (bleep) people cut off."

Rutledge speaks often of natural law, of every natural thing having a purpose, but has few good words to say about flies; he knows a horse without a tail suffers worse from them. He points upward to some turkey vultures circling an adjoining pasture. "See them? They eat carrion, clean up the place, sure, but did you know that anthrax bacillus can't make it through their digestive system? Everything has its role."

Weeds are a case in point. "You can't get rid of them, you can only control them." And because horses create the least amount of soil compaction, they are, to Rutledge, the best way to mechanically control weeds. Indeed, horses are a crucial aspect of all of those parts of the cycle that involve the central resource, topsoil. And Rutledge is a topsoil freak—for the very good reason that there isn't much of it on Copper Hill. The traditional mold-

The Suffolk Punch is bred to farm labor, has a docile temper and great stamina and is built for power rather than speed.

board plow—even though fellow Virginian Thomas Jefferson invented it—is anathema, but the relatively gentle effects of cultivating fields with horses preserve topsoil against erosion.

It takes about 50 years to create an inch of topsoil, he points out, and weeds themselves play an important role—if the farmer adapts to *their* cycles. In the first place, some—like morning-glory and ragweed—are actually good for corn. But they also demand crop rotation. The first year, Rutledge says, after a field is freshly tilled from sod, you can get away with one cultivation. The second year you need to cultivate twice; the third, three times. Then the handwriting is on the wall. Let it go fallow. "Those weeds will grow up *and* down, and their roots will help bring nutrients up to the topsoil." And in the natural course of crop rotation, planting a field to pasture not only helps the land, but it grows the fuel needed for the horses.

Meanwhile, the horses are producing manure. "Manure isn't good for anything until you compost it. Then you've really got something." And once you reintroduce the workhorse into the equation, you are into a different kind of agricultural economics altogether. It's nearly impossible to assign certain costs of horses to any traditional (or recently traditional) category of farm economics. Take manure. Once you have the horses in the barn, Rutledge says, you've got to get the manure out of there. Is that a health-maintenance cost (like keeping a tractor greased)? When you take it out to the field, is that a transportation cost (the horses are going out there anyway)? And once it's spread on the field, is that a fertilization cost or a waste disposal cost or what? A horse is no perpetual motion machine, of course, and it may be more labor intensive. But if it does a significantly better job, Rutledge says, it pays for itself.

He's the first to point out a horse's limits. "For heavy tillage, a tractor is more efficient. But for most of the rest, on a small farm, horses will do the work and add value to the land. That's what I call appropriate technology." They become most efficient in extreme situations—and Rutledge shares the Biblical wisdom of all farmers that an extreme is always around the corner. In times of drought or in times of heavy rains, the horse is at its very best, even for the occasional odd job. Rutledge speaks self-deprecatingly about the time he got a truck seriously mired thanks to a lapse in attention. The tractor was useless in the deep mud, but one of his Suffolks hauled the truck onto dry ground in minutes.

Furthermore, he points out, "You can use a horse on any land where it can stand up. A horse does fine on land that's got over a 12% slope. Use a tractor there and you can end up field pizza." Toward the end of a day, Rutledge hitches up a team of two-year-olds to a large wooden sled he built. "These boys don't know nuthin'," he says. "They're the equivalent of two 15-year-old kids."

Nevertheless, under Rutledge's guidance, they proceed with what could pass for horse wisdom along the edge of a field. Grinning, Rutledge scoops something up from the ground and holds it up. It's a wren's nest, made in part with chestnut-colored hair. "See, it's a rare Suffolkbird nest."

Further along, beside a forested slope, are a dozen mammoth logs. "Sally counted the rings on that big oak. It's 158 years old. These boys hauled it out of there—up the slope—without any trouble." He stops to examine the slightly disturbed ground where the logs had been pulled out of the forest. "Horses are best for selective logging," he says, and indeed they are still widely used for that purpose. "Logging roads and big skidders just wreck the forest, especially in hilly country."

Thunderclouds begin to unfurl in the west, and the sun drops down. On the way back to the barn, Rutledge stops the horses every few yards and hops off the sled to collect the quartz rocks that dot the pasture.

As he tosses the large rocks on the sled, he summarizes his case for the workhorse. "They create fertilizer, not pollution. When you use horses, you get to keep what you made. You grow your own fuel. And a horse appreciates in value. They get better each year for nine years, then they level off till they're about 12. That's a lot different from a tractor. Soon as you get a tractor out of the salesroom, you've lost money. And you don't ever get up in the morning and go into the barn and find a little baby tractor there, do you?"

He pauses and leans one elbow on a chestnut haunch. The sky begins to sprinkle lightly.

"These horses," he says. "They can be part of the job of stewardship. They'll leave this land better off than when I came here. We don't need any more mining of the soil. And these horses are one way of getting back to an old idea. It's called independence."

Back on the sled, Jason Rutledge and his young team set off toward the barn. He tells them what a good job they've done, and a visitor realizes another benefit Rutledge derives from his horses. Out in the fields, working in the quiet of his mountaintop—"playing with his horses," as his wife cheerfully puts it—he is never alone during the long day of the farmer.

Choosing and Using a Tractor

There's one to suit just about every country home and job.

If you live on and work a piece of land of any size, you'll eventually find yourself faced with a task that human muscles alone simply can't handle. Perhaps you'll need to spread five tons of lime over a couple of acres of run-down pasture, or drag some kitchen sink–sized stones from the vegetable garden. Maybe you'll have stumps to pull, logs to skid or acres of brushy land to mow, plow, harrow and seed to grass.

And when that time comes, you'll have two choices. One is to hire someone with a tractor—or perhaps a team of horses—and the appropriate implements to do the job for you. Most communities have a "custom" worker who can be called upon to do plowing, harrowing, seeding, mowing and other tasks for a set hourly rate. If the job you have in mind is a one-shot or occasional deal, such as preparing a new garden patch, that may be the best approach for you.

But if you find that you could use the services of a tractor more or less regularly, you may decide that the money you spend hiring others to work for you might better be put toward a machine of your own. After all, when hiring work out, it's rarely possible to have it done exactly when you'd like it to be—when the field first becomes dry enough in the spring or when the hay is just right for cutting—because there may be others in line ahead of you, or the custom worker may have a job to do on his or her own land.

By owning your own tractor, you'll be able to light into those big jobs when *you're* ready, not when someone else is. And if you have the time and inclination, you may be able to offset some of the cost of that capability by doing some custom work yourself for others in the area.

How a Tractor Works: The Basics

Everyone knows what a tractor looks like: It has two big, cleated tires in back, two smaller ones in front, a steering wheel and a seat for the driver. What's less obvious,

though, is that a tractor is much more than a powerful pulling machine with low gearing and high ground clearance. To understand that fully, take a look at a prototypical "tractor."

In northern New England, the *doodlebug* (Fig. 1) is fairly common. These are make-do farm machines improvised by taking an old pickup truck—usually one so badly corroded from exposure to road salt that it can no longer be used on the highway—and stripping it down to a bare motor and chassis. The springs are blocked up for increased clearance, and oversized tires are mounted, often fitted with chains for better traction. The result is a singularly ugly machine, but one that works surprisingly well for light-duty chores—hauling pumpkins from the back field, dragging a hay rake or cruising the edges of the wood lot for firewood.

Still, there are many more jobs that a doodlebug can't handle, because it lacks two vital features found on nearly all tractors. The first is a *power take-off,* or PTO.

A PTO (Fig. 2) is a splined shaft driven by the vehicle's engine. It's located behind the operator's seat, between the drive wheels, so that when implements like balers, mowing machines, manure spreaders and rotary tillers are drawn by the tractor, they can be powered by a detachable drive shaft extension. The utility of the PTO isn't limited to running field machinery, though. A wide variety of other implements can be PTO-driven as well. And since a *live* PTO can be engaged when the tractor is in neutral, it makes a tractor into a versatile stationary power unit. (Be warned, though, that not all PTO systems allow this!) A partial listing of commercially available PTO–powered devices would include winches, arc welders, air compressors, cement mixers, posthole augers, irrigation pumps and electric generators.

Another advantage the doodlebug doesn't have is a *three-point hitch* (Fig. 3); without one, implements can be fastened only with

a simple one-point arrangement, in the same way you'd attach a small boat trailer to the back bumper of a car. That system is satisfactory for implements that simply need to be dragged along behind—such as a set of smoothing harrows or a wagon—but when closer control is required, things can get considerably more complicated.

Plowing with a one-point hitch, for example, calls for the use of a *trailer plow* (Fig. 4). As its name implies, the trailer plow rides on wheels; the depth of its bite is regulated with a system of levers, ratchets and control rods. While that system works—similar controls have been used with horse-drawn machinery for more than a hundred years—it's cumbersome to adjust and makes for long-bodied implements that are difficult to turn around in a confined space.

The three-point-hitch plow illustrated in Fig. 5 is much simpler. The two *lift arm pins* on the plow fit into sockets in the *lift arms*

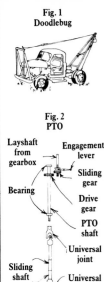

Fig. 1
Doodlebug

Fig. 2
PTO

Layshaft from gearbox

Engagement lever

Sliding gear

Bearing

Drive gear

PTO shaft

Universal joint

Sliding shaft

Universal joint for attaching to machine

on the tractor and are secured with snap-on *linchpins*. The upper end of the plow frame is attached to the tractor with an adjustable *top link*. Once the plow is mounted on the tractor, it can be precisely controlled from the driver's seat. By moving a control lever, the operator activates a powerful hydraulic cylinder that raises or lowers the lift arms and determines how deeply the plow bites into the soil.

The three-point hitch makes it much easier to turn around at the end of a row, too, since the implement fastened to the hitch can be lifted clear of the ground, reducing the assembly's turning radius to that of the tractor alone. Furthermore, three-point-hitch implements are easier to transport, particularly if you ever need to take your tractor on a public road. A set of three-point disk harrows (Fig. 6), for example, can be taken anywhere you can drive the tractor, provided that you raise the hitch enough to keep them

Fig. 3
Three-point hitch

Fig. 4
Trailer plow

from digging into the roadway—but the road commissioner is not going to be pleased if he finds you pulling a set of drag harrows (Fig. 7) along the center line, slicing the asphalt behind you as you go—a use that won't do the harrows much good, either.

Finally, hydraulics provide increased traction for heavy pulling chores. Imagine, for instance, that you want to drag a big stone out of your potato patch. To do that, you'll mount a *drawbar* between the lift arms of the three-point hitch, and fasten a *pin-mounted grab hook* to the drawbar (Fig. 8). Once the offending rock has been dug free to the point that a heavy chain can be fastened around it, the chain's other end can be fastened to the hook. Then you can simply ease the tractor ahead until the chain grows taut, and carefully add more throttle until the stone comes loose.

How do the hydraulics come into play? Well, if the stone gives up as easily as the one just described, you won't need them. In many cases, though, you'll find that the tractor's wheels begin to spin before the stone surrenders its grip on the soil. There's no easy solution to that problem if your tractor isn't equipped with hydraulics. If it is, however, you need only to back up until the drawbar is as close to the rock as possible, refasten the chain to eliminate any slack, and raise the lift arm a few inches. That serves to raise the stone slightly, transferring some of its weight to the drive wheels—the same idea as placing some cement blocks or a bag of sand in the back of a pickup truck for better traction on slippery wintertime roads.

Fair warning, however. There is such a thing as *too much* traction. Attempting to pull too heavy a load with too heavy a hand on the throttle and the drawbar raised too high can cause a tractor to pivot on its rear axle and flip over backward—with perhaps fatal consequences for the operator.

Selecting the Right Tractor

One aspect of choosing a tractor that probably isn't particularly important, except as it relates to the availability of good service or spare parts, is the manufacturer's name painted on the side of the machine. Most of the firms around today produce, and have produced, good and reliable tractors. So don't pay too much attention to the nameplate. Concentrate instead on the features offered.

What are those features? Foremost among them is horsepower. If you delve into tractor manuals, sales brochures or other references, you'll notice that two horsepower ratings are usually given for each machine. *PTO horsepower* is the higher value and refers to the energy output available at the power take-off when the tractor is stationary—the power available, in other words, for operating water pumps, generators and other accessories. (PTO horsepower is sometimes called belt horsepower, since stationary implements driven by older tractors often ran on a flat belt-and-pulley arrangement, rather than on a drive shaft coupled directly to the PTO.)

Drawbar horsepower, typically 10 to 15% lower than the PTO horsepower, measures the pulling force available at the drawbar when the tractor is in motion. It's less than the PTO horsepower—which, roughly speaking, is the total output of the engine—because some power is consumed in wheel slippage and in moving the dead weight of the tractor itself. Drawbar horsepower is the more commonly used power rating, so the recommendations herein are based on it.

For all-around use, a tractor of 25 to 30 horsepower is a good choice. If you'll be do-

Fig. 5
Three-point plow

Top link attachment point

Cross shaft

Coulter stem

Beam

Skim coulter

Wing

Shin

Landside

Disk coulter

Share or point

Moldboard

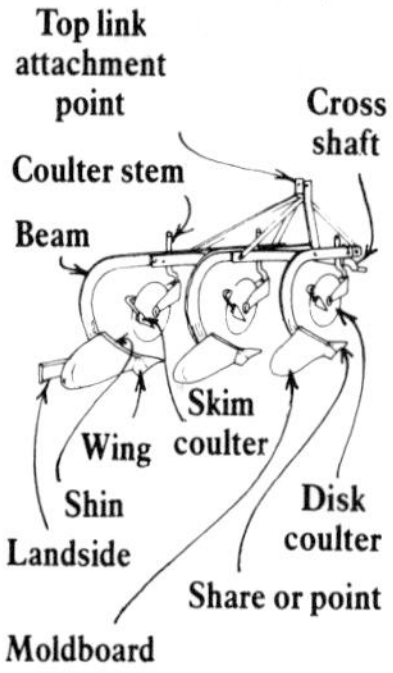

Fig. 6
Disk harrows

Fig. 7
Drag harrows

Fig. 8
Drawbar with grab hook

Fig. 9
Wide-front-end tractor

Fig. 10
Tricycle-type tractor

ing mostly heavy work, however—such as large-scale rotary tilling, mowing brush, skidding logs or plowing heavy clay soil—a 35-horsepower model is even better. There is little point in opting for anything with less than 20 horsepower unless, of course, you're looking for a machine that will only be mowing the lawn and maintaining a one-family garden.

If a small landowner is interested in purchasing a *used* tractor, a gasoline-powered vehicle is probably a better choice than a diesel. Gasoline engines run at a much lower compression than diesels, which means that they tend to age more gracefully. It's easier to get gasoline than diesel fuel, and it's convenient to be able to fill your tractor, lawn mower and tiller—and, in a pinch, your car—from the same fuel container. New diesel engines, on the other hand, are remarkably trouble-free—but when you're dealing with one that's 25 years old, problems are a lot more likely to crop up.

Virtually all tractors manufactured within the past 10 or 15 years are of the *wide-front-end type* (Fig. 9)—that is, the front wheels are spaced as far apart as the rear ones. Before that time, though, *tricycle-type* tractors were more popular. In the tricycle design, the two front wheels are placed very close together or are replaced by a single wheel (Fig. 10). Both types have their advantages and disadvantages. In older tractors not equipped with power steering, the tricycle configuration made turning easier by giving the steering increased leverage against the wheels. Tricycle tractors were—and are—considered good choices for row-crop cultivation, because there's no wide front axle to interfere with forward visibility at ground level.

A disadvantage of the tricycle design is that it does not steer well on slippery surfaces or on light, sandy soil. Under those conditions, the closely spaced front wheels often skid sideways when turned, rather than biting in and bringing the front of the tractor around as they should. Of greater concern is the fact that tricycle-type tractors are inherently less stable than their wide-stanced counterparts, and are more subject to a deadly sideways rollover when driven on irregular or sloping terrain.

The decision in your case should be based on where you will use the tractor and what sorts of jobs you'll be performing with it. If, for instance, you'll be using your tractor primarily for making hay on flat or gently sloping fields, a narrow front end need cause you no anxiety. A wide front end is a better and safer choice for use on rocky or irregular ground or if you plan to venture into the wood lot to move logs or firewood. Many older tractor models were manufactured in both tricycle and wide-front-end versions, so

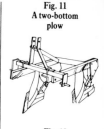

Fig. 11
A two-bottom plow

Fig. 12
Disk harrows, closed position

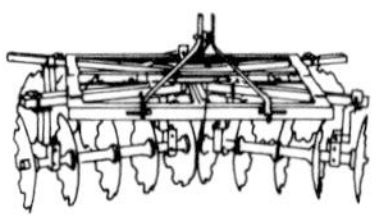

Fig. 13
Disk harrows, open position

Fig. 14
Disks

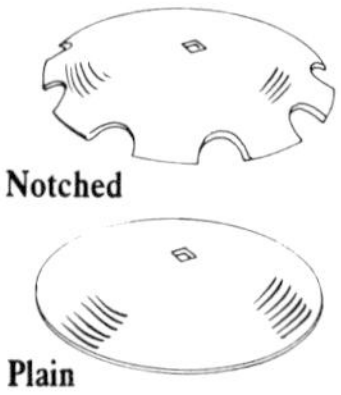

Notched

Plain

Fig. 15
A spiked-tooth harrow

Fig. 16
A bedspring smoothing harrow

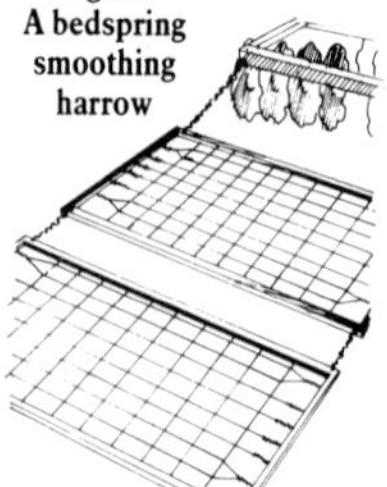

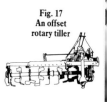

Fig. 17
An offset rotary tiller

if you're responding to an ad for a used implement, and the front end type is not specified, be sure to ask which type it is.

Finally, consider hitch and implement compatibility. While the three-point linkage is now the industry-wide standard, in the past many tractor manufacturers incorporated a hydraulic lift system of their own design, such as Allis-Chalmers' Snap-Coupler hitch and the Farmall Fast Hitch. Those and other designs required matching implements, usually manufactured by the same company.

It's just possible that you'll find a tractor with such a nonstandard hitch already equipped with every implement you need and that you'll buy the whole outfit at once. If, as is far more likely, the attachments don't accompany the machine, you'll probably want to continue looking or else adapt the existing hitch to accept the more widely available three-point-hitch implements you're bound to acquire later. That's not necessarily a severe problem. Conversion kits are readily available to fit most tractor makes and models that require them.

When taking a tractor—particularly a used one—for a test run, think about the same things you would when buying a car. You want a machine that runs well and is in good condition mechanically. Scratched paint, rust spots on the sheet metal body, dents and dings in the fenders—none of these have much bearing on how well the tractor will perform. The following check list includes some of the most important points that *do* have a direct bearing on performance:

1. What is the condition of the tires? New ones are expensive.

2. Check the brakes. Unlike the brakes in your car, which are designed to keep you from running into things, tractor brakes are primarily an aid to steering, so each rear wheel will have its own brake pedal. Brakes that grab unevenly are a sign of bent drums, while squawking brakes probably need new shoes. Oil or grease leaking from the brake drums could point to more serious and expensive trouble.

3. The engine should start easily and run without coughing, misfiring or otherwise misbehaving. Thick, blue or black exhaust smoke probably indicates that the engine is badly worn and needs rings or valves, or both.

4. Check the hydraulic-fluid dipstick—which is usually located near the back of the tractor—and the crankcase-oil dipstick, which will be up front on the side of the engine. Dirty oil is a sign of poor maintenance, as is cloudy hydraulic fluid.

5. Stand next to one of the back wheels, push in on the top of it, then pull outward. If you detect a significant amount of play, the axles and hubs are probably worn and may

Draft Animal or Tractor?

Nothing here should be construed as an argument against horses, mules or oxen. In fact, there are plenty of times when tractor owners find themselves wishing they owned a good strong team of Belgians instead of a 1953 Ford NAA—when the tractor bogs down in snow that horses could easily wade through, say, or when the electrical system starts acting up again.

Animals, moreover, don't use gas or oil, and a team of horses can make more horses. (Mules and oxen, of course, are another story.) The manure that animals provide is a valuable fringe benefit, in contrast to the exhaust fumes emitted by a tractor.

On the other hand, animals eat, and unless you can raise all of your own hay and feed grain, you'll probably end up paying more to fuel your draft animals than you would to feed a tractor—particularly when you consider that animals, unlike machines, need to be fueled whether they're working or not. And although animals don't require replacement parts as such, they do require the high-priced services of veterinarians and farriers from time to time. The bottom line is that there's not a whole lot of difference in price between maintaining a team of draft animals and maintaining a tractor. And it costs at least as much to buy a two-horse team as it does to pick up a used midsized tractor in good condition.

Ultimately, the choice is a personal one. If you've always wanted your own team of horses, if you know what you're getting into and if you can afford it, there's no need for an exhaustive economic analysis. There's more to life than dollars and cents, and in the long run the best choice for you is the one that will make you happiest.

need to be replaced. That will cost several hundred dollars.

6. Look under the tractor for oil or hydraulic-fluid leaks. All old tractors drip a little bit, but excessive leakage should give you pause.

7. Engage the PTO by stepping on the clutch and switching the lever near the driver's seat. It should turn steadily and smoothly—a grinding noise is bad news.

Just about all recently manufactured tractors utilize a 6-splined PTO shaft $1^3/8''$ in diameter, and that's the size most PTO-driven implements are designed to accept. Some older tractors, though—notably the Ferguson T020 and T030, Ford 9N, 8N, and NAA, and several other Ford models manufactured until the mid-'50s—came equipped with smaller, $1^1/8''$, shafts.

Adapters to step those slimmer shafts up to the now-standard $1^3/8''$ diameter are inexpensive and readily available. The adapters, however, often break when subjected to sudden stress. If you will be doing much haying or other demanding tasks that require the PTO, you'll probably want to replace the original shaft with a beefier $1^3/8''$ one. That's a surprisingly simple operation, but it will set you back some money. (Be sure to buy a complete PTO conversion kit, rather than just a bare replacement shaft.)

8. Raise the lift arms with some weight on them—if no implements are handy, you should at least stand on the drawbar—and leave them in the raised position for a few minutes. Occasional "hiccupping" is par for the course, but if the hydraulics can't keep the load up, or if it bobs up and down, the system is in need of an overhaul.

With the above information, you know enough to begin looking for a tractor of your own—and given some patience, common sense and perhaps a little luck, you'll find the one you need.

Implementing Your Tractor

A tractor by itself is not particularly useful. A plot of land with a bare tractor is analogous to a kitchen with a well-stocked pantry but no pots, pans or utensils. Fortunately, though, the tractor itself is the most expensive and complicated component in the system, and if you've chosen a tractor—new or used—that's common in your area, you shouldn't have any trouble finding the right accessories for it. Here, without further ado, are some of the implements most likely to appear on your wish list.

Plows are described in terms of the number of furrows they leave in the soil with each pass. A plow with a single cutting blade is a one-bottom plow, one with a pair of them is a two-bottom plow (Fig. 11) and so on. The monstrous wheat-field tractors used in the wide open spaces of the Midwest can pull a 10-bottom plow without straining—but a small-farm machine, probably in the 30-horsepower range, is intended for use with a two- or possibly a three-bottom model. In heavy clay or rocky soil, the two-bottom is a better bet, since it means less work for the engine.

There are many subtleties to plows and plowing, however, and you should seek advice from neighbors, or perhaps the county agricultural agent, before buying one. These individuals probably know more about local conditions than you do and can help you make an informed choice. If you're using a midsized tractor, be sure to get a plow to fit a Category 1 three-point hitch. (Category 2 implements, by contrast, are for large tractors, while Category 0 implements fit compact or lawn-and-garden machines.)

Disk harrows are used to eliminate the lumps and clods left in the field after plowing. The tandem type illustrated in Fig. 12 is probably what you'll want. Note that it consists of four separate *gangs* of disks—two in the front and two in the rear. The positions of the gangs can be adjusted relative to one another. In the closed position (Fig. 12), the disks will slice deeply into the soil without displacing it very much. Switching them to the open position (Fig. 13) after going over the field with them closed allows the disks to chop up the previously loosened soil, leaving a relatively fine seedbed.

Don't buy a bigger set of disk harrows than your tractor can handle. For a 25- to 30-horsepower machine, an 8'-wide tandem harrow is the practical maximum. Most harrows in that size range will be fitted with 18" disks, either plain or notched (Fig. 14). The notched ones are somewhat more efficient at chopping up sod or stubble, but are more easily damaged when run up against a big stone.

When examining used harrows, check all the disks for damage, and also make sure that each gang turns freely—but without excessive play in the bearings. Very large harrows are often equipped with ball or roller bearings, but the ones you'll be looking at will probably turn on cast-iron sleeve bearings or simple hardwood bushings. Both are acceptable, although the iron bearings will last longer. In any case, each bearing—unless it is sealed—should be equipped with its own grease fitting.

Spike-tooth harrows, sometimes called smoothing harrows, are used after disk harrows when an even finer seedbed is required (Fig. 15). They're ordinarily connected directly to the frame of the disk harrows and drawn across the field behind them, thereby eliminating the need for an extra soil-compacting trip over the field. Because spike-tooth harrows are not linked to the three-point hitch, the depth of their bite is not regulated by the tractor's hydraulic draft control but by a ratcheting lever on the harrows themselves.

A cruder, but absolutely free, smoothing harrow can be improvised by dragging a set or two of discarded steel-framed bedsprings—which you can probably find at the dump—behind the disk harrows (Fig. 16).

Rotary tillers hook up to your tractor's three-point linkage and are powered by its PTO shaft. Like walk-behind tillers, they pulverize the soil and leave it ready for planting in a single pass—in effect combining the operations of plow, disk harrows and smoothing harrows. Various sizes are available, but a medium-sized tractor shouldn't be expected to handle one any wider than 4'—and if you plan on chewing up any sod ground, a three-footer is a better choice. Since the space between your tractor's rear wheels is likely to be greater than that, look for a tiller that can be mounted in an offset position (Fig. 17) to prevent the tractor tires from leaving tracks in the freshly tilled ground at each pass over the field.

Rotary tillers are expensive, and the tractor-mounted units are not as versatile as walk-behind tillers. Come midsummer, for example, you'll have a hard time maneuvering a tractor into the middle of the garden to prepare a few small beds for second plantings of broccoli—a task that's easily handled with a walk-behind type. Still, if you plant a very large garden or plan to do any commercial gardening, the tractor-mounted tiller may be a worthwhile investment. The same quarter-acre piece that would take all day to work up with a walk-behind tiller can be disposed of in an hour with a tractor-powered one. A rotary tiller is also a potential moneymaker in the spring, when you may be able to find work preparing home gardens in your area.

Scraper blades (Fig. 18) are ordinarily mounted behind the tractor, although front-mounted blades are available for some makes and models. They're most often used for plowing snow, although they also work well for scraping and smoothing gravel roads or driveways. If you reverse the blade, the implement can be used to backfill holes or trenches if not too much soil needs to be moved at once. When buying a scraper blade, look for one with a replaceable carbon-steel wear strip where the edge of the blade meets the ground.

Logging winches for farm tractors have become common in this country only within the past few years, but they've been in general use for decades in Scandinavia, where most of them are manufactured. The winch fits in the three-point hitch, as shown in Fig. 19, and is driven by the PTO shaft. With the winch in place, the tractor is taken to within the cable's length—typically 120' to 200'—of the felled trees that are to be skidded out of the wood lot. The cable is pulled out by hand, and the logs are fastened to it with short choker chains and special sliding fittings. The logs are then winched in, lifted at the tractor end and dragged off to the yarding area.

Although a winch is costly, it's a superb tool for the wood-lot owner who wants to do some selective cutting with a minimum of damage to the residual stand. And if it enables you to harvest timber that would otherwise simply fall down and rot, the winch can pay for itself with gratifying speed.

Safety

Some aspects of operating a tractor are easily learned by experience. When you first use a disk harrow, for instance, you may have trouble getting it to bite into the soil evenly—but with practice, you'll soon learn to manage the hydraulic draft control to best advantage. Lower it too far, and you'll find that the harrow leans forward and rides on the front gangs alone, the rear ones lifting free of the soil and doing no work. Don't lower it far enough, and the disks will merely scuff the surface of the soil, rather than slicing deeply into it as they should. Common sense, a willingness to ask questions of those with more experience than yourself, and a certain amount of trial and error will teach you most of what you need to know in short order—and teach it to you more effectively than anything you're likely to read.

Safety is another story. A trial-and-error approach here is lunacy, because the consequences of a single error can be so grave that you'll never have a chance to learn what you did wrong. Some of the hazards involved in operating a tractor, of course, are the same as those that go with handling any motor vehicle. Others, however, are less obvious and deserve special mention.

Foremost among those is the danger of a *rollover*—of turning the tractor over backwards, wheelie-fashion, or flipping it onto its side. Either will probably kill you, and a glance at any farm tractor immediately tells you why. When it goes over, there's nowhere to hide, and no sheltering roof to hit the ground before your head does. (Virtually all new tractors can be ordered with an integral roll bar—Fig. 20—but these guards are not often found on older models.)

A rear rollover sometimes occurs when the tractor's drive wheels freeze solidly in muddy ground during a cold snap. When that happens and the operator tries to free them by yanking back on the throttle, there are only two possible outcomes. The first is that the wheels will break free of the bond holding them to the ground. But if they *don't* break free, the tractor will pivot around the immobile wheels, rather than the other way around (Fig. 21). That can happen with almost unbelievable speed. Tests have shown that the point of no return can be reached in as little as $3/4$ of a second, with the top of the tractor crunching into the soil $3/4$ of a second after that.

That can be avoided, however, by one sim-

Moving bulky material is one of those jobs that beg for a little motorized assistance.

ple precaution. If you suspect that there's the slightest chance of your wheels being frozen in, try moving the tractor in *reverse*, since it's impossible for a rollover to take place in that direction. If it won't budge, you may be stuck until the weather warms up—frustrated, perhaps, but unhurt.

Rear rollovers can also take place if the rear wheels are so heavily loaded that it's easier for the front end to come up than for the wheels to spin. That's most likely to happen when the drawbar is in too high a position and chained to a rock, a log, a stump or some other heavy weight—but it can also happen with nothing more than a set of harrows in the hitch, given an uphill direction of travel, too much throttle and too fast a release of the clutch. No matter what's fastened to the tractor—and even if nothing is—*make a habit of releasing the clutch slowly and carefully when you start moving*, and be prepared to push it in again at any sign of the front wheels lifting off the ground. A set of front-end weights (Fig. 22) will help keep the wheels down—making for more positive steering, as well as increased safety—and are well worth using if you habitually pull or drag heavy loads, as when working with a logging winch.

Sideways rollovers almost always result from venturing onto too steep a sidehill or from allowing the wheels on one side to drop into a ditch or hole. The solution is simply to use your head and watch where you're going. A tractor is considerably less steady on its feet when moving sideways along a slope than when traveling straight down or straight up one—and that makes it imperative that you consider the path ahead from all angles before committing yourself. For example, don't try to drive straight down a slope you wouldn't dare cross; you may slip sideways and suddenly find yourself in big trouble.

Roll bars or cages for older tractors can be difficult to come by, but if you'll be working in steep or uneven terrain, it's well worth trying to find one. For logging in particular, rollover protection is almost mandatory. If a search fails to turn up a ready-made roll cage or bar, a neighbor or farm-equipment dealer may be able to steer you to an expert welder who can make one to fit your machine.

Another hazard is the whirling PTO shaft used when a tractor is operated in conjunction with a powered implement—whether a movable one, such as a manure spreader, or a stationary one, such as a forage blower. Most PTO shafts turn at a speed of about 540 rpm, with an energy output, for the sort of tractor we're talking about, of around 30 horsepower. Consider what can happen if you should reach down to check one of the linchpins on the three-point hitch and the sleeve of your floppy old wool sweater—the one you keep meaning to throw away—momentarily brushes against the whirling shaft.

If the shaft happens to bring the fabric around for one full turn—perhaps because a loose flake of paint lightly snags the wool fibers—the part that first made contact with the shaft will be whipped under more fabric about one second later. A few seconds after that, the shaft will have wound in enough sweater to begin dragging you through the 10"-wide space between the PTO shaft and the tractor lift arm, with grisly results better imagined than described.

That may frighten you, and it should. If you're properly alarmed, you'll give that turning PTO shaft the wide berth it demands, and live to a ripe old age. The fact that every PTO shaft you use should be equipped with a tubular plastic safety shield (Fig. 23) should not temper your respect for it even slightly—any more than you would be careless in handling a loaded gun because the safety was on.

Upkeep, Repairs, Troubleshooting

You need two kinds of tools to keep your tractor running well. If you don't already own a set of mechanic's tools (that's the first kind) when you pick up your tractor, buy some the same day. When you're already in-

vesting a considerable sum in the tractor, an additional $100 or so won't seem like so much. If you don't buy them right away, you'll end up buying them one by one later, as you need them, paying a much higher price in frustration, lost time and probably dollars as well.

A good starter set consists of a $1/2$" drive socket set with sockets ranging in size from $3/8$" to $1\,1/4$", and a set of combination wrenches in the same size range. Add to that a few screwdrivers, an inexpensive set of feeler gauges and a lever-operated grease gun, and you're in business.

The second type of tool is the kind you hold, not in your hand, but in your mind. Fortunately, the information necessary to maintain most tractors is both readily available and less expensive than wrenches and pliers. The place to start is by acquiring the shop manual for your tractor—a storehouse of useful data, including specifications, advice on routine maintenance and detailed instructions on how to perform major repair jobs, such as installing new rings and valves and rebuilding worn hydraulic systems. If you purchase a new tractor, you'll probably be able to find the appropriate shop manual at a local dealer. If you own a used machine, however, you might have to search more widely than that. The Intertec Publishing Corporation in Overland Park, Kansas, is a good place to start.

The wisest course is to pay close attention to routine maintenance. Conscientious preventive maintenance is inexpensive and takes little time, yet it's the single best way to minimize wear and prevent expensive problems from occurring.

Service the air and oil filters at least as often as recommended by the manufacturer —usually every 100 operating hours—and drain the crankcase and install fresh oil with each filter change. If, as is fairly likely, you don't use your tractor for 100 hours each year (that's an average of about 20 minutes every day), service the filters annually anyway.

Every other month or so, take up your grease gun and pump some fresh grease into every fitting on the tractor. You'll find a fitting at each pivot point in the steering gear, in a couple of places on the three-point hitch and at other wear points. Every two or three years, drain and replace the fluids for the transmission, hydraulic system and differential. And every now and then, take a moment to inspect the fan belt—which runs the generator—and make sure that it's tight and in good repair.

Most older tractors were originally equipped with six-volt electrical systems, which tended to be short on cranking power, particularly in cold weather. Whatever you can do to keep such a tractor operating

Fig. 18
A scraper blade

Fig. 19
A logging winch

Fig. 20
A roll bar

Fig. 21
Rear rollover

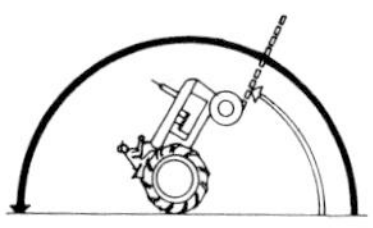

Fig. 22
Front-end weights

Fig. 23
PTO safety shield

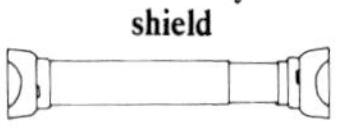

efficiently reduces the chances of your getting on it some damp, chilly morning and finding that it resolutely refuses to fire—something that's bound to happen just when some vital chore needs to be done. It therefore makes sense each year to replace the spark plugs, plug wires, distributor cap, rotor, breaker points and condenser. Would the tractor start just as reliably without such attention? Possibly, but why risk it?

If you someday find yourself with a dead battery anyway, don't succumb to the temptation to stretch a set of jumper cables from the six-volt battery in your tractor to the 12-volt battery in your car. That's a fine way to burn out the tractor's wiring harness by overloading it.

What if you press the starter button and the motor turns over strongly but the tractor will not start? Well, not every problem has a simple solution, but some do. Is the ignition switch turned to ON? It's easier to forget than you might think. If they're honest, most tractor owners will probably admit to having vainly cranked a switched-off engine at one time or another, cursing bitterly as the battery wore down, and finally sheepishly realizing the trouble.

The switch *is* turned on? In that case, one of two things is wrong: either the cylinders are not getting fuel, or the spark plugs are not receiving enough current from the battery and ignition coil to ignite the mixture of air and fuel. There are actually several other possibilities, but those two are the most likely and the easiest to test. Try the gas first. Use the correct size of wrench to unscrew the fuel line where it enters the carburetor; you should see a fine, steady stream of gasoline flowing from it. If you don't, add a few gallons to the tank—even if you can see gas in the tank, there may not be enough to reach the level of the outlet line—and look again. If you still don't see any gas flowing, you have a clogged fuel line, filter or shutoff valve. Examine the system and repair the culprit.

If you find that gas is getting to the carburetor and the engine still won't start, check the spark plugs. Remove the wire from one of the plugs, unscrew the plug, and reconnect the wire to the plug. Now rest the metal base of the plug on the axle, steering rod or some other heavy steel member, rubbing it back and forth a few times to be sure it's well grounded. Take your hands off it—if you don't, you'll soon get a sharp electric shock—and push the starter button, making sure the ignition switch is on. You should see a strong blue spark leap across the gap of the spark plug (Fig. 24). If you don't see a spark, you have an electrical problem. In that case, check that the points are properly gapped, that the rotor and the inside of the distrib-

Fig. 24
Testing the spark plug

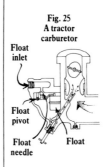

Fig. 25
A tractor carburetor

Float inlet

Float pivot

Float needle

Float

tor cap are clean and dry and that the distributor cap is firmly fastened down. If the plugs still don't spark, it may be because the porcelain insulators are wet or dirty, either of which can temporarily short-circuit the plugs and prevent them from sparking or cause them to spark too feebly. Wipe the exposed porcelain surfaces of the plugs, and if they are very wet or if the tractor has sat unused in damp weather for some time, remove them, and dry them completely by putting them in a warm oven for half an hour.

Still no spark? Take out the ignition coil, and have it tested. If it proves OK, the problem is a bad wire somewhere in the system, or possibly a defective ignition switch.

If you get a strong spark at the plugs and gas is getting to the carburetor but the engine refuses to start, there's probably a glitch in the carburetor itself. In order to give the carb a going-over, you'll need to shut off the fuel line at the tank and remove the carburetor from the tractor.

Before doing that, some people like to give the cast-iron body of the carb a smart tap with a wrench and try the starter again. The tap is sometimes enough to jolt a stuck float valve loose again—at least temporarily. Another worth-a-try approach is to hold the palm of your hand over the carb's air intake, crank the starter for a few seconds, and jerk your hand away as you continue to push the starter button. Sometimes the sudden surge of air pressure that results from this maneuver is enough to blow out any deposits gumming up the carburetor's inner workings.

Most tractor carburetors can be split into two halves, like a clamshell, by removing a few screws or bolts (Fig. 25). Disassemble the carburetor carefully, laying out the parts in an orderly fashion on a clean surface. Make sure the float—which, like the float in a toilet tank, shuts off the flow of incoming liquid when it reaches a certain level—is set to the specification given in the shop manual. Check that the float pivot, needle and seat are free of gum deposits. A commercial carburetor cleaner—such as Gumout—should help clean any sticky parts. Also, examine the float itself to make sure that it hasn't turned into a sinker instead. Reassemble and reinstall the carb, and try the starter again. In theory, you should install new gaskets whenever you take the carburetor apart, but gaskets can often be reused without ill effects.

Still nothing? You've checked all the obvious trouble spots, and it's time to call in a professional mechanic. That's an honorable solution, too, and a good way to learn something new. The chances are, though, that you'll seldom find yourself in that situation. If you select the right tractor in the first place and care for it faithfully, it will serve you well.

Tool Shed Check List

Allow us to offer you our suggestions in this master list of implements for repair and maintenance.

1. Safety glasses

Just about everyone agrees that it's a good idea to wear safety glasses when working with tools; far fewer actually do it. Please make it a habit.

2. Screwdrivers

You need a minimum of two sizes each of flat-headed and Phillips. One good approach is to buy a driver with switchable heads; the kind that stores bits in the handle works well because you always have the right bit with you. Bits or blades with flat, rather than round, shanks can be twisted with a wrench. Quality is very important. Cheap screwdrivers quickly become useless.

3. Hammer

For all-around use, choose a 16- to 20-ounce, rip-claw (flat-tanged) hammer with a smooth face. Only a steel or fiberglass handle will stand up to serious nail pulling.

4. Locking pliers

Often referred to by a brand name, Vise-Grip Locking Pliers. Look for a 10" pair with curved jaws.

5. Tape measure

If you're going to own only one, make it a 25-footer with a 1"-wide tape. Look for a case that's an even number of inches front to back, so there's a convenient number to add for inside measurements. The 1"-wide tape is rigid enough to extend straight out without an assistant to hold it. Thus you can measure horizontal distance by yourself and check vertical distance by bending the tape at the corner and reading the inside.

6. Shovel

Now here's a tool that's hard to get a consensus on. For one thing, what do you call all those different shapes of shovels? There's the standard digging shovel—rounded blade at an angle to the long straight handle. And the digging spade—squared blade nearly in line with the shorter D-handle. And the coal shovel—no good for digging, with its broad blade with angled sides and short D-handle, but great for heaving quantities of loose material.

7. Utility knife

The type with the stout, triangular blade. Blades that retract into the handle are much safer to carry and store but aren't as secure in use as fixed blades. If you use a retractable knife, be sure the handle screw is tight at all times. Should the razor-sharp blade slip through the joint in the case, you could be badly cut.

8. Four-in-hand file

Often called a horse rasp, after one version of the tool. Look for an 8"- to 10"-long item about 1 1/8" wide. One side should be half-round and the other flat. Most designs include round and flat rasps and medium-flat file surfaces.

9. Six-foot stepladder

That which is just out of reach on your tiptoes can often be done with ease from a ladder. A six-footer works well inside the house, and it enables a person of average height to reach gutters and low tree limbs that need trimming.

10. Needle-nose pliers

For yeoman duty, pick out an 8" pair that has a wire cutter and maybe even a stripper. Insulated handles are nice for cold days and for electrical work.

11. Three-eighths-inch variable speed reversible drill

Look for a drill with at least a 4.5-amp motor, a long cord and, if possible, roller or ball bearings. Pick up a set of high-speed bits spanning from $1/32$" to $1/4$" in $1/32$" increments, $1/4$" to 1" spade bits in $1/8$" increments, a couple of Phillips-head screwdriver bits, and maybe even a magnetic hex-head driver for sheet-metal screws.

12. Hacksaw

There's no comparably inexpensive substitute when it comes to cutting metal. Check to see that the handle adjusts blade tension easily and prevents the blade from twisting. Blades with 18 teeth per inch work fine for most work, though a carbide rod comes in handy for very hard materials.

13. Adjustable wrench

A good 10" adjustable wrench will do a reasonable imitation of a set of open-end wrenches. The jaws should open to about 1 1/8" and should be tight even at full extension.

14. Chisels

Unless you plan to get into detailed woodworking, you don't need a full set of chisels. One-half-inch and 1" butt chisels with beveled blades will handle most jobs. Since you'll often be using them to "hog out" wood in a comparatively crude fashion, stout handles that can tolerate pounding with your hammer are important.

15. Circular saw

The standard size carries a 7 1/4"-diameter blade and should have at least a 10-amp motor. Ball or roller bearings are preferable to sleeve bearings. If it doesn't come with a carbide-tooth combination blade, buy one. The carbide costs twice as much and lasts four times as long as a high-speed steel blade—especially if you occasionally use it on nails.

16. Wrecking bar

Really a variant on the time-honored crowbar, this curved piece of flat steel bar is better suited than its ancestor to removing materials without damaging them, and it also does a fine job of pulling nails without marring a surface.

17. Combination square

The 12" sliding square—offering 45° and 90° angles, an accurate steel rule and a built-in bubble level—is a standard for basic carpentry.

18. Extension ladder

A must for do-it-yourselfers who have two-story houses. The 24' size reaches all but the steepest gable ends. Aluminum is lighter than wood and very durable. Fiberglass is best, because it's nonconductive, but is very expensive.

19. C-clamps

For general duty, pick out a pair of 8" clamps. You may find them so helpful that you'll eventually want to get other sizes as well.

20. Maul

With one side configured as a splitting ax and the other as a sledgehammer, you get double duty. The 8-pound size works well for most people.

PART THREE

Husbanding Plants and Animals

We are all of us
midwives, ready to attend
the births of vegetable
and animal bounty.

I farm the soil that
yields my food.
I share creation.
Kings can do no more.
—Ancient Chinese Proverb

Perhaps you spent a dreamy winter day among the sweet promises of seed catalogues, or maybe you've been seduced by the memory of your granny's tomatoes. It could be that the latest ticker tape of grocery receipt provided the trigger, or was it the wholesome fantasy of trading jogging shoes for a hoe? At any rate, you've decided to plant your first-time-ever garden. Congratulations! And welcome to the 44% of American families that share an addiction that we euphemistically call a hobby. Oh, you'll hear the same old rationalizations from most of us: We're gardening to save money, to keep fit, to put good food on the table or to spend time outdoors. And those reasons might have provided motivation at the beginning . . .

As you'll come to know, though, what makes us pull out our tools year after year is the sheer wonder of sticking that pinhead-sized little ball of a broccoli seed into the ground and—*ta-da!*—eventually harvesting something that holds up the hollandaise. Big crop, little crop—it doesn't matter really. As much fuss is made when just one fine head ripens as when we cart off bushels.

In short, it's being smack-dab in the middle of a real-life miracle that makes this pastime pretty hard to resist. Who can get enough of it? Building a cabinet or piecing a quilt just aren't quite the same. Only gardening (and having children) lets you stand so close to the miracle of life that, as in the ancient Chinese proverb quoted above, you feel as if you're sharing in creation.

Yes, welcome to gardening. None of us can ever claim to really know the territory. We're all learning as we grow. Each year's a mystery—a renewed challenge—during which you'll reap plenty of mouth-watering vegetables at the very least. What's more important, you'll occasionally have the opportunity to feel like the only person who ever saw a honeybee wake up after spending the night on a morning-glory, or the only soul who's seen the wind rattle a corn leaf, making the plant appear to be scratching its own back. And like a brand-new parent, you'll be blind to the beauty of any broccoli other than your own.

Getting Started

When learning to ride a bicycle, you don't read up on aerodynamics, physics, gravity and inertia. Instead, you simply ask someone how to start, steer and stop the thing; then you hop on and give it a go. And you keep hopping on until you're pedaling vertically. The same goes for gardening. You might want to read a few good books, and you will want to find at least one neighbor who's gardened in your area awhile and pester him or her to death (the odds are great that most gardeners won't mind at all). Then simply go get your fingernails dirty. The following basic tips and recommendations will help you get started. You'll have to find the neighbor yourself.

1. Learn your zone: It's on that little map you'll see in seed catalogues or comprehensive gardening books. Zones are climatic bands, and seed catalogues will list by number which ones are suitable for certain plants.
2. Memorize your first and last frost dates: Planting times for everything from radish seeds to fruit trees depend on when frosts occur in your location.
3. Know your soil's make-up: Have a soil test done. (See "Fertilization" below.)
4. Be aware of available warm- and cool-

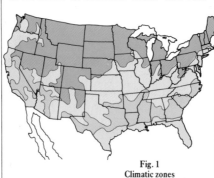

Fig. 1
Climatic zones

weather crops: Some vegetables grow best in warm weather and some in cool.
5. Look into local clubs: Check the library or chamber of commerce for a list of garden-related clubs. Organic-growers' organizations and native-plant societies are widespread, and their members will be more than willing to help you get started.
6. Read one or more of these books on gardening basics: *How to Grow More Vegetables* by John Jeavons; *The Self-Sufficient Gardener* by John Seymour; *The Healthy Garden Handbook* by the staff of *Mother Earth News.*

Fertilization

Soil testing is the map to any good fertilization program; it tells you how to "get there from here." It's all too easy to waste money and risk nutrient imbalances by guessing at what your soil needs. Labs whose personnel are not chemically oriented will give custom-tailored recommendations in terms of compost and such natural amendments as rock powders and animal bone and blood by-products that are dried, ground and bagged. These additives break down more slowly than synthetic fertilizers, are gentler to plants and soil and are much less likely to be leached away.

Best of all, "natural" soil-testing firms speak a language you can understand. Granted, the local agricultural extension service, home kits and many standard labs are much less expensive—but will you know what to do with all those unexplained numbers and equations?

Fall is the best time to send samples for evaluation. That's when preparations should be planned for the next year's garden.

With clean utensils, and without touching the soil with your hands, gather samples at a depth of from six to eight inches, and do so in 10 to 15 places around the garden. Mix the soil thoroughly to create a composite specimen. Secure at least a pound of dirt in a plastic bag enclosed in a small but sturdy box, and mail it off.

Tools

Equip yourself with at least the basics, some of which you may already have. You can always add more equipment if and as the need arises. For starters, round up a wheelbarrow, leaf rake, garden rake, trowel, soil-turning tool of choice (motorized tiller or garden fork), spade, hoe and sharp knife (for harvesting, cutting twine, etc.). Add some quality hoses, a few sprinklers and a hose attachment for watering by hand, such as a fan sprayer or, better yet, a watering wand. You'll also need a hammer, pegs and twine for laying out lines and patterns, plant tags, a file for keeping a sharp edge on things, buckets and an assortment of empty containers such as coffee cans or milk jugs.

After you've obtained the basics, anything you can imagine—from the practical to the absurd—is out there for your pleasure, from ornate brass faucet handles and copper watering cans to a soft-spray nozzle attachment, hand pruners and a minimum-maximum thermometer.

Site Selection . . .

Think big—dream of future orchards, vine-covered walkways and stone walls—but start small. A compact garden will leave you with enough time to get to know your piece of earth and the plants and insects that share it with you; time to do things right.

Think weather. The placement of a garden, even within the framework of a small lot, can significantly determine how much energy you'll have to expend battling the elements. Generally speaking, hillsides are better locations than either the tops, where wind can batter plants, or the bottoms, where wa-

Beginning Gardening

The gardener's world is full of fulfillment and frustration. Here's how to avoid the latter.

Planting peas: The hard work of soil preparation is over and the waiting begins.

ter and cold air accumulate. A south-facing slope gets the most sun and turns its back on cold north winds. Western slopes allow frozen plants to thaw slowly, though higher overall temperatures occur there than on east-facing hillsides, which shelter heat-sensitive plants in midsummer. And even northern slopes can be put to good use as orchard sites, since lingering spring cold can keep early buds from opening too soon.

You might not know it, but there's a great little microclimate on the south side of your house or outbuilding that offers protection against north winds and provides mass to absorb radiant heat during the day and slowly release it at night. Lakes and ponds also reflect heat and light to edge-of-the-water plants, but sometimes they provide open pathways for winds as well.

Watch what happens to rain and snowfall. Does the water drain or puddle? Does snow melt quickly (a sunny spot) or linger for days (possibly too shady)? Will crops get at least six to eight hours of direct sunlight each day?

Think water. Is the area in mind close to a source of reliable, easily tapped water? If not, consider what it will take—laying pipe, installing a pump, etc.—to bring the life-giving liquid to your crops.

All factors considered, it pays to choose a location close to your house. The farther you must go to weed the carrots or pull some greens for dinner, the greater the chance you won't. If you're lucky enough to have several small sites, plant herbs, lettuce, tomatoes—things you cook with most often—within plucking distance of the kitchen door.

Last, but not least, kick the dirt around a little. Dig up a spadeful at each potential site. Handle it, squeeze it, smell it. Crumbly, loose and sweet-smelling earth will be easier to work with than soil that feels like modeling clay, or sand that sifts through open fingers.

There, that didn't take too long, did it? And now—get out the champagne, straw hat and red-ribboned spade—it's time to finally break ground.

. . . and Preparation

If weeds and grass now stand tall where your dreams call for corn and tomatoes, top them with a mower or swing blade, pile the cuttings near the site of your compost heap, and consider yourself fortunate to have found a good source of organic matter. Then pull out any large rocks, and clear the area of trash.

Now stand back and once again envision that garden-to-be. Try to put borders on that dream. To do so, simply ask yourself: How much time will I honestly be able and willing to devote to this garden?

Fig. 2
Take soil samples at various spots in your garden.

6"-8"

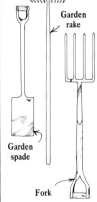

Fig. 3
Essential garden tools

Garden rake

Garden spade

Fork

Fig. 4
There are hospitable microclimates on the south sides of buildings.

N

S

Fig. 5
Double-digging a wide bed

Remove topsoil.

Loosen subsoil, then replace topsoil.

A postage-stamp plot, so called for its tiny dimensions, is perfect for people with busy schedules. One or, at the most, two 4' X 20' raised beds or a single 20' X 20' row plot is garden enough for most folks to start with. For those who can put in four to six hours per week of garden time, four 4' X 20' raised beds or one 20' X 40' row plot can produce all the fresh vegetables needed by a family of four, and then some.

Areas that have been in sod for many years are among the toughest to prepare. So is heavy clay. In the best of all worlds, you'd be able to first turn the soil in fall and plant a winter cover crop to break up hard clods and choke out grass. If you're starting in spring, though, at least plan on the autumn cover crops to come. If the turf has a persistent root system, remove it, roots and all, and shake the topsoil back onto the plot. Small areas can be worked by hand with a spade and fork; large plots will probably require a garden tiller or tractor. You might borrow or rent this tool, at least for the first year.

And how thoroughly should you work your soil? If using a tiller, break up the earth to the maximum depth of which the machine is capable. Then, if you'd like, use a garden rake or even a shovel to pile the loosened earth into wide beds or rows. If you're doing the job by hand, try to break up the soil thoroughly to at least the depth of your garden fork's tines. Once again, a rake can be handy for the final shaping and pulverizing of the seedbed. Double-digging, a technique used to prepare wide, raised beds, is very popular among organic-gardening experts. This involves first using a spade to remove the upper soil to about a foot in depth, then loosening the undersoil to the depth of a garden fork's tines and finally replacing the removed soil to produce a "fluffed" bed that's higher than the surrounding soil and loosened to a depth of almost two feet.

Previously used garden sites are, of course, relatively easy to prepare, and you should think seriously about using one if available. Whatever the situation, as you work and shape the soil, incorporate an inch of compost—purchased, if you haven't had time to make your own yet—and the natural amendments recommended in the results of your soil test. Again, this would best be done in fall to give these slow-releasing fertilizers a chance to break down, though spring is a good second choice.

Now it's time to give yourself a pat on the back. Behind you is some of the hardest work you'll ever need to tackle in the garden.

Seed Starting

Many seeds—peas, beans, carrots, corn and potato eyes, among others—are best

Fig. 6
A homemade seed-starting flat

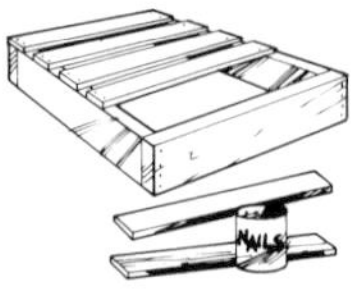

Fig. 7
Don't let seedlings develop a permanent lean.

Fig. 8
A sprout with the first leaves, the cotyledons

Fig. 9
If you must handle a seedling, use the leaves, not the stem.

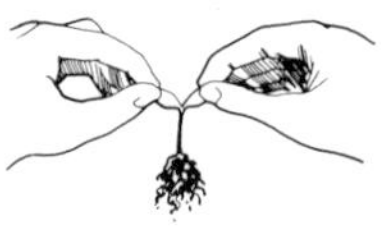

Fig. 10
Lamb's-quarters, a weed you can get even with

Fig. 11
Heavy and light feeders

Heavy:
Beets
Broccoli
Cabbage
Cauliflower
Corn
Cucumbers
Lettuce
Pumpkins
Radishes
Spinach
Squash, summer
Tomatoes

sown directly in the ground. Others, like broccoli, cauliflower, tomatoes and peppers, need to be started indoors. You might wonder if it's worth it to raise them yourself when it's possible to buy seedlings from a local nursery.

Come on. Remember the broccoli seed—the real-life miracle—the sharing of creation? Go for it!

After all, should you fail, the nursery stock will be there to fall back on. Seed starting is a skill worth developing, allowing *you* to decide what kind of broccoli you want (purple-headed, chartreuse cone-shaped, old heirloom or sprouting), instead of settling for whatever the stores offer.

Today there are special-interest catalogues offering seeds and plants to suit nearly every locale or gardener's desire: hot-climate, cold-climate, high-altitude, open-pollinated and nontreated seed; gourmet, unusual and ethnic vegetable varieties; aquatic plants; container vegetables; blue corn and white carrots.

You'll want to send for the next year's seed wishbooks in November and order in December and January. If you're beginning a garden in spring, shop for seeds at the nursery, and buy seedlings for anything that you won't have time to start yourself. Many flower seeds must be planted indoors in February, and some vegetables must be started in March.

Make selections based on the foods your family likes to eat. Grow more of things that you hope to can, freeze or dry. Smaller-than-average seed packets, often labeled "kitchen," "mini" or "trial," are great for little gardens or for growers interested in just trying something new. For your first year, pick varieties specifically listed as "easy to grow." And try to include a few flowers and maybe some herbs. They'll not only help attract beneficial insects and confuse pesty ones, they'll also add bright splashes of color and fragrance that will draw you into the garden often.

Are you the handy type? Then build wooden flats for starting your seeds, preferably out of cedar or any other rot-resistant wood. The standard size is 14 inches wide by 23 inches long. Make some three inches deep and others six inches deep. If scrounging's more your forte, use paper cups, butter tubs or anything deep enough to allow roots to expand. Be sure to punch holes in the bottoms for drainage.

Of the endless variety of commercially available seed starters, two are especially good. Speedling trays are polystyrene pyramid-shaped cells molded into a one-piece solid tray. They're available from Peaceful Valley Farm Supply, 11173 Peaceful Valley Rd., Nevada City, CA 95959. Try model 200

with 72 cells, two inches square by three inches deep.

The APS system is also based upon a polystyrene tray, but one with fewer cells for the money. However, this system features a water-wicking base and a clear cover to automatically keep the growing medium moist for up to a week at a time. It's available from Gardener's Supply, 128 Intervale Rd., Burlington, VT 05401. Try the APS-24 with 24 two-inch-square cells.

Though garden soil can be used with success as a seed-starting medium when incorporated into a homemade mix, if used alone it tends to crust over, carry weed seeds and expose tender seedlings to damping off and other soil-borne diseases. Sterilized soilless mixes are widely available and will ensure a new gardener a greater chance of success.

Seedlings can perform some pretty strange contortions in order to reach available light—don't you let them do it. A sunny south- or southwest-facing window with ample sill will grow some fine specimens, but you'll need to turn the containers whenever you notice plants developing a permanent lean toward the sun, and also to keep them from becoming dangerously spindly or even from touching the glass on cold nights.

If you don't have such a window, you'll have to use artificial lighting. Fluorescent bulbs are preferred over incandescents because they most closely imitate the spectrum of natural light, are cost-efficient to run and give off cool light. Newly started seedlings require from 12 to 16 hours of light each day, so plug in the fixture first thing in the morning, and unplug it just before you retire. Rotate the containers to ensure even exposure. Be sure to keep the light three to five inches above the foliage as the seedlings grow.

Plant extra. If you want five heads of cabbage, plant 15 seeds. Some won't make it, and you'll be able to choose the strongest plants from the ones that do.

Each seed contains enough food to nourish the resulting plant until its first set of true leaves, called cotyledons, appears. After that, a weak fish-emulsion solution is all that's needed. If the seedlings stay indoors longer than four to six weeks, move them to deeper containers so they won't get root-bound.

Transplanting

Young sprouts accustomed to warm temperatures and the cushy life can't simply be plunked outside into the cool spring ground and expected to survive. Instead, toughen them up gradually. This process is called hardening off. Two weeks before setting them out for the summer, move plants outside during the day. Find a location that receives only partial or indirect sun and is

protected from strong winds. At the same time, begin gradually limiting their food and water, but never let them dry out.

A week before setting out the plants, let them experience the joys of direct sunlight. Then, for the last three days or so before transplanting, let them camp out overnight as well.

Late afternoon—or any time during an overcast, drizzly day that is sure to stay that way—is ideal for transplanting. Carefully remove seedlings by tapping on or poking from the bottom of their container, using the leaves as a handle if necessary. Never pick up a seedling by its stem. That's where its delicate food-and-water transport system is located. With open flats, dig out a clump of plants at a time with a garden fork or your hand, and wrap the roots in a damp cloth to keep them moist.

Open a small pocket of earth with your fingers, a trowel or a large kitchen spoon, then bury the young plant a little deeper than it grew indoors. Set cole crops—broccoli, cauliflower, cabbage—in up to their first true leaves to ensure the solid footing they'll need to support those weighty heads. A lush root system is encouraged in tomatoes by pinching off all but the top cluster of leaves and burying the bare stem.

Lightly firm the soil around each plant with your hands, water it thoroughly, and, if you have it, add a dose of manure tea made by steeping a small porous bag of manure in a container of water for at least several days.

Culture

At this stage, the garden looks orderly—but somehow timid—with its small, green points of life hopefully punctuating the brown of the soil. But those green dots will quickly spread, so don't blink or you'll miss something. Make sketches; take notes and photographs. Enjoy the full spring blush of colors and textures, the bounty of late summer and the rebirth of fall, which can be much like a second spring.

Throughout the year, your care will ensure your plants a long and healthful life. Perhaps the most important job is to learn how and when to water. Plants need ample liquid, and what rain doesn't provide, you'll have to. Whenever you think things look dry, dig down a finger's depth to see how much moisture is in the root zone. Sandy soil loses moisture rapidly, while clay can be hard to drain. When you decide it's time to water, do so deeply. Shallow watering encourages shallow roots that become susceptible to drought and are unable to anchor plants.

Early mornings and late afternoons are the best times to water. You'll lose less to evaporation, and plants will have a good supply to carry them either through the night, when much of their actual growing is taking place, or through the heat of midday.

Second, give heavy-feeding crops additional nutrition by side-dressing them with compost or dosing them with manure tea or nursery-purchased fish-emulsion tea. Do this several times a season for nonfruiting plants (spinach, lettuce, cabbage, potatoes), but not after flowering for fruit bearers (tomatoes, cucumbers, squash, eggplant).

Third, be on the lookout for insects and disease. Catching a problem early can mean the difference between a Band-Aid or a coffin to your crops. Actually, many insects are on your side, consuming hundreds of their damaging kin every day. The only way to know which is which is to consult a good reference book.

Fourth, pull weeds when they're young. It's easier on you to cart out handfuls now instead of armfuls later—and it's easier on your plants, too. You can actually get even by eating any edible weeds. Many, like lamb's-quarters, are delicious and vitamin-packed to boot. However, be sure of your identification before sampling any wild edibles.

There's an old saying that your shadow is your garden's best fertilizer, so, finally, be sure to spend time there. Not just time spent working either. Construct a simple bench, picnic table, barbecue or sandbox—put up a hammock—anything to give people an excuse to play in the garden.

General Tips

Crop rotation: Planting the same vegetable in the same place every year concentrates disease and harbors insects. Rotate among light feeders, heavy feeders and legumes, such as beans and peas, which put nitrogen back into the soil.
Thinning: It's hard to pull out anything that's green and thriving, but force yourself. Crowded carrots grow no thicker than pencils, and bunched-up beets are marble-sized at best.
Succession planting: To ensure a steady supply of crops like lettuce, radishes, corn, mustard, carrots and beans, make not one planting but several, spaced about two weeks apart. Plug extra seeds or seedlings into holes that result from harvesting.
Fall gardening: Check catalogues for varieties specifically listed as fall crops, and include seed for these in your initial order. Consult planting charts for when to sow in late summer.
Timing: Plant crops a little earlier or later than normal to miss major insect-pest cycles.
Disease resistance: Should you find that certain vegetables always become sickly in

A carefully dug seedbed (left) will repay your efforts in beautiful, healthy crops (right).

Fig. 11 (cont.)
Light:
Beans, snap*
Carrots
Onions
Peas*
Peppers
Potatoes

(* Givers)

Fig. 12
Mexican bean beetle

your garden, look for varieties specifically labeled "disease resistant."

Wrapping Up the Year

There's a simple way to have a zero-maintenance crop of greenery when other gardens are only a brown memory—to have a crop that checks erosion, aerates soil and supplies spring compost material. Sound too good to be true? As or just before each vegetable crop is harvested, sow a cover crop in its place—perhaps winter rye mixed with hairy vetch. Check your local feed-and-seed store to see what's used in your area.

Before the weather gets too cold, gather up garden tools, clean them, and rub them down with vegetable oil. Run the gasoline out of power machines, and store all tools under cover.

Bring in hoses, trellises, stakes, benches and anything else that winter can damage. Remove plant debris to the compost pile, and tidy up any trash. If you have carrots, leeks, parsnips or other overwintering crops in the ground, mark them with visible stakes for easy location under snow.

Crowfoot, a Blackfoot warrior and orator, was a gardener, though not in our sense of the word. His plot was that which man neither planted nor tended —nature's garden— the out-of-doors. With his dying words he reflects on this garden and the lessons he learned there.

"What is life?" he questions—and answers, "It is the flash of a firefly in the night. It is the breath of a buffalo in the wintertime. It

is the little shadow which runs across the grass and loses itself in the sunset."

There's no end to these little miracles that await your observation in the garden. Soon you'll be adding trees, shrubs and small fruits, or perhaps designing an entranceway of climbing roses. Maybe you'll save your own seeds, build a small pond or a simple birdhouse, or just learn to identify praying mantis egg cases and watch as the tiny hatchlings pour out.

When you think about it, the real miracle, after all, may be not in the procession of growth in the garden, but in the birth and development of a brand-new gardener.

Best Bets for Beginners

Which crops are the best choices for beginning growers? The following vegetables, flowers and herbs should get you off to a good start as a gardener.

Vegetables

Beans: Bush varieties stand upright; pole types need support to climb. Find information on Mexican bean beetles and illustrations of all stages of their development. If you're blessed with cooperative neighborhood youngsters, pay the kids a penny a bug to squash them.
Carrots: Remove all rocks and obstructions to a depth of at least one foot, and loosen the soil well. Manures that aren't well broken down cause root crops like carrots to become misshapen. Remember, a watched carrot bed

Zinnias: The flattened pompom flowers of this fast-growing annual come in a wide range of colors and last a week or two before needing deadheading.

Sunflowers (*Helianthus annuus*): Everyone's watched the cheerful face of this annual as it follows the sun and eventually hangs its head under the weight of ripening seeds.

Jerusalem artichokes (*Helianthus tuberosus*): This perennial sunflower multiplies and comes back each year from underground tubers—tubers that are actually a great-tasting vegetable.

Four-o'clocks or marvel-of-Peru (*Mirabilis jalapa*): This tropical-looking plant bears a profusion of two-inch, funnel-shaped flowers and attracts hummingbirds as well as admiring comments. It's an annual that easily self-sows, but its seeds are poisonous: Don't grow four-o'clocks if small children are around.

Herb flowers: Emerald and All Purple sage, chives, tansy, lavender, yarrow, chamomile, catmint and bee balm are just a few of the herbs that sport beautiful flowers.

Herbs

Chives (*Allium schoenoprasum*): Dried chives are as worthless as lawn clippings; fresh cuttings are wonderful. Plants multiply and come back each year bearing rose-colored spring flowers with their own culinary uses.

Oregano (*Origanum* spp.): For spicing up Italian dishes, start with cuttings or seedlings of Greek or Italian varieties of this herb, because oregano from seed is virtually tasteless.

Mints (*Mentha* spp.): Mints love to run wild under a drippy faucet or in any moist, partially shaded area. Buy plants from a reputable nursery. Mints grown from seed are usually worthless.

Thyme (*Thymus vulgaris*): Thyme's filigreed leaf structure is delicately beautiful. An easy garden or potted plant, thyme comes in interesting colors and scents.

Basil (*Ocimum basilicum*): From mammoth-to tiny-leaved, with varieties like Lemon, Cinnamon and Purple Ruffles, basils are anything but boring.

Sage (*Salvia officinalis*): Poultry stuffing and sausage aren't worth a hoot without sage. And don't forget the ornamental types.

Parsley (*Petroselinum crispum*): Not just for decoration, this vitamin powerhouse takes about three weeks to germinate. Be patient.

Dill (*Anethum graveolens*): Great in pickles, salads and cooked carrots, this upright annual will easily self-sow.

Garlic (*Allium sativum*): Homegrown garlic packs a pungent punch, and garlic braids make useful, on-the-spot gifts. Plant cloves in fall for the largest bulbs.

never germinates. Be patient. It may take three to four weeks of keeping the seedbed constantly moist before the tiny, grasslike shoots appear.

Corn: It's hardly a space-wise plant for the small patch. Nevertheless, every gardener deserves the chance to pick and eat sweet corn right in the field. Be sure to plant in blocks for good pollination. Fertilize and water well, since corn's a heavy feeder, and hill some dirt around stalk bases to anchor their shallow roots and keep them from blowing over in heavy rainstorms.

Cucumbers: Keep 'em watered, and stand back. They share the same pests and problems as squash.

Greens: Swiss chard is an all-season annual green that hail, being trampled on and even being cut back to the ground won't kill. Kale and collards go from strong to sweet after a frost, and spinach, sometimes hard to germinate, can be grown both spring and fall.

Lettuce: A cool-weather crop, lettuce germinates quickly and matures in two months. For such a little plant, it's a heavy feeder and also needs plenty of water to keep from bolting or tasting bitter.

Peas: Plant in spring as early as the ground can be worked, and again in midsummer to try for a fall crop. Kids who snub store-bought peas find that homegrown ones taste as sweet as candy. If sprouts don't emerge in three weeks, replant. Provide a trellis for support.

Potatoes: Once or twice before they bloom, hill up the soil around the stems until just the top leaves are poking out. This practice increases yields. Hand-pick the Colorado potato beetle and larva.

Radishes: Nothing's faster. Remember to thin early and water well.

Summer squash: Second only to radishes in ease of growing, summer squash is also prolific; three plants of any variety will be enough.

Tomatoes: Smokers should wash their hands before any contact with tomatoes, to avoid spreading tobacco mosaic virus. Avoid planting near walnut trees or using leaf mold from beneath them, because of a toxin given off by this tree's roots. If you have 40 acres or just one pot on a patio, you can grow your own vine-ripened fruits.

Flowers

Marigolds (*Tagetes erecta*, African; *T. patula*, French; *T. singata* Pumila or *T. minuta*, Mexican): Easy to grow and keep up with, this annual doesn't require deadheading (removing old blooms) to continue blossoming. Some varieties repel pests. Marigolds will easily self-seed.

Calendulas (*Calendula officinalis*): These big-seeded, easy-to-germinate annuals have cream- to orange-colored flowers that stay attractive from May through early July. They'll easily self-seed.

Nasturtiums (*Tropaeolum majus* and *T. minus*): What a find! Nasturtiums have edible leaves and flowers and insect-repellent qualities, and they also thrive on neglect. The crimson, yellow and deep orange blooms of this annual easily self-seed.

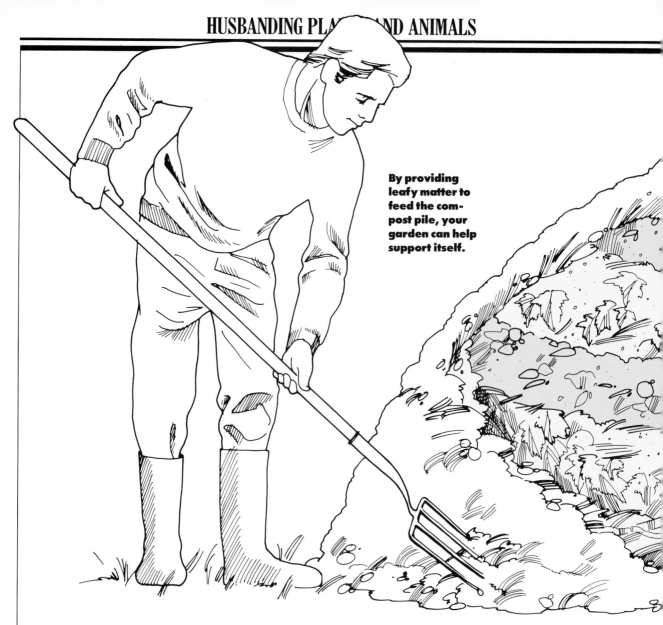

By providing leafy matter to feed the compost pile, your garden can help support itself.

Making Compost

You can turn kitchen garbage, fallen leaves, garden trash and manure into the premier organic soil aid.

The single most important step you can take toward guaranteeing a healthy garden is to make compost. Used for thousands of years, it's become synonymous with good land stewardship, and its benefits are legion: It provides nutrients (and changes those already in the soil into forms plants can use), builds better soil texture, helps bring pH levels into the neutral range, promotes good drainage as well as water retention by opening up heavy soils and binding loose ones, darkens most soils to allow better heat absorption, attracts earthworms, helps plants produce their own growth stimulators, fixes heavy metals and other toxins, keeps water-soluble nutrients from leaching away, allows plants to choose their own nutrition based on individual needs, and much more.

Whew! All that, and it's free, too.

For your own source of this magic soil amendment, pick a site near the garden, under a deciduous shade tree if possible (it will provide shelter from the elements and contribute leaves), and with easy access to vehicles if you'll be importing some ingredients.

Though freestanding piles work fine, a bin or enclosure saves time in shaping and keeps the heap neat enough to buffer the possible objections of neighbors. Whichever you choose, be sure the mass measures at least 3' X 3' X 3' to ensure generation of the heat needed to break down ingredients and destroy weed seeds.

A creative scrounger can use boards, poles, wire fencing, old pallets, hay bales, snow fencing or concrete blocks to create bins. At the other end of things are commercial composters sold through garden-supply catalogues. Somewhere in between lies the bin built mainly from purchased materials. Choose whatever you think best fits your abilities, your pocketbook and the tolerance

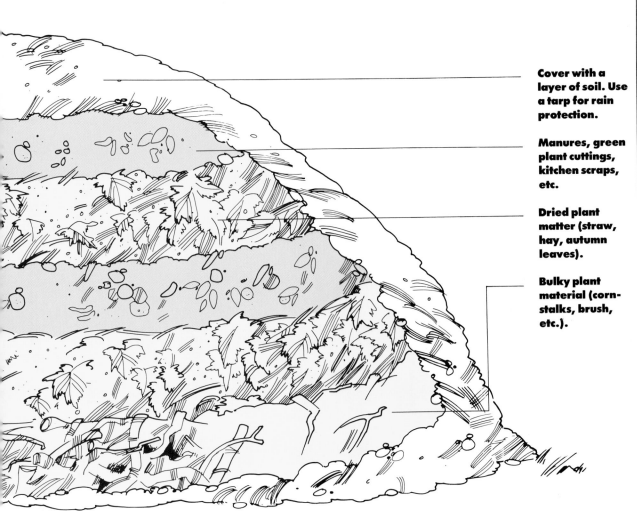

Cover with a layer of soil. Use a tarp for rain protection.

Manures, green plant cuttings, kitchen scraps, etc.

Dried plant matter (straw, hay, autumn leaves).

Bulky plant material (cornstalks, brush, etc.).

of your landlord or neighbors.

You may have heard that everything but the kitchen sink will disappear neatly into the workings of a compost pile. Well, it isn't so. For example, don't add pet feces, large amounts of grease or fat, coal, coal ashes, barbecue briquettes, synthetics like plastic and polyester, floor sweepings (in some homes these can contain up to 500 parts per million of lead), food preserved with BHT (even small amounts can alter plant growth), sludge (it can contain concentrations of heavy metals), diseased plant material (burn it first, then add the ashes), and overly bulky or hard materials (bones, oyster shells, nut hulls, thick stalks or twigs) unless they're first pulverized.

What you *will* need to produce a clean-smelling, effective pile are the following: mass (at least a cubic yard), moisture (the heap should be neither soggy nor dry—just damp), air, beneficial microorganisms (found in garden soils or previously made compost), materials that supply nitrogen (all manures and urines, kitchen scraps and green plant residue, as well as blood, bone, cottonseed, hoof, horn and alfalfa meals) and materials that supply carbon (such dried plant matter as straw, hay and dried leaves, grass or weeds).

There are thousands of different recipes for making compost. Here's one that's fairly basic: 1) Lay down bulky material onto bare soil. 2) Fork on a layer of carbonaceous material from four to eight inches thick. 3) Add a layer of nitrogenous matter two to four inches thick. Fluff all material as you go. 4) Repeat steps 2 and 3 (adding sprinklings of soil and water as needed) until the pile is the desired height. 5) Cover with a layer of soil, sod or stalks or with a waterproof tarp if rain protection is needed. Run-off will leach out valuable nutrients. 6) Turn the pile once or twice at six- to eight-week intervals.

The textbook ratio is 25 parts carbon for every one part nitrogen, but it's easier just to make the carbon layer larger than the nitrogen layer and experiment until you find the proportions that work best for you.

Within four to five days the pile should shrink in size and the interior should become hot (around 140°F). If it doesn't, check the steps above to be sure you've not missed anything. If you notice a strong ammonia odor, there's too much nitrogen. The pile may still break down, but what you smell is nitrogen lost. To correct this, turn the heap, and add more carbonaceous material.

Composting is somewhat magical; an inexact art to be sure. There are as many methods as there are gardeners. Before long, no doubt, you'll have your own family recipe.

Pruning Fruit Trees

It's easy to improve fruit-tree yields.

Gardeners expect surprisingly modest yields from their orchards. A well-known gardener in North Carolina, for example, always has a superb vegetable garden, a wonderful bed of roses and the best strawberry patch in town. Each tomato is a jewel. Every stalk of corn produces two large ears, and every flower in his perennial bed looks as if it is posing for the cover of a garden magazine. Yet, in spite of his gardening skill, he seems to be perfectly satisfied to take whatever his fruit trees hand him.

Often this isn't very much. He has good fruit when conditions are perfect, but it's usually small, misshapen, poorly colored and infested with insects. Furthermore, he typically gets a crop only every other year.

Undoubtedly, when his trees were young, they were full of vigor and produced excellent fruit. Young trees almost always bear large, colorful fruit, because they still have very few limbs, so the fruit gets lots of sunlight. However, as the trees mature and grow more branches, you must prune to keep them producing well. Most trees naturally produce a large crop of fruit every other year, so if you want your trees to grow an annual crop, you must give them some special attention. Pruning is a neglected art, however, and one that novice fruit growers don't completely understand.

Pruning fruit trees doesn't need to be confusing. If you follow the simple, basic rules, you can leave the scientific jargon to those who are intrigued by it.

A major point to be aware of is that most fruit trees are grafted (Fig. 1). The roots usually belong to a type of tree that produces low-quality fruit, whereas the top is a good-bearing variety that has been transplanted onto the rootstock. The two have been grafted together because this is the most efficient way to produce large numbers of quality fruit

trees. Fruit trees grown from seed seldom resemble the parent tree even slightly, and growing trees from cuttings or layers is slow and extremely difficult.

Reasons for Pruning

Some gardeners enjoy pruning their fruit trees and consequently do a good job. However, no one should prune simply for the fun of it—you should know the reasons for pruning. All of the following are equally important to the health and maintenance of your trees:

Prune to get the tree off to a good start. Although it isn't easy, you should cut back any bare-rooted young tree at planting time. When nursery workers prune trees at the nursery, customers typically wince and say that it looks as if the trees are being slaughtered. Yet it is one of the best things you can do to insure good growth and early crops.

Trees enclosed in a ball of soil or growing in a pot will not need any cutback. However, bare-rooted trees have probably been dug recently, and chances are good that some of the roots have been seriously damaged in the process. Most mail-order plants are sold bare-rooted, and unless the directions you receive with the tree indicate that it has already been done, you should prune both the roots and top at planting time.

First, cut off any jagged edges on broken roots so they will heal smoothly. Then cut back the top to make it equal in size to the root surface. Cut back fruit trees that are whips—those with no side branches—by at least a third: If a tree is six feet tall, for example, cut it back at least two feet, and make the cut on a slant just above a bud.

If your fruit tree has branches, cut off those that are weak, dead-looking, broken or too close to the ground. Then cut back the top by a third and each strong, healthy limb by at least a third also. Cut each limb back to an outside bud so that the next branch will form toward the outside and the tree will spread outward rather than inward toward the trunk.

Keep in mind that these directions are only for pruning new trees. Don't neglect the other ingredients for proper planting, like soaking bare-rooted trees for several hours after arrival, using lots of good soil and water while planting, and planting to the right depth. Most fruit tree failures are due to the lack of proper planting as well as neglecting to prune the tree properly at planting time.

Prune lightly to shape the tree during the first years of its life. The old saying, As the twig is bent, so the tree is inclined, is unquestionably true. A little snipping and pinching here and there while the tree is

young will save you a lot of heavy pruning later on.

If you have trained your tree properly early in its life, all subsequent pruning will come easier. Whenever you clip or snip off the buds or tiny twigs, try to keep in mind an image of the mature tree. Prune in accordance with the tree's natural growth habit and for the purpose of developing a strong tree with a branch structure sturdy enough to hold up the crop. Keep the branches sparse enough to allow the sunshine in to ripen the fruit.

You should prune very little during the tree's first years—just enough to help shape the tree. Although it's good to prune heavily at planting time, this process may cause it to grow too many branches close to the ground. By pinching or clipping off all those undesirable new sprouts during the first years, you will be training the new tree to grow upright.

Some trees need more shaping than others. Many varieties of apples, such as Wealthy and McIntosh, seem to grow into a good shape quite naturally. Other varieties, like Delicious and Yellow Transparent, tend to grow very upright, forming lots of tops with bad crotches. If left uncorrected, these weak crotches and the limbs coming from them are very likely to break under a heavy load of fruit.

Fruit loads on plums and cherries are not as heavy as those on pears and apples. Since the former are apt to grow into a bushy shape no matter what you do, early shaping is important mainly to keep them from getting too wide or to prevent the branches from growing too close to the ground.

Some trees grow twiggy naturally, and certain apple varieties, such as Jonathan, as well as many varieties of cherries, plums, peaches and apricots, need additional thinning of their bearing wood to let in sunshine to ripen the fruit.

Direct all of your early pruning to guiding the tree into the desired shape. Fruit trees are usually trained in one of three forms: central leader, modified leader or open center.

Central leader. Trees that bear heavy crops of large fruit, including apples and pears, are usually best pruned to grow with a central leader, or trunk, at least in their younger days (Fig. 2). With only one sturdy trunk in the center of the tree, branches come strongly out from it at fairly wide angles and can safely bear abundant loads of fruit.

Thin out the branches growing from the central leader as necessary to allow open space between the limbs. Thin also the branches that come from these limbs, and so on to the outermost branches. Sunlight produces colorful, flavorful, vitamin-enriched fruit. Sunlight and circulating air also help to prevent scab, mildew and a host

Older trees will require a saw (above). Use shears (right) to make small cuts, being careful not to split any limbs.

of other diseases that thrive in shade and high humidity.

Eventually you will have to remove the top of the central leader because this high-growing leader will gradually sag under a load of heavy fruit, forming a canopy over part of the tree that will shut out the light. Cutting back the top helps prevent a canopy from developing while also keeping the tree from growing too tall.

Modified leader. The modified leader method is initially the same as the central leader method, but eventually you let the central trunk branch off to form several tops (Fig. 3). This training insures that the loads of fruit at the top of the tree are never as heavy as those at the bottom, where limbs are larger. Cut back the tops of larger trees from time to time to shorten the tree or to let in more light. Although the central leader method is preferred by most orchardists for growing apples and pears, the modified leader method is easier to maintain simply because most fruit trees grow that way naturally.

Open center. The open center method, also known as the open top or vase method, is an excellent way to let more light into the shady interior of a tree (Fig. 4). Since this method produces a tree with a weaker branch structure than if it had a strong central leader, the lightweight fruits are the best subjects: quinces, crab apples, plums, cherries, peaches, nectarines and apricots.

Prune so that the limbs forming the vase effect do not all come out of the main trunk close to each other, or they will form a cluster of weak crotches. Even with the whole center of the tree open, you'll have to thin the branches and remove the older limbs eventually, just as you would with a tree pruned in the central leader method.

Prune for good crops of quality fruit. Good fruit needs plenty of sunshine, and a fruit tree fortunately has a potentially large area to produce fruit: A full-sized, standard tree can be well over 30 feet wide and 20 feet high. However, only 30% of an unpruned tree, because of its tight branch structure, gets enough light, while another 40% gets only a fair amount of light. As these percentages indicate, when only the top exterior of the tree produces good fruit, you are getting the use of but a third of your tree, and all that fruit is grown where it is most difficult to pick. Even the most careful pruning won't bring the light efficiency to a full 100%, but you can greatly increase it.

The drawings in Figs. 5 and 6 illustrate the theory of pruning to let the light in. Since a fruit tree is three-dimensional, your tree won't look just like the drawings. They are exaggerated to show why pruning should be done and how it lets more light into the tree.

Another way to improve the quality of your fruit is to remove the surplus fruits whenever your tree sets too many (Fig. 7). Although regular pruning will cut down the number of fruits produced, a tree may still bear a greater number than it can develop to a large size. The production of too many seeds seems to tax a tree's strength, and certain varieties of fruits seem bent on bearing themselves to death, unless you give them a helping hand. When a tree bears too many fruits in any one year, it usually bears few if any fruits the following year. Thin out extras when they are small. Most trees, as well as their fruits, benefit if you leave only one fruit remaining in each cluster. Make sure that each fruit is at least six inches from its neighbor on either side.

Prune to keep your trees from getting too large. Since standard-sized fruit trees can grow to 25 feet or more, they are often pruned to keep them at a more manageable height. A tall tree is difficult and dangerous to work in. And, because so much of the tree is shaded, it often produces poor fruit.

Of course it's best to prune regularly so that your tree won't get too tall in the first place, but if this advice comes too late, consider shortening the tree. First, make sure it is healthy enough to stand major surgery and that there will be enough lower branches left on the tree to sustain it after its upper level has been removed: The leaf surface remaining must be adequate to supply nutrients to the tree. If these conditions can be met, begin to prune back the top in late summer or early fall. Make the cuts in small stages, cutting off only small pieces of limbs at one time, so that the limb weight will be lessened before you begin the heavy cutting. These small cuts lessen the danger of splitting limbs and also help insure that you won't drop heavy pieces of wood onto the lower branches. If possible, have a helper handy to catch the limbs as they fall or to guide them away from the tree (Fig. 8).

Don't cut off more than one large limb in any one year. Make sure that some regrowth has started on the lower branches before you make any further cuts. Like an obese person, the tree got into its overgrown condition over a period of many years, so don't try to correct all its problems at once.

Prune to keep your tree healthy. Even young fruit trees occasionally need to be pruned because of some mishap: Limbs get broken, tent caterpillars build nests, and as the tree gets older, rot and winter injury often take their toll on the branches.

As soon as you notice any damage, clip or saw off the injured part back to a live limb or to the trunk. Even one deteriorating limb is not good for the tree's health, and the accumulation of several sick limbs will speed up the decline, and fall, of the tree.

Rejuvenation is vital to a tree's health, especially when your goal is to produce good crops of high-quality fruit over a number of years. Many trees that produce handsome specimens while they are young or middle-aged often bear only small, poor fruit as they grow older. By replacing and renewing the old bearing wood, you encourage the tree to continue bringing forth large red apples or big crops of juicy plums or peaches.

As with every other kind of pruning, you'll get the best results from rejuvenation pruning when you do it on an annual basis rather than as an occasional event. If you remove a few of the older limbs each year to open up the tree to sunlight and air, the whole bearing surface can be renewed every six or eight years, which is like getting a whole new tree. In addition, because you will seldom need to do any drastic pruning of large, heavy limbs, the tree will suffer less.

A large limb should grow only as an extension of the tree trunk itself, and as a unit from which the small limbs grow. Overlarge limbs are a tremendous strain on the tree, so the fewer, the better. Because fruit trees are pruned more heavily than most other plant life, heavy limb growth is much more likely to result than when a tree is left unpruned or lightly pruned. Cut off crossed branches or branches that might rub to cause wounds in the bark (Fig. 9).

Water sprouts are those upright branches that grow in clumps, often from a large pruning wound (Fig. 10). They are usually unproductive, and they can weaken the tree by causing additional, unwanted shade. You should remove water sprouts promptly.

Suckers are the branches that grow on the lower part of the tree trunk or from the roots of the tree (Fig. 10). Usually they grow from below the graft, so if you don't remove them, they'll grow into a wild tree or bush that will crowd out the good part of the tree within a few years. A lot of sucker growth results on fruit trees when a slower-growing variety is grafted onto a vigorous-growing rootstock. Usually the suckers appear as a cluster of branches close to the base of the tree trunk, but sometimes (especially on plum trees) they may pop up out of the roots anywhere under the tree, even a distance away from the trunk. Mow or clip them off at ground level as soon as they appear.

When to Prune

There is an ever-continuing argument among pomologists about the best time to prune fruit trees. Each professional orchardist and experienced home grower has a favorite time. Meanwhile, beginners can get completely confused when exposed to the

Fig. 1
A grafted fruit tree

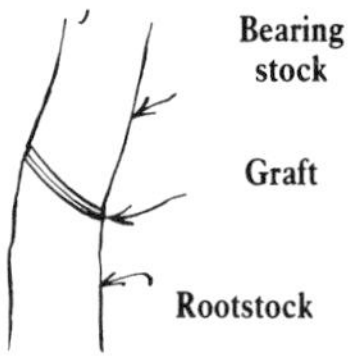

Bearing stock

Graft

Rootstock

Fig. 2
Central leader

Fig. 3
Modified leader

Fig. 4
Open center

Fig. 5
The interior of an unpruned tree gets almost no light.

Fig. 6
All areas of a pruned tree receive light.

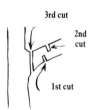

Fig. 7
Thinning fruit

Fig. 8
Pruning a heavy limb

3rd cut

2nd cut

1st cut

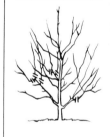

Fig. 9
Prune crossed branches.

Fig. 10
Water sprouts and root suckers

many sides of the controversy.

Perhaps the best way to help answer the question is to describe what happens when you prune at different seasons. Seasonal conditions vary greatly throughout the country, so your location is an important factor in determining when you should prune.

Spring. Most people agree that pruning a fruit tree when it is just beginning to make its most active growth is one of the worst times. The tree will probably bleed heavily, and it may have trouble recovering from the loss of so much sap. Also, infections such as fire blight are most active and most easily spread in the spring. If a book suggests pruning in the early spring, the author often means late winter—before any growth begins.

The only pruning you should do in the spring is to remove any branches that have been broken by winter storms or injured by the cold. Immediately tack bark that has split from the trunk back onto the wood, and seal the wound with tree dressing to prevent air from drying the bare wood.

Early summer. Although early summer is not the best time for major pruning, it is a good time to pinch off buds and snip off small branches that are growing in the wrong direction or in the wrong place. As soon as you notice them, remove suckers, water sprouts and branches that have formed too low on the stem.

Late summer. Late summer is a favorite time for many people to prune their fruit trees. By pruning after the tree has completed its yearly growth and hardened its wood and before it has lost its leaves, you stimulate less regrowth. You still have to take care of any frost injury in late winter, but this late summer–early fall pruning works well if extensive winter damage is not likely.

Wherever growing seasons are short and the extreme cold or heavy snow and ice loads may cause injury to the trees, late-winter pruning is best. Don't cut back the tree in late summer if there's a good chance that the remaining branches will be winter-killed. You'll have to prune away too much of the tree.

Late fall and winter. Late fall or winter is a favorite time to prune in the warmer parts of the country. Orchardists have more spare time then, and the trees are bare, so it is easier to see what needs to be done. You should choose days when the temperature is above freezing, however, to avoid injury to the wood. Because frozen wood is very brittle, it breaks easily when hit by a ladder or pruning tool.

However, if you live in a cold part of the country, or if you are growing tree varieties that are inclined to have winter injury, wait until the coldest weather is over before pruning.

Late winter. This season is probably the most popular time for northern gardeners to prune. As in late fall and winter, the tree is completely dormant, and since the leaves are off, it is easy to see where to make the cuts. You can repair any winter injury, the weather is usually warm enough during the day, and most orchardists are not too busy during this season.

If you prune your trees regularly each year, late winter is a satisfactory time to prune, because you don't have to remove large amounts of wood. However, if the trees have been neglected for a few years and are badly in need of a cutback, late winter is not the best time to prune. Excessive pruning in late winter usually stimulates a great deal of growth the following spring and summer, because the tree tries to replace its lost wood. Branches, suckers and water sprouts are likely to grow in great abundance. If a major pruning job is necessary, do all or at least a large part of it in late summer or early fall so that you won't cause a great amount of regrowth.

Pruning Sanitation

Some of the most serious diseases are carried by pruning tools. Fire blight, for example, a bacteria-caused disease that is lethal to fruit trees, has spread around many orchards this way.

If you suspect disease, think of yourself as a tree doctor as you prune. You wouldn't expect a surgeon to take out your gallbladder with the same dirty instruments he had used to remove his last patient's appendix. Your prized Bartlett pear likewise deserves careful treatment with tools that have been disinfected.

If you feel that there might be disease in your orchard, disinfect your gloves and tools after pruning each tree. Professional orchardists often use a mixture of bichloride of mercury and cyanide of mercury for this purpose, but both of these chemicals are very poisonous and are not recommended for home use. For the home orchardist, it is safer and quite effective to soak the tools in a pail containing full-strength Clorox or a similar household bleach as you go between branches or trees. With these germ-free tools, you can approach your patients with a clear conscience and not feel they are drawing their limbs about them in fear and trembling.

Disease also spreads around the orchard via the wind and insects. A good way to keep fungus, germs and insects out of a tree is to seal up all cuts and open wounds with an antiseptic paint. Most tree infections are especially active in the spring, so do your painting and sealing early in the season before they get started. Remove all of the pruning debris from the area, and either burn it or take it to a dump or landfill.

Training young apple and pear trees

First-year tree

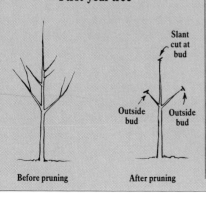

Before pruning · After pruning · Slant cut at bud · Outside bud · Outside bud

Second-year tree

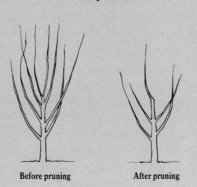

Before pruning · After pruning

Third-year tree

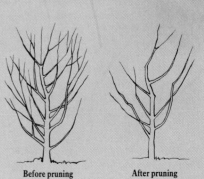

Before pruning · After pruning

Many good folks dream of the day they can exchange the noise, dirt and pressure of city life for the tranquillity of a country place with a cozy house, a big garden—and *livestock*. It's the animals that really make a rural home special, isn't it? Only with a flock of glossy-feathered poultry, a few gentle sheep, a mare with a frisky colt, or maybe even a great-eyed Jersey cow does the picture of country living come alive.

But there's a hitch, a *big* hitch. While the house will wait patiently for its repairs and you can make up for a week's garden neglect with a hose and hoe, livestock demand continual care and attention. Many new country dwellers populate the barn before they're ready for the challenges involved, and then find their long-anticipated rural tranquillity transformed into plain old drudgery. They can't take even a short vacation once Daisy starts turning meadow grass into two or three gallons of Grade A every day.

Don't let yourself become unwittingly indentured by the livestock trap and end up as much servant to your animals as they are to you. Think through each acquisition of a living creature: Know how it will change your life before you take it on, learn essential management techniques in advance, and build your animal facilities ahead of time. Do all that, and livestock can be a major satisfaction of country living.

To repeat, make sure you know what is good and bad about each of the main barnyard creatures *before* you commit yourself. That way you'll be better able to pick the ones that are right for you. Also, bear in mind this crucial rule: *Take on only one type of*

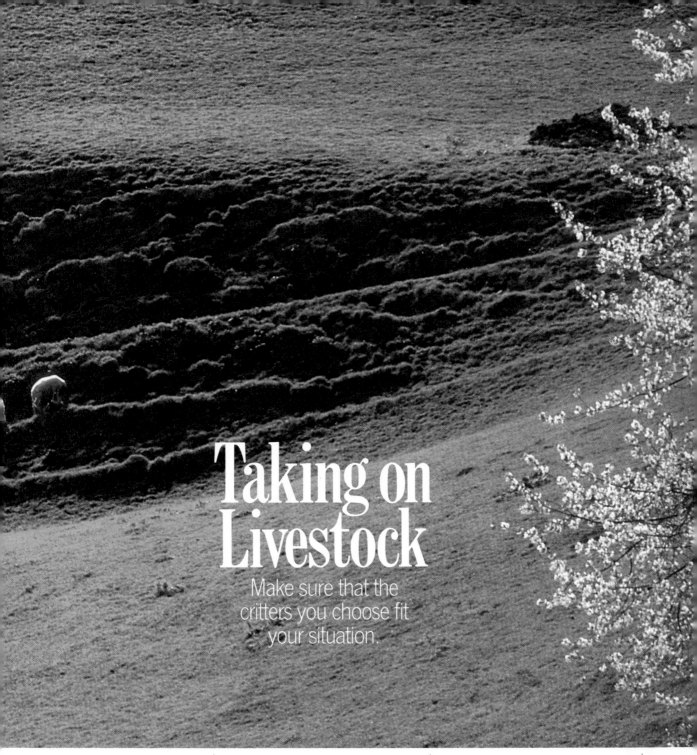

Taking on Livestock
Make sure that the critters you choose fit your situation.

animal at a time. And don't be in too big a rush to get started, either. Be sure you have the garden in, the house livable, the well flowing in reliably and the septic system flowing out even more reliably before you so much as look at livestock. Then get the fences up, pens built, water piped and hay racked before you adopt your first animal.

Bees First

For your first venture beyond gardening, a colony or two of *Apis mellifera* make per-

fect sense: Honeybees don't need pasture, pens, watering or feeding. They take less than a square yard of land per hive and can be put most anywhere, as long as their flight path doesn't interfere with human or animal activity.

And managing a hive takes very little time, only about five to 10 hours a *year* (see Fig. 1). The bees take care of all their breeding, feeding and watering needs, except for the occasional early spring when their own honey stores run short and you have to sup-ply sugar water for a few weeks. What's

more, in most places, the state bee inspector will give your colonies a free annual check-up for disease—whether you want it or not.

You may consider an individual bee to be nothing but a loud buzz with a sting at-tached, but a healthy colony is a warm (90°F or more in the middle) and vibrant commu-nity of up to 100,000 individual creatures. Its intricate workings are more fascinating than the behavior of any poultry or four-legged stock.

There is also a satisfaction to keeping bees that's lacking in most other animal husbandry. You'll experience an altogether different thrill from handling frames of comb covered with thousands of bees. They are gently humming insects pacified by the fumes from your smoker, to be sure (Fig. 2). But almost every one comes equipped with a stinger, and it is your beekeeping skill and patience that keep those stingers sheathed. There's a stimulating sense of risk to working bees—just enough danger to spice up the day.

Then, of course, there's the reward of your own golden, flower-scented honey, pooling with butter on a freshly baked bran muffin. While a good hive in a good location can produce over 100 pounds of honey a year, even an average colony should give you at least 20 to 30 pounds, unless the weather or bees fail completely.

What are the drawbacks to beekeeping? Stings, of course—even the best hive tenders get stung. But an experienced back-yard beekeeper can reduce the occurrence to a rarity, scrape that occasional stinger out quickly to practically eliminate venom intake, and actually develop an immunity to bee venom. (Note: A small proportion of the populace is allergic to bee venom. If anyone in your family has allergy problems, take a trip to the physician for a stinging-insect sensitivity test before you take up bees.)

While small-scale beekeeping doesn't take much time once you know what you're doing, it does take skill. (And it takes considerable time those first couple of beekeeping years to gain those skills.) You have to know what to look for in a hive and how to do it without upsetting the inhabitants; how to reduce swarming, the tendency colonies have to split in half in spring, with one half *leaving* your hive; and several other tricks of the trade, such as harvesting honey *without* harvesting bees. Your management skill is necessary to a colony's health, growth and production. Without it, the colony may, in time, dwindle and die.

How do you get that skill? From reading and experience, sure, but initially the best way to learn—and to see if beekeeping suits you—is to work some colonies with an experienced apiarist. Ask your county extension agent, or at the local feed store, for the names of some teaching beekeepers. An outing or two with an experienced person can help you get over the initial nervousness any novice feels when adopting a few thousand well-armed insects.

Spring is *the* time to start keeping bees. You can buy your equipment—hive body, internal frames and starter honeycomb—from a mail-order or local bee-supply house. The materials for a complete hive come in an easy-to-assemble package (Fig. 3). You can then mail-order a starter colony (Fig. 4). It might be less expensive to purchase an estab-

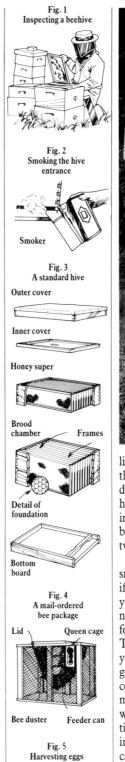

Fig. 1
Inspecting a beehive

Fig. 2
Smoking the hive entrance

Smoker

Fig. 3
A standard hive

Outer cover

Inner cover

Honey super

Brood chamber — Frames

Detail of foundation

Bottom board

Fig. 4
A mail-ordered bee package

Lid — Queen cage

Bee duster — Feeder can

Fig. 5
Harvesting eggs

lished colony locally, but be certain first that the hive has been inspected and is free from disease. Then you'll also need a bee veil and hat, gloves, smoker and hive tool (for opening and manipulating the hive). And remember, many folks recommend starting with two colonies, in case one fails.

Your ongoing expenses, however, will be small: replacement starter combs, when and if necessary, and maybe a queen bee every year or two so you can make sure your colony's egg layer is in top shape. But watch out for another potential drawback: "bee fever." That beginner's overenthusiasm can tempt you to buy lots of hives and such expensive gear as a honey extractor. Stay small for a couple of years until that first flush of excitement passes and you know for sure that you want to stick with beekeeping. If, at that time, you decide you don't, you can sell a going colony in spring—with an ad in the local paper—for most of what it cost you.

Poultry Next

Gathering eggs in the morning is the essence of country living. The sun's just up, the air is clear, the hens on the nest are all fluffed up and fussy, and the straw is almost hot when you reach under for the eggs (Fig. 5). Also, you'll never be able to enjoy a store egg after you've tried one from your own

Using a smoker calms the bee colony, which could have up to 100,000 residents.

Fig. 6
An inexpensive hen house

8' X 6½' floor

4'4"

5'6"

8'

1'X1' hen door

Screened vents

Ramp to human door

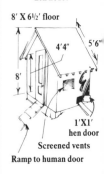

Fig. 7
A simple nest box

12"

12"

3" lip board

2"X2" perch

3"

3"

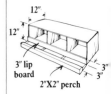

hens. Yolks are a rich yellow, stand up fat and sassy in the pan and have a flavor that fairly sings.

The same goes for the meat. Home-raised broilers have a bright golden skin and a full-bodied taste that seem to have been bred right out of commercial birds.

Chickens can be enjoyable company, too. They're oddly human in their temperaments—fidgety and bordering on hysterical when young, fussy and outrageously indignant as old hens. Roosters are vain and randy little martinets who ruffle their feathers, strut and act tough until you wave your arms and yell at them. Then they shriek, gather their skirts and run off (saving the occasional truly feisty cock that you'd better dispatch to the stewpot).

Chickens don't need a lot of space, but you must provide a predator-proof, well-ventilated, draft-free coop with at least two square feet of floor space per bird. You can use a corner of a shed or barn, build your own coop (see Fig. 6) or adapt a metal or wood prefab lawn building. Each bird needs a foot of roosting space, and you should add at least one foot-square nesting box (two feet off the floor) for every four hens (Fig. 7).

An outdoor run is also essential to an aesthetic home poultry operation. Just to *look* contented—to say nothing of the health benefits—the birds need fresh air, space to move around, dust to bathe in and bugs to chase. A couple of square feet of sun space per bird is fine, but the more room the better. Birds kept in too-close confinement peck one another excessively, a practice that can draw blood and lead to cannibalism.

Pens made of chicken-wire fencing held on steel stakes will do the job fairly inexpensively. If you don't clip wing feathers after every annual molt, build the fence at least six feet high. And if you've got potential predator problems, reinforce the bottom. A two-foot-wide band of small-mesh welded wire extending a good six inches underground should work.

Add automatic dry feeders and waterers,

and—egg collecting aside—your flock will need service no more than once or twice a week. With a neighbor coming in to tend the birds in exchange for the eggs, you can enjoy those occasional vacations away from the place that make coming back such a delight

Chicks come in lots of 25 from large hatcheries "as hatched"—50:50 male and female. (You can get them from a local feed store or poultry breeder, or through the Sears Farm Catalog.) You'll have to tend those chicks carefully in a brooder for a few weeks. The females will grow up in six or seven months to give you a nice family-sized flock of 10 or 12 layers. They'll produce about four eggs each a week for six to eight months a year. Production drops in winter, but can be extended for almost the full year if you augment the sun with enough artificial light in the coop to provide 16 hours of light a day.

The hens will manage fine without a rooster, but think about keeping two males for breeders, both as fertile-egg providers and for the pleasure of hearing them trying to outcrow each other at dawn. Slaughter the cocks you won't be keeping when they reach broiler size at eight weeks, or caponize (castrate) them and harvest still-tender roasters at 11 to 15 weeks of age.

Chickens can be highly productive. A broiler like a Rock Cornish cross yields nearly a pound of meat for every two pounds of feed. A good egg-layer like the Leghorn (pronounced "leggern") gives about a dozen eggs per five pounds of feed. And dual-purpose breeds—such as White or Barred Plymouth Rocks, and Rhode Island or New Hampshire Reds—give a fair supply of both products.

Still, feed costs add up. Each hen will need 80 to 100 pounds of layer pellets per year. Over her eight-month laying period, she'll produce about 12 dozen eggs. Store-bought eggs would cost about the same as your feed bill. Are farm-fresh eggs, then, worth the bother of tending chickens? Emphatically. What's more, you can save money by supplementing up to half that dry feed with ev-

ery kitchen and garden scrap you have. In fact, if you've got the room, you can train your chickens to free-range for much of their food during the day and come home to the roost at night. One hitch here: You will have to fence the fowl out of your garden plot.

What are the drawbacks of keeping chickens? If your country home isn't as isolated as you'd like, you may need to worry about offending the neighbors. (Honeybees and rabbits are both quieter livestock.) Moreover, cleaning the winter's accumulation of droppings is the opposite of homestead happiness. The straw-and-droppings mixture is pried out in heavy slabs that are gray and innocuous on the surface but piercingly redolent of ammonia underneath. Each thrust of the digging fork releases a miasma that clears your sinuses really fast!

Pick a day with strong wind (blowing away from the neighbors) to clean your coop. Compost that high-nitrogen fertilizer (it can burn young plants if applied directly to the garden), then work it into your plot, and watch the sweet corn shoot for the sky.

Nobody enjoys slaughtering, either. If you want home-raised eating birds, though, you've got to do it. String a bird up by its feet, cut its throat, scald it in hot water, pluck off the steaming feathers, gut it, and throw it in the deep freeze.

Laying hens can keep it up for five years, but most are better culled for Sunday dinner after two or three. (Commercial layers are slaughtered after their first—most productive—year, then recycled into feed for their successors.) You'll want to periodically inspect the vents of your layers; you should be able to place two fingers between the pubic bones of a productive hen. Harvest the nonlayers before they get too old. By the time an aged or ill hen begins to look ragged and dull-eyed, it's scrawny and unappetizing.

To dispose of an entire flock, advertise "Old Hens, $1" in a country newspaper, and be willing to take half that. Someone on a strict budget will buy them for stew meat.

A yard full of chickens really says "country." They aren't too difficult to care for, and produce delicious eggs and meat.

Other Fowl

Ducks can be raised in a pen or on pasture as easily as chickens, and grow to a plump maturity quickly on just about any feed you offer or they forage. Unlike chickens, ducks never seem to get tough and gamy with age, either.

The same virtues can be attributed to geese. But geese are mean and aggressive and can harvest your garden to bare soil if you let them "weed" it. Eggs from ducks and geese are delicious, if a little leathery when fried. However, they taste fishy if the birds have a pond to grub in, and tend to come on only in spring. One exception: A good Khaki

Campbell duck can lay almost year round.

Guinea birds, peafowl, domestic quail, pheasants, pigeons (raised for the young off-spring, or squab), turkeys and wild-strain quail and ducks are all projects needing special equipment and skills but offering special rewards. If you have the heart to slaughter milk squab, for instance, you can enjoy some fancy eating. Guineas screech horribly but make great watch birds and roasters. Game birds require state fish and game permits and are terribly nervous, but they sell well for put-and-take shooting. Turkeys convert feed to meat even more efficiently than ducks but are hard to raise. They sicken easily, and young poults are so dumb that if they see one of their number stick its head in an un-screened water bowl and drown, they're all apt to try it.

Rabbits

Rabbits are good for meat (the flesh has more protein and less fat and calories per pound than any other home-raised meat), hides (or fur, if you raise Angoras) and lots of excellent manure (which *won't* burn plants if applied fresh to a garden). They need very little space, won't disturb you or neighbors with noise and—of course—are very prolif-ic. A good doe can produce a half-dozen two-pound (dressed) young rabbits every two to three months. So with a home rabbitry of just one buck and two does, you can enjoy well over 100 pounds of delectable fried rabbit ev-ery year.

Certain domestic rabbits came from bur-rowing European stock, so they'll dig right out if kept in an outdoor pen. Surprisingly, perhaps, adults also will fight—silently but viciously. So the animals require secure in-dividual cages (Fig. 8). You can build sim-ple hanging cages out of wire mesh. The open mesh will let the manure and urine fall below, where you can raise wonderful red worms for fishing. Each doe's cage should contain a nesting box (Fig. 9) if it's exposed to strong drafts or winds.

Your cages must provide protection from the elements—*especially* direct summer sun—and from dogs and wild animals. Caged rabbits are easy prey. The old-style, free-standing, roofed wooden hutches take time to build properly, rot fairly quickly from the strong urine and can leave the rabbits vul-nerable to predators. But don't try keeping rabbits in the cellar unless you're prepared to clean up after them frequently. The urine is strong-smelling and copious. In other words, rabbit cages are best located in a barn or shed.

To start with rabbits, you need only a young buck, a pair of does and six months' time. For meat, get New Zealand Whites

(Fig. 10). They're the most common variety, kindle (give birth to) large litters easily and can interbreed forever with no problems. For pet stock, take your choice: Floppy-eared French Lops are current hot sellers as in-town pets. You can litterbox-train them like cats. Angoras are a good bet if you'd like to try a small fleece operation—perhaps as a tri-al before taking on sheep. A good Angora, or any show-quality animal, will cost two to three times more than a good, breedable New Zealand White.

Buy your feed by the hundredweight sack. A 10-pound adult will consume about 120 pounds of pellets a year, not including an ad-ditional 24 to 30 pounds per pregnancy, and a litter of eight will go through 65 to 100 pounds. As with chickens or *any* home livestock, plan to raise as much feed as you can. Rabbits love root crops, green vegeta-bles and hay.

Breeding is a matter of taking a doe to the buck's cage and letting rabbits do what they are noted for. Does actually ovulate *after* they are bred. Some does produce more young than others, but even the best give out after a year or two. However, old rabbit tastes as good as young.

Drawbacks? Rabbits take more time to care for than poultry. Each one needs at least a daily check. They must have a *constant* sup-ply of fresh water; a doe and her litter will consume a gallon of water a day! And you have to be more careful about feeding them properly. They can't free-range for bugs and won't recycle spoiled milk or fish scraps, so you have to give them enough pellet feed to meet their essential protein needs. And you can't put the adults on self-feeders, as you can chickens: Obesity causes infertility. (You can let young rabbits eat all they want, however.)

The biggest drawback to keeping rabbits is butchering them. In itself the job is easy.

Just hold one by its head and feet, stretch it over your hip, and snap its neck (Fig. 11). They are easier to eviscerate than poultry and shuck right out of their hides, which can be tanned into warm, if short-lived, pelts. The whole procedure takes but five minutes.

But they're so appealing that it takes real will power—at least at first—to slaughter them. (And remember, you'll be repeating the process over and over throughout the year.) If you have children who have made pets of the rabbits, you may find it nearly im-possible. This brings up a crucial point. Differentiate early in your livestock-raising career between beasts to be food and those to be pets. As dirt-farm practical as you may try to be, you'll find it difficult to eat a rab-bit or duck that your children have cuddled or trained to follow them around. Give your meat animals *qualified affection*—love at arm's length. For example, try calling your steers "Hamburger," hogs "Sunday Lunch" and so on. Don't name your too-easy-to-adore meat goats at all.

While rabbit meat sells best in California, live rabbits are easy to dispose of in most areas. Try selling just-weaned bunnies to pet stores for half the retail price—or direct to eager customers around Easter. Anytime you tire of the animals, put an ad in the paper to move adults, cage and equipment; you're likely to recover most of what you've invested.

From raising bees, poultry and rabbits to keeping "real" livestock is quite a jump. Nonetheless, doing so is a move many new-ly arrived countryfolk are eager to make. Most of the time, things work out just fine for novice keepers of cattle, horses, sheep, goats and pigs. Still, it's wise not to commit yourself to large or midsized livestock without first analyzing the vastly greater de-mands on your time, facilities and budget.

You can raise your own pork for well under $1 per pound.

Fig. 8
An all-wire rabbit cage

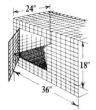

Fig. 9
A nesting box

Fig. 10
A New Zealand White

Fig. 11
Butchering
a rabbit

Fig. 12
Start with a weaned
piglet.

Fig. 13
Butcher the adult
yourself . . .

Pigs

As midsized farm animals go, pigs are easy to care for. They can be purchased inexpensively as weaned piglets (shoats), require only a small pen and rudimentary shelter from the elements, need to be kept just through the warm-weather months to mature and are anything but finicky eaters (Fig. 12). With pigs, you have little to lose and much to gain. Even if your initial experience suggests that "pig ranching" isn't your cup of tea, you'll still have earned both that knowledge and a freezerful of tender, delicious, additive-free pork.

Mature pigs kept as breeders require only four or five pounds of mash daily, plus whatever table scraps you can come up with. To fuel a 20- to 40-pound shoat to maturity—at which point you'll net around 120 pounds of hams, pork chops, ribs and bacon—will require six to seven months and some 500 pounds of hog pellets plus table scraps—or a half-ton-plus of garden excess or restaurant garbage. Including the cost of hog pellets, cholera shots and wear and tear on your equipment, you can still end up with that pork and ham costing well under the wholesale cost per pound, with little more effort than filling the feed and water troughs once a day.

To make pig into pork, you'll need to a) use block and tackle, scalding drum, bell scraper, knives, stunning gun, cutting table, pickling tank and smokehouse (Fig. 13); or b) find the will and a way to haul several hundred pounds of uncooperative hog to a butcher. Custom butchering usually will include salting and smoking the hams and bacon.

Here's a method for simplified pig loading: Feed the chosen porker right at the pen gate for a week or so, then securely pen it alone and let it go hungry through two feedings. At feeding time on the fateful day, lure the hungry hog up into the loading chute with a trail of goodies (Fig. 14). When the animal's rump is clear of the pen gate, close the gate. The pig will then follow the food trail right up into the back of the truck. Now close the truck gate, put the end rail in place, and you're ready to roll.

You can keep hogs from spring until slaughtering time—generally in October, after the first good frost, when most of the flies are gone. The ideal home for that time is a small woodland lot enclosed with dual-wire electric fencing. A simple shed provides adequate shelter (Fig. 15). The pigs sleep most of the time, stay clean and healthy and use a far corner of the lot as a latrine. With trees for shade, they don't need a stream to roll in for a coating of cooling mud. Only

Fig. 14
. . . or truck it to a
slaughterhouse.

Fig. 15
A simple pig shelter

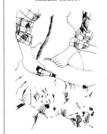

Fig. 16
Shearing is an
annual chore.

Fig. 17
Strong fencing keeps
out dogs.

Fig. 18
Lambing can present
problems.

Fig. 19
Milking a goat

when pigs are kept in close quarters, their slop allowed to rot and their sweetish-smelling manure permitted to accumulate in a swampy wallow, do they become offensive. And that, of course, is no fault of their own.

If you'd like to take raising pigs a step beyond mere spring-to-fall feeding, you can have one or more of your sows bred. Should you decide to take this step, you'll need to provide adequate wintering quarters for the sow and her offspring—a farrowing shed or pen and a heated brood box (creep) for litters born during cold weather—plus some help in castrating boar piglets.

Keeping sows and piglets isn't too much trouble—if you're up for it. But don't keep a boar unless you decide to become a professional hog raiser and are prepared to pay the piper toward that end. Big, strong and mean, boars require stout pens made of boards or hog panels fastened securely to deep-set posts.

No matter what pig-raising approach you decide to take—limited or whole-hog—you can look forward, come fall, to receiving substantial quantities of wholesome pork in return for your efforts.

Sheep

It hardly pays to buy young lambs and feed them to adulthood for strong-flavored mutton. The trick, instead, is to raise your first lambs into adult breeders, then slaughter their offspring as fat, tender lambs. With an acre or two of pasture, a shade tree, a third of a ton of hay for winter and a handful of grain a day, a ewe lamb will mature in a year and, if bred, produce a lamb or two of her own, plus five to eight pounds of wool. After maturing on its mother's milk and a little grain and graze, each of your new lambs will provide you with a wonderful fleece hide and around 50 pounds of delicious meat.

When you're buying sheep, it's wise to spend a few dollars more for pedigreed stock. Stick with a registered breed that's popular in your area—which will greatly increase your chances of selling your animals quickly and profitably should the need arise.

A minimal flock consists of a ram and two or three ewes. A male sheep is about the only stud animal that's docile enough for a beginner to handle; the worst you can expect is an occasional cautionary butt to your backside. A ram needs only grass or a couple of bales of hay per month to stay healthy, and should be able to replenish your herd for at least five years.

Sheep load into a truck more easily than pigs. If they won't drive in readily, chase them down one at a time, cornering them against the fence, where they can be tackled. Once down, they'll go limp and let you tie their feet and hoist them into the truck.

If you're going to keep sheep, you'll have to either get on the shearer's circuit or learn to do the fleecing chores yourself (Fig. 16). Shearing isn't difficult; most sheep sit calmly while you work. Still, you would be well advised to get an electric shearer, since few modern hands have the strength to wield hand clippers for more than a few minutes at a time.

To protect your investment, you'll need to either fence your pasture well or keep shepherd dogs with the flock to discourage feral canines and, in some parts of the country, other predators. As long as feed and water are available, a small flock of sheep will stay put behind a single-strand electric fence strung at (sheep) nose level—but it takes a strong and tight six-foot-high barbed wire, wire fabric or multiple-strand high-tensile electric fence to keep out predatory canines (Fig. 17).

Some small-scale sheep raisers keep pairs of animals in eight-foot-square, wire-mesh-panel pens that are light enough to be picked up and moved to a new spot on the pasture every day. Others rotate their flocks between narrow electric-fenced strips of pasture. In both instances, shepherd dogs stay with the flocks to woof away any four-legged interlopers.

Centuries of genetic manipulation by humans have left the modern ewe with a myriad of birthing problems, including breeches, prolapses, stillbirths and dry udders (Fig. 18). That's why you should arrange for a vet to be on 24-hour call, at least for your first spring lambing. And read whatever you can to familiarize yourself with lambing. You'll also need to invest in a lamb puller, nursing bottles, heat lamps and artificial milk—and plan to stay up nights to see your ewes through their most difficult and dangerous time.

No matter how endearing your new lambs are, resist the temptation to turn them into pets. Sheep get soft, spoiled and soiled unless kept out grazing in the wind and rain and snow. If pan-fed to adulthood, a sheep will loaf happily around your door, bleating stupidly and incessantly, relieving itself indiscriminately and drawing flies.

Dairy Goats

Being flock animals, sheep aren't tremendously interesting as individuals. If you want farm animals with *lots* of individual personality, try goats—which all but insist on being treated as people. However, goats are more expensive to buy, so shop around carefully. A nonpedigreed, "grade" milker will be quite satisfactory, as you'd have to spend even more for an animal with papers. For

A goat can be a prolific milker. Riding horses (right) demand a lot of care and expensive upkeep.

feed, figure on a ton of hay (half that if you have good pasture or browse in the summer) and up to half a ton of mixed grain per year per milker.

Dairy goats require a lot of attention. Twice each day—early and late—you'll have to fetch each doe from pasture or pen to the milking station, wash her down, provide her with a bucket of grain to keep her happy while you milk, then return her to pen or pasture when she's done (Fig. 19). But *you* won't be done at that point: The fresh milk must be strained and cooled, and the milking equipment washed and sterilized, before you can move on to other chores. If you have one or two goats, all of this will take a couple of hours a day.

In light of the purchase expense, feeding costs and daily commitment required to keep dairy goats, you'll understand that, before getting into goats, it's wise to weigh your costs in cash and time against the value of the milk your goats will give. If a twice-daily milking regimen doesn't appeal to you, or the cost of keeping goats averages out to be greater than the purchase price of an equivalent amount of cow's milk—why bother?

Well, for one thing, many countryfolk aren't blessed with the pasture and facilities required to keep dairy cows but want nonetheless to "grow" their own milk. A *good* goat will produce milk that you can't tell from cow's milk—unless you try making cheese. Sure, goat cheese can be grand, but the nonseparating quality of goat's milk requires special recipes.

In addition to producing your own goat's milk and cheese products, you can often market any excess. Since goat's milk is naturally homogenized, colicky children and ulcer-prone adults find it more digestible than cow's milk. Thus, with the help of a two-gallon pasteurizer, the possibility exists of developing a small but lucrative business selling milk for special diets.

Unlike pigs and sheep, dairy goats need substantial shelter against winter's cold and summer's sun and rain. A sound shed will

do for kids and wethers (castrated males), but milking demands strict sanitation. Thus, the perfect living quarters for does consist of a stall housed in a warm barn furnished with a milking bench, nearby grain and hay storage facilities and, of course, running water.

To prevent udder problems, keep your does' bedding clean by spreading straw, wood shavings or old hay over wet and soiled spots every day, gradually building up a self-composting litter bed. Transfer the deep layer of rich mulch to your garden several times a year to provide a superb medium for growing melons, tomatoes and berries.

Does must be bred annually to refresh their milk supply. Well-treated dairy goats are naturally tame and will follow you right up into the bed of a truck, or even into the back of a station wagon, for a trip to the breeder. Helping to offset the expense of the stud fee, plus boarding for three days, is the fact that each of your bred does will produce one or two kids—every one of which you'll have to bottle-feed to weaning age (Fig. 20). If you allow kids to start nursing a doe, they'll be difficult to stop.

If the kids (twins are common) are doe-babies, you'll soon have more milkers, with a promise of even *more* the next year. But if they're bucks, it's decision time. Male goats must be castrated—unless they're stud candidates from blue-ribbon matings of outstanding milk-producing lines. Unless you plan to become a breeder, don't try keeping a billy. They're thoroughly unpleasant creatures that will try to breed with everything and that spread a pervasive musk that turns the stomachs of all but the most ardent goat ropers.

Desexing bucks and branding off the horn buds of all kids (both sexes) are simple but essential chores. However, both tasks require special tools and skills and may be operations you don't care to undertake yourself. If not, your breeder will do it—for a fee, of course. You *will*, however, need to learn to trim hooves and give worm medicine.

To refute an old-time belief, goats *don't* eat tin cans. What they were truly after was the horse glue once used to stick paper labels onto food tins. They're natural browsers, however, and will nip curiously at just about anything—tree leaves, flowers, the bandanna in your hip pocket, your hair. In spite of their healthy and varied appetites, goats are fastidious eaters that will refuse to take hay or grain off a dirty floor and will die of dehydration rather than drink water with a dead fly in it.

Wethers are good only as pets, for pulling goat carts, or to slaughter when young, yielding about 20 pounds of meat that can be delectable if properly handled and aged. And goat hides make wonderfully soft, thin leather. Unfortunately, few custom meatcutters will process goats, so you'll probably have to do the butchering yourself. This can become a major problem for some people. Too many goat fanciers have ended up tending large herds of fussy, nonproductive wethers and retired milkers that they could neither sell nor bring themselves to kill.

Riding Horses

Sad to say, *do not* attempt to keep horses unless you have riding experience, a working knowledge of saddlery and tack, a good understanding of pasture management, sufficient pasture and facilities, and a willingness to give your horses proper—and often expensive—health care. For such large beasts, horses are surprisingly delicate. Those silky flanks can easily be cut and otherwise injured; those gorgeous, slender legs are prone to fractures; and, since horses can't upchuck, one bad feeding can spell disaster.

Immediately upon purchasing a horse, make contact with a good country vet—not an urban cat-and-dog specialist—who's willing to hurry out for emergencies. Put your horses on a country vet's twice-yearly circuit to receive shots, worming and a general checkup. Trimming the hooves of unshod horses isn't a difficult task to master, but shoeing is a skilled trade. Consequently, you'll also need to have the farrier call around at least a couple of times annually.

Fencing needn't be elaborate for tame horses. A single charged wire will generally do the trick—as long as you provide sufficient feed and plenty of clean water. Although most predators are no threat to adult horses, feral dogs will run them, and, in some parts of the West, bears and cougars do occasionally take colts left unguarded in remote pastures. To avoid predation problems, simply see to it that all livestock births take place in the safety of a barn or barnyard.

Fig. 20
Bottle-feed the kids.

While many countryfolk consider goats wonderful company, others find them too sneaky and set on having their own way. And their blatting can be irritating: If goats don't get their grain on time, and if they don't have clean beds, comfortable temperatures in their living quarters and freedom from insect pests, they'll blat all day long.

Being natural climbers, goats will clamber up rocks, trees, walls, low sheds and floppy wire fences. Electric fencing serves as little but a challenge, a board fence is but an appetizer, and a smart old doe will learn to open any latch you can devise. Goats aren't strong, though; they can't bull a fence down or root beneath one like a hog. The answer is a six-foot-high wire-mesh or chain-link fence strung tight. Padlock any gates.

Fig. 21
A draft horse earns its keep.

Fig. 22
A milk cow gives two to three gallons a day.

Horses are capable of enduring even the most severe climates with minimal shelter—a few trees for wind and sun protection—*if* their feed is adequate. An adult horse will consume a quart or more of grain twice a day, plus a third to half a bale of hay. But horses winter best in cozy stalls with dry straw bedding (pitchfork it clean and dry during your twice-daily feeding and watering sessions). In summer, horses *must* have shade and unlimited fresh water.

After feed, water and shade, horses most need exercise—to retain both muscle tone and training. Don't take on an educated saddle horse if you can't provide it with plenty of pasture in which to run—enclosed with electric, mesh or board fence; *anything* but barbed wire—and a qualified rider who's eager to give the animal a good workout at least once a week.

Draft Horses

Driving a team of draft horses is one of the greatest joys country living has to offer. It's also the cheapest and most satisfying way to plow small fields or haul logs out of a thickly timbered wood lot (Fig. 21). But to develop a good team requires years of training, preferably begun when the animals are colts. And *you'll* need special training, as well—to teach the horses to work together, to care for their hardworking lower legs and hooves, and to supply just the right amounts of water, grain and roughage at the proper times.

While you *can* train yourself and your draft animals on the job, it is infinitely saner to have an experienced drover alongside to show the way.

Milk Cows

Finally, there comes the queen of the farmstead, the milk cow.

Before you buy, *think:* Can you honestly find a use for two to three gallons of raw milk per day (Fig. 22)? If you have a large crop of children and enjoy making your own cheese and churning your own butter, then possibly you can justify keeping a cow. But don't plan to make money by selling excess output: Federal laws stringently regulate the sale of raw milk products, and price competition in the commercial dairy-products business is brutal.

For milk cows to produce their full capacity of around 1,000 gallons per 300-day lactation period, they must be bred (or artificially inseminated) annually. This procedure, naturally, will also provide you with at least one calf per cow per year. What to do with the little critter? Well, you can sell it newborn; bottle-feed it in darkness for a few weeks, then slaughter it for milk veal; or raise your heifer calves to maturity for milkers (a two-year endeavor) and your steer calves for meat.

Keeping milk cows all but demands a real barn—and lots of hard, unpleasant work keeping it mucked out. What's more, cleaning dried manure off a cow's flanks and udder can spoil your appetite for dairy products. While you shouldn't be automatically discouraged from keeping milkers, you should be aware of the realities that so often get overlooked by starry-eyed country newcomers anxious to "get back to the basics." Before investing in a milker, at least study a good guide.

Beef Cattle

Feeder cattle are not nearly as difficult and expensive to keep as milkers. Raising a steer calf for meat takes only water, a couple of acres of pasture and enough hay for two winters. But no family can eat through some 700 pounds of beef before it becomes spoiled or freezer-burned. So don't try "ranching" unless you have a big appetite for red meat and a large freezer for long-term storage—or a sales outlet for ungraded beef. (One excellent option is to raise a beef "on the halves" with another family.)

Opinions differ on the palatability of strictly grass-fed beef, especially that of steers from dairy cow stock. Many love it, while others maintain that often such meat is tough, the flavor strong and the fat yellow and soapy. To get the bland-flavored, white-marbled meat you find in most supermarkets takes a month or more of grain feeding in a quiet, low-exercise environment. An isolated, low-light barn stall is ideal.

You should not slaughter and butcher your own beef unless you're equipped with a deer rifle, a heavy-duty hoist, a commercial meat grinder, adequate offal-disposal facilities and plenty of hands-on experience.

Disposing of Unwanted Livestock

An ad in a rural newspaper can almost always sell a partly finished feeder steer for more than your investment. A first-freshening dairy cow from blue-ribbon bloodlines can fetch a tidy sum. And a highbred, well-trained saddle horse can be worth megabucks. But tired old cows, goats and sheep, as well as untrained, unregistered horses, can be difficult to dispose of at more than glue-factory prices.

By planning before buying *any* farm animals, then starting off small and working up, you can avoid the traps that have snared so many others. And you'll also be assuring that keeping livestock will evolve into one of the rewarding experiences of country life.

Would-be horse raisers would be well advised to consider boarding the animals elsewhere.

Whether smoked, corned or turned into delicious sausage, cured meat offers flavor and easy storage.

Curing Meat

Once a necessity, now a flavorful alternative

Few could dwell for long on thoughts of the rural life without envisioning the family cozily tucked away for the winter, substantially provisioned with viands from their own land. However idyllic this picture may be, there are some large gaps to fill between the food on the hoof or in the field and what goes in the pot for dinner. Once the fruit is picked, the vegetables harvested and the cow, pig or lamb slaughtered, what then? Further on in this book is information on putting up produce; here are some of the best ways to preserve and cook meats.

Smoke Curing

Smoke curing ham after soaking it in brine not only lets you keep it without refrigeration for three to five months but improves the flavor as well. Actually, it's the salt that does the preserving. The smoking aids and abets the process and—its real contribution—adds that sugar-and-hickory touch that makes such hams taste so special.

You'll need a smokehouse, unless you've asked the butcher to do your curing for you. The shed is simple to build and can vary in size and shape as long as it meets certain basic requirements. It must be smoke-tight and allow for a constant temperature of between 90° and 100°F. Don't let the temperature go higher, or you'll end up with cooked meat, which will not keep. For this reason, the fire pit is usually built to one side of the smokehouse and the smoke piped in.

Before being smoked, the meat must be soaked in brine. The soaking solution contains, besides salt, a little sugar to counteract some of the dryness that salted meat would otherwise have, and saltpeter, which keeps the meat red. Saltpeter is not necessary as long as you're prepared to cut open a nice gray ham for dinner. Whichever color you make your hams, remember to cook all pork very, very thoroughly to guard against trichinosis. Smoking cures the ham for storage; it does *not* cook it.

For the salting brine, mix together:

1 gallon water
2 cups salt
1 cup dark brown sugar
$\frac{1}{2}$ to 1 teaspoon saltpeter

Stir the brine well so that all ingredients are dissolved. The formula given is for one gallon, to simplify mixing. If you're about to smoke the meat from a whole pig, you'll need a lot more.

Pack the hams and the bacon slabs loosely into a big crock. Cover them with the brine solution, and add a rock to keep them submerged. Set the covered crock in a cool spot (35° to 45°F). Hams usually need to soak one day per pound. That's for each individual ham, not by total weight. In other words, if you have two 15-pound hams, soak them for 15 days, not 30. The minimum soaking period is two weeks; the maximum is about one month. Move the hams around daily so the same areas are not always in contact with each other. Check the water to see that it doesn't turn sour—that is, milky and smelly. If it does, remove the meat at once, rinse it well, and start over, but boil out the container before refilling it.

When they have soaked sufficiently, rinse off the hams and bacon, dry them well, and hang them in the smokehouse. The smoldering fire should be started several hours before you tote them in, to ensure that the temperature and smoke are adequate. Your smoky fire can be of hardwood chips—many people prefer hickory for its special flavor—ground corncobs or fruit-tree chips. Do not use birch, beech or soft resinous woods unless you like strangely flavored hams.

Smoke bacon continuously for one to two weeks, hams for two to four weeks. After removing a ham from the smokehouse, cover it with a cheesecloth stocking or a coating of paraffin, and hang it in a cool place free from dampness and protected from flies and insects. An older method is to bury it in salt or in the grain bin, to exclude air. It will keep safely for three to five months in a cool, dry spot.

Cured Ham

The ham butt can be baked uncured as a roast or can be cured first and baked. One or more slices can be cured at a time and the shank used for boiling, or the bones can be removed and the boneless meat used for making sausage.

To dry cure the ham butt, apply two tablespoons of Tender-Quick for each pound of meat. Put the meat into a plastic bag, and allow it to cure 36 hours per pound. The slices are cured by applying one tablespoon of Tender-Quick per pound of meat or per average slice of ham. When the cure has been ap-

plied, put the slices of ham in plastic bags. Tie the open ends of the bags, and place them in the refrigerator for curing. Ham slices are ready to use after curing for 24 hours. It is advisable to use the cured slices within five days.

It's practical and economical to first cut the hams and store them in your home freezer, and then, many months later, to thaw and cure them or make sausage. This method eliminates the storing of hams whole or in pieces that are difficult to wrap. Such unwieldy packages also take up a lot of extra space in your freezer.

Sausage Making

Sausage is to pork what hamburger is to beef. And bulk sausage is just as simple to make. Take whatever meat you care to use, and feed it into a meat grinder. Add pepper, salt and any herbs and spices you may like— bay leaves, caraway, cumin, sage, thyme, oregano—to the ground meat. The proportions are strictly up to individual taste, but most sausage lovers feel that, except for salt, it's pretty hard to overseason. Put the spice-and-meat mixture through the grinder one more time. What comes out is bulk sausage, ready to cook.

Fry it up like hamburger, or brown it for a favorite casserole, but make sure it's well done. Pork in the United States is still often riddled with trichinae. Also, don't let ground meat get warm sitting around between grindings. Always keep it cool or refrigerate it.

If you want to make real sausages, you'll need casings. Originally, casings were made from the small intestine of the pig that contributed the stuffing. Nowadays you'll probably find it easier to buy synthetic cellulose casings, which are edible. You've been eating hot dogs in them for years. Usually they will need to be soaked in tepid water for 15 minutes before use to soften them.

Attach a funnel over the meat grinder where the meat comes out. Pull the casing over the tip, stocking-fashion, and you have an instant sausage-making machine. Hold the casing snugly around the tip of the funnel as you grind the meat once more. As the casing fills, guide it with your hands as it winds its way across your kitchen worktable,

or it will break. Tie it with string into links, any length you want. A two-foot sausage curled around a mound of scrambled eggs makes a fantastic family country breakfast.

Sausage will keep without preservatives two or three weeks refrigerated. You can smoke cure it, but all this does is improve the flavor; it doesn't enhance its keeping qualities.

Experiment with other meat flavors. Try beef and pork sausages, or chicken and pork, for instance, and of course grind in a little garlic from your garden sometimes, or perhaps some wheat germ.

Country Sausage

10 pounds ground pork
4 tablespoons brown sugar or honey
3 tablespoons salt
8 tablespoons ground sage
2 tablespoons pepper
2 teaspoons paprika
2 teaspoons nutmeg
1 teaspoon garlic salt

Thoroughly combine all the ingredients. Because you should never taste raw pork, you can check the amount of spices by making a small sausage patty, cooking it thoroughly and tasting that. Correct the seasonings if needed. Freeze the sausage in 1-pound packages.

Cured Corned Beef

Fresh beef or beef from the freezer can be brine cured or dry cured.

Make a brine by mixing one pound of Tender-Quick, or another similar type of commercial tenderizer, to two quarts of water; for small batches, one cup of Tender-Quick to three cups of water.

Place the beef in a clean container, allowing some space for the curing brine. Pour enough brine over the meat to completely cover it, and weight it down to keep it submerged. Cure this in a refrigerator, not over 45°F, for 14 to 20 days, depending on the thickness of the piece of meat. If the meat is not used at the end of the curing time, leave it in brine seven days longer. If it is not used then, it should be taken from the brine, washed, dried and refrigerated. Cook it within five days.

To cure small pieces for boiled dinners or for making corned beef hash or a loaf, prepare the curing brine as directed above. Place the pieces of meat in a clean bowl or jar, and add enough brine to cover. Allow it to cure for six to seven days. When the curing time is up, remove the meat from the container, and cook it.

To dry cure beef, use two tablespoons of commercial tenderizer for each pound of meat. Rub the cure into the meat, slip the beef into a plastic bag, and refrigerate it for seven to 14 days depending on the thickness of the meat.

Pork Cookery

Fresh pork: Loins, legs (fresh hams), blade Boston shoulders (butts), arm picnic shoulders, and tenderloins (whole) should be roasted at 325° to 350°F to a final internal temperature of 170°F. Chops, steaks, cubed steaks and patties are usually cooked by braising, broiling or pan-frying.

Chops and steaks should be cooked at a low to moderate temperature so they are well done in the center but are not dry on the surface. To cook sausage links or patties, place them in a cold frying pan, add two to four tablespoons of water, cover tightly, and cook slowly five to eight minutes, depending on size and thickness. Pour off the drippings, and cook the sausage uncovered until browned.

Smoked pork: Large, "fully-cooked" cuts (hams, loins, arm picnic shoulders, shoulder rolls and Canadian-style bacon) should be roasted at 300° to 325°F until the meat thermometer registers 130° to 140°F. Roast "cook-before-eating" cuts to 160°F. Slices of ham and Canadian-style bacon, bacon and smoked chops are broiled, pan-broiled or pan-fried.

Beef Cookery

It's important to choose the proper cooking method to produce flavorful, juicy and tender beef entrées. Your choice depends on the tenderness of the beef cut itself. Cook tender cuts—rib, short loin and sirloin—by dry-heat methods. Some less tender cuts—chuck, round, flank and brisket—can be prepared by moist- or dry-heat methods, depending on beef quality and the cooking time and temperature used. Quality is influenced by the age of the animal and by marbling. (In general, the younger the animal, the more tender the beef; and the higher the degree of marbling, the greater the flavor and juiciness.) The combination of lower temperature (300°F) and longer cooking time enables some less tender cuts to be prepared by dry-heat cookery methods.

Other less tender cuts—short plate and shank—should be prepared only by moist-heat methods. It's also possible to tenderize less tender beef cuts by marinating them in a food acid such as vinegar or lemon juice for six to 24 hours before cooking. Marinades will also add flavor. Pounding the meat with a heavy object (such as a meat mallet or the edge of a sturdy plate) will aid tenderness by helping to break down connective tissue.

There are four types of dry-heat cooking: roasting, broiling, pan-broiling and pan-frying. Stir-frying and deep-frying are variations of pan-frying. Moist-heat cooking involves either braising or cooking in stews or soups.

Meat Snacks

Using pemmican is an art in itself. While old-timers may regale you with stories—some may even be true—of wolfing down pemmican straight from the sack and then snowshoeing or driving the dog team 20 miles to school, you'll probably like pemmican better after you lightly fry it. It makes a fine breakfast food with hash browns, eggs, sourdough hot cakes or buttermilk biscuits. Then you can regale acquaintances and strangers with accounts of wolfing down pemmican to stave off starvation, braving blizzards and any of the other daredevil doings on which tall tales depend.

Yukon Pete's Rare Pemmican
$^1/_3$ lean bear meat
$^1/_3$ lean moose meat
$^1/_3$ lean pork scraps
Salt, pepper, sage
Berries (see below)

First, you catch a bear and a moose (or a deer or an elk). Please do so at such times of year when these may be safely considered "food" and not "wildlife." Grind the various meats with the medium blade of a food chopper, mix well, and season with salt, pepper and a little sage. Cook the whole shebang in a kettle with just enough water to steam, rather than boil, the contents. When the meats are nearly done, remove the lid to let moisture evaporate, while retaining rich juices in the meat. If you choose to add fruit (cranberries, serviceberries, chokeberries or whatever), add fresh fruit early in the cooking process or canned fruit when the meat is nearly done.

Boil a white cloth sack made from worn sheeting, and fill it with the steaming mixture of meat and berries. Pour some hot grease over the contents. Yukon Pete's mother used a big dipper to ladle out the melted bear fat that she used—about a quart for 20 pounds of meat. Pete says he used lard the last few times he made pemmican, since "there ain't no bear grease" in really lean bear meat. Pete's mother might ask, "Well, what did you do with the rest of the bear, Pete?" If you, like Pete, don't have the portly parts of a bear on hand and decide to use lard, be aware that it foams when heated and should be melted in a large container. Pour it into the sack at once so that the hot fat will seep down and mingle with the hot meat mixture. The lard also coats the sack and makes a tight casing which effectively preserves the pemmican. "Keep pemmican cold and it's good for 10 years," allows Yukon Pete. You'd most likely prefer to store small batches in the refrigerator for short-term use and freeze the rest.

Easy Beef Jerky
5 pounds beef flank steak
$^1/_2$ cup soy sauce
$^1/_2$ teaspoon garlic salt
$^1/_2$ teaspoon lemon pepper

Trim *all* the fat from the steak, and cut the meat lengthwise into long, thin strips no thicker than $^1/_8$ inch. Combine the soy sauce, garlic salt and lemon pepper, and coat the steak strips with this mixture. Place the strips close together—but not overlapping—in a single layer on a rack over a baking sheet (to catch drips), and bake overnight in a 150°F oven. Store the cooled, finished jerky at room temperature in an airtight container. If all fat was trimmed away from the meat before it was cooked, the jerky should keep indefinitely.

Lamb Cookery

Since lamb is naturally tender, most cuts can be prepared conventionally, using dry-heat cooking methods. Rib, loin, shoulder, sirloin and leg cuts are excellent when roasted, broiled or pan-broiled. Chops cut one inch thick or more should be broiled; cuts less than one inch thick are usually best pan-broiled. Ground lamb may be roasted (baked) in loaves, broiled or pan-broiled as patties or browned and included in casseroles or other combination dishes. To insure maximum tenderness, cuts from the neck, shank and breast are usually cooked by moist-heat methods, such as braising or cooking in liquid, although riblets from the breast can be broiled. With all cooking methods, it is important that lamb be cooked at a low to moderate temperature and that overcooking be avoided.

The fell (the thin, paperlike covering on the outer fat) should not be removed from the roasts and legs, because it helps these cuts retain their shape and juiciness during the cooking process. The fell is usually removed at the market from smaller cuts such as chops.

At one time, lamb was served only well done. Now more people are enjoying lamb cooked rare (140°F) and medium (160°F), as well as well done (170°F). To determine doneness in roasts and legs, a meat thermometer should be used. Since lamb will continue to cook after it has been removed from the oven, the thermometer should register about 5°F lower than the desired doneness. For easier carving, allow the lamb to sit 15 to 20 minutes.

Organ Meats

Take the plunge into culinary exploration!

As your carefully raised livestock leaves for the butcher, you eagerly look forward to roasts, chops, steaks, bacon, stews and ground meat. But when you put those familiar cuts into storage, you also find feet, hocks, tongues, tripe, kidneys, tails, heads, hearts, brains—all sorts of overlooked extras. Sometimes you may skillfully continue to forget them until they're all that is left in the freezer. Then it's time to decide what to do with those puzzling leftover packages.

Two types of meat are included here: organ meat (heart, kidney, brains, etc.) and muscle meat (hocks, tails, heads, etc.). If you depend on the markets for some or all of your meat consumption, you know that most of these cuts are more reasonably priced than the common ones.

Kidneys

Most of us find the kidney aroma unpleasant but the taste fantastic. One way of combating the odor is to soak the kidneys in salted water for half an hour, rinse them, cover them with water in a pan, and boil them slowly for 10 to 20 minutes, depending on their size. Discard the water.

Kidney Stew

1 beef kidney, or 2 veal, 2–3 pork or
  6–8 lamb kidneys
3 medium onions, sliced
4 medium potatoes, quartered
4 carrots cut in 2" sections
2 green peppers, quartered
6 stalks celery, cut in 3" sections
2 tablespoons flour

Slice the deodorized kidneys about $1/2"$ thick. In a kettle, sandwich the onion and kidney slices, then add the rest of the vegetables, and cover with water. Simmer until the vegetables are done, about 20 minutes. Mix the flour into $1/2$ cup of the broth, and stir it into the stew. Cook until thickened. Serves 4–6.

Kidneys in Wine

2 pork or veal kidneys or 6–8 lamb
  kidneys
1/4 cup flour
1 tablespoon butter or margarine
1/2 pound mushrooms
1/2 cup port wine

Cut the deodorized kidneys in half length-wise, and cover with flour. In a frying pan, melt the butter, and fry the kidneys briefly until browned. Add the mushrooms, and brown them. Lower the heat, and add the wine. Simmer 15 to 20 minutes, turning the kidneys over a couple of times. Serve hot. Serves 4.

Tripe

Tripe is the lining of beef stomachs. To prepare tripe for cooking, put it in a kettle, and cover it with water and 1 cup of vinegar. Cover the tripe tightly, and cook it 3 or more hours over very low heat (a slow cooker is ideal), or place it on the back of a woodstove where the heat is such that you can just about put your hand flat down. When the tripe is done, rinse it thoroughly in cold water. Cut off what you will use, and refrigerate the rest. It will keep for a few weeks.

Tripe from the supermarket is usually pickled, which means it has been prepared and is probably too vinegary. If pickled, boil the tripe 10 minutes, throw out the water, and rinse the tripe in cold water.

Tripe also makes an interesting addition to homemade brothy soups.

Fried Tripe

1–1 1/2 pounds tripe
2 beaten eggs
1/2 cup flour
1 tablespoon butter or margarine

Cut the tripe into individual serving piec-es; dip them in egg and then in flour. Melt the butter or margarine in a frying pan, and fry the tripe over low to moderate heat until lightly browned. Serve hot. Serves 4.

Brains

Brains are a delicacy, and they're best the day the animal returns from the butcher. Before putting the animal's head in the freez-er, pick out the brains. Since they spoil very easily, they shouldn't be allowed to sit at room temperature. To prepare brains for cooking, remove and throw out the mem-branes. Soak the brains for about half an hour in cold water with 1 teaspoon of salt and 1 tablespoon of vinegar. Rinse them, place them in a saucepan, cover them with fresh water, and boil them slowly over low heat for half an hour.

Brains and Scrambled Eggs

Brains, prepared
1/2 cup flour
1 beaten egg
1 tablespoon butter or margarine

Cut the brains in half lengthwise. Dip them in flour, then in the beaten egg. In a frying pan, melt the butter, and fry the brains over moderate heat until the outside is crisp. Serve with scrambled eggs.

Barbecued Brains

Brains, prepared
1 1/2 cups tomato sauce
1 tablespoon parsley and celery leaves
1 teaspoon oregano or marjoram
1 tablespoon Worcestershire sauce

Combine all the ingredients except the brains. Marinate the brains in this mixture for about an hour. When the coals are ready, barbecue the brains, turning them regular-ly and basting them with the sauce. They are done when browned evenly.

Heart and Tongue

Before cooking the heart, remove all gristle, valves, arteries and excessive fat. No precooking or soaking is needed.

Stuffed Heart

1 heart
1 cup bread crumbs
1 medium onion, diced
2 stalks celery, diced
1/2 cup diced mushrooms
1 teaspoon thyme
1 tablespoon parsley
1 beaten egg
1/4 cup milk

Slit the heart open. Combine the remain-ing ingredients, stuff the heart, and tie or sew it closed. Bake in a covered dish in a 300°F oven—about 3 hours for a beef heart, 2 hours for pork or lamb heart. Serves 4–6.

Boiled Tongue

1 beef or veal, or 2 pork or lamb tongues
8–10 peppercorns
2 stalks celery, diced
8 sprigs parsley, diced, or 3 tablespoons
  dried parsley

Put all the ingredients in a kettle, and cover them with water. Simmer this slowly for 1 hour for pork or lamb, 2 hours for beef or veal. When it's done, remove the tongue from the heat, skin it, and slice it. Serve it with mustard or horseradish. Serves 4–6.

Liver

Liver is a well-known organ meat that peo-ple seem to either relish or detest. This recipe is for liver dislikers or their parents.

Donna's Liver Pâté

1 pound liver
1/4 cup flour
1 tablespoon butter or margarine
1 large onion, diced
1/2 pound mushrooms, diced
4 hard-boiled eggs
2 tablespoons mayonnaise
1 cup yogurt

Cut the liver into 1" squares, and coat it with the flour. Melt the butter or margarine in a frying pan. Fry the onion and liver, turn-ing them frequently. When the liver is almost done, add the mushrooms, and continue cooking until the mushrooms are done. Grind or blend the liver, mushrooms, onions and eggs in a bowl, and add the mayonnaise and enough yogurt (about 1 cup) to make the mixture formable. Refrigerate it in the bowl or in a mold for a couple of hours or more. When you're ready to eat, turn the pâté out on a plate, and serve it with your favorite mild crackers.

Tails

At first glance, livestock tails, especially pig tails, don't look like much of anything to bother with, but here's a tip: Barbecue them. Whittle a sharp point on a green switch, stick the tail on it, and broil the tail over a bon-fire or barbecue until the meat, skin and all, is ready to fall apart. Then eat it. Of course, this method doesn't allow for more than a couple of bites, but it's a fun-filled ritual at butchering time.

For more nutritional mileage from the waggers, especially if only one is available, use them with hocks and feet (of the same species) or for soup stock.

Legs: Hocks and Feet

Each animal lends it own flavor to organ meat, but with muscle meat the differences are even more distinct. You can repeat the same recipe with various kinds of meat and end up with different dishes. Although hocks and feet are more bone than muscle, they can be the most versatile cuts of all. Section the legs into 3" lengths (or ask your butcher to do it).

New England Boiled

For each person you'll need:
1–2 pork legs
1 potato
1–2 carrots
2–3 stalks celery
1 onion
1/2 cup green beans and/or peas
1 wedge cabbage

Place the legs in a kettle, cover them with water, bring this to a boil, reduce the heat,

Since the days of the family butcher are pretty much gone, you'll have to do some looking to locate fine cuts like this beef tongue.

and simmer the meat slowly for 1 hour with a lid on the pot. Add the potato (cut in half if it's large), carrots and celery, and simmer for 30 minutes. Add the onions and green beans and/or peas, and cook another 15 minutes. Put in the wedge of cabbage, and simmer until it's tender, about 15 minutes. Serve hot with warm biscuits or bread.

Lamb Stew

Prepare the same way as the New England Boiled, but omit the cabbage, and add some Swiss chard or spinach.

Beef Stew

Prepare the same way as the New England Boiled, but omit the cabbage, and add green peppers and Swiss chard or spinach. When the meat is done, mix 2 to 3 tablespoons of flour in $^1/_2$ cup of the broth, adding this to the stew and cooking until it's thickened.

Buraki With Pigs' Legs

Basically, this is a regional form of borscht. It's good cold as well as hot.

3-4 pork legs
2 pounds raw beets, grated or shredded
1 small onion, diced
1 tablespoon vinegar
2 tablespoons flour
1 cup milk

Put the legs, beets and onion in a kettle, and just barely cover them with water. (This "barely covering" is a tricky business because the beets want to float. Press down on the beets—not hard—and make sure the water would cover but not drown them.) Add the vinegar, and cook over low to moderate heat until the meat is ready to separate from the bones ($1^1/_2$ to 2 hours). When the meat is done, mix the flour in $^1/_4$ cup of the milk. Stir this mixture into the buraki, and add the rest of the milk. Bring the buraki to the boiling point—but don't let it boil—and it's ready to eat. Serves 4.

Lamb and Greens

Prepare the same way as buraki, but use beet greens, spinach or Swiss chard, and less water.

Sauerkraut and Pigs' Legs

This dish is a fine alternative to the more classic sauerkraut with spareribs.
4 legs
1 quart sauerkraut
4 large potatoes, cooked and mashed

Put the legs, sauerkraut and enough water to cover the meat in a kettle. Cook over low to moderate heat until the meat is done, $1^1/_2$ to 2 hours. Serve the sauerkraut and legs over the mashed potatoes. Serves 4.

Heads

Minestrone

$^1/_4$–$^1/_2$ beef, pig, calf or lamb head
1 clove garlic
12 whole peppercorns
1 tablespoon each oregano, basil and sage
$^1/_3$ cup each dried kidney beans, chickpeas and small limas
$^1/_2$ cup each diced onion, green pepper, carrot, Swiss chard (or spinach), celery and cabbage
1 quart stewed tomatoes or 4-6 fresh tomatoes
$^1/_2$ cup uncooked macaroni
Grated Parmesan or Romano cheese

Put the head, garlic, peppercorns, seasonings and dried beans in a kettle. Cover them with water, add a lid, and simmer over low to moderate heat for $2^1/_2$ hours. If the soup becomes too thick, add more water to keep the ingredients floating free. After 2 hours add the diced vegetables and tomatoes. Simmer the soup for another $^1/_2$ hour, or until the vegetables are done. In a separate pot, cook the macaroni according to package directions until done; add to the minestrone. Cook another 10 minutes, and serve with lots of grated cheese sprinkled on top.

Head Cheese

1 beef, lamb, pig or calf head
2 onions
6 stalks celery
2 cloves garlic
1 teaspoon thyme (or other favorite herb)
2 tablespoons parsley
12-14 peppercorns
2 tablespoons vinegar
2 cups dry white wine (optional)

Put all the ingredients except the wine in a kettle, cover them with water, and simmer until the meat is falling from the head—about 1 hour for a lamb, 2 hours for a pig or calf, 3 to 4 hours for a beefer. Remove the head, pick off the meat, and dice it very fine. Strain the stock, add the wine, and simmer until reduced by $^1/_3$ to $^1/_2$. Add the diced meat, and simmer 10 minutes. Pour the "soup" into molds (loaf pans are ideal). Chill this until set—a few hours. Slice it to serve.

Fresh Chicken

It may sound imposing, but preparing chicken "from scratch" was, not long ago, the *only* way to do it!

Grace Firth is a classic country cook. The following account of how to kill and clean a chicken is adapted from her book, Stillroom Cookery.

"Every girl should learn to cook chicken," was my grandmother's pet phrase, and to her way of thinking, "cook chicken" started with the ax.

It all began the evening before, when we sneaked into the chicken house and selected our dinner, head under its wing, snoozing on a roost. If the hapless fowl was to be a fryer, Grandma felt the breastbone to "feel for the meat," while thoughts of Hansel and Gretel danced in my head. For a chicken destined for the stewpot or roasting pan, she directed that I snatch a hen that she had noted to be a lax layer.

We let our selection sleep overnight in a cage. The next morning we immobilized the poor chicken's head between two nails on the chopping block. One hand would hold the feet, and the other, the hatchet. The end was mercifully quick. The chicken was allowed to bleed neck down for a minute, while the wings were held to diminish the splatter.

Picking the chicken, or removing its feathers, is a simple task if the bird is scalded; that is, dipped in and out of hot water, about 208°F (98°C). Hold the scalded chicken by one foot, and pluck its feathers by pulling downward or toward the neck, taking little tufts or handfuls at a time. Start on the legs, and pluck everything until you get to "the spot where the head ought to be." Dip the chicken in and out of the hot water if the feathers put up a fight. Rinse your hand from time to time, work fast, and pull wing and pinfeathers last, using a dull knife.

Singe the body hairs over a fire or candle, cut off the feet, and you are ready to draw the bird.

"Always kill and clean a chicken in one sitting," my grandmother advised. There is an awful temptation after the feathers are plucked to take a breather. Don't! It's much easier working with a warm and pliable bird than one that has turned cold and stiff.

To draw a chicken, slit the skin from the vent, cutting around the vent. Insert your hand into the cavity along the inside of the rib cage. Follow the backbone toward the tail, and scoop out the cavity. Remove the lungs (located along each rib pocket), and tuck your hand way into the bird; at the base of the neck, feel the craw, and, on the far side, the windpipe. With your forefinger take a turn around the windpipe and, without squeezing the craw, pull the craw out, together with the pipes.

Rinse the cavity with cold water. Remove the gizzard, heart and liver, being careful not to rupture the greenish gall sac as you cut it away. Let the chicken cool for two or three hours before cooking.

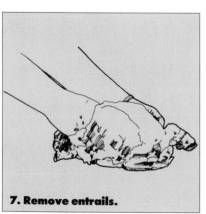

1. The dispatch

2. Scald; pull off feathers.

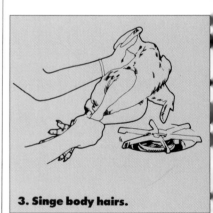

3. Singe body hairs.

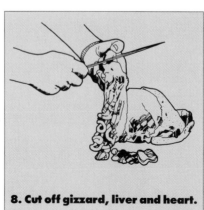

7. Remove entrails.

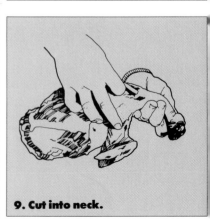

8. Cut off gizzard, liver and heart.

9. Cut into neck.

Four Classic Chicken Recipes

Red Wing Stew

2 large cans of tomatoes packed in purée
2 pounds chicken wings
4 unpeeled potatoes, cubed
Several pods of okra, sliced
1 pound green beans
2 green peppers, sliced
2 carrots, sliced
2 onions, cut in rings
1 clove garlic, minced
1 hot pepper pod
1 bay leaf
1 tomato can of water
Salt, pepper, basil and marjoram to taste

Combine the first 12 ingredients in a large pot, and cook over low heat until the chicken wings are tender. Add some salt, pepper, basil and marjoram to taste, and simmer the stew for another 30 minutes. Serves 6.

Stewed Chicken With Biscuits

1 stewing chicken
Water to cover
2 small onions
Salt and pepper
1 1/2 tablespoons flour

Wash the chicken, cut it up, and place it in a pot of water (skin side up). Add the onions, and simmer until the chicken is tender (about 2 1/2 hours). Season with salt and pep-

per. Thicken the broth with slowly sifted-in flour, whisking it smooth. Serve the chicken with split biscuits and gravy. Serves 4.

Creamed Chicken

3 tablespoons chicken fat or butter
1 tablespoon chopped bell pepper
2 tablespoons finely chopped onion
1/4 cup flour
1 cup chicken broth
1 cup milk
2 cups diced cooked chicken
3/4 teaspoon salt
1/4 teaspoon pepper

Heat the fat, and cook the pepper and onion in it until tender. Blend the flour into the fat and vegetable mixture. Stir in the chicken broth and milk. Cook to a smooth sauce, stirring constantly. Add the chicken, and season with salt and pepper. Heat thoroughly, then serve on rice, biscuits or toast. Serves 4.

Annie's Southern Fried Chicken

This recipe was handed down from Annie Kate Jones, a cook in Charleston, South Carolina, around the turn of the century. It's slightly modernized, but the basic result remains the same—delicious.
1 frying chicken, cut up
2 cups flour
2 tablespoons each salt and pepper
2 teaspoons each paprika, thyme
  and dried parsley

1 teaspoon each sage, rosemary, garlic powder and onion powder
1 quart corn oil (enough to fill 2 medium frying pans to a depth of 1 inch)

Wash the chicken, removing excess fat. Pat dry. Mix the flour and spices (you can vary to taste) in a paper or plastic bag, add the chicken a few pieces at a time, and shake well, turning the bag to make sure the chicken's well coated. (Hold tight so it won't leak!) Remove the chicken, and let it sit a few minutes while you pour an inch of oil into each frying pan. Place the pans over high heat. Put the chicken back in the bag; shake again. Wait until the oil is hot (just before it smokes—if your hand can't stand the heat an inch away from the oil, it's ready). Carefully ease the chicken into the oil with tongs or forks; try not to dislodge the flour. Add the pieces one by one to maintain constant high heat. Don't overcrowd. Cook at high heat until golden on the bottom side (5 to 10 minutes); be gentle when you lift the chicken to peek. Turn; fry until that side's golden. Reduce the heat to medium, and cook another 20 minutes or so. The chicken is done when it is golden brown, feels solid as you push against it with the flat side of a fork, and starts to float a bit in the oil. Smaller pieces will be ready before the breasts and drumsticks. Drain the meat on paper towels for 15 minutes; the chicken will stay warm while the crust "ages." Serves 4.

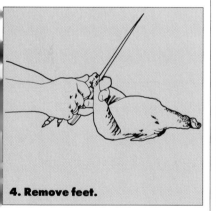

4. Remove feet.

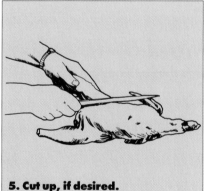

5. Cut up, if desired.

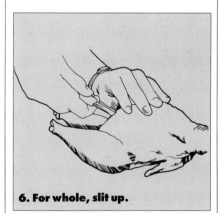

6. For whole, slit up.

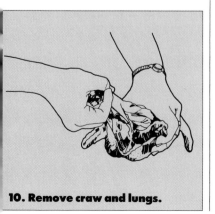

10. Remove craw and lungs.

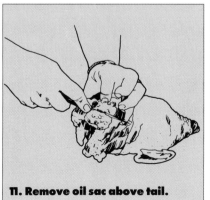

11. Remove oil sac above tail.

12. *Voilà!* Ready to go.

Gourmet Seafood

You'll never turn
out great seafood meals
unless you learn how
to handle and prepare the
main ingredients.

A freshly caught fish, water still streaming from its sides, can give a whole new meaning to the overworked phrase "living color." And the sight seems more vivid because those hues, apparently lit from within and perhaps brightened by the thrill of the catch, fade rapidly as the fish dies. The dulling of that beauty, however, doesn't have to imply a loss of flavor or nutritional value. In fact, it's the responsibility of any angler to either release caught fish unharmed or care for the meat in such a way that it will reach the table in a form fit to be not only appreciated but raved over.

Fortunately, it doesn't require much time or talent to clean and cook fish, whether purchased at the local market or lured to a feather-fancied hook.

First, Keep Freshly Caught Fish Fresh

It stands to reason that the best way to keep your catch in top condition during a long day on the water is to keep the fish alive. If you're in a modern fishing boat with an aerated live well, that won't be much of a chore. Simply handle the fish with dampened hands, remove the hook as quickly and gently as possible, and slip the catch into the well. While most of us don't own such a boat, we can still keep our fish swimming during the day on a stringer. Small fish—those up to, say, 10 pounds—can be held on a chain link stringer equipped with locking metal clips, with the pin on each clip passed through both the upper and lower lips. Larger fish are probably better held on a heavy-duty stringer with a metal spike on one end and a ring on the other—simply run the spike through both lips, then through the ring. In either case, when you're tying the stringer to boat or pier,

1. Make a cut behind the gills.

2. Follow the backbone to the tail.

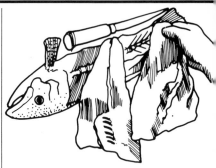

3. Repeat on the other side.

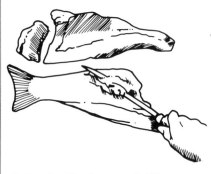

4. Cut the ribs from each fillet.

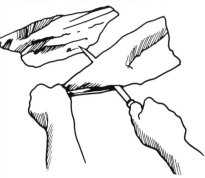

5. Cut between the flesh and skin.

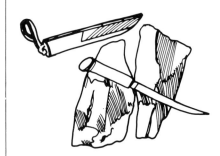

6. They're ready for the pan.

allow enough slack to let the fish swim in the cooler, shady water beneath you.

Another option, best suited to the trout angler who is working a small stream, is the wicker or canvas creel. A creel can be used to keep the catch for several hours, but be sure that the stored fish aren't touching; a separating layer of dry grass is probably the best bet. In this case, and in the case of *all* fish that are dead—even if they've been cleaned—remember that water is the enemy of freshness. Keep them dry and cool.

No-Fuss Filleting

Anyone who has had the opportunity to watch a professional at work with a fillet knife is likely to be a bit intimidated by the experience. Fishing guides and fish market employees work with such speed and deftness that they can make the simple separation of meat from bones look more like alchemy than the basic kitchen skill it is. Don't plan on getting that fast yourself, at least not before you've taken your fillet knife to a *lot* of fish. Do, however, be confident that, with the right knife and a little care, you can slice off beautiful, nearly boneless fillets the first time you try.

There are a number of fine fillet knives on the market, each characterized by a thin, flexible blade that tapers toward the point. Choose one of a size appropriate to the fish you'll be cleaning (a blade of about six inches is a good multipurpose compromise), keep it sharp, clean it after each use, and it should be slicing fillets for generations to come.

Alternatives to Filleting

Fillets are probably the most common, convenient and (if you're purchasing your fish) costly seafood cuts, but some fish are either too large or too small to lend themselves to this handy boning technique. And there are times when the successful angler doesn't want to take the time to fillet a large catch before heading home. *Dressing* the fish provides an easy alternative. Simply remove the head, slicing just behind the gills, then open the stomach cavity all the way back to the anal vent, trying to avoid piercing any of the internal organs. Now scoop out the innards, and be sure to scrape away the kidney, which looks like a long stripe of blood running along the inside of the spine. Once that's done, remove the tail and fins (if you want a "packaged"-looking fish; some people prefer to keep them on), and dry the interior of each fish with a paper towel or dry

grass. Fish cleaned in this way can be either pan-fried as is or, if large enough, separated into steaks by slicing off sections perpendicular to the backbone.

If you have a long drive home, *wrap* your cleaned fish—in newspaper, brown paper bags or plastic refrigerator bags—to protect them from moisture and, as much as possible, from air until they can be refrigerated. If the drive (or flight) will take more than an hour or so, plan to store the fish on ice for the trip. Have some waterproof plastic bags handy in which to store your hard-won seafood—sealed *well* to keep out moisture.

Here's to a Fine Kettle of Fish

You should now be able to prepare the raw ingredients for any number of delicious fish fries, bakes, roasts and barbecues. Of course, it will still be up to you to meet that often unprinted first instruction for *any* seafood recipe: "First, catch a fish."

At the Market, or "Is Your Fish Fresh?"

Buying "fresh fish" and *getting* fresh fish are, unfortunately, not always one and the same. In order to make sure that your purchase will perform as well as just-caught seafood when it reaches the table, keep the following tests in mind.

1. Ask if the fish has been frozen. (This straightforward approach isn't guaranteed to work, of course, but most people *are* honest.)
2. Smell it. Fish that has a strong "fishy" odor isn't fresh.
3. Touch it. The flesh should spring back.
4. Look closely. The eyes should be round and bright, not sunken. The skin should not appear dull, and scales should still be firmly affixed.

Rabbit Fare

Lean, healthful, delicious and easy to raise, rabbit is livestock made easy.

Robert C. Winans of Lutz, Florida, keeps several dozen rabbits (along with a flock of laying hens, a few beds of fishing worms and a year-round productive vegetable garden) on the acre of land to which he and his wife have retired.

And when it comes time to eat one of his homegrown hares, Winans doesn't rely on a cookbook. Nor does he fall back on some time-honored but ordinary cooking method. What he does is call upon his imagination in order to invent new ways to prepare the tasty meat as he goes along.

George Fournier of Charlton City, Massachusetts, on the other hand, prefers to adhere to one favorite rabbit-cooking formula that has never let his family down. "It's a recipe my Canadian wife, Monique, brought to Massachusetts with her as part of her dowry, part of the accumulated farm-kitchen wisdom that's passed down from generation to generation in a land where tradition is still a part of one's inheritance."

The first three recipes on these pages will give you some idea of Bob Winans' creative flair, and the fourth will present you with the chance to experience a wonderful Canadian tradition!

Rabbit Fried With Grapefruit Juice

1 cup all-purpose flour
1 teaspoon Season-All (or other all-
   purpose seasoning)
1 teaspoon garlic powder
$^1/_4$ teaspoon pepper
$^1/_4$ teaspoon thyme (optional)
$^1/_2$ teaspoon salt
1 3- to 4-pound rabbit, cut into pieces
Juice of 1 grapefruit
$^1/_2$ cup cooking oil (or enough to measure $^1/_4$ inch in bottom of pan)
1 medium onion, chopped

Combine the flour with the seasonings. Dip each piece of rabbit in grapefruit juice, then roll it in the flour mixture until the meat is thoroughly coated. Pour the oil and the chopped onion into a deep, heavy pot, and heat over a high flame. Place the floured rabbit in the pot, and brown each chunk first on one side and then the other. Lower the flame, stir together the remaining grapefruit juice and flour mixture, and add to the pot. Cover and let everything simmer together until the meat is tender, being careful to turn the rabbit pieces from time to time to keep them from sticking.

Rabbit Sausage

Coarsely ground meat and fat of 1 large
   rabbit (save the bones for soup stock)
$1^1/_2$ teaspoons salt
1 teaspoon pepper
Pinch of ginger
2 or more teaspoons sage (to taste)
1 teaspoon thyme
Pinch of garlic powder
Dash of cayenne pepper, or 2 or 3
   dashes of hot pepper sauce (optional)

Combine the seasonings with the ground meat (everything together should total about 2 pounds), and regrind (this helps to get everything well blended). Refrigerate overnight. The next day, test the flavor by frying and eating a small patty, and adjust the seasoning if necessary. Form 1-pound rolls of meat, wrap in freezer wrap, and place the ready-to-slice rolls in your freezer (frozen sausage can be cut quite easily when you're ready to use it).

Rabbit Soup

Bones of 1 or more rabbits
1 to 2 quarts water
Sliced carrots
Chopped onions
Presoaked lentils or split peas
Fresh or canned tomatoes
Salt, pepper and garlic powder to taste
A few pieces of suet or a little butter
   (Note: The exact amounts of the above ingredients are purposely not specified, to allow you to vary them according to your preference or what you have on hand.) Boil the bones in the water in a good-sized stockpot. Remove the bones from the stock, and scrape all the meat from them. Return the chunks of rabbit to the broth, and add the carrots, onions, lentils or split peas and tomatoes . . . plus any other vegetables you may wish to include. Season, add the suet or butter, and simmer until the vegetables are tender.

Canadian Rabbit Stew

1 large, whole rabbit
1 quart water
2 tablespoons cornstarch
6 sliced carrots
6 medium potatoes, diced
1 cup whole kernel corn
1 cup green peas
1 cup wax or green beans
1 medium onion, chopped
1 cup diced celery
1 bay leaf
Salt and pepper to taste

Boil the rabbit in the water until the meat is tender, then remove it from the pot, and bone it. Put the meat into a large kettle, add 2 cups of broth in which the rabbit was cooked, bring to a boil, and add a thickening sauce that you've made by stirring cornstarch into $^1/_4$ cup of the remaining broth. Allow the kettle's contents to boil for another minute, then reduce the heat. Add all remaining ingredients.

"Now for the topping that makes this stew stand head and shoulders above the rest!" says George Fournier.

1 cup flour
$1^1/_2$ teaspoons baking powder
$^1/_2$ teaspoon salt
2 tablespoons chilled shortening
$^1/_4$ to $^1/_2$ cup milk (the less you use, the
   better the dumplings seem to hold
   together)

Sift the dry ingredients together into a bowl, then cut in the shortening with a pastry blender until the mixture resembles coarse meal. Add the milk all at once, stir lightly just until the dough holds together, and then drop by rounded tablespoonfuls on top of the gently bubbling stew. With the heat adjusted so the liquid just simmers, let the dumplings cook—uncovered—for 10 minutes, then cover, and let them cook 10 minutes longer, or until the steam has fluffed them up nicely.

If you need to thicken the stew, do so after removing the dumplings. And George recommends serving homemade tomato relish and cranberry sauce on the side, to give your hearty meal just the proper finishing touch.

Herb and Spice Chart

Herbs	Appetizers	Eggs & Cheese	Fish	Poultry & Game
Allspice	Pickled beets, pickles, relishes, fruit compote, spiced fruit, spiced wine	Egg casseroles, cream cheese	Poached fish, oyster stew	
Angelica	Vermouth, Chartreuse, gin, marmalade, preserves, tea		Fish dishes	Poultry dishes
Anise	Liqueurs, cordials, tea		Marinade	
Balm, Lemon	Wine cups, crab apple jelly, melon			
Basil	Seafood cocktails, tomato and vegetable aspics, tomato preserves, cheese balls and spreads	Scrambled eggs, soufflés, rarebits, cream cheese, egg casseroles	Lobster, mussels, shrimp, sole, scallops, clam chowder	Rabbit, venison, duck
Bay leaves	Aspic, tomato juice, pickled beets, pickles		Boiled and steamed shrimp and lobster; chowders	Venison, chicken
Bergamot	Tea			
Borage	Summer drinks			
Burnet, Salad	Summer drinks			
Caraway seed	Dips, soft cheese spreads, pickles	Cottage cheese, cream cheese	Tuna casserole, clam chowder	Roast goose
Catnip	Tea	Scrambled eggs	Fish and oyster stews, chowder	
Celery seed	Cream cheese and ham spreads, dips, deviled eggs, pickles, tomato juice	Boiled, fried and deviled eggs; omelets, cheese sauces, rarebits		Chicken pie, chicken and turkey hash, croquettes
Chervil	Mushrooms, dips, vegetable juice	Cream and cottage cheese, cheese casseroles, rarebits, cheese soufflés, deviled, fried and scrambled eggs; omelets	All fish, especially crab, fish balls, haddock, halibut	Chicken casseroles, baked, boiled and roasted chicken and turkey; poultry stuffing
Chives	Dips, egg rolls, vegetable and tomato juices, cheese balls	Egg casseroles, deviled, scrambled and fried eggs; omelets, cottage and cream cheese, cheese soufflés, cheese casseroles	All fish, especially fish balls, fish cakes; see soups	Venison, chicken, turkey, poultry stuffing
Cinnamon	Hot spiced beverages, pickled fruit, sweet gherkins		Poached fish	Steamed chicken
Cloves	Fruit punch, hot spiced wines, hot tea, spiced fruit, pickles			Baked chicken, chicken à la king, roast chicken, croquettes
Coriander	Pickles, liqueurs, tea		Fish curry	Chicken curry
Cumin	Deviled eggs	Deviled eggs, cottage cheese, cream cheese, Cheddar cheese	Fish dishes	
Curry powder	Deviled eggs, dips, salted nuts, tomato juice	Deviled eggs, cottage cheese, cream cheese, cheese sauces	Baked fish; shrimp, oyster stew, chowders	Curried chicken and turkey, hash, croquettes
Dill	Anchovy and Cheddar cheese spreads, sour cream dips, pickles, relish, deviled eggs	Cottage cheese, cream cheese, deviled eggs, omelets, poached and scrambled eggs, egg salad	Baked fish; lobster, shrimp, crab, haddock, mackerel, salmon	Creamed chicken

A sprig of this and a hint of that turn plain old "meat and taters" into a palate-pleasing adventure.

Meats & Sauces	Salads & Dressings	Soups	Vegetables	Pastry & Desserts
Baked ham; lamb; beef and lamb stews, hamburger, meat loaf, meat gravies, cranberry sauce	Cottage cheese and fruit salads, cheese dressings	Asparagus, green pea, tomato and vegetable beef soups; minestrone	Beets, cabbage, carrots, collards, eggplant, spinach, squash, turnips	Molasses cookies, fruitcake, spice cake, pies, puddings, tapioca, mincemeat
		Asparagus and chicken soups	Angelica roots cooked in butter	Candied angelica stems, gooseberries, rhubarb, stewed apples
				Breads, cakes, cream fillings
	Green and fruit salads		Chopped vegetables	Custards, rice pudding, cake, cookies
Beef, lamb, liver, meat loaf, sausage, tomato sauces	Garnish; French and Russian dressings	Bean, beef, pea, tomato and turtle soups; clam chowder	Eggplant, onions, peas, potatoes, spinach, squash, stewed tomatoes, string beans	
Corned and roast beef, lamb, veal, meat pies and stews, pot roast, gravies, marinades	Beef and seafood salads, aspics, French dressing	Beef, oxtail, potato, tomato and vegetable soups; minestrone, fish chowders, bouillon	Artichokes, beets, carrots, eggplant, onions, potatoes, squash, stewed tomatoes	
	Green salads			
	Green and fruit salads	Pea soup	Cabbage	Candied borage flowers
	Green and fruit salads	Mushroom and bean soups		
Beef à la mode, kidney stew, liver, roast pork, sauerbraten	Potato salad, coleslaw, sour cream dressing	Cream and vegetable soups, borscht, clam chowder	Beets, broccoli, Brussels sprouts, cabbage, carrots, cauliflower, celery, onions, potatoes, tomatoes, turnips	Coffee cakes, cookies, muffins, rolls, rye bread, baked apples
Stewed beef and lamb	Green salads			
Braised lamb, roasts, meat loaf, stews, stuffings, cream sauces	Bean, egg, potato and tuna salads; coleslaw, sour cream dressing	Cream of celery and vegetable soups, fish chowder, bouillon	Cabbage, cauliflower, potatoes, stewed tomatoes, turnips	Biscuits, rolls, salty breads
Roast beef, beef stew, lamb, meatballs, ragouts, veal; béarnaise, butter, fish, shellfish and white sauces; marinades	Chicken, egg, green, potato, seafood and tuna salads	Leek, sorrel, spinach and vegetable soups; vichyssoise	Beans, beets, carrots, chard, cucumbers, green peas, potatoes, spinach	Croutons, biscuits, rolls, white bread
Garnish for grilled pork and steaks; barbecued beef, beef stew, lamb, meat pies, pork, pot roast, rabbit, spareribs; barbecue, butter, fish, shellfish, spaghetti, tomato, white, and tartar sauces; brown gravy	Chicken, egg, green, macaroni, potato, seafood and tuna salads; French, mayonnaise, sour cream, oil and vinegar, yogurt dressings	Bouillabaisse, chowder, gumbo, minestrone, oyster stew, vichyssoise; chicken, leek, tomato and turkey soups	Chard, cucumbers, eggplant, green beans, lima beans, mushrooms, potatoes, squash, zucchini	Biscuits, Cheddar cheese bread, corn bread, cottage cheese bread, croutons, potato pancakes, rolls
Ham, pork chops, sauces for pork and lamb	Fruit salads		Pumpkin, squash, sweet potatoes	Buns, coffee cake, spice cake, cookies, pumpkin pie, custards, rice and chocolate puddings, tapioca, apple desserts, stewed fruits
Baked ham, boiled tongue, pot roast, sausage, stews, gravies	Fruit salad topping	Bean, beef, cream of pea and cream of tomato soups	Baked beans, beets, squash, candied sweet potatoes	Apple and pumpkin pies, mincemeat, rice pudding, tapioca, stewed fruit
Marinades and garnish for pork, ham and veal				Cakes, biscuits, milk puddings, cookies
Chili con carne, hamburger, meat loaf			Cabbage, sauerkraut	Fruit pies
Curried lamb, stews, veal croquettes, cream sauces	Meat and fruit salads, French dressing, mayonnaise	Cream of mushroom and tomato soups; clam and fish chowders, oyster stew	Carrots, celery, corn, creamed onions, lima beans, potatoes, scalloped tomatoes	
Corned beef, kidneys, lamb, pork, veal, hamburger, barbecued beef, stews	Chicken, cucumber, egg, fruit, green, macaroni, potato, seafood, tuna, vegetable and Waldorf salads; coleslaw; French, yogurt, mayonnaise, oil and vinegar, and sour cream dressings	Bean, chicken, navy bean, tomato, and vegetable soups; borscht, chowder, vichyssoise	Avocado, beans, beets, cabbage, carrots, cauliflower, cucumber, eggplant, green pepper, lima and snap beans, potatoes, squash, tomatoes, turnips	Apple pie, dill-seed bread, pound cake, cookies, applesauce cake, apple fritters, biscuits

Herbs	Appetizers	Eggs & Cheese	Fish	Poultry & Game
Fennel	Sweet pickles		All fish dishes, especially poached	
Garlic	Dips	Egg dishes	Shellfish	Chicken
Ginger	Chutney, conserves, pickles, candied ginger, syrup			Squab, roast chicken, Cornish hen, curries
Marjoram	Lemonade, tea, vegetable cocktail, fruit punch, tomato juice, herb butters; cheese dips, spreads and balls; stuffed mushrooms, liver pâté, pickles, jelly, deviled eggs	Cheese casseroles, cottage and cream cheese, rarebits, soufflés, omelets, cheese sauces, deviled eggs, scrambled eggs	Baked and broiled fish; salmon loaf, crab, trout, clam chowder	Venison, pheasant, rabbit, duck, goose, turkey, chicken; stuffings
Mint	Cheese dips, fruit compote, jelly, syrup, tea, hot chocolate, fruit punch, juleps, wine cups	Cream cheese, soufflés	Any mild fish	
Mustard	Deviled eggs, mustard sauces, pickled onions, pickles	Deviled eggs, cheese sauces	Poached fish; shrimp; creamed and stewed oysters	
Nutmeg	Eggnog			
Oregano	Avocado dip, cheese dips and spreads, vegetable and tomato juices	Scrambled and boiled eggs; omelets, cottage and cream cheese, soufflés, rarebits, cheese sauces	Clams, crab, lobster, baked white-fish, stuffings, butter sauce	Chicken, duck, pheasant, rabbit, venison; poultry stuffing
Parsley	Cheese spreads, dips, and balls; tea	Scrambled, fried and deviled eggs; omelets, cottage and cream cheese, soufflés, casseroles	Bisques, chowders	All poultry and game, especially chicken, duck, goose, pheasant, turkey, venison; stuffings
Rosemary	Deviled eggs, fruit cup, pickles, sour cream dip, cream cheese dips and spread, honey, jam, jelly, fruit juice and punch, vegetable juice, wine cups	Scrambled and deviled eggs; omelets, soufflés, cottage and cream cheese, rarebits, cheese sauces	Creamed seafood; crab, halibut, salmon; chowders	Broiled chicken; duck, goose, turkey, grouse, pheasant, quail, venison, rabbit; poultry stuffing
Sage	Cheese dips and spreads, deviled eggs, pickles, honey, tea, wine	Deviled, fried and scrambled eggs; omelets, casseroles, creamed eggs, soufflés, Cheddar cheese, cheese sauces	Baked fish; stuffings, chowders	Rabbit and venison stews; chicken, duck, turkey, goose, pheasant; poultry stuffing
Savory	Deviled eggs, vegetable and tomato juice cocktails, tea	Deviled, scrambled and fried eggs; omelets, soufflés	Broiled and baked fish; chowders	Rabbit and venison stews; chicken, duck, turkey; poultry stuffing
Sorrel, Garden	Cream cheese dips, garnish, tea	Cream cheese	Sauces	
Sweet cicely	Fruit drinks, wine cups, herb butter, mulberry jam			
Tarragon	Cheese spread, herb butters, pickles, seafood cocktails, tomato and vegetable juice cocktails	All egg dishes, cottage and cream cheese, rarebits	All fish, shellfish; sauces, chowders	Chicken, duck, turkey, goose, rabbit, venison
Thyme	Seafood, tomato and vegetable juice cocktails, cheese dips and spreads, deviled eggs, jellies, honey	Omelets, shirred eggs, soufflés, cottage and cream cheese	Broiled, baked and fried fish; croquettes, oyster stew, chowders	Venison, fricassees, stuffings

Meats & Sauces	Salads & Dressings	Soups	Vegetables	Pastry & Desserts
Beef stew, roast pork, veal	Salad dressings		Sauerkraut, squash	Breads, buns, coffee cakes, muffins, sugar cookies, apple desserts
Grilled meats, kebabs; meat casseroles, lamb, veal; spaghetti, tartar and béarnaise sauces	Green, potato, seafood salads; mayonnaise; sour cream dressing	Bouillabaisse; chicken, vegetable beef and tomato soups	Corn, green beans, potatoes, spinach, squash, tomatoes	French bread, rolls
Broiled and chopped beef; lamb, veal, pot roast, stews, curries	Ginger pears, French dressing	Black and navy bean, onion and potato soups	Baked beans, beets, carrots, squash	Cookies, gingerbread, spice cake, pumpkin pie, custards, Indian pudding, applesauce, stewed and baked fruit
Pork, veal, roast beef, lamb chops, beef hash, beef stew, brains, meat loaf, roast pork, meat pies; brown gravy; mustard, pizza, spaghetti and tomato sauces	Asparagus, chicken, egg, fruit, green, seafood, tuna and vegetable salads; French, oil and vinegar dressings	Chicken, onion, oxtail, oyster, tomato, turtle and vegetable soups; clam chowder, minestrone	Broccoli, carrots, celery, eggplant, green pepper, green beans, lima beans, onions, peas, potatoes, spinach, squash, sweet potatoes, zucchini	Cheese bread, white bread, biscuits, croutons, dumplings
Hamburger patties, roast lamb, shish kebab, lamb stew, meatballs, pork chops, veal roast; lamb and veal roast sauces, marinades, shellfish sauces	Coleslaw; fruit, green and cottage cheese salads; honey and mayonnaise dressings, oil and vinegar dressing	Bean, fruit and split pea soups; vichyssoise	Cabbage, carrots, celery, green beans, peas, potatoes, spinach	Devil's-food cake, candies, cookies, custards, fruit salads, fudge, frostings, gelatins, ice cream, chocolate pie, sherbets
Ham, kidneys, pickled meats; cheese and fish sauces	Dressings		Asparagus, beets, broccoli, Brussels sprouts, cabbage, celery, onions, snap beans, squash, white potatoes	Molasses cookies
Meat loaf			Cabbage, glazed carrots, onions, snap beans, spinach, squash, sweet potatoes	Cakes, cookies, doughnuts, pumpkin pie, custards, ice cream, puddings, stewed fruit, whipped cream
Kidney, pork, veal, roasted and broiled lamb, meat loaf, tamale pie, sausages, sweetbreads; gravies, marinades; tomato, butter, barbecue, fish, mustard, pizza, spaghetti and white sauces	Avocado, green, potato, seafood, tomato and vegetable salads; aspics; French, oil and vinegar dressings	Bean, beef, lentil, onion, tomato, vegetable soups; borscht, chili, chowder, minestrone	Broccoli, cabbage, eggplant, leeks, mushrooms, onions, peas, potatoes, spinach, stewed tomatoes, string beans, white potatoes	Bread sticks, cheese bread, croutons, pizza dough, rolls
All meats and stews, especially beef pies, beef roasts, beef stew, hamburger patties, lamb, tongue, veal; gravy; butter, barbecue, meat, mustard, spaghetti and tartar sauces	Coleslaw; chicken, fish, green, macaroni, potato, seafood and tuna salads	Bean, chicken, cream, mushroom, onion, potato, split pea and vegetable soups; bisques, bouillabaisse, chowder, gumbo, minestrone	All vegetables, especially carrots, peas, buttered potatoes	Corn bread, white bread, croutons, rolls
Roast beef, beef stew, lamb, liver, meat loaf, sausage, ham loaf, ragouts; brown gravy, marinades; butter, barbecue, mustard and tomato sauces	Chicken, fruit, potato and seafood salads; honey and mayonnaise, oil and vinegar dressings	Chicken, cream, potato, split pea and turtle soups; chowders	Broccoli, cauliflower, chard, eggplant, green and lima beans, onions, peas, mushrooms, potatoes, spinach, squash, tomatoes, turnips	Biscuits, corn bread, white bread, cake, cornmeal mush, croutons, cherry pie, pizza
Hamburger patties, kidney, liver, pork dishes, pork stuffing, veal, roast lamb, meat loaf, pot roast, stews	Green and tomato salads; French and oil and vinegar dressings	Cream, onion, potato and tomato soups; consommé; corn and fish chowders	Brussels sprouts, cabbage, carrots, eggplant, lima beans, onions, peas, potatoes, tomatoes, turnips, winter squash	Biscuits, corn bread, corn sticks, croutons, crusts for meat pies, waffles
Beef, hamburger, kidney, liver, meatballs, meat loaf, roast lamb, roast pork, pot roast, stews	Coleslaw; bean, green, potato and tomato salads; dressings	Bean, split pea and lentil soups; consommé, chowders	Asparagus, avocado, beans, beets, Brussels sprouts, cabbage, peas, sauerkraut	Croutons, biscuits
Fricassees, ragouts	Green salads	*Soupe aux herbes*		
	Green and fruit salads			Fruit cups
Aspic, steaks, pot roast, stews, veal, butter sauce for steak; gravies, meat marinades, Yorkshire pudding	Coleslaw; asparagus, bean, chicken, crab, cucumber, egg, green, lobster, potato, seafood, shrimp, tomato, turkey and vegetable salads	Bean, chicken, mushroom, pea, tomato and turtle soups; consommé, bisques, fish chowders	Asparagus, beans, beets, broccoli, cabbage, carrots, cauliflower, kale, mushrooms, peas, potatoes, spinach, tomatoes	Croutons
All meats	Tomato aspic; green, potato, seafood, tomato and vegetable salads	Bean, potato, tomato and vegetable soups; borscht, chowders, consommé, gumbo, oyster stew	Artichokes, beans, beets, broccoli, cabbage, carrots, eggplant, mushrooms, onions, peas, potatoes, spinach, squash, tomatoes	Biscuits, cheese bread, white bread, croutons, rolls

Putting Up Produce

Pick, boil, cool, cut, pack, and put away.

The only problem with gardening is winter. You can grow your own fresh, wholesome, great-tasting produce until black frost hits. Then—blam!—the garden dies, and until next spring it's back to the supermarket.

There's one way out of this seasonal bind, however: Preserve part of your harvest. Freeze it, can it, dry it, or cellar it—those four techniques allow you to enjoy your back yard's best any time of year. But it's work, as you will discover if you try to freeze, say, five bushels' worth of corn in one day.

Pick, haul, husk, desilk, boil, cool, cut, pack, put away. "Two hours field to freezer!" Go back. Pick, haul, husk, desilk, boil, cool, cut, pack, put away. "Let's get two more bushels." Pick, haul, husk, desilk, boil, cool, cut, pack, put away. Done. Five bushels of fresh corn become 22 quarts of frozen. The time? Five minutes to midnight.

Is it worth it? You bet. Those frozen kernels will taste worlds better than any store-bought fresh, canned or frozen corn.

Freezing

Freezing is far and away the most popular method of home food preservation. According to a recent survey by the National Gardening Association, for example, 42% of American households—37 million families—preserve some produce by freezing. In fact, more people freeze food than grow it.

And with good reason: Freezing does a good job of retaining flavor, texture and nutritional value. It's easy, too. Just blanch, cool, pack, and store away. And the job demands only standard kitchen implements and a supply of freezer bags or boxes.

There is one big drawback, though. It takes a full-sized chest freezer or an upright freezer to store any substantial amount of food. That appliance is expensive, both to purchase and to operate. Worst of all, in the

event of a power blackout, if the electricity is off for more than a day and if you can't find alternate cold storage, the frozen produce may spoil.

Canning

Canning takes second in the preserving popularity contest: 24 million households (27%) put up food in jars. It probably deserves to be only number two. Canned foods don't have the flavor, texture and nutrient value of frozen ones for the simple reason that they must be cooked for so long. Quart jars of green beans, for instance, are processed for 25 minutes at 240°F, while beans destined for the freezer are blanched for a mere three minutes in boiling water!

Canning also takes more time and labor than freezing. It means cleaning and heating special jars and lids; slicing, precooking (usually) and packing all the food; and then processing each run on the stove for a half-hour or more. And the operation has more room for error. If each jar rim isn't cleaned carefully before the lid is screwed on, for example, the processed jar won't seal.

Still, the method has real advantages. There is not much expense for equipment—the most costly item is a pressure cooker. There's also some initial outlay for a water bath canner, canning jars and lids, and a few inexpensive kitchen implements like jar lifters and funnels. But after that, all it takes each year is to buy new lids.

The other advantage canning has over freezing is storage. No power-consuming, shortout-vulnerable, space-tight appliance here—just stack the jars on a shelf!

Drying

Only 4 million households (5%) practice food drying. In terms of texture, flavor and nutrition, drying and canning are about equal. Most dried foods require soaking before being used; as a result, some flavor is lost, and most rehydrated foods must be incorporated into some sort of cooked dish, like a casserole or a stew. However, a few dried foods—mostly fruits such as apples and apricots—are legitimately delicious in their own right.

Drying is slow, too. It takes one to three days to dehydrate most foods, so putting up much produce by this technique becomes pretty time-consuming. Of course, drying foods don't take constant watching. Once the pieces are sliced, possibly blanched or treated or both, and then trayed, they need only to be checked and rotated once or twice a day.

A dryer, either electric or solar, is necessary for volume drying. (Small batches can be dried in the oven or in sunlight.) Those

appliances are relatively expensive but cost little or nothing to operate. And the end product is easy to store: Just keep it in airtight bags in a dark place. And because dried food is so lightweight, it makes great camp and trail fare.

Cellaring

Cellaring—storing fresh food in a cool, dark place—has a lot going for it. The flavor, texture and nutrient value stay intact, since the food isn't processed at all. There's little labor or time involved. Sort and store—that's basically it. And cellaring adds nothing to the electric bill.

So how come only 2 million households (2%) resort to cellaring? Because there's a hitch; actually, two hitches. For one, it helps to have a root cellar—an insulated underground or earth-bermed storage room—and that might cost $1,000 or more to build. However, many root vegetables can be stored in the ground or in buried containers, and other vegetables, such as onions and garlic, can be kept in dry storage.

The other hitch is that only certain foods cellar well—root vegetables, some cabbage family members and a few fruits.

A wise preserver uses a variety of methods, each resulting in a food prepared with an individual touch and with taste that's a lot better than that midwinter fare from the store.

Which Method for Which Food?

Cellaring	Freezing
Apples	Asparagus
Cabbage	Berries
Carrots	Broccoli
Celery	Brussels sprouts
Onions	Cauliflower
Potatoes	Corn
Pumpkin	Green beans
Sweet potatoes	Greens
Turnips	Peaches
Winter squash	Peas
	Rhubarb
Canning	Summer squash
Apples	Sweet peppers
Tomatoes	
Berries	**Drying**
Carrots	Dry beans
Corn	Herbs
Green beans	Hot peppers
Peas	Apples
Peaches	Berries
	Peas

Canning

Before refrigeration, heat and pressure preserved our foods.

There's great satisfaction in storing the fruits of your summer's labor to enjoy in the dark of winter.

Canning is obviously a more involved process than freezing, and it takes more time and equipment. If it's done carefully, however, it's a good, safe way to preserve food. As with freezing, foods fall into acidic and nonacidic categories and require somewhat different processing.

Fruits—as well as tomatoes—are acidic. Since that acidity will kill any heat-resistant bacteria, these foods can be preserved by being processed at 212°F in a boiling water bath. The common water bath canner has room for seven or nine quart jars of food and has a rack to keep them from touching each other or the kettle's bottom.

Vegetables (and meats as well) are low-acid foods, so they must be superheated to 240°F to kill harmful bacteria. To process food at that high a temperature means using a steam pressure canner—a heavy kettle with a steam-tight lid. It will also have a safety valve, a vent and some form of pressure gauge. The canner will build up enough heat and steam at 10 pounds of pressure to reach that bacteria-killing 240°.

There are also two different ways to pack the jars: with the food either hot or cold. *Hot packing* is commonly used with firm food to make it softer so that more of it can be stuffed in the jars. *Raw packing* is better for softer foods, including most vegetables and many fruits. Actually, the choice is rarely crucial: Many foods can be either hot or raw packed.

Canning Precautions

While canning is basically a simple procedure, there are certain precautions that must be followed to avoid accidents and food spoilage. Ever read about "summer sickness" in one of those quaint olden-days cookbooks? We call that *food poisoning* today.

Always use tempered-glass canning jars. (You can *try* using old mayonnaise jars for water bath canning—but *NEVER* use them for pressure canning!) And always use new rubber-sealed lids to ensure a tight seal that will keep out any invading bacteria. Most people today use the two-piece vacuum lids with sealing rings. Use high-quality food with no signs of spoilage. And make sure jarred food is completely covered with liquid,

but leave enough air space (one-half inch for acid foods and one inch for nonacid ones) in the tops of the jars to allow for expansion during processing.

Once the food has been processed and cooled, check to see that the jars have sealed. Vacuum lids curve in—often with a soul-satisfying "pop!"—when they're sealed. Push any lids down that haven't popped in on their own. If they come back up, don't store those jars. Reprocess them, or use their contents soon. Never consume any stored food that has mold, gas, an off-color, cloudiness, suspicious odor or a bad seal. It's not worth the risk. In fact, most canning guides recommend *re*boiling low-acid foods for 15 or 20 minutes before eating them.

Canning Procedures

Check all jars for any nicks or cracks around the rim that could ruin an airtight seal. Discard defective jars. Wash the good ones well, and leave them in hot water until ready to be used. Don't ever expose the jars to sudden drastic temperature changes—for instance, don't put a cold jar of food in a canner filled with boiling water. Simmer the vacuum lids at 180°F.

Wash, peel, core, slice—prepare the food as needed. Precook it if you're going to hot pack it. Then, one by one, fill the jars. A canning funnel is a big help here. Pack the jars tightly, and fill them with water as necessary to cover the food, while leaving the necessary headspace. Use a nonmetallic utensil to force out any air bubbles.

With a clean, damp cloth, carefully wipe the rims clean—any food specks here could interfere with the seal. Then put on the lids, and hand-tighten the screw bands.

Put the jars in the canner. If using a water bath canner, make sure it's filled so the lids are covered by an inch or two of water. Hot-packed jars can be added to boiling water. Cover the kettle, and crank up the heat until you have a nice rolling boil. Start timing the batch, keeping a steady boil going until the required time has passed. Add more boiling water during processing to keep the jars covered, but don't pour it directly on them. Remove the jars as soon as they're done, and set them to cool so they don't touch each other, in a place with no drafts.

If you're using a steam pressure canner, put two to three inches of water in the bottom, add the jars, fasten the cover securely, and heat. Let steam come out the vent for 10 minutes to drive out excess air. Then use your gauge (follow the manufacturer's instructions for your model of canner) to let you know when 10 pounds of pressure has been reached. Start timing, and maintain the pressure until the required time is up. Turn off the heat, and let the canner cool for 10 minutes or more before carefully removing the cover. Set the jars out to cool.

Store the properly processed and sealed jars in a cool, dark, dry place. The space should be cool, because too much heat accelerates decomposition; dark, because light destroys some vitamins and hastens oxidation; and dry, because too much moisture can corrode the seals.

Canning is work, and, unfortunately, you often have to do it during the hottest, garden-busiest days of summer. But the warm, secure feeling that comes from gazing at that pantry full of food-bright jars in midwinter and knowing you and your family have good food to eat come hell or high water—*that* makes it all worthwhile.

Jams, Jellies, Pickles, Sauerkraut

Jams, jellies, fruit butters, conserves, marmalades, preserves, pickles, relishes, sauerkraut—all are made by variations of canning. Actually, jellies and other sweet spreads use so much sugar as preservative that often they do not need to be processed, but can just be poured hot into sterilized jars and sealed (with either canning lids or paraffin). Pickles, relishes and sauerkraut are partially preserved by the salt and vinegar they contain, but do need the water bath canning typically given to acid foods.

Jellies are clear spreads made from strained fruit juices. Pectin and acid are added to the cooked juice to help it gel. Sugar sweetens and preserves it.

Jams are similar to jellies except they use crushed or chopped fruits rather than strained juice.

Butters are slowly cooked fruit pulps.

Conserves are jams with two or more fruits. Often they contain nuts and raisins as well.

Marmalades are soft fruit jellies that contain little pieces of peel or fruit.

Preserves are like jams, but are cooked carefully so that the fruit pieces retain their natural shapes.

Pickles are vegetables either fermented in salt (brined) or packed in vinegar.

Relishes are chopped fruits or vegetables, or both, that are canned in a spicy vinegar solution.

Sauerkraut is chopped, pickled cabbage. It's fermented in salt.

Methods and Times

Food	Method	Hot or Raw Pack	Minutes Processing Time	
			Pints	Quarts
Apples	Water bath	Hot	20	20
Asparagus	Pressure	Raw or hot	25	30
Beets	Pressure	Hot	30	35
Berries	Water bath	Raw	15	20
Carrots	Pressure	Raw or hot	25	30
Cherries	Water bath	Raw	20	25
Corn	Pressure	Raw or hot	55	85
Grapes	Water bath	Raw	15	20
Green beans	Pressure	Raw or hot	20	25
Greens	Pressure	Hot	70	90
Lima beans	Pressure	Raw or hot	40	50
Okra	Pressure	Hot	25	40
Peaches	Water bath	Raw	25	30
Peaches	Water bath	Hot	20	25
Pears	Water bath	Hot	20	25
Peas	Pressure	Raw or hot	40	40
Plums	Water bath	Hot	20	25
Potatoes	Pressure	Hot	30	40
Rhubarb	Water bath	Hot	10	10
Sweet potatoes	Pressure	Hot	65	95
Tomatoes	Water bath	Raw	35	45
Tomatoes	Water bath	Hot	10	15
Turnips	Pressure	Hot	30	35

Family Favorites

The following foods can all be bought in a grocery, of course, but your own home-canned versions will make the difference between "ordinary" and "outstanding!"

Soup Mix

What could be nicer in the middle of winter than reaching into the pantry and pulling out a jar of already-prepared vegetable soup? This recipe makes enough for a full 7-quart canning run with some left over to eat fresh.

5 quarts chopped tomatoes
1 quart sliced okra
1 quart lima beans
2 quarts corn
A few chopped carrots (optional)

Mix and heat the vegetables until they cook down a bit. Pack into quart jars, and process in a pressure canner for 85 minutes (the time required for the slowest-processing ingredient). Store. To serve, reheat, with cooked meat if desired.

Grape Juice

This is absolutely the easiest way to home-can grape juice. Measure two cups of whole stemmed grapes into a hot, clean quart jar, add one cup of sugar (more or less to taste), fill the jar with boiling water, and process for 10 minutes in a boiling water bath.

To serve, strain out the liquid, dilute the concentrate by half with water, and enjoy nearly two quarts of tasty grape juice!

Cider

You know how much better fresh cider tastes than ordinary apple juice, right? This recipe falls right between the two. It doesn't have quite the tang of that freshly squeezed ambrosia, but because it hasn't been boiled, it beats the socks off the pasteurized kind.

Heat a potful of cider (do not boil) until the sediment rises to the top. Skim that off. Pour the hot cider into hot, clean jars. Seal, and process in a water bath canner for 20 minutes at 180°F.

Chunky Applesauce

Any homemade applesauce is a treat, but *chunky* sauce tastes especially good. Peel and core the apples, then cut them into bite-sized chunks. Cook, with a bit of water, until the fruit is partially broken down (do *not* put through a food mill). Pack in clean jars, and process in a hot water bath for 20 minutes.

Ketchup

The difference between homemade ketchup and the purchased product is as great as the difference between summer-grown and winter-bought tomatoes. If you've never tried a home-brewed sauce before, you're in for a pleasant surprise.

48 medium tomatoes
4 sweet peppers, seeded
4 onions
3 tablespoons dry mustard
1/2 teaspoon ground cayenne pepper
3 cups white vinegar
1 1/2 teaspoons whole allspice
1 1/2 teaspoons whole cloves
1 1/2 teaspoons broken stick cinnamon
3 cups sugar or honey
3 tablespoons salt

Mix the vegetables in batches in a blender until puréed. Add the mustard and pepper, and set aside. Pour the vinegar into a nonaluminum pan, tie the allspice, cloves and cinnamon in a cloth, and add them, then simmer this mix gently for 30 minutes. Add the purée, sugar (or honey) and salt. Cook the ketchup carefully in the oven or over low heat until it reaches the consistency you desire. Then pour it into hot, clean canning jars, seal, and process for 10 minutes in a boiling water bath.

Freezing

Probably the
safest, simplest and most
convenient method

A lmost any fruit or vegetable will store well when frozen. It is worth remembering, however, that while freezing sharply reduces aging damage, it does not sterilize food. So frozen produce should be consumed within six months or a year.

Freezer burn and other possible storage damage can be avoided by the use of sound, airtight containers. The two most popular are reusable plastic boxes and plastic freezer bags that can be fitted into cardboard boxes. Each package should be labeled with the name of the food and the freezing date to make it easy to keep track of the food's time in storage.

What happens in the event of a power loss? Food in a half-filled freezer should stay frozen for a day; in a full freezer for two days. In either case, opening the freezer to check will just make things worse. After the critical period, dry ice can be added to the freezer to keep it cold, or, as a final option, the contents can be moved to a locker plant or another freezer that is working.

Food that becomes partially thawed should be safe to refreeze if it still has ice crystals in it or if it has been held at refrigerator temperature for only one or two days. It will lose some quality when refrozen, so it should be consumed as soon as possible.

No matter the process, only the highest quality of unbruised food should be preserved. Overripe or blemished food won't store well. Food should also be washed clean and be cut and trimmed as necessary.

Freezing Vegetables

Most vegetables are low-acid foods, so they need to be *blanched*—boiled briefly—to help kill enzymes, bacteria, molds and yeasts that might otherwise damage them in storage. Green peppers and onions are the exception: When cut up and put in airtight bags, they can be stored straightaway. And broccoli, pumpkin, sweet potatoes and winter squash can be steamed instead of blanched.

To avoid their becoming an overcooked, unappealing product, vegetables should not be boiled any longer than recommended. And they should immediately be cooled— *all* the way through—to completely stop the cooking process. Then they can be drained, packaged, labeled, sealed and stored.

Freezing Fruits

Most fruits are so acidic they don't need blanching. Besides, these soft foods get mushy after even just a few minutes cooking.

So start off by washing them, and peel, trim, pit and slice as needed. Then it's decision time: Should they be packed in sugar syrup, with sugar or without any sugar?

The only drawback to using no sugar at all is that most fruits won't keep as well without sweetener. (Gooseberries, currants, cranberries, rhubarb and figs freeze just fine without sugar.) After all, sugar is a preservative—think of all the jams and jellies it's kept fresh. But you *can* freeze fruits without it—all that's needed after cleaning and preparing the fruit is to pack it in containers, seal them well, label and store them.

Most fruits are packed in a 40% sugar syrup (three cups of sugar to four cups of water). Cover the fruits, and leave an inch of headspace to allow for expansion.

Dry sugaring is a third method. Simply stir an appropriate amount of sugar into the prepared fruit right before packing it. The sugar draws out the water in the fruit and makes for a solid, good-keeping block of food. Also, although most freezing guides recommend specific amounts of sugar (generally, three-fourths cup of sugar per quart of berries), it's best just to sweeten to taste.

If your frozen fruits tend to darken, try mixing in crystalline ascorbic acid (one-fourth to three-fourths teaspoon per quart) before you pack it.

Most fruits are packed in a sugar syrup, but there are other methods that some feel preserve more of the fruit's true flavor.

Blanching Times for Common Vegetables

Vegetable	Minutes
Asparagus	2-4 (depending on size)
Beets	until tender
Broccoli	3 (or steam 5)
Brussels sprouts	2-4 (depending on size)
Carrots	2
Cauliflower	3
Corn	4 (corn on the cob, 7-11, depending on size)
Green beans	3
Greens	2 (3 for collards)
Lima beans	2-4 (depending on size)
Okra	3-4 (depending on size)
Peas	1-1½
Pumpkin	until soft
Summer squash	3
Sweet peppers	0
Winter squash	until soft
Turnips	2

Sugar Amounts for Frozen Fruits

Fruit	Syrup Pack (% sugar)	Dry Sugar Pack (cups per quart)	
Apples	40%	½	2½ cups sugar + 4 cups water = 35% sugar syrup
Apricots	40%	½	
Blackberries	40–50%	¾	
Blueberries	40%	0	3 cups sugar + 4 cups water = 40% sugar syrup
Cherries (sour)	60–65%	¾	
Cherries (sweet)	40%	¾	
Cranberries	50%	0	4¾ cups sugar + 4 cups water = 50% sugar syrup
Currants	50%	¾	
Figs	35%	0	
Gooseberries	50%	0	7 cups sugar + 4 cups water = 60% sugar syrup
Grapes	40%	0	
Peaches	40%	⅔	
Pears	40%	⅔	8¾ cups sugar + 4 cups water = 65% sugar syrup
Plums	40–50%	0	
Raspberries	40%	¾	
Rhubarb	40%	0	
Strawberries	50%	¾	

Family Favorites

Frozen Pesto

Basil's a wonderful herb and easy to grow, but it loses some of its zing when dried. So why not make it into pesto, a tangy green paste that's good with noodles, scrambled eggs, vegetables, Italian dishes and in soups and stews? You can even freeze it in ice cube trays before you store it in containers, so you'll have small portions readily available.

3 cups packed fresh basil leaves
2 big cloves garlic
½ cup piñon nuts, walnuts, almonds or sunflower seeds
¾ cup Parmesan cheese
½ cup olive oil

Blend everything together (you can add more basil if your blender can handle it) and freeze it. A simple process—and a *very* basily result!

Berry Freezer Jam

Sort and wash three cups of ripe, crushed blackberries, raspberries or strawberries. Mix in five cups of sugar, and let stand for 20 minutes. Stir occasionally.

Dissolve one package of powdered pectin in one cup of water. Boil for one minute. Add the solution to the berries, and stir for two minutes.

Pour the jam into canning jars, leaving one-half inch of headspace. Cover, and let stand for 24 hours. If the jam has set, store it in your freezer. (It will spoil if left at room temperature.)

Freezing Green Beans: Step by Step

1. Thoroughly wash tender green beans.
2. Cut the beans into one- or two-inch pieces. (If you prefer, you can French-cut them—slice them lengthwise into long, thin pieces.)
3. Cook the beans in boiling water for three minutes. (If you use a blanching basket, you can easily use the same hot water for subsequent batches.)
4. Plunge the beans into cold water to cool. Once they are thoroughly cooled, drain them.
5. Pack the beans into an airtight container.
6. Seal the container tight. Leave one-half inch of headspace to allow for expansion once they are frozen.

Drying

Getting the water out and leaving the best of the flavor in

Dehydration, humanity's oldest method of preserving food, involves just a few basic principles:
• Moderately high temperatures are used to remove moisture and retard the growth of decay-causing organisms. If food is dried at too *low* a temperature, it will spoil before it dries; too *high* and it will "caseharden"—that is, form a shell on the outside that traps moisture inside.
• Good air circulation helps food dry evenly. Food should be turned and rotated as needed to promote even drying.
• Dried food should be stored in airtight containers and kept dark and cool.

Methods

Sun drying—setting food out in the sun— is the age-old dehydration technique, and it's free. But it takes two to three times longer than using a well-designed dehydrator. Food must be protected from insects and brought in at night to prevent it from spoiling. You can speed sun drying by setting your food trays in a car parked in the sun. Keep a couple of windows cracked to promote air flow.

Oven drying is faster than sun drying, but you need to carefully monitor temperature. Also, it will work better if you leave the oven door cracked—and even have a fan blowing across it—to increase air flow. Oven drying is most convenient if you have a gas stove with a constant pilot light.

Bag drying is the simplest way to dry home-grown herbs. Simply tie the plants together, put them in a paper bag, and hang the bag in a dry place.

Solar drying involves using a homemade or purchased solar dryer. It works faster than sun drying, but unless the unit is really well designed, temperature and air flow can vary extremely.

Electric drying means using an electric food dehydrator. Good ones are expensive but are nevertheless the best devices for serious food drying. They can hold up to 20 pounds of produce at a time, do not burn or spoil the food, dry evenly and quickly, yet don't use a lot of electricity.

If you're just starting out, try some sun or oven drying. And, of course, bag dry your herbs. Then, if you like drying food, move up to a good solar or electric dryer.

Drying Fruits

The main difference between fruit and vegetable drying is the pretreatment. There are several possible ways to pretreat fruits to retard oxidation—including soaking the pieces in various dips or smoking them with sulfur fumes. Most vegetables, however, should receive one pretreatment: blanching. It softens their fibrous tissue, letting water escape more easily while drying and re-enter more rapidly during rehydration.

To dry fruit, select firm, ripe, bruise-free fruits, and wash them in cold water. Slice them into uniform pieces about one-fourth inch thick.

Pretreat them if desired. You might want to soak the pieces for five to 15 minutes in a solution of one tablespoon of sodium bisulfite per gallon of water, though this added liquid will increase drying time. Or you can sulfur the fruit by burning flowers of sulfur in a closed container with the fruit. This is the most effective treatment for retarding oxidation and vitamin loss, but it must be done outdoors—sulfur fumes are poisonous. The food should then be dried outdoors as well. Research has shown no harmful effects from the sulfuring process, which is widely used in commercially dried food.

Set the food, well spaced, on screened trays so air can circulate underneath. The screening should be fiberglass or stainless steel; galvanized screens contaminate food.

Load the dryer. If using a dehydrator, set the temperature at 145°F until most of the moisture is removed, then lower it to 125° to 135°F. Check the food every two or three hours, turning and rotating it if needed. It's done when it feels pliable and leatherlike and contains no moisture pockets.

Let the fruit cool, then store it.

To reconstitute the fruit, steam or boil it for a few minutes until plump, or let it soak in water or fruit juice.

To make your own fruit leather, purée the fruit. You can use overripe fruit for this, and sweeten it if desired. Then spread it out on trays covered with sheets of plastic wrap. After it's dry, roll it up and store it.

Drying Vegetables

Vegetable drying is much the same as fruit drying. You *do* need to blanch vegetables beforehand, however. They are dry when they feel brittle or papery. Storage is crucial because these low-acid foods are more apt to spoil than fruits are. Use sealed plastic bags set inside airtight containers, and put only a small batch of vegetables in each bag. Store them in the coolest part of the house. And check them occasionally during the first few weeks: One still-moist piece can cause an entire batch to mold.

Drying authorities disagree on whether vegetables need to be soaked for rehydrating or should just be cooked up right away. However, soaking for 15 minutes to two hours before cooking produces tenderer vegetables.

Dried fruits are popular snacks, the basis for numerous camping-food mixes and the "raw" material for surprising tarts and pies.

Jams and Jellies

These are two of the easiest, and most satisfactory, methods of preserving spring and summer's abundance.

Almost any fruit can be made into a delicious spread: Jelly is made from fruit juice; jam is prepared from crushed or chopped fruit; preserves contain whole fruit or large chunks; butters are thick fruit purées; conserves are made from two or more fruits and often contain nuts and raisins; and marmalade is soft jelly containing slivers of citrus fruit.

Consulting a good canning guide before preparing any food for open-shelf storage is a must. In general, however, jellies can be cooked and put into sterilized (boiled 15 minutes) jars, which without further processing are then capped with either self-sealing lids or paraffin. It's recommended that jellies prepared in this way be used within six months and that the entire contents of any jar in which mold starts to form be disposed of. Any other preserved fruit should be prepared as indicated in the recipes. Spoon it into clean, dry, hot jars; cap them with self-sealing lids; and process them in a boiling water bath for at least 10 minutes. A pressure canner is not necessary for fruit.

Pectin, either dry or liquid, is added to fruit to help it jell. Follow the directions on the packages as these two types of pectin are not interchangeable. Some fruits, such as apples, contain an ample amount of natural pectin, so adding it is not necessary. (In fact, combining apple juice with other fruits will often supply the needed amount of jelling substance.) You will find that adding pectin reduces the amount of cooking time needed to make fruits jell, and this often results in a tastier, more attractive preserve. While the recipes here call for the standard commercial types of pectin, you may want to experiment with a product generically called low methoxyl pectin, which is made from the inner peels of citrus fruits. When this jelling agent is used as instructed, the amount of sugar or honey used can be decreased considerably. Since sugar acts as a preservative, though, jellies made with reduced amounts must be capped with self-sealing lids, and the jars processed for 10 minutes or more in a boiling water bath.

Some recipes call for honey as a sweetener and others specify sugar. Substituting one for the other is often a matter of taste-testing. As a guideline, try substituting three-fourths cup of honey for one cup of sugar, or vice versa. A recipe using honey may have to be cooked a bit longer, or the liquid decreased slightly, in order for the spread to jell. The amount of sweetener in any recipe should be adjusted according to the sweetness of the fruit and to your own tastes.

Mountain Tomato Jam

$4^1/_2$ pounds tomatoes
$1^1/_2$ cups vinegar
$4^1/_2$ cups sugar
1 tablespoon cinnamon
$^1/_2$ teaspoon allspice
1 teaspoon cloves

Wash the tomatoes thoroughly, and then scald, peel, and quarter them. Put them in a pot to cook, adding the vinegar, sugar and all the spices. Slowly simmer until thickened. Pour into sterilized jars, and seal. Makes 5 pints.

Rhubarb Conserve

3 oranges
1 lemon
10 cups small rhubarb pieces
8 cups sugar
$1^1/_2$ cups seedless raisins
1 cup chopped nuts

Squeeze the juice from the oranges and the lemon, and grind up the rind of 1 orange. Combine the liquid and the peel with the rhubarb, sugar and raisins in a saucepan, and cook slowly, stirring often, till the mixture thickens. Add the nuts, remove from the heat, pour into clean, hot jars, cap with self-sealing lids, and process in a boiling water bath for 10 minutes. Makes 6 pints.

Strawberry Jam

2 quarts ripe strawberries
1 box dry pectin
5 cups honey

Wash, stem, and crush the strawberries to make about $4^1/_2$ cups of fruit. Blend the strawberries and pectin in a saucepan, and bring the mixture to a full boil. Mix in the honey immediately, and boil and stir for 2 minutes. Remove from the heat, and stir for 5 minutes longer. Pour into clean, hot jars; cap, and process in a boiling water bath for 10 minutes. Makes $4^1/_2$ pints.

Red Raspberry Jam

4 cups red raspberries
4 cups sugar
1 cup water

Boil the sugar and water together until the syrup threads. Wash and drain the berries, crush with a masher, and measure. Add them to the syrup, and cook rapidly—while stirring—for about 20 minutes. Place the mixture in sterilized jars. Cool, and seal. Makes about 2 pints.

Blackberry Jam

6 cups blackberries
$^1/_2$ cup water
6 cups sugar
$^1/_4$ cup lemon juice
1 cup orange juice
1 tablespoon grated orange peel

Cook the blackberries in the water until hot. Rub the berries through a sieve, and then add the sugar, lemon and orange juice, and grated peel. Cook over low heat until thick. Seal in hot, sterilized jars. Makes about 36 ounces.

Spicy Blueberry Jam

2 pounds blueberries
$^1/_2$ teaspoon cloves
$^1/_2$ teaspoon cinnamon
$^1/_4$ teaspoon allspice
7 cups sugar
Juice of 1 lemon
1 bottle liquid pectin

Boil the berries with the sugar, spices and lemon juice for 2 minutes. Stir the mixture as needed to prevent it from burning. Remove from the heat, and add the pectin. Skim the jam, pour into sterilized jars, and seal. Makes about 3 pints.

Baking Bread

When we conspire with yeast, we enter into humanity's oldest symbiosis. It is like ranching beneath a microscope, like gardening on a glass slide . . . and is as close to magic as most of us will ever come.

A woman who bakes bread can comfort children with a glance, converse with elms, invent with colors. A man who bakes bread—why, he can gentle animals with a touch, talk to teenagers, look good in his undershirt. Or so we are likely to believe. Such is our reverence for this elemental food that the people who create it seem to tap an ancient communal memory, to possess powers that the rest of us can only dimly imagine.

Staff of Life

Bread pervades our language and literature, a metaphor for physical and spiritual sustenance. We petition for our daily bread, live not by bread alone, break bread together. (The word *companion* derives from the Latin *companio*, "one who shares bread.") The satirist Juvenal lamented that his fellow Romans cared only for "bread and circuses," a concern we still share: A modern man who is short of bread could use a little dough to see him through.

And substance preceded the image. Ten thousand years ago, the domestication of wild grasses made the domestication of humanity possible. Freed from the necessity to roam constantly in search of food, humans could settle down and invent civilization. Heroic images of fur-clad, spear-wielding hunters notwithstanding, we soon fed ourselves primarily on grains.

Before bread, grain was dried on hot rocks or boiled into a paste or gruel. By the late Stone Age, flat breads were common. (Remnants endure: Mexican tortillas, Chinese pancakes, Indian chapaties.) The Egyptians began making leavened bread about 4000 B.C., probably when a neglected gruel, contaminated by wild airborne yeasts, fermented and rose. With characteristic virtuosity, the Greeks became master bakers who served up 62 varieties.

Both Greeks and Romans preferred white bread, the food of the upper classes; slaves and servants ate the dark. Since extra labor was required to refine dark flour into light, it was more expensive and thus a mark of status. Europe followed the classic tradition. For centuries, coarse, hard rye bread was the daily fare of peasants—often secondhand, at that. The masters ate their dinners served up on rock-hard slabs of bread, called trenchers. When they'd eaten their meat and gravy, they fed the sopping trenchers to the servants and the dogs.

Dark bread continued to get bad press until the Reverend Sylvester Graham, nineteenth-century reformer and grump, began a campaign to popularize whole grains. They were healthy, he nagged; they alleviated a wide range of digestive problems. Besides, milling the bran and germ from the flour was tantamount to "putting asunder what God has joined together." (Whole-wheat flour is often called graham flour, in the reverend's honor; graham crackers are another namesake.) With the publication in 1974—a mere 100 years later—of an article in the *Journal of the American Medical Association*, touting the benefits of dietary fiber, the respectability of whole-grain bread was assured.

During the Industrial Revolution, baking bread became less of a private enterprise and more of a commercial one. Even so, packaged bread was not plentiful in grocery stores until 1930; and until the beginning of World War II, 50% of the baked goods consumed were produced at home. Now 95% are store-bought.

In the 1970s and 1980s homemade bread has enjoyed a minor renaissance. Lured by an honest, unadulterated loaf, by the fragrance and taste of perfectly fresh bread, by the sensuous pleasure of working the dough, by the pride of accomplishment, by participation in an art as old as humanity itself—more and more of us are doing it ourselves.

Basic Bread

The simplest loaf contains just flour, water, yeast and salt. Almost always, the flour is made from wheat (Fig. 1). Alone among cereals, wheat contains substantial amounts of gluten—long, sprawling molecules of protein that, with the addition of water and handling, mesh into an elastic network that can stretch and expand, permitting the loaf to rise. Other grains—rye, oats, corn, millet—may be added for flavor, texture and nutrients. But if we are to have leavened bread, we must have wheat. (Rye has only traces of gluten; used alone, it will produce a loaf hard enough to break a peasant's tooth. Other grains have none. Bioengineers hope to be able to transfer gluten's genetic codes into corn, millet and sorghum, a development that would revolutionize bread making.)

Yeasts are fungi, one-celled plants—160 species of them. The *Saccharomyces cerevisiae* are particularly useful to brewers and bakers. In an anaerobic environment like bread dough, they metabolize starches and sugars, giving off carbon dioxide and alcohol as by-products. As the bubbles of CO_2 increase and expand, they stretch the gluten, and the loaf rises.

Since the Pharaohs, bakers have transformed flour and yeast into bread by the same ritual. 1) *Making the dough*. All the ingredients (except part of the flour) are combined and beaten, by hand or (these days) by machine, to mix the dough and start developing the gluten. 2) *Kneading*. Pummeling the dough, stretching and folding it, disperses the yeast, develops the gluten and evaporates the alcohol. At this stage, the remaining flour is worked into the dough. 3) *Rising.* While the dough sits in a warm place, the yeast multiplies and produces carbon dioxide, and the dough rises. Then it's deflated and allowed to rise either once or twice more. 4) *Baking.* In a hot oven, the yeast dies and the elastic gluten solidifies, now able to support all other ingredients—the character of which will govern the taste and texture of the bread.

Ingredients

Flour. Three principal types of wheat dominate the 600 million acres planted in the crop worldwide. *Hard* wheat has a hard kernel and ample protein, including gluten. It is made into bread flour. *Soft* wheat, with little gluten, is milled into pastry and cake flours (pastries are toughened and ruined by gluten). *Durum* wheat is so hard that it isn't even good for bread, which must have some elasticity; it becomes pasta.

Whole-wheat flour contains the entire ground-up kernel (Fig. 2): the germ or embryo, rich in oil, vitamins and minerals; the endosperm, or main body of the kernel, filled with starch and protein (including the gluten); and the bran, or hard seed coat. Compared to white flour, which contains only the endosperm—the germ and bran are milled out and sold separately—whole-wheat is rich in flavor, fiber, nutrients and fat. Alas, fat turns rancid quickly. While white flour is virtually imperishable, whole-wheat keeps only about a month at room temperature, or two under refrigeration, before it starts to become bitter. It pays to check the expiration date on supermarket packages, or to question the shopkeeper when buying from bulk bins. The unused portion should be wrapped in an airtight package and stored in the refrigerator.

Because whole-wheat flour contains heavy, solid particles of bran and germ, it may produce a dense loaf. Thus, many recipes for "whole-wheat" bread call for a portion of white flour, some additional yeast or an extra rising.

Whole-wheat pastry flour is milled from whole kernels of soft wheat. With too little gluten for bread, it makes crisp, light biscuits and pastries.

The market supports a greater variety of white flour, since most bread, whether commercial or homemade, is light. By law, white flour must be enriched with niacin, thiamine and riboflavin (the B vitamins that got milled out with the germ).

Bread flour is made from hard wheat, rich in protein and gluten; it makes a high, light loaf. Some brands are treated with ascorbic acid (vitamin C) or potassium bromate, to

make the gluten more elastic and more resistant to overworking by heavy commerical machinery. Overkneading dough—which leads to the collapse of the gluten and the failure of the loaf—is rarely a problem for hand kneaders, who give out long before the gluten does. Food processors, however, can overwork dough in a heartbeat.

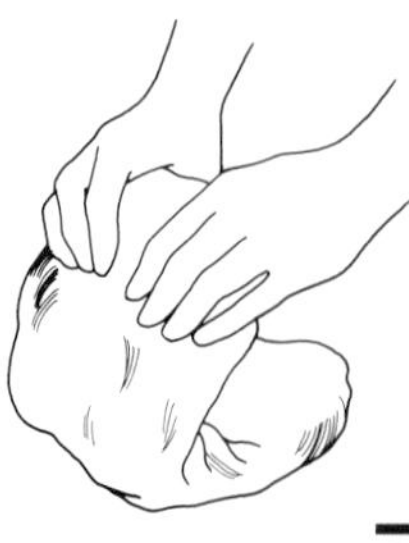

All-purpose flour is a blend of high-gluten hard wheats and low-gluten soft ones, produced by large mills to satisfy a wide range of baking needs, from pastries to breads. Like most compromises, it does everything adequately and nothing superbly. The *unbleached* variey works well.

Pastry flour is too gluten-poor for bread.

Yeast. the most common yeast on the market—and the one used in all recipes here—is active dry yeast, universally available in small foil packets of one-fourth ounce each. Alive but dormant, it has been dehydrated and becomes active when dissolved in warm liquid. Freshness is vital; yeast that's past its pull date is a license to fail.

Fat. Butter, margarine, shortening, oil, lard—in small amounts, all add volume (by lubricating the gluten, making it more elastic), tenderness, flavor, moistness and richness. Too little fat will produce a dry, coarse loaf; too much, an oily, crumbly one.

Salt. Saltless bread tastes bland and flat. Although too much damages the yeast and produces a heavy loaf, a little improves the flavor, strengthens the gluten and regulates fermentation.

Sugar. Sweetening in its various forms (sugar, honey, molasses, maple syrup) contributes flavor, tenderness, moisture and a rich brown crust. It also delays staling. In small amounts, sugar increases the activity of yeast, so it's usually dissolved with the yeast in warm water. But too much upsets the water balance in the yeast cells, at which point fermentation declines sharply. That's why recipes for sweet doughs often call for extra yeast (and why it's a bad idea to add more sugar to the dissolving yeast than the directions suggest). Except in very sweet doughs, the choice of sweetener doesn't affect the flavor.

Liquid. Although water is the most common liquid, others can be substituted—everything from fruit or vegetable juices to broth or beer. Obviously, flavor varies. Milk makes the texture softer, delays staling and creates a rich brown crust.

Et cetera. Fruits, nuts, seeds, cheese, vegetables, cornmeal, oats, wheat germ—the list goes on for flavor, character and fun.

Equipment

Assuming a kitchen stocked with the usual measuring cups and mixing bowls,

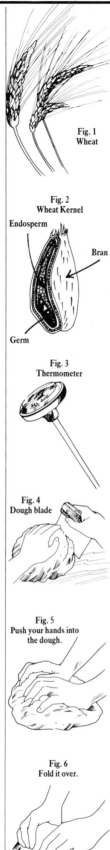

Fig. 1
Wheat

Fig. 2
Wheat Kernel

Endosperm

Bran

Germ

Fig. 3
Thermometer

Fig. 4
Dough blade

Fig. 5
Push your hands into the dough.

Fig. 6
Fold it over.

Fig. 7
Well-kneaded dough

Fig. 8
Check the risen dough.

Fig. 9
Punch it down.

Fig. 10
Fold the long edges to the middle.

Fig. 11
Fold the oval in half.

Fig. 12
A free-form loaf.

Fig. 13
Slashing

only a few extra tools are required.

Thermometer. Like other living organisms, yeast cares about temperature: too cool, and it will remain dormant; too hot, and it will die. The most useful thermometer is an instant-response one with a metal spike and a gauge that measures from freezing to boiling (Fig. 3). With it you can check the liquid you add to the yeast and the place where the dough rises.

Dough blade. Also called a dough scraper or cutter, this handy tool is a rectangular piece of steel (about 4″ X 5″) with a wooden handle (Fig. 4). It is useful for kneading dough in the early, sticky stages, for dividing it and for scraping off the kneading surface afterward.

Pans. Bread bakes well in a variety of materials. Most widely recommended are dark metal loaf pans, which absorb heat readily and produce a uniformly brown crust. Shiny metal pans reflect heat and produce pale sides and bottoms. (If the baked loaf is re-

Since the Pharaohs, bakers have transformed flour and yeast into bread by the same ritual—making, kneading, rising and baking the dough.

moved from the pan and returned to the oven for five or 10 minutes, the crust will brown up nicely.) Glass baking pans also work well; lower the heat by 25°F when using them. Recipes are most apt to call for loaf pans that measure 8″ X 4″ (medium) or 9″ X 5″ (large). You'll also need a baking sheet for round peasant loaves.

Oven thermometer. Equally certain are death, taxes and an inaccurate oven thermostat. Considering the odds, a good oven thermometer is a sound investment, so that you end up with neither a cinder nor a semibaked lump of dough.

Techniques

Because of yeast's sensitivity to temperature, all ingredients need to be at room temperature (except, of course, the liquid for dissolving the yeast, which should be warmer). If your whole-wheat flour is stored in the refrigerator, take it out in time to warm up; if you've melted butter, let it cool. **Making the dough.** Although details vary, there are three general methods of adding the yeast to the other ingredients. Directions vary from cookbook to cookbook and, frequently, from recipe to recipe.

Method 1. Dissolve the yeast in warm (105° to 115°F) water with a small amount of sugar, then add the other ingredients. Older recipes direct you to let the dissolved yeast sit for five to 10 minutes, until it becomes frothy—a means of "proofing" the yeast, or making certain that it's still alive. These days, when yeast is virtually always reliable, this delay is simply unnecessary, unless the pull date has expired or you have some other reason to question the yeast's viability.

Method 2. Mix the yeast with some of the flour and the other dry ingredients; add hot (120° to 130°F) liquid to form a batter, then add other ingredients.

Method 3. Make a sponge: Combine the yeast, half the flour and other ingredients (except fat and eggs), and let it all ferment for several hours or overnight. Then add the rest of the flour and any other ingredients to form the dough.

Regardless of the method, it is vital to check the temperature of the liquid before you add it to the yeast. Once yeast is heat-killed, nothing will resurrect it.

Kneading

Kneading is like dancing: As long as you've got the rhythm, there's lots of room for individual moves.

Do find a work surface that's the right height. You should be able to extend your arms downward with palms resting flat on the surface. Unless you're tall, a kitchen counter is too high; you won't get full power from your arms. Too low a worktable will break your back. Sprinkle the surface lightly with flour, dump the dough onto it, dust your hands lightly with flour, and get it on.

Form the dough into a rough ball. Using the heels of your hands, push into the dough, moving it down and away, stretching and flattening it (Fig. 5). Then lift the back end and bring it forward, folding the dough in half (Fig. 6). Give it a quarter turn, and push it out again. Push, fold, turn—the elements of kneading.

As you knead, add sprinkles of flour as necessary, to make the dough workable. Try not to overdo it; the dough will become less sticky as you work it, and too much flour will produce a dry, heavy loaf. It's impossible to specify how much extra flour should be kneaded in, so recipes give a range. Flours absorb varying amounts of water, depending on what type they are, what crop they came from, how they've been stored and whether the day is humid or dry.

At first, when the dough is especially sticky, try for a fairly light touch, so your hand doesn't become stuck. In these early stages, a dough blade is helpful; use it to lift, fold and turn the dough. As the mass begins to firm up, your strokes can become more aggressive.

Kneading isn't a delicate operation; put your whole body into it. Some apparently rational experts even suggest that you periodically lift up the ball of dough and slam it down on the table, insisting that it will do the dough (and you) a world of good.

When can you stop? The standard estimate is 10 minutes to knead one loaf, but time varies with the flour, the weather and the energy of the baker. Most cooks judge by look and feel. Well-kneaded dough loses its stickiness (whole-wheat stays tackier) and becomes smooth and shiny. Small blisters sometimes appear on the surface, especially on white dough. Most important, the dough (like the gluten) becomes elastic: It can be stretched into a thin sheet without tearing (Fig. 7). As you knead, it begins to resist your advances; when you push into it, it springs back.

The Dough Also Rises

During rising, the yeast does the work. The only thing you have to provide is the right environment for the yeast to multiply and metabolize.

Lightly grease a large mixing bowl—large enough to allow the dough to double in size. Round the dough into a ball; place it in the bowl, and turn it once (to grease the surface lightly so that it doesn't form a crust); cover the bowl with plastic wrap, a platter or a damp towel; and set it in a good rising place: free of drafts (which will make the dough rise slowly and unevenly), with a temperature of about 80°F. Slightly cooler will slow the rising; slightly warmer will speed it up. Just try to stay in the 80° range. (Whip out your trusty thermometer.)

Good rising places range from the ordinary to the whimsical. Some cooks put their dough in a gas oven; with the door closed, the pilot light supplies just the right warmth. (Make sure to test your oven; many are far too hot.) Others turn their electric oven to 200°F for one minute, turn it off, then insert the dough. A few place it atop a refrigerator or water heater or on a washer or dryer that's been used recently. Some set it on a heating pad; a few lay it on a water bed. (Where does your cat nap? It's probably a warm, draft-free place.)

Normally, dough rises until it doubles in bulk, which takes about an hour. To test whether it's ready, poke two half-inch-deep holes in it with your fingers (Fig. 8). If the holes start to fill in, more time is needed. If the indentations remain and the dough feels spongy, your time is up.

Now punch the dough down (Fig. 9): Double up your fist and push it into the center of the dough (gently or viciously, as your conscience dictates). The dough will collapse as the gas sighs out. Knead for a minute or two to force out the rest.

Most recipes direct you to shape the dough into a loaf and put it in the pan for the final rising (or "proof"). Some call for a second rising in the bowl before the proof (a total of three risings). Whatever the recipe says, you can always opt for that additional rising. There's plenty of life in the old fungus yet, and the texture will become finer with each rising. Since there is more yeast to do the work, second and third risings take half to two-thirds as long.

Once you decide to let well enough alone, the dough needs to rest for two or three minutes so the gluten can relax. Then shape the loaf—a process as individual as the bakers who do it. You can simply pat the dough into a roughly loaflike shape and place it in the pan. Or roll it flat with a rolling pin and then roll it up like a jellyroll. You might pat the dough into an oval, fold each of the long edges into the middle, then fold up the ends (Fig. 10). A simple method is to fold the oval in half (Fig. 11), pinch the seam tightly to seal it, tuck the ends under, and place it, seam side down, in the pan. For a freeform peasant loaf, just shape the dough into a round, flatten it slightly on top, and set it aside to proof (Fig. 12).

The dough is now ready for its final rising. Set it in the same kind of place where it rose before, until it doubles in bulk. (Try to select your pans so that the kneaded dough doesn't fill them more than two-thirds full; otherwise, it's likely to rise more than an inch above the pans—the desirable height.) If your loaf has risen particularly well and looks as if it's bursting at the seams, make a few slashes across the top with a very sharp knife or razor blade (Fig. 13). If the loaf continues rising in the oven—a phenomenon known as oven spring, a baker's joy that occurs when everything has gone absolutely right—the slashes will allow the loaf to expand without tearing.

Baking

First, try not to open the oven door for at least 15 to 20 minutes; you can instantly lose as much as 25% of the heat. Second, rely on your own on-site evaluation of whether the bread is actually done.

The top crust should be golden brown.

Speeding It Up

Although the actual work of bread making is relatively brief, the risings and baking keep you in or around the house for three hours or more. With occasional help from modern technology, it doesn't have to take that long.

1. Food processor. A food processor doesn't provide much in the way of sensuous pleasure, but it's fast. Instead of a minimum of 10 minutes for hand kneading, the machine takes about 45 to 60 *seconds*.

While machines vary (consult the owner's manual), the general pattern is this: Dissolve the yeast in warm water. Place the dry ingredients in the work bowl, and pulse to blend. Add dissolved yeast; then with machine running, add other liquid ingredients slowly until the dough forms a solid mass. Process 45 to 60 seconds more.

2. Fast-acting yeast. Recently, genetic engineers have developed new strains of yeast that cut the rising time in half (Fleishmann's RapidRise and Red Star's Quick-Rise). Since the risings are the most time-consuming part of the bread-making process, the savings are significant.

3. Microwave. Few people would find bread baked in a microwave acceptable; the dough forms no crust, and it comes out of the oven the same color as when it went in. But some long-time bakers use these ovens to raise their bread, thus reducing rising time by two-thirds. Consult your manual, but here's how it generally works:

Microwave three cups of water in a one-quart measure until it's steaming hot. Cover the bowl of dough with a towel, and put it in the oven next to the water. Microwave at 10% power (the lowest possible setting) for 18 to 20 minutes. Check the risen dough in the usual way.

When this technique fails, it's usually because the oven can't maintain a low enough power. If the microwave can't be set at 10%—if, for example, it registers only low, medium or high—forget it. You'll end up with an unrisen, semibaked blob.

Among both expert bakers and devoted eaters, evaluations of these techniques vary widely. Some argue that all three compromise flavor, texture and keeping quality; others maintain that the final loaf is every bit as good as a traditional one. Considering the time savings involved, it's probably worth your while to find out what you think.

Now check the bottom: With oven mitts on, turn the loaf out into one of your hands. When it slides out easily, that's a good sign; as bread cooks, it shrinks away from the sides of the pan. Tap the bottom crust with a fingernail; the loaf should sound hollow. A dull, liquid thud says you're holding uncooked dough. Squeeze the sides. If the bread bounces back, it's probably done. If it retains the impressions of your fingers, it's probably not. If your loaf fails these tests, return it to the pan and the pan to the oven for five minutes, then check again. Cool the finished loaf on a wire rack; on a solid surface, escaping steam will condense and produce a soggy bottom.

A really silly piece of advice: Don't slice the bread until it's completely cool—that is, for two or three hours. OK, at least wait 30 minutes, if you can, and resign yourself to a soggy texture even then. (It will improve in a couple of hours.) A still-warm loaf doesn't cut so much as it tears—a minuscule consideration when compared to the allure of fresh, warm bread. Whenever you eat it, don't wrap the remainder in any air-tight way until it's completely cool; otherwise, the steam will soften the loaf and encourage mold.

Recipes

If you master these recipes, you'll be able to bake almost any kind of bread.

Whole-Wheat Batter Bread

Batter breads involve no kneading; the gluten is activated solely by beating. Thus, their texture is open and coarse. Their flavor, however, can be the stuff that memories are made of.

1 package active dry yeast
1¼ cups warm water (105°-115°F)
2 tablespoons honey
2 tablespoons butter or margarine, melted and cooled to room temperature
1 teaspoon salt
1½ cups white flour
1½ cups whole-wheat flour

In large mixing bowl, add yeast to water and stir to dissolve. Add honey, and stir until dissolved. Add butter or margarine, salt, white flour and ½ cup whole-wheat flour. With electric mixer, beat on low speed until blended. Then beat at high speed 1 minute. Scrape bowl; beat 1 minute more. Stir in remaining flour with wooden spoons. Cover and let rise until doubled in bulk, about 45 minutes.

Grease an 8″ X 4″ loaf pan. Deflate batter by stirring 30 strokes with a wooden spoon. Spoon batter into pan. Cover and let rise 30–40 minutes, or until batter rises just to rim of pan (not above the rim, for batter breads). Bake in preheated 375°F oven for 40 minutes, or until done. Cool on wire rack. Makes 1 loaf.

Basic White Bread

1 package dry yeast
1 teaspoon sugar
¼ cup warm water (105°-115°F)
3 tablespoons sugar
1 tablespoon salt
1¾ cups milk, room temperature
3 tablespoons butter, melted
6–6½ cups unbleached or bread flour

In large mixing bowl, stir yeast and 1 teaspoon sugar into water until dissolved. Add remaining sugar, salt, milk, butter and 1½ cups flour. Beat on medium speed with electric mixer 2 minutes, or 200 strokes by hand. Stir in enough remaining flour to make a workable dough, adding flour by quarter cupfuls toward the end. Turn dough out onto lightly floured surface, and knead 10 minutes, or until smooth and elastic. Place in greased bowl, turning once to coat. Cover and let rise in warm, draft-free place until doubled in bulk, about 1 hour. Punch down, knead 2 or 3 minutes, and divide in half. Let dough rest 2 or 3 minutes, then shape into loaves and place in 2 greased 8″ X 4″ loaf pans. Let rise until doubled in bulk, about 45 minutes to an hour. Bake in a preheated 375° oven 35–40 minutes, or until done. Makes 2 loaves.

Honey Grain Bread

2 packages dry yeast
½ cup warm water (105°-115°F)
¼ cup honey
¼ cup brown sugar, firmly packed
1¾ cups milk, room temperature
¼ cup butter, melted
1 tablespoon salt
1½ cups rye flour
2½ cups unbleached or bread flour
2½–3 cups whole-wheat flour
½ cup raisins

In large mixing bowl, stir yeast into water until dissolved. Stir in honey, brown sugar, milk, butter, salt, 1 cup rye flour, 1 cup white flour and 1 cup whole-wheat flour. Beat at medium speed with an electric mixer 2 minutes, or 200 strokes by hand. Stir in raisins, remaining rye flour, remaining white flour and enough whole-wheat flour to make a workable dough. Turn out onto lightly floured surface. Knead 10–15 minutes, or until smooth and elastic. Place in greased bowl, turning to coat. Cover, and let rise in warm, draft-free place until doubled in bulk, about 1½ hours. Punch down, and knead for 2 or 3 minutes. Divide in half, and let rest for 2 or 3 minutes. Shape into round loaves, and place on a large baking sheet that has been greased and sprinkled with cornmeal. Let rise until doubled in bulk, about 1 hour. Bake in preheated 375°F oven 35–40 minutes, or until done. Cool on racks. Makes 2 large loaves.

Butter

It may just be fat by another name, but you can't beat it on homemade bread.

Forget about buying an expensive cream separator or butter churn. Forget anything anyone ever told you about butter being hard to make. Because if you want to produce your own flavorful, creamy "high-priced spread" from fresh cow's milk, you can do it—quickly, easily and without any expensive equipment—in just four easy steps. Here's how:

Skim (and Ripen) the Cream

Start by pouring one gallon of milk (fresh from the cow) into a clean container. Chill the milk quickly, and keep it in the refrigerator for at least 12 hours. Then skim the cream off the top of the fluid with a spoon. When watery, bluish-colored skim milk appears in the spoon, stop skimming.

Next pour the cream into a jar, cap the container tightly, and let it sit at room temperature for approximately 12 hours, or until the cream is about 75°F and smells slightly sour. This is called *ripening* the cream and develops its acid content. (Only ripened cream will produce butter with a good "butter flavor.") Experience will teach you when your cream smells too sour (or too ripe) and when it's just perfect.

Shake It Up

For this step, it's imperative that you use a jar that is only one-third full. (If you need to pour your cream into a larger container at this point, do so.) The "empty" two-thirds of the jar allows the cream to expand as you shake it and also allows the thick fluid to splash against the walls of the container more violently when the jar is shaken. (This splashing—technically known as *concussion*—is what turns cream into butter.)

Now sit down in your favorite chair, and start shaking the one-third-full jar of ripened cream, keeping in mind that concussion is what makes the butter form. Practice agitating the jar so that a heavy impact occurs between the cream and the walls of the container.

The length of time you'll have to shake the liquid before you'll begin to see butter depends on a) the cream's temperature, b) the enthusiasm with which you agitate the jar and c) the amount of cream in the container. Hence, it's better to *look* for butter rather than to try to make it "by the clock." (In case you're wondering, though, you'll probably have to continue shaking for 15 to 30 minutes.) What do you look for? Just before you get butter, you'll notice that the churned cream is becoming "heavy." Then you'll begin to see a definite separation between the buttermilk and a heavy mass of butter.

At this point, you don't really have butter yet, but you're very close, so keep right on shaking the jar, but with somewhat less vigor. Within seconds, the heavy mass will turn yellow, become firm and separate from the milk. Do not shake the jar much beyond the point where the butter has formed into slightly firm granules. Too much concussion will make the finished spread "hard."

Rinse the Butter

Return to the kitchen now, and strain the butter from the buttermilk with the aid of a colander. (And save that delicious buttermilk!) Then rinse the solids thoroughly with cold water. (Warm water will make the butter soft; the warmer, the softer.) Your butter should now be crumbly.

Water Out and Salt In

Next, put the butter in a bowl. (The size of the bowl will depend, of course, on how much butter you have.) With very clean hands, work the butter around the sides of the bowl, tipping it to one side to let all the water run out.

After you've worked the water out of the butter, and the mass has become fairly firm, sprinkle some salt over it (try about a half teaspoon of salt per half pound of butter). Work the salt in, turn the butter over, and work it in some more. Taste the butter, and—if necessary—add more salt.

All that's left now is to put your lusciously creamy homemade spread into a covered container, place the marvelous buttermilk in a capped jar or bottle, and store both containers in the refrigerator until needed.

Time was, butter churning was a regular (and not eagerly anticipated) chore. These days the experience can be a rewarding novelty.

Cheese Making

The conversion of milk to delicious solid foods is a very human miracle.

Their story began when they purchased several milk goats, each of which produced a generous gallon a day. At first Robert and Ricki Carroll of Ashfield, Massachusetts, tried drinking the milk as quickly as their does manufactured it. Couldn't be done. Next, they tried their hand at making yogurt. But, as with milk, one can consume only so much yogurt before it spoils—so their chickens inherited the surplus. *That* was when they decided to try making cheese.

For their premier attempt, they employed a homemade bricks-and-orange-juice-cans press in an effort to turn out a few pounds of feta, a brine-cured goat's-milk cheese of Greek origin. The homespun press got the job done, but only barely, and it soon became apparent that if they were to continue pursuing their new hobby-of-necessity, they would have to purchase some specialized equipment.

After drawing a blank in their initial search for a domestic cheese-making supplies house, they wrote to the embassies of just about every country in the world that might produce small-scale cheese-making equipment. During the course of that search, they opened a correspondence with the Wheeler family, who, from their farm in the south of England, produce and market a beautiful, handcrafted cheese press. Eventually, the Carrolls made a pilgrimage to the Wheeler farm.

During their stay, Mrs. Wheeler thoroughly indoctrinated them in the craft of cheese making, giving special attention to the hard English varieties. One evening she served a tasty homemade Cheddar she called "Lilly cheese." The Carrolls assumed it was a variety peculiar to that locale until Mrs. Wheeler took them to the barn after dinner and introduced them to Lilly, her Jersey cow. Cheese flavors can be that specific.

Upon returning home from England, the Carrolls purchased their own Jersey milk cow, Nelly, who turned out to be good company for the goats and provided ample amounts of raw material for making a greater variety of cheeses.

Through trial and error, the Carrolls eventually perfected recipes for making a number of delicious cheeses at home—with a minimum of hassles and at the lowest possible cost—finally founding the New England Cheesemaking Supply Company as a result. What follows is the essence of their cheese-making craft, as they acquired it over the years.

Milk Requirements

Any milk used for cheese making must be fresh and of the highest quality. It shouldn't be mastitic, that is, drawn from an animal with inflamed udders; nor should it contain the residues of antibiotics, pesticides, herbicides or sanitizers.

Do you own a dairy goat or cow? If so, special precautions are in order; raw milk contains a variety of natural bacteria. Consequently, if you intend to make a raw-milk cheese that's aged less than 60 days, you must be absolutely certain that the milk contains no pathogens: disease-causing organisms. Because of the high acid content of raw-milk cheeses, varieties that are aged *more* than 60 days are generally free of pathogens. If there's any doubt as to the quality of your raw milk, it should be pasteurized before use.

Pasteurization is a process in which the raw milk is heated in a double boiler or in a home pasteurizer to 163°F, kept at this temperature for 30 seconds, then cooled as quickly as possible to below 40°F. The pasteurized milk should then be refrigerated until you're ready for cheese making.

But don't depend entirely on pasteurization to provide you with wholesome milk. Rather, begin taking precautions at milking time by maintaining strictly sanitary conditions. Be especially careful to avoid gross contamination. If a cow or goat should put a foot in the milk pail, for instance, the entire bucket would become contaminated. In such an event, if you can't afford to dump the contaminated milk, strain it through a milk filter, and *then* pasteurize it.

Milk should be collected only in containers that can be easily cleaned and sterilized. Stainless steel is best, though enameled and glass containers are satisfactory. Avoid using cast-iron or aluminum pails, since they're difficult to clean and can introduce metallic salts into the milk.

If you purchase your milk from a store, attempt to find an unhomogenized brand. The process of homogenization breaks down milk's butterfat, which prevents the cream from rising to the top, thereby rendering it useless for making hard cheeses—the homogenized fat globules are too small to produce a proper curd. Homogenized milk *can* be used, however, for making soft cheeses.

Getting A-culture-ated

Cheese making requires the efforts of *two* dairy animals—the cow or goat from which the milk is drawn, and a microscopic bacterium that lives in milk, consumes milk sugar (lactose) and produces the lactic acid that enhances flavor and gives cheese its natural resistance to spoilage. Today, these specialized bacteria are bred in dairy labs and marketed in freeze-dried packets.

The two main types of cheese-starter cultures are thermophilic and mesophilic.

Thermophilic, from the Greek, means a lover of heat. It follows, then, that a thermophilic starter culture is used in making cheeses that are processed at high temperatures—ranging from 105° to 132°F. This includes the Swiss cheeses, plus such Italian varieties as mozzarella, Parmesan, Romano and several others.

Mesophilic refers to a lover of moderate temperatures. Mesophilic dairy bacteria thrive in temperatures ranging from 70° to 104°F, and are used in making such hard and semihard cheeses as Cheddar, Colby, blue, Muenster and others.

The majority of cheeses made at home use mesophilic starters. Fortunately, the process of culturing this variety of bacteria is no more complicated than making yogurt.

To prepare a mesophilic starter culture, you'll need a half-gallon canning jar with a lid or two one-quart jars with lids. Sterilize both the container and its cap by immersing them in boiling water for at least five minutes. After removing the jar from the sterilizing bath and allowing it to cool, begin the culturing process by filling it to within half an inch of the top with skim milk—mesophilic bacteria don't need cream in order to survive and prosper. Now screw the lid tightly onto the jar, and lower the container into a pot of water that's deep enough to cover the top of the jar by at least a quarter of an inch. Place the uncovered pot on a stove-top burner, and bring it to a slow boil (Fig. 1). After 30 minutes, remove the jar from the boiling water, and allow it to cool to room temperature, which may take several hours.

Heat-treating the milk in this fashion kills any harmful living organisms and provides a hospitable environment for the starter-culture bacteria.

When the milk has cooled to room temperature (72°F is perfect, but don't risk contaminating the milk at this point by dipping

In terms of taste, texture and aroma, few foods can excite the senses as can a fine cheese.

in a thermometer), add a packet of starter culture: Remove the lid from the jar, pour in the powdered bacteria, then quickly replace the lid (Fig. 2). After swirling the jar around a bit to dissolve the powder, store the milk in a spot where it will remain at or near room temperature. After 15 to 24 hours, the bacteria will have created so much acid that the milk protein and butterfat will have coagulated into a semisolid curd, thickening the milk to a yogurtlike consistency.

Once the starter culture has coagulated, refrigerate it immediately, and use it within a week, or pour it into sterilized ice cube trays, and freeze it in the coldest part of your freezer. Later, you can remove the cubes from the trays, place them in heavy, airtight plastic bags, and return the bags to the freezer. A starter culture can be kept for 30 to 60 days this way, with the cubes providing convenient one-ounce portions of culture that can be thawed for use in cheese making, or—sourdoughlike—employed to start *another* culture. One cube of frozen dairy culture equals one packet of powdered starter.

The Rundown on Rennet

Whole milk consists mostly of water, with smaller proportions of sugar, protein, butterfat and minerals. One of the primary goals of the cheese-making process is to *remove* much of that water, thereby concentrating the protein and butterfat into a delicious, easily preserved form.

To do this, cheese makers employ *rennet.* Rennet was discovered in prehistoric times, when glass and plastic jugs weren't nearly as easy to come by as they are today. Back then, the best milk containers people could come up with were animal stomachs. Just about any old stomach would do. But, as people soon discovered, if fresh milk was stored in the stomach of a *young mammal* for any length of time, strange things began to happen; the milk separated into a white curd and a greenish watery liquid. This discovery was to cheese making what the invention of the

wheel was to transportation.

Modern science has developed a method for extracting *rennin,* the active enzyme from calf stomachs, which is then refined and marketed in liquid and tablet form. If liquid rennet is protected from direct sunlight and kept refrigerated but not allowed to freeze, it will remain effective for up to a year. Rennet *tablets,* if stored in a cool place, including the refrigerator or freezer, will hold their strength for *several* years. Furthermore, if you're a vegetarian, you'll be happy to know about vegetable rennet, which also comes in liquid and tablet forms and has about the same strength and properties as calf rennet.

Recipe No. 1: Lactic Cheese

It's best for novice cheese makers to start with the soft cheeses, since they're by far the easiest and quickest to make, especially *lactic cheese,* also known as bag cheese, farmer's cheese and acid-curd cheese. This is a soft, spreadable dairy treat that's a perfect replacement for cream cheese in such dishes as cheesecake and dips.

To make a batch of lactic cheese, you'll need a large stainless-steel (or enameled or glass—but never cast-iron or aluminum) pot, a dairy thermometer, a colander, some cheesecloth, a gallon of milk—either raw from a cow or goat, or homogenized from the grocery store—some mesophilic starter culture and cheese rennet.

Begin by pouring the entire gallon of fresh milk into the pot. Now heat the milk to 72°F by placing the pot in a basin filled with heated water.

While the milk is warming, measure out one-third cup of mesophilic starter culture, stirring it with a sterile spoon to remove any lumps. When the milk has warmed to room temperature, add the culture (Fig. 3). Now dilute one drop of liquid rennet in two tablespoons of cool water, add it to the pot of milk, and stir gently for several minutes.

With the mixing completed, cover the pot, and store it at 70° to 72°F (room tempera-

ture) overnight. After 15 to 24 hours, the milk will have coagulated into a white curd with (usually, but not always) a clearish liquid—whey—floating on the surface.

After lining your colander with fine-weave cotton cheesecloth, place it in the kitchen sink, and gently pour in the pot of curds and whey (Fig. 4). If the curd is so thin that it flows right through the cheesecloth and colander and down the drain—you lose. But don't give up just yet; such a disaster simply means that you need to add more rennet, perhaps two drops rather than one, to the milk next time around. If the curd stays in the cheesecloth, you're in business. Gather up the four corners of the cheesecloth, and tie them together to form a crude bag, then hang the bag over a sink or other catch basin, and allow the curd to drain for four to six hours (Fig. 5).

After draining, remove the cheese, which the curd has now become, from the bag, and place it in a bowl so that you can conveniently mix in herbs, salt and honey to taste. If, when you go to mix salt or herbs into the cheese, it feels like a rubber ball, it's an indication that you need to use less rennet next time. Your finished lactic cheese should now be refrigerated and will keep for up to two weeks.

Many of the problems associated with making lactic cheese result from contamination. While you don't have to keep your kitchen hospital-sterile in order to successfully make this dairy food, you do have to keep your *cheese-making* equipment very clean. Additionally, if you attempt to make lactic cheese during the hottest part of summer when temperatures are running above 90°F, you'll be risking coliform bacillus contamination, which can lead to a very unpleasant stomach upset. Of course, if your house stays cool—in the 70s—and you pay close attention to cleanliness, there should be nothing to worry about, even during the dog days.

Recipe No. 2: Caerphilly

An excellent hard cheese for the beginning cheese maker is caerphilly—a mild, white, crumbly cheese of Welsh origin, sometimes referred to as children's cheese, that requires only three weeks of aging. Most hard cheeses must be aged from three to six *months* before they're ready to eat, which is a long time to wait to find out if a pioneering cheese-making attempt was successful.

There are 11 steps involved in making any hard cheese, including caerphilly: 1) ripening, 2) renneting, 3) cutting the curd, 4) cooking the curd, 5) draining, 6) salting, 7) molding, 8) pressing, 9) drying, 10) waxing and 11) aging. But it's not as difficult as all

Steps for Making Hard Cheese

1. Ripening the milk

2. Adding cheese rennet

6. Salting the curd

7. Molding the cheese

8. Pressing the cheese

those steps make it sound, so let's get with it.

Step 1—Ripening the milk: Pour two gallons of whole milk (cow's or goat's, unhomogenized) into a stainless-steel pot, and warm it to 90°F in a basin filled with heated water. Since you'll need to maintain the milk at 90° for some time, a dairy thermometer that attaches to the side of the pot is required for this step.

Now stir six ounces of mesophilic starter culture in a glass measuring cup until all lumps are dissolved, add the smoothed culture to the warmed milk, and stir gently but thoroughly. With that done, cover the pot, and allow the milk to ripen at 90°F for 30 minutes. *Ripening* refers to the process of the bacteria converting milk sugar into lactic acid, which will aid in coagulation when the time comes.

Step 2—Renneting: Add one-half teaspoon of liquid rennet to two tablespoons of cool water, then take the lid off the pot, add the diluted rennet to the heated milk, and blend gently for one minute, using an up-and-down stirring motion. Now "top-stir" the milk for three more minutes, using a spoon or ladle to disturb only the upper quarter inch of milk. This is to keep the cream from rising to the surface. Consequently, if you're using goat's milk, you can skip the top-stirring, since goat's-milk cream won't rise anyhow.

Next, cover the pot again, and allow it to sit undisturbed at 90°F for 45 minutes, after which time the milk should have congealed into a white, semisolid curd. To

Fig. 1
Preparing starter: sterilizing the milk

Fig. 2
Preparing starter: adding the culture

Fig. 3
Lactic cheese: adding starter

determine whether or not the curd is ready for cutting, insert a clean finger at a 45° angle, then slowly lift up. If the curd breaks cleanly around your finger, it's ready for cutting. If, however, the test shows that the curd is not yet ready to be cut, allow it to sit another five minutes or so. Also, add a bit more rennet the next time you try the recipe.

Step 3—Cutting: For this operation, you'll need a long-bladed knife and a flat, slotted ladle. Begin by using the knife to cut the curd into one-half-inch-thick vertical slices. Now rotate the pot a quarter turn, and cut again, working perpendicular to the first series of cuts.

The third step requires a bit more finesse: Insert the blade of the ladle a half inch down into the curd, and move it slowly back and forth until you've cut through the entire curd on something approaching a horizontal plane. Now go down another half inch, and do the same thing, then down another half inch, and so on until you reach the bottom of the pot.

Step 4—Cooking the curd: Warm the pot of cut curds to 92°F by placing it in a basin of heated water, taking the pot out and replacing it in the water as necessary to hold the temperature for 40 minutes. In order to keep the curd squares from matting together while cooking, stir them gently and frequently. This process helps to eliminate water by drawing the liquid whey from the curd pieces, which will gradually become smaller and firmer.

Fig. 4
Lactic cheese: pouring off the whey

Fig. 5
Lactic cheese: draining the curds

3. Cutting the curd

4. Cooking the curd

5. Draining the curd

9. Drying the cheese

10. Waxing the cheese

11. Aging the cheese

Step 5—Draining: At the completion of the cooking period, remove the pot from the warming bath, and allow the curd to rest for several minutes before carefully pouring off the whey. After this initial draining, dump the curds—which will probably now look more like one big glob than separate pieces—out onto a clean chopping board or a similar surface, and cut it into inch-thick slices. Turn the sliced curds over twice, at five-minute intervals, to further drain the whey.

Step 6—Salting: Use your hands to break the curd slices into bits approximately the size of a quarter. Do this immediately after draining it, before the curd has a chance to cool. Next, place the curd bits into a bowl, and gently stir in two tablespoons of salt, or less if you wish. If you want to add herbs, now is the time to do it.

Step 7—Molding: Sterilize a cheese mold and a section of cheesecloth in boiling water. The mold should be a container made of stainless steel or food-grade plastic and capable of holding at least two pounds of curds. Avoid using coffee cans as molds, since many such containers are seamed together with solder that contains lead. The cheesecloth should be of pure cotton in a medium to fine weave and be cut to fit the mold.

Place the mold in a place, such as a sink, where it can drain without causing a mess, then line it with cheesecloth, and pour in the curds. Use your fist to press the curds firmly down into the mold, then pull the cheese-cloth up tight around the sides to eliminate bunching and wrinkles.

Step 8—Pressing: Any good specialty cheese mold will come with a *follower*—a device that fits snugly into the mold and applies uniform downward pressure on the curd when a weight is placed on its top. (One of the advantages of caerphilly is that it doesn't require a great deal of pressure for pressing, as other hard cheeses do, and thus it eliminates the need for a cheese press.)

With the curds firmly fist-packed into the mold, fold one layer of the cheesecloth over the top of the curds, smoothing out any wrinkles. Now place the follower on top of the curds. And, finally, weight the follower with a pint-sized canning jar filled with water.

After 10 minutes of pressing, remove the curd, which is now officially cheese, from the mold, gently unwrap the cheesecloth covering, and turn the lump upside down. Now rewrap the cheese in the cheesecloth, and return it to the mold. After making certain that what was originally the top of the cheese is now the bottom, replace the follower and the weight. Repeat this flip-flopping procedure twice more, at 10-minute intervals, then leave the cheese undisturbed, under pressure, for 16 hours.

Step 9—Drying: After the final pressing, remove the cheese from the mold, and gently unwrap the cheesecloth covering. Now place the cheese on a clean surface at room temperature to dry. During this phase, turn the cheese several times each day, until it feels dry to the touch, which could take anywhere from one to three days, depending on the weather.

Step 10—Waxing: When your cheese is dry, it can be waxed to keep it from drying out *too* much, and to help retard the growth of mold. It's best to use specialty cheese wax, which doesn't crack as easily as paraffin. Find an old pan that's sound but dispensable, and melt the wax, very carefully, over low heat. The safest method is to use a double boiler.

The waxing will go easily if you cool the cheese in a refrigerator for several hours prior to beginning, then paint the wax on with a natural-bristle paintbrush. Don't use nylon, which can dissolve in molten wax. Paint the top and sides first, wait 30 seconds or so for the wax to cool and solidify, then turn the cheese over, and paint its bottom.

Now's the time to date your cheese with a self-adhering label.

Step 11—Aging: Store your waxed cheese on a clean shelf in a slightly damp environment at between 35° and 55°F. Most root cellars or basements meet these requirements—but if yours doesn't, play it safe, and age your cheese in the refrigerator. During the first week of aging, the cheese should be turned frequently—top to bottom—to keep moisture from collecting on its under surface and decomposing it.

As with any new recipe, making this and other cheeses will become easier and result in a better cheese with each attempt.

Ice Cream

Freeze with ease.

Ice cream, probably America's favorite dessert, wasn't invented by Americans, of course. The original frozen dessert has long since melted into the annals of antiquity, but there is solid evidence that widely separate cultures were cooling their palates with delicious concoctions while the glory of the Roman Empire was at its height.

Charles I, king of England, felt so strongly about ice cream that he didn't want the majesty of the delicacy tarnished by lower-class palates. He paid his French chef handsomely to keep the recipe classified. But the chef must have been working both sides of the Channel, for by the latter part of the seventeenth century, exclusive cafés in Paris were peddling small amounts of the frozen delight for outrageous sums. It seems fair to say that ice cream originated as a treat for the rich.

The American upper class featured it as a special touch of elegance at dinner parties. George Washington provided his family and guests with $200 worth of frosty during the long, hot summer of 1790. The first advertisements for ice cream in the New World appeared during the Revolution. But it took American mechanical genius and Yankee ingenuity to make it really pay off.

That incredibly inventive period that brought us the cotton gin and the assembly line culminated in 1846 with the invention of the churn-type ice-cream freezer, brought to perfection by Mrs. Nancy Johnson, a New England housewife. With the slight improvement of adding a crank to the top of the churn, the crank ice-cream freezer, much as we know it today, was patented by William Young in 1848.

Before Nancy Johnson's day, ice cream was strictly a handmade item. Rather than a wooden (or most often today, plastic) tub to hold the ice and salt for freezing, our forefathers and foremothers used a pewter bowl. A smaller container of the same material held the concoction of milk, cream, eggs, sugar and flavorings. The small pot was shaken up and down by one person while another held the bowl with the ice and salt. George Washington had such pots (and the slaves to do the shaking) at his Mount Vernon estate.

Such primitive manufacturing methods, coupled with the unavailability of ice in large quantities, made ice cream a rare and expensive treat. It took the development of the insulated ice house, the "Johnson Patented Ice Cream Machine" and the addition of a motor to bring ice cream to the masses. America ate well and often of this wonderful, healthful dessert for the next 50 years or so.

As America changed, however, so did its ice cream. Just as the automobile and mass communications were speeding up and homogenizing American society, a comparable development revolutionized the ice-cream industry: the air-inject freezer in 1927. Until this invention, ice cream was a fairly heavy, textured product with no need for gelatins, chemicals, stabilizers or such. But all the rules were changed when *air* could be directly injected into the mix. While old-fashioned ice cream contained 10 to 15% air, it now became possible to make a product containing as much as 60% air, bound into the mix by stabilizing chemicals. The ice-cream industry learned (much as the baking industry was to learn a few years later) how to sell air. The process was quicker and cheaper, large-scale volume became possible, and the industry quickly leaped into the modern era of mass merchandising.

While eggs and cold had been enough to hold the product together before, the air-inject freezer required chemical stabilizers to keep all that air in long enough for the customer to buy it. The first stabilizers were animal gelatins and cornstarch, both somewhat foreign to real ice cream but harmless enough.

Then along came the chemical companies. Their marriage to the dairy industry resulted in the addition of stabilizers, improvers, emulsifiers, smoothers and whatever else could be foisted off on the unsuspecting public. Some brands of commercial ice creams today are 80% artificial.

Of course, synthetic ice cream doesn't taste the same as the genuine thing. Ice cream should have a real texture, not be a smooth, glutinous mass that never melts. It's supposed to melt, and fairly rapidly. It should be icy and refreshing and *not* leave a sickeningly sweet aftertaste. Today's commercial ice creams made from prepared mixes contain as much as 25% sugar, usually glucose, while old-fashioned ice creams contain from 10 to 12% of 100% cane sugars. Synthetic ice cream has a flavor as subtle as a jackhammer, while the real thing—diluted naturally by cream, milk and fresh eggs—is delicately delicious. When you make strawberry ice cream, for example, it is impossible to use more than 20 to 25% strawberries without

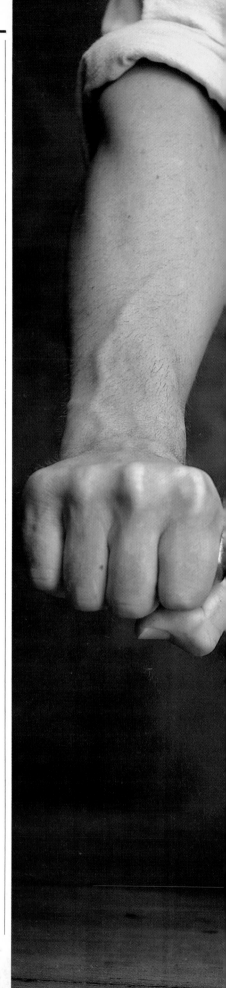

Sure, you can buy electric models, but the hand-cranked freezer just plain makes ice cream taste better.

getting an "icy" end product. So when you dilute this naturally subtle flavor, the end product, of course, is also subtle in taste. And the color will be pale pink or even off-white, not the fire-engine red that often passes for strawberry at the local ice cream store.

The Ice-Cream Freezer

To make your own ice cream, you need a machine not unlike the original one devised by Nan Johnson and improved by Bill Young. There are several suitable freezers on the market.

The tub most often used today is plastic. Though many people prefer wooden containers because they give about 25% more cooling power, there have been some recent developments in plastic vacuum-molded tubs with extra-thick walls that react conductively like wood. These specially thick tubs have the added advantage of being unbreakable.

If you choose a wooden tub, it may leak the first time you use it. After that, the water and salt will swell the wood and create a permanent seal.

Whichever tub you choose, notice the hole in the side. Never let it get clogged with ice and salt. As you freeze the ice cream, keep poking your finger into this small hole to permit smooth passage of the brine. It would never do to let the brine seep over the top of the can and into your ice cream.

Inside the tub, at the bottom, is a spindle. The can rests on this, and it must be kept rust free, be dried after each use and be greased fairly regularly.

The crank-and-gear assembly fits over the can lid and keeps it spinning, turns the paddle and makes the whole machine work. It's a simple mechanism and requires little maintenance other than a bit of oil or light grease semiannually or whenever it is stored for a long period of time. Again, don't over-oil it, or the lubricant will run into your ice cream through the hole in the can lid.

The can and lid are usually tin-plated metal. Try not to let the tin be scraped off by using metal spoons and such. Use a rubber spatula to clean out your can and a soft sponge when washing. Never scour it.

The paddle is the heart of the machine. Revolving on its spindle, jogging up and down, this is the mechanism that makes old-fashioned ice cream smooth. The cream nearest the sides of the can freezes first. The wooden, or plastic, scraper blades on the paddle (usually set at the factory to revolve a specific distance from the sides of the can) keep the ice cream from sticking. When you put the paddle into the can, make certain it is seated in the small hub at the bottom.

To be sure all the parts are put together correctly, turn the crank to see that the whole

Ten Easy Steps to Making Ice Cream

1. Wash the freezer can, lid and paddle in hot, soapy water. Let them air-dry.
2. Assemble the ingredients: milk and cream (or half-and-half), eggs, salt, sweetener (sugar or honey) and flavorings.
3. If you are making a fruit ice cream, wash, chop, crush and sugar the fruit and set it aside for later. (Finely chop about a quarter of the fruit to add as chunks.)
4. Crack the eggs into a small bowl, and beat them well.
5. Into a large bowl pour one-fourth of the milk and cream, then add the beaten eggs, salt and sweetener. Blend with a wire whisk or hand beater.
6. Pour the remaining milk and cream into the freezer can, add the blended ingredients and the fruit, and mix it up well.
7. Taste! If necessary, add more of whatever it's lacking, but add in small quantities—a quarter-ounce of extract, a tablespoon of sugar. Mix it up again and taste. Keep this up until it's perfect for you. Remember that cold will inhibit flavor just a bit.
8. Place the paddle in the can, put on the lid, seat the can in the tub, and secure the crank in place.
9. Prepare the crushed ice and rock salt (about 1 cup of ice to $1/4$ cup of salt). Layer the salt and the ice evenly around the can.
10. Crank, slowly and steadily, until the ice cream is hard.

mechanism moves freely without any binding.

How about the ice and salt? Crushed ice is best; small cubes, next best. A five-pound bag of ice should be sufficient for a two- or four-quart freezer. Rock salt is available in most supermarkets and grocery stores. If you run short or can't find it, use common table salt. It will cost more and may cause a slight freezing problem until you get used to it. But sodium chloride is still salt, no matter how you crack it.

Take a cup of crushed ice, and distribute it evenly around the opening between the can and the tub. Now spread a quarter cup of salt evenly over the ice. Start turning the crank, smoothly and slowly, and don't stop until the ice cream is finished. Continue filling the freezer sides with alternate layers of ice and rock salt; about four parts ice to one part salt is a safe formula. Keep that crank turning. Don't cover the can lid with ice or salt. Put them only as high as the bottom of the lid. When the ice melts and goes down a bit, add more ice, then another layer of salt on top. Keep churning away, mixing up the rich cream.

If after 15 or 20 minutes the ice cream isn't getting too hard to turn the crank, then it's probable that you've used too little salt. If it gets too difficult to crank after 10 minutes or so, then you've probably used too much. Experience will help you hone in on the exact time it takes your particular freezer to freeze a particular batch. If it's done properly, you should have ice cream hard enough to dish out in about 18 minutes or so.

The cranking will become more and more difficult. No heroics here, no strong-arm tactics necessary, just steady as you go. Finally, when the crank is nearly impossible to turn, the paddle will have beaten the cream

into a frozen mass that won't mix any further. No problem, you're done!

The ice cream will come out of your freezer at about 25°F. For it to hold its shape—for a cone, for instance—it should be served at a much lower temperature. Doing this at home is simple. After you remove the paddle, place a piece of waxed paper over the top of the can, replace the lid, and put a small paper plug in the hole at the top of the lid where the paddle shaft fits. Drain off all the water, and re-ice and salt the freezer, using the same proportions of ice and salt as before. This is called curing, or packing, the freezer. It permits the ice cream to get much harder within a relatively short period of time. Packing, if done properly, will hold the ice cream for up to six hours.

Ingredients

Milk and cream, eggs, sweetener and salt—no matter what else you add, old-fashioned ice cream always includes these ingredients.

Since cream is fairly expensive, the recipes given here offer commercial half-and-half as an alternative to the milk and cream combined. Try making your favorite recipe both ways, check the costs—and perhaps the calories. Either way, the ice cream will have about 11% butterfat, much the same as that of most commercial ice creams. If you prefer a richer taste, add half a pint of whipping cream to each quart of liquid, which will bring the butterfat content to about 15%.

You can substitute honey for sugar, but it will definitely affect the flavor, so when using honey, use it sparingly and rarely in the same proportion as sugar. Start out by using half as much honey as you would sugar. From there, sweeten to taste as you mix.

Fresh eggs are the stabilizing element; they hold the ice cream together. A good rule of thumb is to use one egg for every two quarts of finished ice cream. You will wind up with about 3% egg, which technically speaking qualifies your ice cream as a custard. Use both the yolk and the white. While the yolk does the stabilizing, the white tends to lighten up the end product.

Salt is an excellent flavor enhancer, but about one teaspoon per gallon will do nicely. Those on salt-free diets can forget this ingredient with little cause for concern.

This homemade ice cream *can* be stored in a freezer, and should last a week if the compartment is cold enough. But a word of caution here: When old-fashioned ice cream is kept at such low temperatures, ice crystals will form, and before you eat it you should let these crystals melt a bit. Spoon each serving into a dish, and let it sit out at room temperature for about 15 minutes before you dive in. It will come back to the same creaminess as before.

Make It Yourself!

Old-Fashioned Vanilla

The all-time favorite. Enjoy it plain, or add your own special topping. It's a classic, so don't change anything in this one, please.

2¹/₂ cups cream
2 cups milk
 (or 4¹/₂ cups half-and-half)
2 fresh eggs
¹/₄ teaspoon salt
¹/₂ cup dark brown sugar
3 tablespoons white cane sugar
2 tablespoons pure vanilla extract (or to taste)

Lotus Cream

This unusual ice cream is very refreshing and makes a superb dessert. Lemons and almonds are an unforgettable combination.

2 cups cream
1¹/₂ cups milk
 (or 3¹/₂ cups half-and-half)
1 fresh egg
¹/₄ teaspoon salt
1 cup cane sugar
1 lemon (grate the peel, squeeze the juice)
4 tablespoons additional lemon juice
¹/₂ teaspoon almond extract
¹/₃ cup sliced almonds

Banana Honey

Smooth and delicious! Mash the ripe bananas well, using a blender if one is available. Bananas will vary in sweetness, so taste the mix as you discreetly add the honey.

2 cups cream
1¹/₂ cups milk
 (or 3¹/₂ cups half-and-half)

¹/₄ to ¹/₃ cup honey
1 fresh egg
¹/₄ teaspoon salt
2 or 3 ripe bananas

Chocolate

The world's second most favorite ice cream flavor. You can vary the intensity of the chocolate flavor by the brand you use and the amount. Blend cocoa well with a bit of milk, as it has a tendency to form lumps.

2¹/₃ cups cream
2¹/₃ cups milk
 (or 4²/₃ cups half-and-half)
1 fresh egg
¹/₄ teaspoon salt
²/₃ cup cane sugar
³/₄ cup cocoa

Chocolate Chip

Two kinds of chocolate chips, sherry and vanilla. A terrific ice cream.

2¹/₄ cups cream
2 cups milk
 (or 4¹/₄ cups half-and-half)
1 fresh egg
¹/₄ teaspoon salt
¹/₂ cup cane sugar
1 tablespoon pure vanilla extract
1 tablespoon sherry
¹/₂ cup chocolate chips (blend semi-sweet and milk chocolate chips to taste)

Coffee

Use your own favorite brand of instant coffee, or try something exotic.

2 cups cream
2¹/₂ cups milk
 (or 4¹/₂ cups half-and-half)
1 fresh egg
¹/₄ teaspoon salt
²/₃ cup cane sugar
3 tablespoons instant coffee

Rum Raisin

Real rum improves this ice cream but makes it a bit more "icy." Dark Jamaican rum is the best. Delicious!

2 cups cream
2¹/₂ cups milk
 (or 4¹/₂ cups half-and-half)
1 fresh egg
¹/₄ teaspoon salt
¹/₂ cup cane sugar
3 tablespoons dark rum (or 1¹/₂ tablespoons rum extract)
¹/₂ cup raisins soaked overnight in the rum

Strawberry

This can be made with fresh or frozen berries, but if using fresh fruit, add from 20 to 30% sugar to taste to the mashed

berries. Mash ³/₄ of the berries well; add whole berries or chunks at the end.

2 cups cream
1 cup milk
 (or 3 cups half-and-half)
1 fresh egg
¹/₄ teaspoon salt
¹/₄ cup cane sugar, to taste
1¹/₂ cups mashed strawberries
¹/₂ cup strawberry chunks

Tutti-Frutti

This is the real thing, worth the bother.

2 cups cream
1¹/₂ cups milk
 (or 3¹/₂ cups half-and-half)
1 fresh egg
¹/₄ teaspoon salt
¹/₂ cup cane sugar
¹/₄ cup raisins
¹/₄ cup cherry pieces with juice
¹/₄ cup crushed pineapple
¹/₄ cup crushed strawberries
1¹/₂ tablespoons sherry
¹/₂ cup chopped nuts

Eggnog

A special holiday treat that's bound to please your friends. The recipe contains a blend of brandy, rum and sherry that makes it the hit of the season. The eggnog mixture can be either frozen as ice cream or served warm as a sauce.

2¹/₂ cups cream
2 cups milk
 (or 4¹/₂ cups half-and-half)
2 fresh eggs
¹/₂ teaspoon salt
²/₃ cup cane sugar
1¹/₂ teaspoons nutmeg
¹/₂ teaspoon cinnamon
1 tablespoon brandy
1 tablespoon sherry
1 tablespoon rum
1¹/₂ teaspoons pure vanilla extract

Pumpkin Raisin

Reminiscent of the mellow glow of Granny's holiday desserts, this flavor has proved popular year-round. And since we all had different grannies, you can really experiment here with spicing the mix to your own particular taste memory.

2 cups cream
2 cups milk
 (or 4 cups half-and-half)
1 fresh egg
¹/₄ teaspoon salt
²/₃ cup cane sugar
³/₄ cup pumpkin, mashed
¹/₄ teaspoon ginger
¹/₄ teaspoon nutmeg
¹/₂ teaspoon cinnamon (spices to taste)
¹/₂ cup raisins

Yogurt

Two decades ago, a comic had only to mention eating yogurt to get a laugh. Today it's an American staple.

The story begins with the tiny organisms that convert milk to yogurt—primarily the same varieties of *lactobacillus* bacteria that like to set up a living factory in your digestive system, where they continuously produce an onslaught of beneficial B vitamins.

The *lactobacilli* thrive—and make yogurt —by converting milk sugar (lactose) to lactic acid. This end product produces yet another of yogurt's amazing health benefits: The toxic bacteria that cause intestinal gas and putrefaction (the rotting decomposition of food) cannot survive in an environment containing significant amounts of lactic acid. The resulting absence of such toxic organisms in the digestive system may be one reason for the long and vigorous lives of the people in yogurt-loving societies.

In addition, yogurt is a digestive aid that helps the body absorb protein, calcium and iron. In fact, many people who literally can't stomach fresh milk can easily assimilate the healthful lactic acid found in yogurt.

The first step in making yogurt is to gather up your equipment and ingredients. You'll need some jars with lids (any clean glass containers will work fine), a large container for keeping the brewing batch warm—either a plastic-foam picnic cooler or a canning pot you can wrap with heavy towels will do— and standard kitchen equipment, including a measuring cup, cooking pan and stirring utensil. A food thermometer can come in handy, too, but if you don't have one, you can estimate the crucial temperature limits of 100° and 115°F by dabbing some heated water on your inner wrist: Liquid at 100° feels comfortably warm to the touch, but at 115° there's a bit of a sting.

Your cooking ingredients will be skim or whole fresh milk, a bit of honey (the sweetener is optional) and either some fresh

(unflavored) yogurt—a quality commercial brand made without gelatins and fillers will suffice—or a package of freeze-dried culture. You can get these special packets from health food stores and some drugstores.

You'll be ready to cook once you've thoroughly cleaned the food containers and utensils to eliminate any unwanted microscopic organisms. The recipe given here produces one quart of finished yogurt, but you can make any amount by proportionally raising or lowering the various quantities.

Start by drizzling two to four teaspoons of honey around the bottom of a two-quart cooking pot to sweeten the culture and also to help prevent "milk burn" on a metal surface. If you'd rather not add sweetener, you can eliminate this step. However, *don't* incubate yogurt with honey if you have trouble digesting lactose, because in that case you'll want to ensure that the only sugar the *lactobacilli* can "work on" comes from the milk.

Next pour in four and one-half cups of milk, cover the pot with a dark lid (to help retain vitamin B_2), and slowly heat the liquid until a skin—with bubbles trapped underneath—forms on top of the milk, a bacteria-killing step that should take about 25 to 35 minutes. Let your heated liquid hold its temperature a few minutes. Then cool it— quickly *or* slowly—to around 115°F.

You're now ready to stir in either the starter packet or one tablespoon of fresh yogurt. Some people also add two tablespoons of powdered milk to thicken the yogurt's texture. With that done, pour the warm liquid into your clean jar or jars, screw on the lids, set the jars in the canner or plastic-foam cooler, and pour 115°F water into the large container until the levels of the milk and water are equal. Covering this incubator will help the curdling process.

Yogurt-making equipment

Cool the liquid to 115°F before adding starter.

The trick is to keep your yogurt hatchery warm and undisturbed for at least a few hours. People have devised ingenious ways to accomplish this. Some with gas-powered stoves will place the yogurt kettle in the oven and let the pilot light warm it. Others with electric stoves will put the culture container in the oven anyway, but will heat the batch with a light bulb on an extension cord or by replacing the small appliance light inside with a 100-watt bulb. Still others place their brew in an airtight pressure cooker and set the pot at an experimentally determined appropriate distance from a woodstove or other constant source of warmth. On a sunny day, you can even drape the brewing vessel with black material, place it outside, and make yogurt with solar power.

After the yogurt has had time to start coagulating, tip a jar gently—don't joggle it any more than you have to—to see how firm it is. Once the creamy product is set to your liking, chill it immediately. The refrigerated culture will continue to gradually thicken and sour, but at a much slower rate than warm yogurt.

You don't have to buy more starter to make your second and succeeding batches of yogurt; just save a tablespoon or two from one culture to "seed" the next. You should, however, start the next round within two to five days. If you can't meet the deadline, simply freeze some fresh yogurt, and then thaw it when you're ready to brew again.

The first batch from the original starter will firm up in anywhere from four to 12 hours, but subsequent rounds will set ever more rapidly—and taste ever more acidic— until you finally have to give up and buy some new starter.

One clever way to delay even an occasional starter-shopping expenditure—as well as to ensure that every batch of yogurt will have a uniform "beginning"—is simply to freeze in ice cube trays a quantity of yogurt brewed from your original starter. You can then thaw one or two of the cubes whenever you need a new starter.

Like many novice yogurt makers, you may find that it takes a couple of tries to get a feel for fixing your own. If so, you'll become an experienced bacteria breeder all the sooner if you learn from any initial mishaps. To help you cope, here's a Yogurt Maker's Troubleshooting Guide:

● Be forewarned that a pot of innocent bubbling milk can swiftly turn into a raging, lid-lifting mess, and that a hard-to-clean layer of the scorched liquid will coat the bottom of the cooking pan if you heat the milk too quickly.

● Did you successfully complete the brewing process but find that a thick coat of cream rose to the top of your yogurt? This outcome, which happens only when using nonhomogenized milk, can be prevented if you hasten the setting process by using less milk or more starter, and also by making sure the brew stays at its optimum cooking temperature.

● Did the yogurt separate into lumpy curds and watery whey? You probably let the brew get joggled around too much or incubate too long. You can remedy this problem by stirring the whey back into your curds, though doing so will liquefy the yogurt's texture. Better still, turn the accident into an achievement: Strain the loose glop through cheesecloth and have a bowlful of delicious and dietetic "sour cream."

● The batch didn't set at all? Such a calamity can have several causes. Your starter may have been too old; perhaps you forgot to add the seeding culture; you may have brewed the batch for too short a time or at too high or low a temperature; or the animals that your milk came from may have been dosed with penicillin, and the antibiotic traces could have wiped out the *lactobacilli*.

● Does the finished batch have an off-flavor? The problem most likely is that some mold or foreign bacteria got into the incubator from unclean equipment or the milk wasn't heated enough initially to kill the liquid's natural microorganisms. In either case, don't use the "strange" batch as a starter for your next one.

Yogurt is a versatile food that can be served at any meal, enjoyed as a quick snack or eaten plain. For extra nutrition, mix yogurt with applesauce or cranberry sauce and top it with granola and sesame seeds. Or you can use it in salad dressings, for making dips and spreads, and in bread, soups and casseroles. Remember, though, any cooking that heats the yogurt up to more than 120°F will kill the *lactobacilli*.

Here's a recipe for cream cheese that's simpler than unwrapping the tinfoil around those rectangles you find in the supermarket. Just mix up a super-large batch of yogurt. Don't make it too tart. Keep what you'll want for lunches, and pour the rest into a cloth bag; several layers of cheesecloth will do. Hang the bag over a pan to catch the whey, which you can use later for baking or in soups. Hang the yogurt overnight (10 to 12 hours), and it will turn into cream cheese. Add some chopped chives from the garden, and spread the cheese on home-baked whole-wheat bread. Makes a meal in itself.

An old-fashioned way to make "yogurt" is simply to take a couple of spoons of sour milk and add them to a quart of regular milk. Stir the mixture, and pour it into shallow dishes or casseroles. Let them stand on the windowsill but not in the sun. This will usually set in a day.

Use a warm water bath to maintain incubation temperature.

Too much joggling spoils the brew.

Nonhomogenized milk can cause separation.

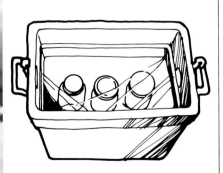

Soups and Stocks

The original health food, and still a champion!

A fine soup needs the inspiration of the artist, the care of the craftsperson and the daring of the adventurer.

He told the story at a party and may have been pulling everyone's leg. Still, it caused a stir—partly because it revealed something of the magic of soup making and partly because it sounded like a fairy tale. An anthropologist, he had done fieldwork in a small rural village in northern China before the Communist revolution. As far as he could determine from local records and lore, he said, the fire beneath the large, black, communal iron cooking pot in the village center had been kept going for at least 400 years. Each day—as they had evidently done for more than 15 generations—the villagers would toss in fresh greens, herbs, spices, rice, knucklebones, chicken feet, birds' nests, what have you. And each day the soup changed. He had nourished himself, he said, over an entire cold and bleak winter from that ancient pot. "Moreover," he added with a wink, "the special qualities of the soup undoubtedly account for the fact that I am now 120 years old."

Although there is plenty of magic in soup, and a good bowl of it can convince you that you will live forever, there is controversy over how long a decent one should be kept going. The truth is that after repeated heatings the vegetable fibers break down and become mushy, while herbs and spices lose the pungency that brought them to the pot in the first place. What had been a symphony of distinct flavors turns into homogenized noise. The French, who worship soup, would never allow one to go downhill, knowing full well that the key to a distinguished serving lies in utterly fresh ingredients: greens, herbs and, in Marseilles, fish. The Chinese know this as well—despite the anthropologist's story—having raised the art of soup making to positively Zen heights.

Even in America, before the advent of canning and dehydration, self-respecting country cooks continually urged their pupils (usually their daughters) to make the time between garden and pot as short as possible.

And yet, soup is obviously more than liquid salad. Rather, it is the wedding of the momentary and the established, the fresh ingredients and the long-simmered broth. This stock, a responsive and enduring substance that can be nurtured and tended for days and even weeks, is the base for the magic.

Inevitably, the education of a soup maker begins with stock. Marjorie M. Watkins knows this well: She learned her soup making from her great-grandmother, who began married life and bore the first six of her 12 children in a sod house on the Kansas plains. "If Great-grandma's pantry contained only a bone, a handful of carrots, a couple of onions and a few potatoes," writes Watkins, "she simmered them in half a bucket of spring water and a few magical herbs from her kitchen doorstep until the tantalizing aroma lured workers from the field and children from play."

The Watkins' beef stock recipe has been the basis for innumerable delicious meals:

Beef Stock

3 pounds stewing meat with bones, cut up
1 pound marrow or soup bones
3 quarts cold water
1 cup dry red table wine
1 large onion, quartered
2 carrots, chopped
2 celery stalks and tops, chopped
2 tomatoes, quartered
2 garlic cloves, minced
1 thyme sprig
5 parsley sprigs
1 bay leaf
5 peppercorns
1 tablespoon salt

Brown the meat in a lightly oiled skillet, then place it in a kettle with the water. Pour the wine into the skillet, and use it to scrape up the browned meat juices, then add this mix to the kettle. Bring to a boil, lower the heat, and simmer partly covered for 2 hours, occasionally skimming the froth from the stock's surface. Then add the remaining ingredients, and simmer for 2 hours more. Remove the meat and bones, reserving the meat for some other use. Strain the stock through a coarse vegetable sieve, then through a double layer of cheesecloth. Cool the stock to room temperature before refrigerating or freezing it in a covered container.

Do not defat stock if storing it, for the fat will rise and congeal on the surface, acting as a sealant. Prior to use, it can easily be removed. (Since freezing separates ingredients, thawed stock should be briefly reboiled.)

If fresh stock is to be used immediately, however, spoon off as much fat as possible from the surface. Floating an ice cube in the stock will congeal the rest, or you can sweep the surface with a chilled lettuce leaf. To clarify fresh or stored stock, add to each quart an egg white slightly beaten in 2 teaspoons of water, and 1 crushed eggshell. Stir, heat, and boil for 2 minutes, then let stand unstirred for 20 minutes. Strain through a double layer of moist cheesecloth. Now you're ready to make some serious soup.

Chicken Stock

5 pounds chicken, cut up, with giblets (less the liver)
3 quarts cold water
2 onions, quartered
2 carrots, chopped
2 leeks and tops, chopped
5 parsley sprigs
2 thyme sprigs
1 bay leaf
4 peppercorns
1/2 teaspoon poultry seasoning
1 tablespoon salt

Add the chicken and giblets to the water, and slowly bring to a rapid boil. Simmer for 1 hour, periodically skimming off the froth. Add the remaining ingredients, except the salt, cover, and simmer for 1 more hour. Remove the meat from the bones but return them to the kettle, then add the salt, and simmer 45 minutes. Strain the stock through a fine sieve, and cool to room temperature. Refrigerate or freeze in a covered container, or use at once. Hundreds of recipes call for this versatile base.

Fish Stock

2 pounds fish heads, bones, skin, tails, but no gills
2 small onions, diced
1 stalk celery with top, chopped
2 1/2 cups cold water
2 cups dry white wine
3 parsley sprigs
1 bay leaf
1 thyme sprig
1/4 teaspoon fennel seeds
5 peppercorns
Salt to taste

Combine everything but the salt in a kettle, bring to a boil, and simmer covered for 45 minutes, now and then skimming off the froth. Add the salt at the last moment. Strain, cool, and refrigerate. The stock can be stored and frozen, although fresh is best.

A Miscellany of Country Soups

No claims of enhanced human longevity attach to the following country soups, yet each can be replenished and stretched over several days at least, and each supplies plenty of high-grade fuel.

La Soupe aux Pois Canadienne

"Venez, garçons et filles, mangez la soupe aux pois. Ça se mange en famille prés du grand feu de bois." (Come, boys and girls, eat some pea soup. Eat it together near the open fire.)

This burly soup, which is listed in Joan Nathan's fine *An American Folklife Cookbook*, was the favorite of French-Canadian lumberjacks who earlier this century migrated south of the border to sign on at logging camps in both New England and the Pacific Northwest.

2 cups dried yellow peas
8 cups water
2 onions, chopped
1/2 pound salt pork or 4 slices bacon, cut into 1" pieces
2 teaspoons salt
1 teaspoon pepper
1 teaspoon sage
2 tablespoons chopped parsley
4 russet potatoes, peeled, boiled and diced
1 16-ounce can white hominy corn

Soak the peas in the water overnight. The next day, replace the water with 8 cups of fresh water in a 4-quart casserole. Add the onions, pork, salt, pepper, sage and parsley. Cover and cook over low heat 3 hours, stirring every 30 minutes. Add more water if necessary, but the soup should be fairly thick. After 3 hours, add the potatoes. Cover and simmer 45 minutes. Then add the corn, correct the seasonings, and simmer, covered, 15 more minutes. Remove the salt pork. If desired, sprinkle with more parsley before serving. If a purée is preferred, put the mixture through a blender or food processor. Serve with bread dipped in molasses.

A Soop or Pottage

Here is a slightly more challenging concoction from long ago. This excellent recipe appeared in the first cookbook printed in America, in 1742. It was, in fact, a shortened and Americanized edition of the *The Compleat Housewife* by E. Smith, first published in England in 1727. According to John and Karen Hess, authors of *The Taste of America*, this sturdy, well-constructed soup is typical of the soups served up in the early seventeenth century. The directions are very clear, say the Hesses, for "this is a cook speaking to cooks." *Colworts*, incidentally, refers to kale or other nonheading members of the cabbage family; *spinnage* is spinach.

"Take several Knuckles of Mutton, a Knuckle of Veal, a Shin of Beef, and put to these twelve Quarts of Water, cover the Pot close, and set it on the Fire; let it not boil too fast; scum it well, and let it stand on the Fire twenty four Hours; then strain it through a Colander, and when it is cold take off the Fat, and set it on the Fire again, and season it with Salt, a few Cloves, Pepper, a Blade of Mace, a Nutmeg quarter'd, a Bunch of sweet Herbs, and a Pint of Gravy; let all these boil up for Half an Hour, and then strain it; put Spinnage, Sorrel, green Peas, Asparagus, or Artichoke bottoms, according to the Time of Year; then thicken it with the Yolks of three or four Eggs; have in Readiness some Sheeps Tongues, Cox combs, and Sweetbreads, sliced thin, and fried, and put them in, and some Mushrooms, and French bread dried and cut in little Bits, some forc'd-meat Balls, and some very thin Slices of Bacon; make all these very hot, and garnish the Dish with Colworts and Spinnage scalded green."

Iowa Vegetable Soup

When Sylvia and Bob Chenault of Walcott, Iowa, devised this recipe, it was December 2 and the temperature on their farm hovered right around the five degree mark. Simple to prepare, the Chenaults' warming recipe relies heavily on produce from the family's garden.

4 quarts beef stock
1 1/2 pounds soup meat
1/2 cup sliced onions
1 cup diced green pepper
1 cup diced kohlrabi
2 cups sliced carrots
1 cup snow peas (or shelled peas)
1 cup long-grain brown rice
1 quart home-canned tomatoes
1 pint tomato sauce
Salt and garlic powder to taste

Warm the beef stock, add the meat, and let simmer about 1/2 hour. Add the other ingredients, and simmer 1 hour or until the vegetables are tender. Makes 5 quarts.

Chestnut Soup

1 cup chestnuts
2 quarts chicken broth
1/2 teaspoon salt
1/8 teaspoon pepper

Shell and blanch the chestnuts. Place 2 cups of the chicken broth in a large pot, and cook the chestnuts in it until they are tender. Remove the chestnuts with a slotted spoon, salt them lightly, and set them aside. Add the remainder of the broth to the hot broth in the pot, and bring to a boil. Put the chestnuts in a soup tureen, pour the broth over them, and serve at once.

Shrimp Gumbo

2 shallots, diced
1/2 green pepper, diced
1 teaspoon olive oil
2 cups sliced okra
2 stalks celery with tops, sliced
1 teaspoon salt
3 cups water
1 pound small, peeled, deveined shrimp
2 1/2 cups fish stock
1 cup cooked long-grain rice
Salt and pepper to taste

Sauté the shallots and peppers in the olive oil. Add the okra, celery, salt and water, and bring to a boil. Cover and simmer at low heat for 10 minutes. Add the shrimp and stock, and simmer 5 minutes more, no longer; shrimp are delicate. Add the rice, stir, and season with salt and pepper.

Green Soup

2 tablespoons cooking oil
2 or 3 green onions, thinly sliced
4 cups stock or broth
1 teaspoon salt
1 large potato, peeled and shredded
1 cup tightly packed, washed and chopped sorrel leaves

Sauté the onions lightly in the oil for 3 minutes. Add the stock, salt and potato, and bring to a boil. Reduce the heat, and simmer uncovered for 5 minutes. Add the sorrel, cover, and cook for 1 minute until the sorrel is limp but still flavorful. Serves 4.

Turnip Chowder

2 tablespoons chicken fat or oil
1 small onion, diced
2 small white turnips, diced
1 medium-sized potato, peeled and diced
2 cups chicken stock
2 cups milk
Salt and pepper to taste

Gently sauté the onion in the fat or oil until the bits are transparent. Add the turnips, and fry until they're lightly browned. Add the potatoes and the chicken stock, bring to a boil, reduce the heat, and simmer with the cover on for 10 to 15 minutes. Stir in the milk, and reheat thoroughly. Add salt and pepper to taste. Serves 4.

Lentil Soup

1 pound lentils
1 bay leaf
3–4 tablespoons bacon grease
2 medium onions, chopped
4 stalks celery, chopped (include leaves)
2 cloves garlic, minced
4 scrubbed, unpeeled potatoes, cubed
Ground coriander, ground cumin, curry powder, lemon juice, salt and pepper to taste
Crumbled bacon (optional)
Sour cream (optional)

In a large pot, cover the lentils with water; add the bay leaf, and simmer over low heat for about 30 minutes. Melt the bacon grease in a heavy skillet. Sauté the onions, celery stalks and leaves and minced garlic until the onions are translucent but not brown. Add the sautéed vegetables to the stockpot along with the potatoes. Simmer over low heat, stirring frequently to prevent sticking, until the vegetables are tender. Season to taste with coriander, cumin, curry powder, lemon juice, salt and pepper. Simmer for another 15 minutes, and serve garnished with crumbled bacon or sour cream. Serves 6.

Black Beans Supreme

1 pound black beans or turtle beans
1 medium carrot, cut in julienne strips
2 medium onions, finely chopped
2 stalks celery, finely chopped
2 cloves garlic, minced
1 1/2 cups tomato purée
1 teaspoon sweet basil
1 tablespoon vegetable salt
1 tablespoon arrowroot starch in water (optional)
Lime slices as a garnish

Pick over and wash the beans. Soak them overnight, and cook in enough water to cover, replacing the liquid as necessary, for about 1 1/2 hours. When the beans are soft but not mushy, add the carrots, onion, celery, garlic, tomato purée, sweet basil and vegetable salt. Simmer until the vegetables become tender. If the soup seems thin, whisk the arrowroot starch into a little water, and pour into the soup. Stir to avoid lumps; serve when the soup reaches the desired consistency. Garnish with fresh lime slices. Serves 4.

Naturally Navy Bean Soup

1 ham bone or 3 ham hocks
2 quarts water
1 large onion, chopped
1 cup tomato concentrate or 1 can tomato sauce
1 pound navy beans, soaked overnight or pressure-cooked
Salt and pepper

Cook the first 5 ingredients for a couple of hours or until the beans are tender. Remove the ham bone, and return any scraps of meat to the soup. Season to taste. Serves 6.

Millet-Mushroom Soup

1 cup hulled millet
2 quarts boiling water
1 green pepper, chopped
1 medium onion, sliced
1 stalk celery, chopped
2 cloves garlic, minced
1 teaspoon sweet basil
1 tablespoon vegetable salt
6 fresh tomatoes, peeled and cubed
1 1/2 cups tomato purée
1/2 cup sliced mushrooms

Pour the millet into the boiling water in

a large pot; reduce the heat, and let simmer for 20 minutes. Add the rest of the ingredients, except the mushrooms, and simmer until the vegetables are almost tender. Add the sliced mushrooms, and simmer until softened. Serves 8.

Watercress Soup

3 tablespoons margarine or bacon
   drippings
1/3 cup chopped onion
2 cups finely chopped watercress
1/2 cup sliced mushrooms (optional)
2 tablespoons flour
3 cups milk
1 cup diced potatoes
Salt and pepper to taste

Melt the margarine or bacon drippings in a saucepan, and sauté the onions, watercress and mushrooms for about 2 minutes. Remove from the heat; sprinkle in the flour, and whisk it into the mixture. Return the pan to the stove, and add the milk and diced potatoes. Season with salt and pepper to taste. Simmer the soup over low heat until the potato cubes are tender. Serves 4.

Clam Chowder

1 pint tomato concentrate
1/2 teaspoon baking soda
3 pints milk
2 cups clams
1 large potato, diced
1 or 2 carrots, sliced
1 medium onion, chopped
1 bunch celery leaves, chopped
Butter

Warm the tomato concentrate, and add the baking soda. Heat the milk in a separate pan. Stir the warm milk into the tomato mix. Blend in the rest of the ingredients, except the butter, and simmer the chowder for 20 minutes. Float pats of butter atop each serving, and pass oyster crackers. Serves 6.

New England Fish Chowder

2 tablespoons oil or 2–3 slices bacon or
   2 ounces salt pork, diced
1 large onion, diced
2 cups peeled and diced potatoes
   (approximately 1 to 2 large potatoes)
2 cups water
1 teaspoon salt
1 pound fish fillets (cod, perch or
   halibut), cut into 1″ pieces
2 cups milk
3 drops Tabasco sauce
Fresh minced parsley or basil

Brown and reserve the bacon or salt pork, and then gently fry the diced onion in the pork fat or oil. Add the potatoes, water, salt and fish chunks, and bring to a boil; cover and simmer on low heat for about 20 minutes or until the fish flakes easily with a fork and

For Soup-erior Broths

• To make your own curry powder, combine 1 ounce each pepper, ginger and mustard; 3 ounces coriander seed and turmeric; 1–3 ounces cayenne; and 1–2 ounces cardamom, cumin seed and cinnamon. Powder all the ingredients, sift them together, and store the mix in a tightly capped bottle. You can use it to season soups, rice, gravy and some stews.

• Sheep sorrel and wood sorrel thrive in neglected gardens and alongside houses and fences. Sheep sorrel has light green, arrow-shaped leaves, which have an acidic, sour taste. In small amounts, they make a zesty addition to soups. Wood sorrel has triple heart-shaped leaves and yellow flowers. The pointy seedpods taste lemony and are great in salads, and the leaves are nice to cook in soups or to eat raw in sandwiches.

• Homemade dumplings are the crowning touch to many hearty meat soups. In a bowl with a flat bottom, break an egg, beat it, and slowly stir in the following dry ingredients, combined: 1/2 cup flour, 1 teaspoon baking powder and a pinch of salt. Continue to beat with a fork until you have a bowl of dry, lumpy dumplings. Add these to your soup, and simmer another 15 minutes.

• If you're unfamiliar with the preparation of fresh seafood, here's how to carry out the preliminary shellfish and fish cleaning for making bouillabaisse. Scrub the clams. If you dug them yourself, keep them in clean seawater for 24 to 48 hours so that they'll expel the sand they contain. You can kill a rock

crab by dipping it in rapidly boiling water, holding it by the shell so that its claws can't nip you. Pull off the back, wash out the mustard, break the body in half, and pull off the claws. Clean the small fish, and scale or skin them. Clean and fillet the larger ones, cutting the fillets into serving-size pieces.

• A handful of spinach leaves, pounded and added to a soup 5 minutes or so before serving, will produce a fine green color. Parsley and celery work well, too, and both can be dried in a slow oven for future use. With parsley, pick out the stems, and place the leaves in an airtight container. Grate the dried celery stalks and roots, and store in an airtight container. You'll need only 2 tablespoons of dried parsley to season 4 quarts of soup.

• Rolled oatmeal will sometimes make a fine substitute for rice in a soup, depending on the recipe. Also, it's easy to make homemade noodles for soups. Stir in all the flour that 1 egg will absorb. Add a dash of salt. Roll out the dough as thin as possible, and let it dry. Roll the dough up jellyroll fashion, and slice the noodles off in narrow strips. Drop them in boiling soup about 15 minutes before serving time.

• Millet is an often-neglected small grain that's ideal for extending soups, stews and casseroles. It's the seed of a grass and is available in many health food stores or groceries that feature gourmet food. Millet is inexpensive, has a nutty flavor and crunchy texture, and is prepared like rice.

the potatoes are tender. Add the milk and Tabasco. Garnish with bacon or salt pork bits and minced parsley or basil. Serves 4.

Bouillabaisse

This classic soup is not as complicated to make as it may seem, and it will guarantee your reputation as a gourmet chef.
Bouillie:
1/2 cup olive oil
1 large onion, diced
1 leek, sliced
4 large cloves garlic, sliced
1 teaspoon marjoram
1 green pepper, diced
2 stalks celery, sliced
3 large tomatoes, peeled and diced or
   1 pint home-canned tomatoes
Herbs:
1 sprig fresh fennel or 2 teaspoons
   dried parsley
1/2″ by 2″ strip of orange peel (remove
   the white pith)

1 teaspoon salt
1/4 teaspoon fresh-ground pepper
Basil and thyme to taste
Fish:
1 pound perch fillets
1 pound halibut steaks
1 pound cod fillets
1 pound red snapper
2–3 rock crabs
12 oysters
12–24 steamer clams
Fish stock (optional)
Saffron

To make the *bouillie*, combine all the ingredients, except the tomatoes, and sauté until the onion is golden, stirring occasionally. Add the tomatoes and all of the herbs. Arrange the fish ingredients on top, and pour in enough boiling water, or hot fish stock, to cover. Add a generous pinch of saffron. Cover, and boil for 15 minutes or until the fish flakes easily but does not lose its shape; the oysters and clams should be open. Divide the

Use only the freshest of ingredients, and cook only until they add a shy promise of their flavor to the blend of the broth. Strive for a taste flirtation, not complete surrender.

fish and shellfish among 10 to 12 bowls, place a piece of hard bread or toast atop each serving, and ladle the fish soup over this. Serves 10 to 12.

French Onion Soup

2 tablespoons cooking oil or bacon
   drippings
1 large or 2 medium onions, sliced
1 1/2 teaspoons fresh (or 1 teaspoon dried)
   marjoram, minced
Bones from 2 veal steaks, pork chops
   or other leftover meat
6 cups water
1 bay leaf
4 slices toasted day-old bread
1/2 cup grated Swiss or Parmesan cheese
Salt and pepper to taste

Brown the onions in the oil in a heavy kettle over medium heat. Sprinkle the marjoram over the sautéing onions. Add the other ingredients, except the bread and cheese. Cover the kettle and simmer for about 25 minutes. Remove the bones, pick off the meat, and return the scraps to the broth. Ladle the soup into bowls. Top each with a slice of toasted bread, and sprinkle with cheese. If you like, set the bowls under a broiler to melt the cheese. Use canned chicken or beef stock instead of making your own if you're in a hurry. Serves 3 to 4.

Good Woman's Thick Soup

1 chicken carcass or chicken bones with
   some meat left on them

2 large potatoes, thinly peeled and cut
   into 1" chunks or unpeeled and cut
   into 1/2" chunks
2 medium leeks, cut lengthwise into 1"
   pieces
1 teaspoon salt
1 1/2 teaspoons chopped fresh marjoram
   (or 1/2 teaspoon dried marjoram)
1 1/2 teaspoons fresh basil (or 1 to 2
   teaspoons dried basil)
1/4 teaspoon coarse-ground fresh pepper
4 cups water
2 cups milk
Salt to taste

Combine all the ingredients except the milk in a large kettle. Cover, bring to a boil, reduce the heat, and simmer for 1 hour. Cool, remove the chicken carcass or bones, pick off the meat, and return it to the kettle. Process the soup 1 cup at a time in a blender or food processor to combine the ingredients. You could also whip the ingredients in the pot using an eggbeater. Reheat the mixture just to the boiling point, and add the milk. Stir, taste, and add more salt if you wish. Serve with garlic toast, cheese and fresh apples for a hearty meal. The soup also may be served without puréeing. Serves 6.

Good 'n' Garlicky Soup

6–7 cloves garlic, crushed
6 tablespoons oil
Pinch of red pepper
6 slices light bread, cubed
6 cups water

1 teaspoon salt
4 eggs, beaten
2 tablespoons chopped fresh parsley
1 carrot, grated (optional)

Sauté the garlic in the oil until lightly browned; add the red pepper, then remove the seasoned garlic from the pan. Cook the bread cubes in the seasoned oil until brown. Pour in the water, salt and garlic. Cover and let simmer for 30 minutes. Blend in the eggs, and simmer another 5 minutes. Garnish with chopped parsley and grated carrot. Serves 6.

Root Chowder

1 medium parsnip, cored and sliced
1 small turnip, sliced
1 medium carrot, sliced
1 small onion, chopped
2 small potatoes, peeled and cubed
3 medium salsify, sliced
4 cups milk
Garlic powder, red pepper flakes,
   parsley, oregano and celery seasonings
   to taste
Butter
Salt and pepper to taste

Steam the parsnip, turnip, carrot, onion, potatoes and salsify in a covered container until completely tender. Mash or process the vegetables in a food processor or blender; combine with the milk. Bring to a near-boil over low heat. Add seasonings to taste. Pour the chowder into bowls, top with pats of butter, and season with salt and pepper to taste. Serves 4.

It has been said that one of the things that sep-arates man from the higher primates is the ability to brew beer.

Beer

Believe it or not, if you can boil water, you can brew fine beer.

There are four likely reasons why you may not have tried making your own beer: 1) You don't like beer, 2) you've read about making beer and decided it was too difficult or time-consuming, 3) you tried someone else's home-brew and decided you'd never tasted anything quite so awful, or 4) you have tried brewing and met with unqualified disaster.

Little can be offered to overcome reason one. If you don't like the stuff, that's that. But if you've hung back for any of the other reasons, read on.

If you can boil water and stir, you can brew beer—and we're talking *premium* here.

Things have come a long way since home-brew was legalized in 1979 (a single-person household can make up to 100 gallons a year; a family household, 200 gallons). Not only have techniques been refined, but the variety and quality of brewing ingredients and supplies now available virtually assure pleasing results.

True, home-brewing in some circles has reached a state of high science. Serious home-brewers dabble in a world of alpha and beta hop resins, custom-made wort chillers and tenth-degree temperature control. Most malt their own barley; some even grow their own

The only real requirements for becoming a home-brewer are a taste for quality, an appreciation for economy and a compelling pride in doing things for yourself. If there also happens to be a certain amount of mad scientist in you, well, so much the better.

Gearing Up

Finding the necessary equipment and ingredients for home-brewing is not, fortunately, the formidable challenge it used to be. Chances are good there's a well-stocked beer- and wine-making shop near you, and even if there isn't, you can easily acquire all the supplies you need by mail.

Here are the basic components for a five-gallons-per-batch home brewery:

1. A boiling kettle. Get one that's copper, stainless steel or enamel. The pot should hold at least two gallons, preferably more. Copper and stainless steel are best, but expensive. An enamel canning kettle works nicely, but be sure the porcelain coating isn't chipped or scratched. The exposed metal could give beer an off-flavor.

2. A kitchen strainer and/or cheesecloth. A wire-mesh strainer six to 10 inches across is perfect. If you don't have a strainer, cheesecloth will do.

3. A long-handled stirring spoon. Stainless steel or enamel are good choices.

4. A thermometer. Any good kitchen thermometer with a range from freezing to boiling will do.

5. A hydrometer. This is a simple instrument that measures the density of a liquid (known as specific gravity) compared to that of water. Water has a specific gravity of 1.000 or, because hydrometer readings are commonly expressed in terms of their last two digits, zero. Home-brewers use the hydrometer to tell them how much sugar and alcohol are in their brew. Sugar is heavier than water, and alcohol is lighter. When beer ferments, yeast converts the sugars in the brew to alcohol. So by measuring the sugar content of a just-mixed, unfermented batch of beer, you can calculate its potential alcohol content. Likewise, you can use the hydrometer to tell you when your beer has stopped fermenting and is ready to bottle. Some beer recipes give you the formulation's anticipated final specific gravity. With those that don't, you can assume that the brew is done when the specific gravity remains essentially unchanged for two or three days.

A hydrometer looks like a large thermometer with a heavy weighted bulb on one end. Some made specifically for brewing come with a graduated cylinder in which you draw off a sample of the brew for taking a reading. In either case, to use the hydrometer you simply place it upright in the liquid, spin it once or twice to dislodge air bubbles, and let it float freely. When it stops bobbing, take a reading at the surface of the brew, just below the point where the liquid clings upward along the sides of the hydrometer.

Most hydrometers are calibrated to read accurately at 60°F. Chances are you'll be taking readings when the brew is warmer than that, so take a thermometer reading as well, and add two to three points (.002 to .003) to the specific gravity for every 10 degrees above 60°F.

6. Fermentation containers. You'll need two: one for primary fermentation and one for secondary. Food-grade plastic buckets are acceptable; the primary container should be big enough to hold at least eight gallons; the secondary can be as small as five gallons. Each should have an airtight lid, and each lid should have a hole in its center to accept a rubber stopper and a fermentation lock. Plastic fermenters are inexpensive and widely available at beer-making supply outlets—or in a pinch you can use food-grade containers purchased from a local restaurant. Many home-brewers use plastic fermenters with great success, and most home-brew kits come with plastic fermenters. But plastic *is* hard to keep clean, particularly if it has picked up a few scratches through normal wear and tear, so you run at least some greater-than-normal risk of contaminating your beer with unwanted bacteria.

The material of choice for fermenters, therefore, is glass, which is easy to sanitize. Many (but not all) beer- and wine-making shops sell five- or six-and-one-half-gallon glass carboy fermenters—large jugs like the ones used for bottled water. Carboys are ideal for this purpose, but they are heavy, more expensive than plastic and sometimes hard to find. An acceptable but less convenient alternative is to use five or six one-gallon glass jugs.

7. Fermentation locks. You'll need one for each fermenter. Also known as bubblers or air locks, these inexpensive little valves, available at all home-brew shops, keep outside air from contaminating your brew but allow fermentation gases to escape. A glass fermenter with a threaded neck will accept a screw-on holder for the lock; otherwise use a drilled rubber stopper to hold the lock in place.

8. A siphon hose. About six feet of ³⁄₈-inch (outside diameter) clear plastic tubing is required for transferring your brew from one container to another.

9. Bottles. You'll need about 60 cappable (nonscrew-top, nontwist-top) brown or green glass bottles; that'll be enough for five gallons, plus some extra to allow for breakage or to accommodate any surplus beer. Brown bottles do a better job of protecting your beer

brewing hops and grains and cultivate their own preferred strains of yeast. These are the home-brewing possessed, intrepid souls who explore the netherworlds of fermentation. They produce extraordinary beers.

But you don't have to practice high science just to make very good beer. Brewing is an eminently inexact science, forgiving of many mistakes and allowing for much experimentation. Just look at any half-dozen books on the subject. Each will describe a different procedure for brewing and fermenting, and each will include recipes unlike those in the other books. All will produce good results.

from light, but green bottles are easier to fill since they let you see the level of the liquid more readily. Most brewers are content to use either. Returnable bottles are usually stronger than nonreturnables. In any case, don't use clear glass bottles or any bottle not designed to hold a carbonated beverage.

10. A capper and caps. There are several different kinds of bottle cappers on the market, and all will do the job. The easiest to use, though, is the bench-style bottle capper. It's also the most expensive, but its efficiency and durability make it a worthwhile investment. Metal crown caps are usually sold by the gross for just a few dollars.

Ingredients

Beer cannot be made without four essential ingredients: malted barley, hops, yeast and water. The first two are the yin and yang of beer—malted barley (more commonly referred to as malt) adds body and flavor; hops provide characteristic bitterness and aroma. It is the mixing of these two ingredients—varying their relative proportions, their cooking times, the varieties used, the points in the process at which each is added—that makes each beer distinctive and different.

1. Malted barley. Barley that has gone through a complicated, carefully controlled process of steeping, partial germination and kiln-drying is said to be malted. In the process, soluble starches and sugars in the barley are released. Before the malt becomes brewable, however, the grain must be *mashed*, another complex procedure involving steeping the grain in water at precise temperatures for specific time periods. Mashing develops the fermentable malt sugars that give beer its alcohol potential and distinctive body and flavor.

But you don't have to bother with malting or mashing barley to make good beer. Instead, you can buy ready-to-use concentrated malted and mashed barley extract, sold in two forms: syrup (referred to in recipes as malt extract) or powdered (usually designated dry malt). Literally hundreds of different varieties and brands of light, amber and dark malt extracts (both syrup and dry) are now available in this country. Always buy the best you can afford. (Munton & Fison, Edme and John Bull are three highly regarded British brands.)

Hopped malt extract, in which hops have already been boiled, is also sold. Because it saves the beginning brewer a step in the process, hopped extract is often included in beer-making kits. Most experienced home-brewers who use hopped extracts, though, maintain that additional hops are necessary to produce a proper bouquet.

Common Hops and Their Characteristics

Variety	Bitterness	Flavor, Aroma, Etc.
Brewer's Gold	High	Strong, full-flavored bittering hop
Bullion	High	Strong, full-flavored bittering hop
Cascade	Medium	Mild bittering, flowery aromatic
Cluster	Medium high	Widely used bittering hop
Eroica	Very high	Strong bittering; use sparingly
Fuggles	Low	Spicy aromatic
Galena	Very high	Strong bittering; use sparingly
Hallertauer	Low	Pungent, spicy aromatic
Northern Brewer	High	Flavorful bittering hop, can also be used as an aromatic
Nugget	Very high	Strong bittering; use sparingly
Saaz	Low	Distinctive, spicy aromatic
Spalt	Low	Full-flavored, blends nicely with bitter varieties
Styrian Golding	Medium	Mild, spicy
Talisman	Medium high	High-quality bittering
Tettnanger	Medium	Bittering hop, can be used as aromatic
Willamette	Medium	Similar to Fuggles

Specialty malts are used in some malt extract–based recipes to add color and/or flavor. Any of several kinds of specialty malts are commonly called for in recipes: Black patent, chocolate and roasted barley malt are used in dark beers to add color and character. Crystal malt is lighter, giving beer a golden color and adding a bit of sweetness. The first three malted grains can be added whole to the brew. Crystal malt should be crushed first—simply run a rolling pin over the grain once or twice to crack the shells. Don't, however, pulverize the grain in a blender or coffee grinder.

As you gain experience as a home-brewer, you may eventually decide to quit using malt extract and make all-grain beer, mashing malted grains yourself to convert the necessary sugars. For now, though, rest assured you can produce superb beers using malt extracts and—if you want—small amounts of specialty malts.

2. Hops. These are the cone-shaped flowers of the female hop plant (*Humulus lupulus*). Besides adding characteristic bitterness and aroma to a beer, hops act as a preservative; the acids released during cooking kill fungi that would otherwise spoil the brew.

It's not the flowers themselves, but the resin glands, called lupulin, at the base of the petals that give hops their distinctive properties. The resin itself contains acids that produce bitterness; the volatile oils in the glands yield aroma.

Hops are usually added to the brew in several stages. "Bittering" hops—those varieties that are high in acid content—are added to the brew first, and cooked the longest, in order to extract the desired hop tartness. "Aromatic" hops—which generally have a low acid content—are added only in the final few minutes of boiling, so that the pungent oils are retained in the brew rather than cooked away. Some varieties of hops are used exclusively for bittering or aroma, while others, usually those with a medium acid content, can produce either characteristic, depending on when they're added to the brew.

You can buy whole dried hops or hop

Fig. 1
Home-brewing equipment

Primary fermenter

Boiling kettle

Fermentation lock

Secondary fermenter

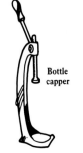

Siphon tube

Hydrometer

Thermometer

Stainless spoon

Bottle capper

pellets. Pellets are made from pulverized and compressed hop resin glands. They're somewhat easier to use than whole hops—you just stir them into the brew. Whole hops need to be strained off, or "sparged," before fermenting or bottling. In any case, be sure the hops you buy are fresh. Whole and pellet hops should appear green, not brown. Many home-brew shops now keep their hops refrigerated, a desirable precaution since hops deteriorate rapidly at room temperature.

The accompanying chart lists the basic characteristics of a number of popular hop varieties. Feel free to experiment: If a recipe calls for a kind of hop that's unavailable in your area, substitute another with similar properties.

3. Yeast. This of course is the fuel of fermentation, the stuff that makes beer *beer*. Just as important as knowing what kind of yeast to use is knowing what kind *not* to use—specifically, bakers' yeast or brewers' yeast (sold as a nutrition supplement in health food stores). The former won't work satisfactorily; the latter won't work at all.

Use only high-quality *beer yeast*, which is generally classified as either *ale* (top fermenting) yeast or *lager* (bottom fermenting) yeast. Most of the recipes you'll find here call for ale yeast. Lager yeasts are generally used only to produce lagers, which are specially fermented at temperatures below 55°F and are best reserved until you have at least a couple of batches of ale under your belt.

Many strains of ale and lager yeasts are available. Most are sold in the form of dried granules, sealed in foil packs. Different brands and strains of yeast impart different flavors; if you're a beginner, you might want to try a different strain each time you make a new batch of the same beer, to get better acquainted with the possibilities.

4. Water. Since water is by far the main ingredient in beer (up to 95%), its quality naturally has some effect on the quality of the brew; just how *much* effect is one of many minor controversies that rage among homebrewers. Generally, any water that tastes good is acceptable for malt extract–based beers. Most public water supplies are, however, quite soft—in other words, low in minerals—so many beer recipes call for the addition of gypsum, noniodized salt, epsom salts or other conditioners to enhance flavors and foster ideal brewing conditions.

In Addition

Many recipes call for ingredients beyond the four basics.

1. Adjunct sugars. Any sugar that is added to the brew, other than priming sugar (discussed in the section on bottling), is called

Fig. 2
Adding malt extract

Fig. 3
Stirring the extract

Fig. 4
Adding the hops

Fig. 5
Adding malt grain

Fig. 6
Transferring to primary fermenter

an adjunct. All-malt beers produce all their alcohol from the malt sugar (maltose) derived from the grains. But all-malt beers are, by nature, full-bodied. To produce a lighter-bodied beer, some brewers simply use less malt and add an adjunct to provide the sugar necessary for fermentation and proper alcohol content.

By far, corn sugar (dextrose or glucose) is the most widely used adjunct because it converts to alcohol readily without producing the "hot" taste characteristic of fermented cane sugar. Too much of either, however, can make your beer taste cidery or can produce an unpleasantly high alcohol content. As a rule of thumb, never use corn sugar in an amount greater than one-third, by weight, the combined amount of malt extract and adjunct sugar in a recipe (some say that the upper limit should be one-fifth, by weight, and others say that *any* adjunct constitutes beer blasphemy).

2. Optional refinements. The emphasis is on "optional" here. The following are listed in many recipes and used by many brewers, but others consider them entirely unnecessary.

Ascorbic acid (vitamin C), an antioxidant, is sometimes added to the brew just before bottling. (Don't use vitamin C tablets; most contain additional ingredients you don't want in your beer.) *Citric acid* is used to raise the acidity of the brew to a level conducive to fermentation and hostile to unwanted organisms. *Finings* (Irish moss, fining gelatin, papain, Polyclar) are substances used to clarify beer by precipitating proteins that supposedly create cloudy brew. *Yeast nutrient*, also called yeast food or yeast energizer, is designed to make your unfermented brew a great place for yeast to live and reproduce.

Before You Brew

Assuming you've gathered up your supplies and ingredients, now you're ready to get cooking. First, though, you'll have to take what may be the most important step in the entire brewing process: *Sanitize* all equipment and utensils.

Don't use soap or detergent; they can leave residues that are virtually impossible to rinse off completely. Instead, use a dilute solution of household chlorine bleach. Make up a solution of two tablespoons of bleach in five gallons of water, and let it stand 10 minutes. While you're waiting, rinse all your equipment in hot (not boiling) water. Then soak everything in the solution for a half-hour or so, and let it drip dry. There's no need for rinsing with water; the chlorine solution is much too dilute to have an effect on the beer.

Commercial sterilants are sold in homebrew shops. They, too, are diluted in water (about one tablespoon per five gallons; follow the package instructions). Soaking is unnecessary; simply slosh the solution around in the containers, and pour it over utensils, then give everything a quick rinse in water.

Get Brewing

To brew your first batch of beer, just pick one of the following lists of basic ingredients, and carefully follow the instructions given in each step.

All-Malt Ale

2 3½-pound cans light, amber or dark malt extract
½ teaspoon noniodized salt
1 teaspoon gypsum
½ pound crushed crystal malt
2 ounces bittering hops (Brewer's Gold, Hallertauer, Northern Brewer or Bullion)
1 ounce aromatic hops (Fuggles or Cascade)
Ale yeast
Water to 5 gallons
¾–1 cup corn sugar for priming
Starting specific gravity: 1.044 to 1.046
Final specific gravity: 1.010 to 1.012

Light Summer Ale

1 3½-pound can light malt extract
1½ pounds corn sugar
1 teaspoon gypsum
½ teaspoon noniodized salt
2 ounces bittering hops (Northern Brewer or Bullion)
½ ounce aromatic hops (Fuggles, Tettnanger or Cascade)
Ale yeast
¾–1 cup corn sugar for priming
Starting specific gravity: 1.036 to 1.038
Final specific gravity: 1.006 to 1.008

Dark Beer

2 3½-pound cans light malt extract
2 cups corn sugar
1 teaspoon gypsum
½ teaspoon noniodized salt
1½ ounces Talisman bittering hops
¼ ounce Bullion bittering hop pellets
1 cup black patent malt
2 cups crushed crystal malt
2 ounces aromatic hops (Hallertauer)
Lager yeast
¾–1 cup corn sugar for priming
Starting specific gravity: 1.049 to 1.051
Final specific gravity: 1.009 to 1.011

Step 1: Boiling the wort. Put two gallons of water in your kettle, and bring it to a boil. While you're waiting for the liquid to heat, place the can or cans of malt extract in a container of hot water to liquefy (or, if you're

Fig. 7
Sparging the wort

Fig. 8
Adding yeast

Fig. 9
Transferring to secondary fermenter

Fig. 10
Adding priming sugar

substituting dried malt extract, make up the necessary batter by adding water according to the package instructions).

When the water comes to a rolling boil, switch off the heat, and stir in the extract. When the malt is thoroughly dissolved, turn the heat back on, and add the salt, gypsum and crystal malt (if called for). This mixture is called the *wort* (pronounced wart). Continue heating to reestablish a rolling boil, but keep a careful eye on the pot. Just before the wort boils, it will begin to froth up. Stir the liquid (and reduce the heat, too, if necessary) to keep the contents from overflowing. The foam will recede after a few minutes.

Keep a slow but strong rolling boil going for 20 to 30 minutes. Then add half the flavoring hops, and boil for 45 minutes, stirring occasionally. Add the remaining flavoring hops and any dark specialty malts (roasted barley, black patent or chocolate malt), and boil for 30 minutes, adding the finishing hops during the last five to 10 minutes.

Step 2. Transfer to the primary fermenter. Remove the kettle from the heat, and pour the hot wort into the primary fermenter. To separate out the spent hops and grain, pour the liquid either through your kitchen strainer (with or without an added lining of cheesecloth) or through cheesecloth stretched tightly across the fermenter. (Don't forget to sterilize the fermenter and strainer.) Then pour a quart or two of hot boiled water over the retained hops and grains (and into the fermenter) to extract as much of the remaining flavors and starches as possible; this is called *sparging* the wort.

Next, using a sterilized spoon, stir in any sugar called for (but *not* sugar designated for priming). Make sure the sugar is dissolved completely.

Add enough more water (boiled, but not boiling-hot) to the fermenter to make five gallons. Don't fill the fermenter more than about two-thirds full, however; some air space is necessary to accommodate the foam and gases created by the first few days of active fermentation. If your fermenter's not big enough, add only enough water to bring the liquid up to the two-thirds level. You can add the remaining water to the brew when you transfer it to the secondary fermenter.

If you're interested in monitoring the sugar content of your brew, this is the time to check the specific gravity with your sterilized hydrometer. If you weren't able to add all the water, you'll have to adjust the gravity reading: To do so, multiply the reading by the number of gallons actually present, and divide the result by five. Even when the recipe doesn't provide anticipated starting and final gravities, it's a good idea to take and record readings. They'll be helpful references when you brew your next batch.

Fig. 11
Sterilizing the bottles

Fig. 12
Siphoning into bottles

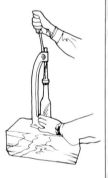

Fig. 13
Capping the bottles

Fig. 14
Enjoying a home brew

Byron Burch's All-time Favorite Irish Stout Recipe

Widely known for his excellent, landmark book, *Quality Brewing* (recently updated and retitled *Brewing Quality Beers*), Byron Burch is considered one of America's preeminent home-brewers. This is a favorite recipe.

Irish-Style Stout (5 gallons)
5 pounds light dry malt or 6 pounds light malt extract
2 pounds amber or dark malt extract
$1/4$ teaspoon salt
Water to 5 gallons
$2 1/2$ ounces bittering hops (Northern Brewer or Bullion)
1 pound roasted barley (added whole)
$1/2$ ounce aromatic hops (Fuggles or Styrian Golding)
$3/4$ cup corn sugar for priming
$1/2$ ounce ale yeast
Starting specific gravity: 1.058
Final specific gravity: 1.020

Thoroughly dissolve the dry malt, malt extract and salt in 2 to 5 gallons of water. Heat this to a rolling boil. Stir in half the bitter-

After the labor of creation, an artist enjoys his reward.

ing hops, and boil it for 30 minutes, stirring occasionally. Add the rest of the bittering hops and all the roasted barley, and boil for 30 more minutes, adding the aromatic hops during the last 2 minutes.

At the end of the boil, cool the wort as quickly as possible to between 70° and 85°F. (This can be done by placing the kettle in a bathtub and running cold water around it.) Add the yeast, and siphon the beer into a fermenter. Ferment and bottle the beer.

Step 3. Add the yeast. Check the temperature of the wort with a sterilized thermometer. When it has dropped below 80°F (70° to 75°F is ideal for ale yeast), sprinkle the yeast on the brew, let it activate for about 10 minutes, and then stir it in. This is called *pitching* the wort. Some brewers *proof* the yeast first, to make sure it's viable, by drawing off about a half-cup of wort into a small sterile container and then adding the yeast to that. When it is apparent the yeast is active, the wort is pitched.

Now put the lid on the fermenter, attach a fermentation lock (sanitize the stopper and lock), and fill the lock one-third to one-half full of boiled (but not boiling) water. Put the fermenter in a cool, dark place where it won't be disturbed and where temperatures won't go above 75°F or, when using ale yeast, below 60°F. Strong light can affect the beer's flavor and aroma in short order; some brewers slip a black plastic garbage bag over the fermenter and cut a small hole for the fermentation lock to poke through.

Step 4. Transfer to the secondary fermenter. Over the next two or three days the beer will ferment actively and develop a foam layer called the *krausen*. After about four days the

krausen will fall back to the surface. When this happens, it's time to transfer the beer to the secondary fermenter. Sterilize the siphon tube, the fermenter and its fermentation lock. Then siphon the beer into the secondary container (if you haven't added all the water yet, do so now, before adding the beer). Keep the siphon tube off the bottom of the primary to avoid picking up sediments; at the same time, try to keep the other end of the tube *on* the bottom of the secondary, to avoid splashing the brew, which can cause it to pick up airborne bacteria. (This can be a bit like trying to thread a needle on each end of a wet noodle; home-brew shops sell special stiff tubes you can attach to the siphon to make it more controllable.)

Now cap the fermenter, attach the lock (one-third to one-half full of water), and allow the beer to finish its fermentation. Keep an eye on the fermentation lock. In three to 10 days—depending on the room temperature and the amount and vitality of the yeast—when apparent fermentation has stopped, when the rise of bubbles through the lock has ceased, and when your hydrometer reading is near where the recipe indicates, your brew is ready to bottle.

Step 5. Bottle and cap the beer. Wash the bottles in hot water, making sure to rinse away any residue in the bottoms. Then sterilize the bottles. If you're using the chlorine solution described, soak the bottles the prescribed time, and turn them upside down to drip dry. If you're using a commercial sterilant, put about a tablespoon of the solution in each bottle, put your thumb over the bottle, shake it, dump it, and rinse the bottle lightly with water. Also clean and sterilize the primary fermenter and the siphon tube.

Now put one to two cups of water in a pot, add the three-fourths to one cup of corn sugar for priming, and boil the solution for five minutes. In the meantime, siphon the beer back into the now-clean primary fermenter (or any other sanitized container big enough to hold the brew). Add the boiled sugar-water, stirring thoroughly. This "priming syrup" puts just enough fermentable sugar into the brew to carbonate the beer after it's bottled. Those who prefer low carbonation should use only three-fourths cup of corn sugar for priming; if you like a somewhat fizzier beer, use one cup.

Now carefully siphon the beer into the bottles. *Don't splash it*; put the sterilized siphon all the way to the bottom of the bottles as you fill them. Leave about a one-inch air space in each bottle, and after they're all filled, cap them. Store the beer in a cool, dark place. After about a week, chill a bottle or two in the refrigerator, and give your beer a try. If it's carbonated, it's ready to drink, although it may be a bit "green." Many home-brewers let their beer age at least a month before sampling it; whether or not aging improves the flavor of beer is a favorite subject of home-brew debate.

Pouring a bottle of your own beer—for yourself or for a friend—is a celebration of achievement, an act to perform with pride and proper care. There'll be a bit of yeast sediment in the bottom of each bottle; it's rich in B vitamins and can't hurt you, but it can give your beer a cloudy look in the glass. One mark of an artful home-brewer is the ability to pour a clear beer, slowly filling a tilted glass until the yeast approaches the lip of the bottle, then deftly tipping the bottle back at the last moment to catch the yeast while wasting barely a half-swallow of the brew itself. This is a skill that demands practice, a task no home-brewer seems to mind.

There you have it: basic brewing from start to finish. Chances are this is only the beginning. There's a phenomenon in home-brewing that compels those who make a first batch to try a second, and then a third, and then—before you know it—you, too, are among the home-brewing possessed, on a quest for the perfect beer.

Wine

Making wine may be an art, but almost anyone can do it superbly. All it takes is fruit, sugar, yeast—and time.

Bottling your homemade wine is the best part of the whole wine-making process. Except, of course, for that great day when you can finally drink it!

Really good wine can develop *only* over time. And, unlike the owner of a commercial winery, many of us have this one ingredient—time—in abundance. This is the edge that you have as a home wine maker. This is the advantage which—used wisely—will allow you to make better wine than you can buy.

If you can fall out of bed in the morning, you can make good wine. It's that easy. But you'll never do it if you try to just blunder along, follow a recipe, throw in a little bakers' yeast now and then and see what happens.

To make superb wine, you must understand the fundamentals of each step of the process. And you must learn to be absolutely religious about keeping everything in your miniwinery spotlessly clean at all times. Master these two basics of the art, and you'll be able to produce exceptional wine from almost any fruit and a variety of vegetables. (Don't laugh. The English even make the drink from hedge leaves, and one of the best wines you'll ever taste is made from beets.)

To most people, the seemingly mysterious world of fermentation is actually as straightforward and easy to comprehend as any other chemistry experiment. A solution—called *must*—of water, sugar, fruit juice and fruit pulp is prepared in a scrupulously clean container, and wine yeast is then introduced to the must.

That's wine yeast, and *not* bakers' yeast. Bakers' yeast is bred for the taste it leaves in baked goods, while wine yeast has been carefully developed over hundreds of years to leave no taste at all in wine. Bakers' yeast is "top fermenting" (most of its action, when it's used to make wine, takes place in the up-

per few inches of the must), while wine yeast "bottom ferments." Bakers' yeast is sometimes killed by the first few percentage points of alcohol that develop in a container of must, whereas wine yeast can withstand as much as a 16% concentration of alcohol.

When the yeast plants (actually, very minute fungi) are added to the must, they rapidly reproduce themselves and release carbon dioxide. Once this carbon dioxide has flushed all the oxygen from the must, the yeast settles down to consume the sugar in the solution and produce alcohol in earnest. Then, when all the sugar is gone (when the must has been converted to wine), the yeast expires and drifts slowly to the bottom of the container.

Our job as wine makers is not to *make* wine, but to *allow* the yeast to make wine. Our task, to put it another way, is simply to set up and control the conditions under which the process takes place, so that the best strain of yeast we can obtain is protected and nurtured and left free to make the finest wine it's capable of producing.

Equipment

Here are all the important items of hardware you'll need to set yourself up as a vintner:

1. An open container of at least eight gallons capacity
2. A two-gallon stainless-steel or enameled bowl or pot
3. A two-quart, small-mesh sack
4. Nine one-gallon, small-mouth jugs
5. One half-gallon, small-mouth jug
6. Six feet of flexible, clear plastic tubing

7. 25 screw-top wine bottles with plastic caps
8. A roll of plastic food wrap
9. An assortment of rubber bands
10. A dependable hydrometer

The first item on the list will be used as a primary fermentation vat. Some people prefer that this container be made of the traditional wood or crockery. But, since both wood and crockery are porous and almost impossible to completely clean and disinfect, many other home wine makers feel that a better bet is a primary fermenter made of food-grade plastic. Try a brand-new plastic (remember, of *food* grade) wastepaper can or garbage pail.

Beware of most metals (anything except stainless steel) when you're selecting the primary fermenter and other utensils for your home winery. Metal almost always leaves a haze and an off-taste in wine. Stick with wood, glass and plastic. And make sure your main fermenting vat will hold at least eight gallons. Primary fermentation is often quite vigorous and can overflow a smaller container.

The small-mesh sack will be filled with fruit pulp and left in the main vat during primary fermentation. Make sure it's large enough to hold two full quarts and still tie off securely at the top. The bag can be made of any porous material: You might, for instance, want to sew up several sacks from a section of nylon drapery.

Cider jugs make very fine gallon and half-gallon bottles for secondary fermentation. Colored glass and plastic jugs will do, but clear glass allows you to look right into the containers and watch the wine develop its polish.

You'll use the plastic tubing to siphon your wine from one container to another at various times during its production. This piece of equipment is more important than it may at first seem because the wine, except for the first time it's moved, should *never* purposely be exposed to the air. Oxygen can react with a green (undeveloped) wine to produce a nutty flavor (which, although desirable in a sherry, is considered a flaw in a normal table wine). Worse, if oxygen is allowed into a new bottle of wine, it can foster the growth of something you don't want at all: vinegar bacteria.

You'll probably have less trouble rounding up the 25 wine bottles than anything else on the equipment list. Most states require all restaurants, bars and caterers to throw out all their wine and liquor bottles as soon as the containers are empty. As a result, such establishments are usually happy to have you haul the empties away. And if you prefer the heavier champagne bottles, just check out the next few weddings and parties in your section of town.

Consider storing your wine in bottles that close with screw caps. The plastic corks that come in those lovely champagne bottles are reusable too, but only for a few times before the ridges around the stoppers become so worn and mashed down that the corks will no longer positively reseal.

The plastic wrap and rubber bands will be used as air traps or air locks. Sure, you can buy "real" wine-making glass or plastic locks (with the nifty little water trap inside) for "only" 35 to 50¢ each. That doesn't sound too bad *one at a time*, but, for the five-gallon batch we're going to make, you should have

Equipment for Making Wine and Beer

Primary fermenter

Bottle capper

Beaker

Thermometer

Hydrometer

at least eight of the little beauties on hand. And if you plan to ever have more than one vat of wine going at a time, your total investment in air locks—even at 35¢ a shot—can quickly mount.

Fortunately, there's a very simple and inexpensive way around this problem. Because, after all, what *is* an air lock anyway? It's nothing but a trap that lets *out* the gas generated by the yeast in a developing bottle of wine, while refusing to let *in* the outside air. A 10-inch square of plastic wrap placed loosely over the mouth of a gallon jug and secured with a doubled rubber band will do that job as well as anything.

Don't pull the sheet of plastic tight, and *don't* go crazy doubling up your rubber bands. (The tighter the bands, the more pressure it'll take to stretch them enough to let the generated gas out. Also, if the plastic is taut enough, there's always the chance it'll rupture before the bands stretch.) *Do* make sure the film of plastic is caught under the doubled band all the way around the jug's neck. Then, as pressure builds in the container, the band will have to stretch a little to let the gas out, and you'll have a positive seal at all times so that no outside air can get in with the wine.

This plastic-wrap trap, by the way, is not a new idea, and it does have one significant advantage over even the most expensive water-type trap: When left unattended for a long period, the water can evaporate from its trap and leave your wine unprotected. The plastic-wrap trap, for all practical purposes, is unaffected by time.

The most important item of equipment, a good hydrometer, is an absolute necessity for anyone who expects to make quality wine consistently.

Hydrometers seem to intimidate a great many people, and they shouldn't. They are simple devices that measure the density of liquids, and the one you'll be using is very similar to the hydrometer that your local garage mechanic uses when he tests the strength of the battery acid and antifreeze in your car.

Some wine-making hydrometers are nothing but a sealed and weighted, graduated tube that is floated right in a vat or bottle of wine. Others consist of the sealed, weighted, graduated tube inside a hollow, transparent cylinder of glass or plastic that has a short length of tubing on its bottom and a squeeze bulb on the top. By squeezing the bulb, dipping the tubing into a liquid and then releasing the bulb, a quantity of the fluid can be drawn into the instrument's main cylinder. This will cause the little weighted tube inside to float higher or lower in the liquid, depending on the fluid's density. It's then very easy to read one of the graduated scales on the side of the floating tube where it sticks up out of the liquid and thereby determine the specific gravity of the fluid being tested.

For instance, the specific gravity scale (marked "S.G.") on a hydrometer is set up so that plain, ordinary water—when tested—will give you a reading of 1.000. Any fluid that is "thicker"—say a solution of water and sugar—will cause the indicator tube to float higher and yield a higher specific gravity reading. But if we convert some of the sugar in that solution to a "thinner" liquid such as alcohol (pure alcohol has an S.G. of only about .800), then we will lower the spe-

cific gravity of the fluid we are testing *in direct proportion* to the amount of change that takes place.

What this means, of course, is that we can use a hydrometer to tell us exactly how much sugar to add to a given amount of water to produce—months later—precisely the percentage of alcohol we want in a finished batch of wine. We can also use the instrument to monitor the wine's progress during its development and to "fine-tune" the fermentation as it goes along.

Complete instructions come with a new hydrometer, and you should buy one (instead of borrowing) if you plan to make a lot of wine.

Two final points about reading a hydrometer: First, make sure the little weighted tube inside is floating freely (give the instrument's cylinder a "spin" between your fingers, if necessary, to shake off any bubbles that might be clinging to the scale inside) before you try to read it. And make that reading with your eye exactly level with the top of the solution in the cylinder. Second, remember that the density of a fluid changes with temperature. Thus, your hydrometer will be strictly accurate at only one temperature (most wine-making S.G. testers are calibrated for 68°F). The variations you'll be dealing with won't be enough to worry about, though, as long as you make some effort to test your wine only at something close to this standard temperature. (If your wine has been stored at—say—40°F, let it warm to room temperature before you test it.)

And that's it for the equipment. Everything you'll need—even if you have to go out and buy it all new—should cost you very lit-

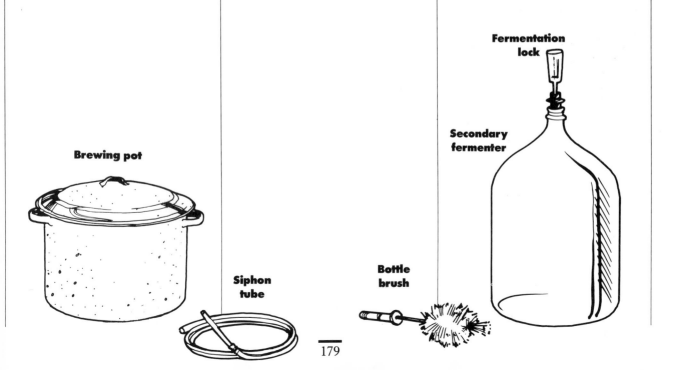

Brewing pot

Siphon tube

Bottle brush

Fermentation lock

Secondary fermenter

tle. And everything can be used over and over again.

Blackberry Wine

Blackberry is a favorite homemade wine, so start with that one. (The recipe will work for all berry wines.) You'll need the following ingredients:

15 pounds blackberries
$1/2$ cup raisins
$1/2$ teaspoon ascorbic acid (vitamin C)
5 gallons water
1 tablespoon acid blend (or the juice of 1 lemon)
10 pounds sugar
1 package dry wine yeast

If your fruit has been sprayed, wash it. Otherwise, don't. Then crush the berries in the two-gallon bowl to release their juice.

Once you've turned your berries to mush, empty them into the nylon sack while you hold the bag over your eight-gallon plastic can. Squeeze the sack gently against the side of the can to force the juice free from the pulp, then fill the bowl half full of berries again, mash them, add the new pulp to the mass already in the sack, and so on. Repeat until all the fruit has been crushed and all the pulp is in the bag. Then dump in the raisins, tie the top of the sack closed, and leave it in the can with the fruit juice.

Add the ascorbic acid next. If you can get it, the powdered form of the vitamin is less expensive than tablets. The purpose of the ascorbic acid, by the way, is to prevent the wine from oxidizing and changing color when it's later exposed to air and light.

Now you're ready to heat five gallons of water almost to boiling and add it to the fruit juice in the eight-gallon can. The hot water will kill most of the wild yeast and bacteria in the juice and pulp and keep them from competing with the wine yeast that you'll soon introduce to the must. There's no need, however, to boil the juice and pulp to make them absolutely sterile, since boiling would set the pectin they contain and make your wine difficult to clear later.

Empty in the acid blend next. This is a powdered mixture of three naturally occurring acids (tartaric from grapes, citric from citrus fruits and malic from apples). Any wine-making supply house will have it in stock.

In a pinch, you can substitute the juice of one lemon for the acid blend. It'll work about as well, although wine made with the straight citric acid will be somewhat more susceptible to oxidation than a batch made with the blend. *Do* add the acid in one form or the other, however, or your wine will be rather flat and insipid.

Once the acid is in, it's time for the sugar and a test of your expertise with the hydrometer. Pour in about two-thirds of the 10-pound bag of sugar, vigorously stir the solution in the big primary fermentation vat to dissolve the sweetener, cover the can with a towel, and let it cool to room temperature. This will take 10 hours or so.

When your must has reached room temperature, check its specific gravity with your hydrometer. Then add a little bit of sugar at a time, stir the must until the sweetener has dissolved, and again test the solution's specific gravity. Stop when the little bulb in the hydrometer floats at the 1.095 mark. Unless your blackberries are really ripe, you'll use most of the rest of the sack of sugar. And if you accidentally overshoot the S.G. you're after, don't worry. Just add enough water to bring it back down to 1.095, a level that will produce a wine that contains about 14% alcohol by volume.

Finally, once you've adjusted the sugar to your satisfaction, you can sprinkle the dry yeast—straight from its foil packet—onto the surface of the must. Do not stir. Some of the yeast will sink directly to the bottom of the can, but most of it will float. That's fine. Let the yeast do what it wants to do.

Primary Fermentation

Within 12 hours, more or less, you should start to see obvious signs of fermentation. Small bubbles will begin to form a circle of foam a few inches in from the wall of your vat. Any yeast that is still floating will be surrounded by this foam, and there will be a distinctly heady smell in the air.

Now that the fermentation is under way, you should stir the must twice a day with something made of wood (never metal!), such as an old broom handle. Punch down the bag of pulp a few times while you're at it. And always re-cover the big can of fermenting must with the towel to keep dust and fruit flies out.

Check the specific gravity of your fermenting brew at least once a day, and keep a record of the developing wine's S.G. As the yeast eats the sugar, it will produce carbon dioxide and alcohol. The gas will bubble off as it forms, but the alcohol will remain in the must. And—as you already know—as the quantity of sugar decreases and the amount of alcohol increases, the specific gravity of the must will drop. When the S.G. reaches 1.030, that's your signal to transfer the wine into closed bottles for secondary fermentation.

Why *closed* bottles? Because, up to this point, the yeast organisms were very active and were producing enough carbon dioxide to cover the surface of the must. The fungi are beginning to slow down now, though, and—from this time on—they'll steadily release less and less of the gas. Which means that it's only a matter of time before oxygen reaches the must, unless it's protected in some way.

Secondary Fermentation

Wash eight of the nine one-gallon jugs superclean. *Don't use soap.* It leaves a film that's almost impossible to rinse away. If some deposits are stuck really hard in any of the containers, swish a handful of gravel around in the bottom. If that doesn't do the trick, throw that jug away, and get another one. Rinse each container several times with cold water.

Squeeze the bag in the primary fermenter until the sack is completely dry (it'll be much smaller than when you put it in). Then throw away the pulp, rinse the bag in clean water, and hang it where it will stay dry until you want to use it again.

Stir the must and sediment together in the primary vat, and, using a cup or bowl as a ladle, fill each of the gallon jugs *to the shoulder* with the mixture. Don't be tempted to fill the containers any higher than their shoulders. The yeast may be slowing down, but it contains enough "kick" to produce some foam yet, and you must leave enough space for it. If there's still some of the fermenting brew left in the primary vat after the eight jugs have been filled shoulder-high, ladle the excess into any available container that— shoulder-high—will hold it. Then cap the eight jugs and the extra container with plastic wrap and rubber bands.

As soon as you've sealed the secondary fermentation jugs, rinse out the original plastic can with plenty of clean water. Immediately is not too soon to handle this job: If you leave it until later, the residue in the vat's bottom will be doubly hard to remove. Then store the can in an airy place until you're ready to start another batch of must.

The nine secondary fermentation jugs should be covered in some way to keep light from reaching their contents. Keep the containers in the coolest spot you can find (a dark cellar is ideal).

Racking

When the foam has disappeared from the surface of the must in the gallon jugs, you should *rack* (siphon off) the green wine into clean containers.

Rinse out the ninth gallon jug (the one you haven't used yet), and run clean water through your siphon hose. Then place the first gallon to be racked off up on a chair or table, and set the empty jug beneath it on the floor. Stick one end of the plastic tubing beneath the surface of the must in the upper jug, and—keeping your head lower than the liquid—gently suck on the other end of the hose. Then, before the must reaches your mouth, cap off the end of the tubing with your thumb. (If you're not quick enough with this last step, you'll get a mouthful of must. Don't worry—it's good for you.)

Now you're in business. Bring the thumb-capped end of the hose to the mouth of the lower jug, and, while you take care to keep the other end of the tubing beneath the surface of the liquid in the upper jug, remove your thumb and start the siphon. As the lower container begins to fill, push that end of the hose down beneath the surface of the accumulating wine. This minimizes the exposure of the must to the air.

When the upper jug is almost empty, slowly tilt it toward you, and draw the last of the wine off its sediment. *Make sure that you don't accidentally stick the tube into those dregs.* As the first bit of sediment begins to sneak up the hose, pull the tubing from the upper jug. This whole siphoning operation is much easier when done by two people.

All right. Carefully rinse the jug you've just emptied, siphon the next filled one into it, and so on. If you plan to start a new batch of wine within the next day or so, you can use the sediment in any of the bottles to inoculate the new must. Just put a few teaspoons of the culture in a closed jar, and keep it in the refrigerator until you need it.

This time around—unlike the last—you'll want to fill each of your gallon containers to within an inch of their rims, since fermentation is over and there's no longer any danger of the wine foaming up. After racking, you should find yourself with approximately five and a half gallons of wine on your hands. Put the odd half gallon into the half-gallon jug included on your equipment list, seal all six containers with plastic wrap and rubber bands, and store the jugs in a cool place.

Rack the wine again after three weeks and again at the end of three months; or, if it has already cleared, at the end of two months.

First Aid for Unclear Wine

There is a slim chance that your wine won't have cleared at the end of even three months. If that's the case, your best cure for the problem is time. Given enough of that magic ingredient, almost any wine will eventually lose its haze; some apple wines habitually take as long as a year to clear.

If you feel that you can't wait your must out, you can sometimes clear a wine by presenting it with a large surface area of something—traditionally, wood—on which

its particles of haze can settle. Try boiling some oak chips for a few minutes, draining them and then putting a couple of tablespoons of shavings into one of the gallon jugs. The chips of oak should help clear the wine, mellow it, darken the must and give it character, and add a distinctive oak flavor to the brew. Although the addition of the shavings should speed the wine's clearing, it will still take time for the haze to settle. So taste the wine every few weeks to see if the oak taste is becoming too strong.

Beechwood shavings or chips—which won't add any taste to your must—can also be used to clear a stubborn batch of wine. Again, add a couple of tablespoons per gallon, and leave them in until the wine clears. Or until you give up.

Yet another way to settle the haze out of your bottles involves the use of egg whites, which have been pressed into service for this purpose for centuries. Using one egg white per gallon of wine, beat them well, and pour them into the jugs. As the whipped white drifts to the bottom, particles of haze will adhere to it. Shake each jug gently once a day for a week or two until the wine has completely cleared.

None of the methods outlined here are foolproof, and you'll find that some wines simply will not clear unless they're filtered. To hell with filtering. Just drink the wine as it is. The haze won't affect its taste in any way, just its visual appeal.

Bottling

Next to drinking, bottling is the best part of wine making. Your fresh batch of the beverage—finally!—doesn't look or smell so bad anymore. It's even beginning to taste pretty good! Hey, this is all right! Bring on the bottles.

But first, you'll want to make absolutely certain that all the action of the yeast is over. Just looking at the wine, or tasting it, won't tell you. But your trusty hydrometer will. If it reads below 1.000 S.G. and your wine is acceptably clear, you're safe. It really *is* time to bring on the bottles.

Wash your 25 wine bottles thoroughly with a bottle brush and plenty of water. If you don't have a brush, use gravel again as you did with the gallon jugs.

Next, mix up a solution of chlorine cleaner or a commercial sterilant (both are available at wine-making supply houses), and rinse each of the containers with it. Then rinse each one at least twice with clean water.

Assuming that your bottles are each the standard fifth-gallon containers common in the United States, the five gallons of wine (with maybe a little over) that you probably racked at the end of two or three months will

just fill all 25 of your bottles to within an inch of their tops.

Start your siphon, and begin the filling. You can, if you like, purchase a small shutoff valve that will allow you to stop the flow of wine as you move from bottle to bottle. It's simpler and less expensive, though, to just fold the hose in your hand and crimp it down whenever you want to slow or stop the stream of wine.

When the bottles are full, seal them with the plastic caps. That's it. If you like the taste of your creation as is, you can begin drinking it immediately. Or, if you find the new wine still a little green, store it away in a cool, dark place, and try it again in about two months. You'll probably find it much smoother and far less astringent at that time.

The blackberry drink we've just made is a *dry* wine, which means that almost no sugar remains in the beverage after it has fermented. The wine, in short, is not sweet. It is, however—if all has gone well—superb.

Variations

Once you realize how easy wine is to make, you'll probably want to try whipping up a batch or two from other fruits, and from vegetables as well. No problem.

Other Berries: The basic recipe for blackberry wine will work with *any* berry.

Apples and Pears: Use a whole ounce of the vitamin C (since this fruit oxidizes so easily), and sprinkle it right into the pulp as you crush it. That crushing, by the way, is easier done with some sort of pestle, since apples and pears are a little tough on the knuckles. A wooden pestle is ideal, but you can use a jar filled with water (don't ram it into the fruit, and it won't break). Go easy, though, when you use any kind of tool to crush your fruit. Seeds contain tannin, which can make a wine taste harsh (the idea, then, is *not* to break up the seeds). You can vary the basic recipe for apple or pear wine by using five pounds fruit for each gallon of water and by adding one and a half (instead of one) teaspoons of the acid blend.

Chokecherries or Rose Hips: Use two pounds of fruit for each gallon of water and one teaspoon of acid blend.

Beets and Carrots: Try three pounds of either of the vegetables per gallon of water and use two teaspoons of the blend.

Grapes: The perfect fruit for wine. Forget the recipe if you have California grapes, and add nothing at all (not even water or acid blend) except the sugar you need to bring the must to 1.095 S.G. Native American wild grapes are a little different: Thin their juice by half with water, and add sugar until you have a specific gravity reading of 1.090. The wild grapes need no acid blend.

Not long ago, an age-yellowed little slip of a book called *The Secret of Better Baking* surfaced in the offices of *Mother Earth News* magazine. The period cover art showed a smiling homemaker with bobbed hair, a bowl of bread dough in one hand and a copy of this same book in the other. Written by Mary D. Chambers and published in 1925, the book is still one of the most concise, entertaining sources of wood cookstove selection/use/care/cooking knowledge around. The paragraphs that follow are from Mary Chambers' book; her 1920s' observations are included here because of their nostalgic charm and the valuable country baking secrets they offer. They also prove that some of the better things in life—such as the joys of preparing a delicious meal on a wood-burning cookstove—never change.

In one of the comedies of a generation ago, there is a love scene in which the hero picks up a leathery-looking object and makes a show of trying to bend it over his knee.

"What is it?" he asks.

The maid hangs her head in embarrassment, but replies courageously, "It's a pie. I made it."

"I'll eat it!" exclaims the delighted lover.

But the lady, with an eye to the future, recovers the pie and persuades the youth to prove his valor in less hazardous ways.

Baking a crisp, juicy pie or a deftly browned loaf of bread or managing a Thanksgiving dinner are worthwhile accomplishments. The kitchen range is close to the center of the home. It provides not only the main sustenance of life but also needed warmth from winter's cold as well as plentiful hot water.

Hundreds of cookbooks and collections of recipes by famous chefs witness the desire for variety in palatable and wholesome dishes. The implements of cooking have made equally rapid strides until they approach perfection. But a recipe book and the finest-equipped kitchen in the world do not make a cook. A good cook has learned how to handle her range so that it does her bidding without effort or "off days." And the cookbooks do not tell her how. There seems to be very little help for those who are making their first acquaintance with a modern range. This booklet is an introduction to your stove—just a few hints to make the acquaintance ripen more rapidly and to help you to a fuller enjoyment of the hours spent in the kitchen.

Building the Fire

No other article in the home means so much to the entire family as the kitchen range. Health and comfort are dependent upon it. No wonder a good housekeeper takes pride in the contentment of her family over the good things for the table that she provides: the extra heat in cold weather, the abundance of hot water on tap all the time, and many other things for which the modern range is equipped.

A good modern range is designed to get the greatest cooking and heating value out of the fuel used. When the range and chimney draft are right, a properly controlled fire will do all the work required, without wasting fuel.

It is therefore necessary to bear in mind that the first problem of better baking is an understanding of the fire. If a match is lighted, the flame shoots upward. The hot blaze causes a draft, drawing fresh air from below and supplying the oxygen necessary for combustion. The range simply makes use of this basic principle on a large scale.

To start the fire, then, have on hand plenty of free-burning fuel—dry paper and wood—cut small. A folded newspaper will not burn freely, but a few sheets, lightly twisted, make a good first layer. Then add a moderate supply of kindling wood, laid in loosely.

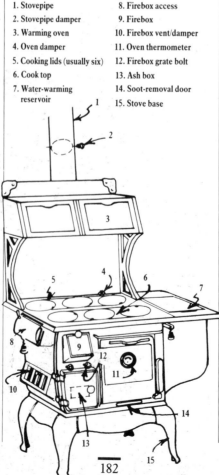

Fig. 1
Wood-burning
cookstove

1. Stovepipe	8. Firebox access
2. Stovepipe damper	9. Firebox
3. Warming oven	10. Firebox vent/damper
4. Oven damper	11. Oven thermometer
5. Cooking lids (usually six)	12. Firebox grate bolt
6. Cook top	13. Ash box
7. Water-warming reservoir	14. Soot-removal door
	15. Stove base

Before lighting, open the door or vent *under the fire*, the direct draft to the chimney (over the oven), the check slide at the base of the smoke pipe, and the damper in the smoke pipe. The purpose is to promote a free passage of air up through the firebox to the chimney by the most direct route.

Remember that no stove has a draft of itself. The draft is furnished by the chimney through the stovepipe, which obviously must be tight in all its joints.

Light the fire from below, and allow it to get a good start. If it burns too slowly, it needs more oxygen, which can be supplied by opening the door wide under the fire. If it burns too fast, it will produce more smoke than the chimney can draw off, and the excess will be thrown out into the room. Partly closing the door under the fire will retard it. (The first fire in a new range usually causes a little surface smoke and oily odor. This is harmless and soon passes off.)

Before applying larger pieces of wood or coal, add a little more kindling. The grate should be well covered with a brisk fire, both to support and ignite the larger fuel evenly and to prevent waste through the grate.

Never use kerosene to quicken a slow fire.

When the bigger fire has a good start, the oven damper may be closed.

The process of keeping up a good fire is merely one of adding more fuel and occasionally "shaking down" to remove the ashes under the fire.

Do not allow ashes to collect close up under the grate. They will kill the fire and cause the hot coals above to burn out the grate.

Some housekeepers who depend upon the kitchen range for heating adjoining rooms or for continuous hot water maintain the same fire for months at a time. When not in use for cooking, the oven door may be left open to help heat the adjoining rooms.

Checking the Fire

If the draft of air through the firebox continues unchecked, the fuel soon burns out, and the top of the range gets red-hot—a bad thing for the stove. Frequent overheating causes warping and expanding and sometimes cracking of the cover. The fire needs to be curbed. This may be accomplished in various ways: by tightly closing the door and slide under the fire, by partially closing the damper in the stovepipe or pushing in the slide near the stovepipe collar on top of the range, by opening the slide in the broiler door at the end of the range *over the fire* or by tipping the lids or covers over the fire. The chimney keeps pulling for air, and the fire is checked by reducing the amount of chimney suction or by allowing the air to rush in *over the fire*, instead of through it.

Wood-Burning Cookstove

Though it sounds impossible, wood-cooked food just *tastes* better.

A home-heating stove can offer numerous cooking options and will heat better than a full-fledged cookstove will.

Closing the damper over the oven also checks the fire, but the real purpose of this damper is to send the heat around the oven on its way to the chimney.

Advantage of a Large Firebox

The range should have a firebox large enough to keep a fire overnight. Under proper damper control, it will smolder all night and have sufficient life to rekindle quickly in the morning. Then, too, it requires far more fuel to start new fires frequently than to keep an old fire. If it is found that the fire does not keep overnight, probably the draft is too strong, causing the fire to burn out.

No directions can be given in advance to cover every case because chimney drafts vary so much, but there is a happy medium that can be determined by a little experimenting.

Generally speaking, it's necessary to fill the box with the biggest hardwood pieces it can hold, and to close all drafts, closing the stove-pipe damper last.

In any case, it is essential in the morning

to get rid of quite a large body of ashes which has accumulated in the firebox. At least half, and perhaps two-thirds, of the contents of the firebox usually consists of ashes and coals that give no heat and must be removed every morning to reestablish a good fire for baking. A half revolution of the dock-ash grate will usually do this very nicely, and in fact this grate is designed for this particular pur-

The venerable "kitchen dragon" once dominated homes across the country. Is it time for a comeback?

pose. If a stove is equipped with a plain grate, considerable shaking is necessary. The triangular grate may be handled similarly to the dock-ash grate, turning a one-third or two-thirds or sometimes even as much as a full revolution.

The ashes should be removed from the ashpit or the ashpan, both to improve the draft and to prevent the risk of terminal injury to the grate.

It would be difficult to overemphasize the trouble that can be avoided by a regular and systematic cleaning out of ashes and dying embers under the fire. A fire may look bright on top and yet be almost out. Its body of clinkers and ashes has little heating value, and unless there are enough live coals on top to rekindle easily, it is better judgment to dump the fire and start anew.

Naturally, a deep fire will do more work than a shallow fire. Once well built up, a deep fire can be maintained more easily and with less fuel than a fire that half fills the firebox. However, the box should not be filled above the top of the bricks, as doing so will increase the danger of overheating and warping the lids.

Using the Range

The first question that enters the mind in regard to any range is, How well does it bake? For that reason, this book is called *The Secret of Better Baking*.

But the range does many equally important things, all at the same time. Broiling may be going on at the firebox end, boiling or frying in the center, simmering along the outskirts, baking in the oven, keeping dishes hot in the warming oven, heating adjoining rooms and supplying a tankful of hot water.

So long as there is a fire going, it should be cooking something or keeping cooked food warm. The old-fashioned stockpot is an example. It remained on top of the stove all the time, taking anything that would contribute to wholesome soups and stews. The stockpot can be used to advantage where canned soups are not easily obtained. Hot breakfast cereal, cooked the night before, will be improved if kept warm on the back of the stove.

Cooking on Top of the Stove

Fill the teakettle before lighting the fire to get all the advantage of the first flames. When a new fire is built, the strong, direct draft up the chimney tends to draw the hot flames close under the center of the stove. Over a fresh wood fire, the breakfast coffee sometimes boils faster in the center of the stove than on the less heated lids directly over the firebox. Perhaps the dish of water for the four-minute egg refuses to come to a boil. Why? Because the cook has not learned that water will boil more quickly if a cover is put on the dish. A cover on the spider has the same effect and also keeps the stove cleaner. A little later, when the fire is going well, the whole top of the range is hot enough for boiling liquids in large kettles or heating the flats for ironing when electric ironing is not practicable.

Broiling should be prepared for in advance. The fire should be built up high and show an even surface of clear, red-hot coals. Good broiling requires intense heat for a short time, over coals that are past the flaming and gas-producing stage.

Open the oven damper so the smoke will go directly up the chimney. Also give the fire

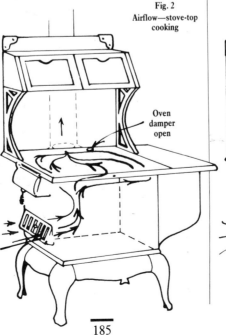

Fig. 2
Airflow—stove-top cooking

Oven damper open

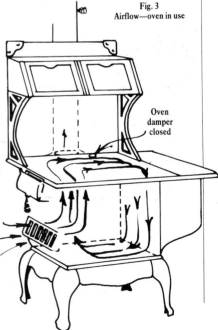

Fig. 3
Airflow—oven in use

Oven damper closed

some draft underneath. Take off the two lids over the fire, and sear over your sirloin, chop or fish as quickly as possible, with frequent turning. This quick searing of the surface tends to prevent the escape of the juices and rewards the cook with a toothsome article of food impossible to produce in any other way. (A little olive oil on the steak before or after broiling gives a wonderful flavor.)

A coal or charcoal fire is the selection of the world's finest chefs for broiling.

Anything broiled should be served as soon as it comes off the fire. If that is impracticable, put it on a platter and keep it hot in the oven.

Use of the Oven

The real test of the range is in the baking. Nothing but individual experience is a safe guide in handling any particular range, but the general principle is the same.

When the fire is first started, the flames rush over the top of the oven and thence directly to the chimney. This heats the top of the oven, while the bottom remains comparatively cool. The entire oven must be heated and the body of fire must be sufficient to maintain an even heat for a considerable length of time. The oven becomes evenly heated by closing the oven damper, forcing the flames and smoke down one side and under the oven, entirely around and up again to reach the chimney.

Foods prepared for baking or roasting differ widely in the time and temperature required for cooking. A little practice will determine the correct temperature and best location in the oven for different bakes.

In a wood or coal range, baking is done directly on the bottom of the oven or on the raised rack. Never attempt to bake with the rack placed on the bottom of the oven.

Use of the Warming Oven

Plates may be kept warm in the warming oven, but this is not all that may be done in it. Dried fruit, such as prunes, figs and raisins, may be put to soak in water in the warming oven and left there for hours and hours, developing a richness and sweetness that cannot be otherwise produced.

One of the attributes of a good cook is a knack for serving hot dishes *hot*. This is not always easy when there is considerable variety in the menu. Here is where the warming oven may play an important part and cause the guests to wonder "how she does it."

For example, take a thick sirloin: If properly timed, it may be broiled just short of completion. Then, while the accompanying dishes are made ready to serve, put the steak on a platter, with plenty of butter, and place

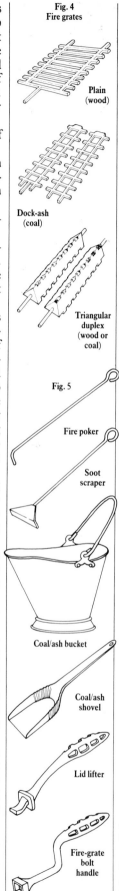

Fig. 4
Fire grates

Plain
(wood)

Dock-ash
(coal)

Triangular
duplex
(wood or
coal)

Fig. 5

Fire poker

Soot
scraper

Coal/ash bucket

Coal/ash
shovel

Lid lifter

Fire-grate
bolt
handle

it in the warming oven. The heat contained in the meat combined with the heat contributed by the warming oven completes the cooking, and your steak is done to a turn, juicy and delicious, on a platter that will keep it hot.

Puddings, such as creamy rice pudding, Indian pudding, apple tapioca, steamed fruit pudding and others, may be much improved by being placed in the warming oven for an hour after baking or steaming.

Stale bread may be dried out in the warming oven for rolling and sifting, and if pulled bread and croutons for soups are put into the warming oven, they will cook of their own accord, without being looked after.

Jelly that has not jelled will sometimes jell after a day or half a day in the warming oven, and even fruit that is only half ripe will ripen after a time in this convenient place if a dish of water is set beside the fruit to keep it from drying out.

Use of the Baking Oven

We all know the New England boiled dinner. Not everyone knows the "Atlantic" baked dinner. About an hour and a half before dinnertime, put into the oven, heated as for bread baking, a four- to five-pound chicken or a cut from a leg of veal or lamb, and a dish of scalloped potatoes. Keep the temperature even. Three-quarters of an hour later, add three large carrots, scraped and cut in halves lengthwise, placing them on the rack of the pan that holds the meat. In another 15 minutes, put in six tomatoes, in an earthen baking dish. By the time the tomatoes are done—in 15 or 20 minutes—a baked dinner for six persons will be ready to serve. After removing the meat and vegetables from the oven, if you place in it six fruit patties,

or six cup-custards in a pan with an inch or more of water, these will be ready to serve when your guests are ready for dessert.

Popovers, cream puffs and éclairs, angel cake and sponge cakes are easier to bake successfully if put into a cool oven and the temperature gradually increased.

Flour mixtures that are of a special shape which should be preserved, like the fancy braided loaves and Parker House rolls, ought to go into a very hot oven so that a crust will immediately form to preserve the shape, and then the baking may proceed at a low temperature.

All meats, fish and poultry are also better cooked at a high temperature to begin with to hold in the juices—then with a gradual reduction of heat. Baste frequently.

Bread, cakes, pies and vegetables may be baked at a uniform temperature, or with a slight gradual increase or decrease.

In many cases, cooking started at a low temperature, gradually increasing, will develop a different taste from the same food started at high heat. Boiled custards, if made with cold milk, are more delicate than if the milk is added very hot.

Scrambled eggs or omelets cooked on a fiercely hot pan from the start take on a richer flavor than when started on a rather cool pan. It is necessary to work fast, however, as overcooking on a very hot pan produces a result that resembles rubber in texture.

Those who enjoy a really good cup of coffee will agree that there is a surprising difference in taste. A cup of real coffee has much more to it than hot water and dark brown color. It should be good if you start with a good blend (ground at home just before using) and are not too economical of the quantity used. For some reason, coffee made in one-cup portions lacks the character of the larger brew. Adding the shells of fresh eggs or a raw egg beaten up with the coffee before boiling both enriches the flavor and produces a much clearer beverage.

Coffee tastes quite different when started with cold or hot water. It is the general opinion that a better result is obtained by mixing with a little cold water and bringing to a boil—then adding boiling water and setting back a few minutes to allow it to settle.

Cereals take on a different flavor, depending on whether they are started in cold or hot water. Which is the *better* flavor is a matter of taste.

All good cooks know the most important secret of all: While the bake is on, make a job of it.

No two conditions of range and draft are exactly alike—in fact, they will differ in your own home, depending on the weather or the direction of the wind. A set of exact rules for one situation would not fit another. In any case, there must be a good body of fire to hold the oven at a cooking temperature. The articles that are being baked or roasted may do better on the rack than on the bottom of the oven, or vice versa.

But no definite rules made for one situation would be at all valuable when compared with the stored-up knowledge gained from your own *experience*—remembering how the oven acted before under similar conditions, and making it serve you better and better with every day's acquaintance.

The foregoing hints are confined very largely to the mechanical operation and care of the range. So much depends upon the preparation of foods for cooking that the temptation to add several pages of palatable recipes is very strong. Recipes are easily obtained, however, and the real purpose of this booklet is to suggest ways of getting consistently better results with the range and draft as they are. If the range works well all the time, both the stove and the draft are all right. If the range has off days, the chimney draft needs attention. A cleaning out may help, or perhaps an extension of the chimney to a point where the air currents will improve the draft.

If you are getting good results only part of the time, you should get much *better* results the rest of the time by making a study of the conditions of fire and draft when the stove is at its best.

If the range fails to give satisfaction the greater part of the time, look for serious defects in the range itself or in the conditions of its installation or operation. If it is cracked or broken, it is past its usefulness. Its operation becomes rapidly more wasteful and irritating, and the early installation of a new range will be good economy and good sense.

The kitchen range usually does its work so well that its virtues are taken for granted. When it breaks down from old age, the whole family realizes what an advance has been made since the days of kettles hung in fireplaces and cuts of meat slowly roasted on wooden spits.

Credits

Cover: Michael Soluri
Table of Contents: Richard O. Springer Photography
p. 6: William Waldron
p. 8: William Waldron

Part I

p. 11: Leonard Lee Rue III/Photo Researchers, Inc. **13:** Jeff Gnass/ West Stock, Inc. **pp. 14-15:** Photo, Joan Baron/The Stock Market **pp.15-16:** Illustrations, Kay Holmes Stafford **p. 17:** Photo, Weststar Photographic **pp. 20-22:** Illustrations, Kay Holmes Stafford **pp. 20-21:** Photo, Pat Stone **pp. 22-23:** Photo, D. Lyons/Bruce Coleman, Inc. **pp. 25-29:** Photos, Clyde H. Smith/f-Stop Pictures, Inc.; illustrations, Kay Holmes Stafford **pp. 30-33:** Don Osby **pp. 34-39:** Photographs, Phil Schofield; illustrations, Don Osby **pp. 40-41:** Don Osby **p. 42:** Kay Holmes Stafford **p. 45:** Top illustration, Don Osby; other illustrations, Kay Holmes Stafford **pp. 46-47:** Sydney Thomson/Animals Animals **pp. 48-49:** Illustrations, Kay Holmes Stafford **p. 49:** Photo, Pat Stone **pp. 50-54:** Illustrations, Kay Holmes Stafford **pp. 50-51:** Photo, Jeff Gnass/ West Stock, Inc. **pp. 56-57:** Steve Kohler **p. 58:** Left, Renee Purse/ Photo Researchers, Inc.; middle, Stephen Green-Armytage/The Stock Market; right, John Bova/Photo Researchers, Inc. **p. 59:** William Waldron **p. 60:** Left, Tom McHugh/ Photo Researchers, Inc.; right, Michael P. Gadomski/Photo Researchers, Inc. **p. 61:** Photos, Leonard Lee Rue III/Photo Researchers, Inc. **pp. 62-63:** Photo, Susan McCartney/Photo Researchers, Inc.; illustrations, Kay Holmes Stafford

Part II

p. 65: Ken Forsgren **pp. 66-70:** Photos, Ken Forsgren; illustrations, Kay Holmes Stafford **p. 71:** Photo, Drew Leviton, illustrations, Kay Holmes Stafford **pp. 72-74:** Photo, William Waldron; illustrations, Kay Holmes Stafford **pp. 76-77:** Photo, Brownie Harris; illustrations, Kay Holmes Stafford **p. 80:** William Waldron **p. 81:** Kay Holmes Stafford **p. 83:** Photo, Weststar Photographic; illustrations, Kay Holmes Stafford **pp. 84-87:** Kenneth Garrett/Woodfin Camp and Associates **pp. 88-89:** Photo, John Deere **pp. 89-94:** Illustrations, Kay Holmes Stafford **p. 93:** John Deere **p. 95:** Kay Holmes Stafford

Part III

p. 97: Philip Ashwood/The Stock Market **p. 98:** Map by Don Osby **p. 99:** William Waldron **p. 100:** Kay Holmes Stafford **p. 102:** Illustration, Kay Holmes Stafford **p. 103:** Pat Stone **pp. 104-105:** Kay Holmes Stafford **p. 107:** Photos, Lee Foster/ Bruce Coleman, Inc. **pp.108-109:** Kay Holmes Stafford **pp. 110-111:** Saul Mayer/The Stock Market **p. 112:** Photo, Richard Kolar/Animals Animals; illustrations, Kay Holmes Stafford **p. 113:** Philip Ashwood/The Stock Market **p. 114:** Bud Titlow/f-Stop Pictures, Inc. **p. 115:** Kay Holmes Stafford **p. 116:** Clyde H. Smith/f-Stop Pictures, Inc. **p. 117:** Photo, Jerry Howard/Photo Researchers, Inc.; illustrations, Kay Holmes Stafford **pp. 118-119:** Phil Schofield

Part IV

p. 121: Grant Peterson **pp. 122-123:** Thom DeSanto Photography, Inc. **p. 124:** Culver Pictures, Inc. **pp. 126-127:** Al Clayton **p. 129:** Al Clayton **pp. 130-131:** Kay Holmes Stafford **pp. 132-133:** Grant Peterson **p. 134:** Kay Holmes Stafford **p. 141:** Grant Peterson **p. 143:** R.J. Erwin/Photo Researchers, Inc. **p. 144:** Peter Miller/Photo Researchers, Inc. **p.145:** Brownie Harris **p. 146:** Thom DeSanto Photography, Inc. **pp. 148-149:** Illustrations, Kay Holmes Stafford; photo, Grant Peterson **pp. 152-153:** Mike Hutmacher/*The Wichita Eagle-Beacon* **p. 155:** Claudia Parks/The Stock Market **pp. 156-157:** Kay Holmes Stafford **pp. 158-159:** Grant Peterson **pp. 162-163:** Illustrations, Kay Holmes Stafford **pp. 164-165:** Grant Peterson **p. 169:** Grant Peterson **pp.170-171:** Roy Morsch/The Stock Market **pp.173-174:** Kay Holmes Stafford **p. 175:** Patricia Arian **pp. 176-177:** Grant Peterson **pp. 178-179:** Kay Holmes Stafford **pp. 182-186:** Illustrations, Kay Holmes Stafford **p. 183:** Craig Blouin/f-Stop Pictures, Inc. **pp. 184-185:** Culver Pictures, Inc. **pp. 186-187:** Photos, Walter Wick **p. 188:** Leonard Lee Rue III/Photo Researchers, Inc. **p. 191:** Renee Purse/Photo Researchers, Inc. **p. 192:** Thom DeSanto Photography, Inc.